Human Capital

The settlement of foreigners in Russia 1762–1804

Лѣоентъ медали на приглашеніе въ Россію иностранныхъ для
поселенія.

На первой сторонѣ: Портретъ
Ея Величества съ обыкновенною
подписью.

На оборотѣ: Богиня Земли
или плодородія, сѣдящая на хол-
микѣ и имѣющая на главѣ город-
скую корону, опирается на щитѣ
съ гербомъ Всероссійской Имперіи;
въ правой рукѣ держитъ плугъ,
а лѣвою Меркурій, имѣющему
въ рукѣ палъ мощу питье, въ
знакъ спокойнаго и мирнаго со-
тія, указываетъ пути прихо-
дящихъ иностранныхъ выходцовъ
на опредѣленныя имъ для поселенія мѣста. Я за ногахъ
Богини лежитъ двойной рогъ изо-
билія, изображающій превосходное
богатство по всякихъ Земныхъ
произращеніяхъ. Сдали видны
съ одной стороны земля пашу-
щей поселянинъ, а съ другой стро-
ющейся у рѣки нашой городъ. Под-
пись притомъ: Новыхъ присо-
вокупляетъ подданныхъ.
Внизу: Приглашеніе иностранныхъ на поселеніе въ Россію
1763 года.

Sketch for a medal in commemoration of the Manifesto of 1763 (see p. 323)

Human Capital

The settlement of foreigners in Russia 1762–1804

ROGER P. BARTLETT

SENIOR LECTURER IN RUSSIAN STUDIES
UNIVERSITY OF KEELE

CAMBRIDGE UNIVERSITY PRESS

CAMBRIDGE

LONDON   NEW YORK   NEW ROCHELLE
MELBOURNE   SYDNEY

Published by the Press Syndicate of the University of Cambridge
The Pitt Building, Trumpington Street, Cambridge CB2 1RP
32 East 57th Street, New York, NY 10022, USA
296 Beaconsfield Parade, Middle Park, Melbourne 3206, Australia

First published 1979

Printed in Great Britain by
Western Printing Services Ltd
Bristol

Library of Congress Cataloguing in Publication Data
Bartlett, Roger P. 1939–
Human capital.
Bibliography: p.
Includes index.
1. Russia – Emigration and immigration – History.
2. Land settlement – Russia – History. 3. Russia – Foreign
population – History. I. Title.
JV8182.B37   325.47   78–68337
ISBN 0 521 22205 2

FOR MY PARENTS

The first principle which presents itself, the most general of all and the most true, is that the real strength of a State consists in the number of its subjects.

Frederick II of Prussia, *Political Testament* (1768)

Russia, far from having sufficient inhabitants, has immense stretches of land which are neither peopled nor cultivated. We cannot therefore do too much to favour population increase.

Catherine II of Russia, *Instruction*

Contents

Maps

Weights and Measures

1 arshin = 28 inches
1 desyatina = 2.7 acres
1 chetvert' (area) = 0.5 desyatinas
1 chetvert' (volume) = 5.75 bushels, Winchester measure
1 pud = 40 Russian pounds = 36 pounds avoirdupois
1 verst = 3,500 feet (0.663 miles)

Abbreviations

1. Manuscript sources

a. Soviet

ORGPB	Otdel Rukopisey Gosudarstvennoy Publichnoy Biblioteki (Saltykov-Shchedrin State Public Library, Leningrad, Dept. of Mss.)
TsGADA	Tsentral'nyy Gosudarstvennyy Arkhiv Drevnikh Aktov (Central State Archive of Ancient Documents, Moscow)
TsGIAL	Tsentral'nyy Gosudarstvennyy Istoricheskiy Arkhiv S.S.S.R. (Central State Historical Archive of the U.S.S.R., Leningrad)
TsGVIA	Tsentral'nyy Gosudarstvennyy Voyenno–Istoricheskiy Arkhiv (Central State Military–Historical Archive, Moscow)

(References to individual archives, files, folios, etc. in Soviet sources are given in general according to Soviet usage: f. (fond) – archive or series number; op. (opis') – catalogue or register; kn. (kniga) – book; d. (delo) – case, file, volume; l. (list) – folio; ob. (obratnaya storona) – obverse.)

b. Additional

AN AE	Archives Nationales, Paris, Archives Etrangères
MAE CPR	Ministère des Affaires Etrangères, Paris, Correspondance Politique, Russie

2. Other abbreviations

AKV	*Arkhiv Knyazya Vorontsova*

xii   *Abbreviations*

Auswahl ökon.	*Auswahl ökonomischer Abhandlungen, welche die*
Abhandlungen	*freye ökonomische Gesellschaft in St. Petersburg,*
	in teutscher Sprache erhalten hat
Buckingham	*Despatches and Correspondence of John, Second*
Correspondence	*Earl of Buckinghamshire. . .1762–65*
Chteniya	*Chteniya v Obshchestve Istorii i Drevnostey*
	Rossiyskikh pri Moskovskom Universitete
HBR	*Heimatbuch der Deutschen aus Russland*
JbfGO	*Jahrbücher für Geschichte Osteuropas*
MIRF	F. Veselago, sost., *Materialy dlya istorii russkogo*
	flota
NF	Neue Folge
NS	New Style or new series
OS	Old Style
PSZ	*Polnoye Sobraniye Zakonov Rossiyskoy Imperii*
	(Sobraniye Pervoye)
RBS	*Russkiy Biograficheskiy Slovar'*
SA	*Senatskiy Arkhiv*
SEER	*Slavonic and East European Review*
SIRIO	*Sbornik Imperatorskogo Russkogo Istoricheskogo*
	Obshchestva
SKRKGP	*Svodnyy Katalog Russkoy Knigi Grazhdanskoy*
	Pechati 1725–1800
SPb	St Petersburg
TVEO	*Trudy Vol'nogo Ekonomicheskogo Obshchestva*
ZhMGI	*Zhurnal Ministerstva Gosudarstvennykh*
	Imushchestv
ZhMVD	*Zhurnal Ministerstva Vnutrennykh Del*
ZOO	*Zapiski Odesskogo Obshchestva Istorii i*
	Drevnostey

Preface

In the eighteenth century, Russia appeared to many people as a land of promise. Immigration both from the west and from the south – principally the Balkans and Transcaucasia – took place on a considerable scale, and involved a variety of nationalities and social classes. Among the many and varied foreigners who entered Russia at this time, the present study is concerned with one basic category: those who settled in the Russian Empire in response to the Imperial Manifestos of Catherine II, published in 1762 and 1763, and subsequent similar legislation.

Catherine's invitation to foreigners to settle in her domains formed the starting point of a long process. The Manifestos of 1762 and 1763 laid the foundation for compact settlements of foreigners on the Volga and in the southern Ukraine, as well as for small groupings elsewhere, during the eighteenth century; and although in 1804 the government of Alexander I set new conditions for the extensive European immigration into southern Russia of the early nineteenth century, Catherine's legislation was influential here as well. The year 1804 has been taken as the terminal date of the present study, but in one form or another the foreign immigration and settlement inaugurated in the 1760s continued through much of the nineteenth century.

The foreign colonies which resulted from the Russian immigration programme provoked controversy from the outset, and their history, and the attitudes of the authorities towards them, have been chequered. The latter history of the Volga Germans, in particular, has attracted much attention. They were the first ethnic group to receive autonomous status under Soviet rule, with the creation in 1918 of the Autonomous Workers' Commune of the Volga German Region, transformed in 1924 into the Autonomous Soviet Socialist Republic of the Volga Germans. But with the German invasion of Russia in 1941, accusations of treason were made against them. They were deported eastward, with other exiled national groups, and their republic abolished; subsequent rehabilitation measures have stopped short of its reconstitution. More generally, the descendants of Catherine II's immigrants are today members of national minority groups in the Soviet Union, or have been assimilated into Soviet society. Many also re-emigrated, in the last decades of the Imperial regime and during the Soviet period: Russian Germans and Mennonites, for example, now live in Germany and in North and South America; Swedish re-emigrants from the Ukraine have returned to Sweden. In this context it may also be of interest to note personal connections between the foreign colonies and the early leadership of the Soviet state: Lenin's maternal grandmother was a Volga German, while Trotsky's father came from a Jewish agricultural colony in the Ukraine which was originally established under the foreign colonist administration.

We are concerned here, however, only with the early period of the foreign settlement system begun by Catherine II; and the focus of the study is essentially upon the activities of the Russian Imperial government and government apparatus. This is primarily an account of the formulation and implementation of government policy; furthermore, it is based mainly upon sources compiled by official bodies, or deriving from government records. Consequently, although care has been taken to present as clear and balanced an account as possible, the view is largely that from the Russian, official standpoint. The viewpoint of the migrant and settler receives less space; and problems which loom large in that perspective – conditions in the country of origin, for example, the often very harsh day-to-day realities of pioneer migration and settlement, relations between immigrants and their native neighbours – are dealt with only briefly or incidentally. This is not for lack of sources to elucidate them: central and regional Soviet archives, as well as German repositories and others elsewhere, hold ample further documentary material which would fill out, and extend, the present work. Similarly, there has not been scope here for an extended treatment of other aspects of Russian life and society which were touched by the immigration scheme: the role of foreigners in the eighteenth-century Russian economy, for example, or the overall development of the borderlands of European Russia. But within these limitations I have tried to show the way in which immigration policy and foreign settlement evolved in their first decades, and their relationship with the wider context of government policies and Russian life.

It is a pleasure to record the numerous debts which I have incurred to
institutions and to individuals who have contributed in different ways
to the completion of this book, and of whom only a few can be acknowledged here. My work in this field first began as doctoral research at
St Antony's College, Oxford; I owe much to the College's generosity.
Research in the Soviet Union was made possible by awards from the
British Council. The director and staff of the Central State Archive of
Ancient Documents in Moscow, the Central State Historical Archive
in Leningrad, the National and the Foreign Ministry Archives in Paris
made available essential documentary material, as did the archivists in
the manuscript departments of the Saltykov-Shchedrin Public Library,
Leningrad, and the Bibliothèque de l'Arsénal and Bibliothèque de la
Ville de Paris, Paris. Besides the resources of the British Library,
London, and the Lenin Library, Moscow, I have drawn heavily upon
the holdings and the services of the Bodleian Library, Oxford, where
my particular guardian angel has been Mrs Carole Menzies of the
Slavonic Department. How to manage, too, without the ready help of
the Inter-Library Loans Desk in my own university library? And in the
field of loans the librarians of the Institut für Auslandsbeziehungen, in
Stuttgart, have also given generous help on different occasions over a
number of years.

During research in the USSR I received valuable assistance from
Academician M. P. Alekseyev, from V. M. Kabuzan, and from Pro-
fessor N. S. Kinyapina. At home, Dr W. H. Parker gave me patient
and effective support in my early work and I benefited greatly at that
stage, as often since, from the bibliographical wisdom of Mr J. S. G.
Simmons. Many individuals have made contributions on individual
points – especially Professor E. Amburger, Dr R. Beerman, Professor
D. Griffiths, Messrs W. S. Johnston and B. Karidis, Drs D. G. Rempel,
D. Shaw and J. Urry, and Dr Olga Crisp, who first suggested the title.
My use of Latvian sources would have been difficult, if not impossible,
without the expert assistance of Mrs Jutta Barlow and Mr V. Eksts;
valuable help with maps was given by Mrs Marian Bartlett. The manuscript has been read and effectively criticized at different stages by
several friends and colleagues – Dr P. Dukes, Dr Isabel de Madariaga,
Miss Wendy Rosslyn, Dr R. Service and Mr H. Willetts. The final
draft was typed by Mrs Nicola Pike and Mrs Joan Heath. To all of
these I am most grateful; responsibility for the final version, warts and
all, belongs of course to me.

For transliteration I have used the British system, modifying name endings and using accepted English forms of proper names where these exist; modern Russian orthography is followed throughout. Unless otherwise indicated, dates are given in the Old Style, according to the Julian Calendar.

Keele   Roger P. Bartlett
April 1978

Introduction

The history of Russia is the history of a country which is being colonized. Her area of colonization expanded together with her state territory. Now falling, now rising, this age-long movement continues up to our own time.

For Klyuchevsky colonization was, indeed, the 'basic fact' of Russian history.[1] When the Empress Catherine II issued her Manifestos of 1762 and 1763 inviting immigration into Russia, most of the foreigners who responded joined, and became part of, this colonization process. Their settlements took root in regions which were in the process of population and development; and they were commonly referred to as 'colonies'.

However, 'colonization' in its usual sense is an ambivalent concept for our present purposes, since it frequently carries quite inappropriate associations. In the global history of colonization and colonialism, Russia occupies a place somewhat apart. While the Muscovite state and its successors have had in common with most other Imperial powers a tradition of expansion, the more or less deliberate acquisition of new outlying territory, they differ in that Russia's colonial regions have been contiguous with metropolitan territory. 'Other empires were divided by the sea, but the Russian empire was a continuous land mass stretching from Poland to the Bering Strait.'[2] Similarly, while some aspects of the colonization process were akin to those of other powers – in the focus on colonial economic resources, or, on a different plane, in the use of colonial regions for penal purposes – there have also been important differences: in the nature and speed of the spread of settlement, in relations between settlers and indigenous populations. General discussions of colonization and colonial expansion in the Imperial sense have consequently tended to include Russian Siberia and Central Asia, but to take little account of Klyuchevsky's 'basic fact' as it applied to the older areas of Muscovite and Russian settlement.

In terms of overseas, 'Imperial' colonization, the closest parallel to the Russian experience overall is provided by settlement colonies such as those of Australia or North America; and North American expansion westwards in the eighteenth century and the post-colonial period has provided an obvious and fruitful comparison with the Russian situation.[3] Within Europe, Russian internal migration and settlement presents a form of the 'inner colonization' by which many of the lands of East Central Europe were also settled. It is the concept of colonization essentially as settlement, and the concepts of frontier and of *innere Kolonisation*, which will be most valuable for an appreciation of the broad geographical and historical setting within which the establishment of Russia's foreign settlements took place.

Within the narrower framework of the eighteenth century, however, and viewed in all its aspects, Catherine's pursuit of mass immigration involves more varied factors. The autocratic state whose throne the Empress ascended in 1762 was underpopulated in relation both to the size of its territories, and to the needs both of the government and the landowning classes. The natural increase in population which began in Russia at the turn of the seventeenth century, and which formed part of the general rise in European population of the eighteenth and the nineteenth, made little impact at first on official thinking. At the same time the modernization of the country inaugurated by Peter the Great in the first quarter of the eighteenth century, on Western lines, and carried further by his successors, including Catherine, made greater demands on existing population resources. But it also produced greater awareness of the country's needs in various respects, and it brought with it closer knowledge of contemporary ideas and practice in the field of economics and political science, including population policy.

In fact, in issuing her Manifestos, Catherine was acting very much in accordance with European practice of her time. Her immigration programme derived its theoretical justification from the mercantilist and cameralist theories of statecraft prominent in Europe in the early and middle decades of the century. It reflected, too, a concern with population which was common to most European states in this period and which resulted in recruitment of settlers by almost all the major powers, for colonies either within the metropolitan country or overseas. This international recruitment in turn affected, and was affected by, European politics and international relations. The Russian programme also stood to some extent in the well-established international tradition – most commonly identified with Peter the Great in Russia, though considerably antedating his reign – of welcoming skilled foreigners for technical purposes.

At home, in the immediate context of Russian internal affairs,

Catherine's theories and measures on immigration form part and parcel of the contemporary economic and social history of Russia. In the sphere of social policy, they represent one strand in a general population policy. They had close connections with the Empress's views on 'police' and on popular welfare, and at some points with aspects of the peasant question: the problems of the fugitive peasant, the amelioration of agriculture, even – at the beginning – the question of landlord–peasant relationships. The majority of the immigrants settled in closed colonies and were consequently described by the term *kolonist*, which was current from 1764 in this context. In the nineteenth century *kolonist* became an official category in social legislation; while the special status and administrative structure granted to the colonies ensured their survival as separate entities throughout the Imperial period.[4]

Apart from social policy, immigration also bore upon government plans for the development of the economy, both generally through population increase – its main immediate purpose – and specifically through the use of immigrants to encourage trade, industry and agriculture. It provided, too, a tool for use in dealing with the various problems and possibilities presented to Catherine and to later rulers by the border regions of the Empire: the Baltic provinces, with their special status and exclusive aspirations, the lands of the Volga, the Urals region, and the North Caucasus, now being progressively drawn into the sphere of settlement and economic development, and the relatively empty southern territories successively conquered from Turkey.

These different aspects of government activity are examined here in the course of a roughly chronological study of policy on immigration and of its results, over a forty-year period. The first chapter examines the antecedents and background to the policy, principally in earlier decades of the eighteenth century; the question of urban and entrepreneurial settlement is treated by itself in Chapter 5. The concluding date chosen for the study, 1804, represents the end merely of one stage in the ongoing history of immigration and of the foreign colonies. The full development of the settlements established under Catherine came only in the nineteenth century, when many new immigrants also came to Russia. The present study examines the workings of Russian government policy in a specific field in the second half of the eighteenth century. It also seeks to show the foundations on which the later developments in immigration and the life of the colonies took place.

I

Antecedents

General patterns of settlement in eighteenth-century Russia:
Orenburg Province

The first large-scale settlement under Catherine's policies took place on the lower Volga around Saratov. At that time this was still frontier territory. During the seventeenth century, Muscovite control over the relatively empty lands around the old Muscovite centre had advanced rapidly. In the south, the political boundaries and the frontier of settlement had reached the lands of the Zaporozhian and Don Cossacks, and close confrontation with the Turks and their Crimean Tatar vassals. The middle Volga region and the lands to the west of it were now relatively secure: on the Don and in Voronezh province the land was being settled by noble landowners (*pomeshchiki*) and the limits of the Don Cossack territories defined. Further south and east, however, the situation was less settled. East of the Volga the Bashkirs, and further south the Kirgiz and the Kalmyk, grazed their flocks and herds over vast, almost empty spaces. On the right (western) bank, the towns established in the sixteenth century remained relatively isolated points of settlement and the land southwards was open to attack by freebooters and brigands, or by the Crimean and Kuban Tatars, as successive defence lines built across the southern Ukraine and as far as the Volga testify. The Tatar threat faded progressively through the eighteenth century, but was only finally eliminated with the annexation of the Crimea and the Kuban in 1783. By 1800 all the lands on the Volga and the northern littoral of the Black Sea had been assimilated, and under the increasingly firm grasp of the civilian administration native immigration was continuing at a rapid pace.

On the lower Volga the completion of this process during the eighteenth century ran parallel with similar developments to the north-east, in Bashkiria. The assimilation of this region was a prerequisite for the final security and full development of the Volga steppes to which Catherine II was to direct her new settlers; and the foreign colonies on the Volga were part of increased government activities in that area from the 1760s onwards. In 1744 much of Bashkiria was included in the newly-formed Province of Orenburg; and, particularly under the able governorship of I. I. Nepluyev (1742–58), Orenburg Province provides a case study of eighteenth-century Russian internal colonization and development, as well as a clear picture of the kind of population elements involved. In addition, Nepluyev's activities had direct bearing on some matters which were to arise during the immigration proceedings of the 1760s.

Official methods of settlement in border regions reflected the fluidity and uncertainty of conditions on the frontier. In the organized process of controlling and colonizing such areas, military considerations inevitably took precedence over civil requirements, in so far as the two were separated at all. It was only in the eighteenth century that non-military types of agricultural colonization in these regions became fully distinct from their military counterparts; and even then the peasantry could be called upon if necessary to perform military functions for which it was not normally liable.

But organized, state-sponsored colonization represents only one side of the picture. On the other stand the figures of the individual settler – estate-holder or peasant – and, equally important, of the fugitive – pioneer, fortune-seeker, dissenter, and in the eyes of the state, criminal. Fugitives (*beglyye*) came from every group among the lower classes of Russian society, and they fled from a multitude of ills: military service, religious persecution, heavy taxation, oppression by landlord or government official. As serfdom grew and the peasant population increasingly lost its legal freedom to move, the government was correspondingly concerned to control such movement and also to prevent population loss from the older territories. In the eighteenth century measures to secure the return of fugitives were closely interwoven with policy on settlement at large.

Orenburg Province was a focus of colonizing activity for several reasons. It covered most of western Bashkiria, a huge area which was sparsely populated, undeveloped, and – until the middle of the century – without effective administration or reliable communications. Both the instability of the region and its economic potential attracted the attention of the government. The gains to be drawn from trade and natural resources were obvious. In 1735 Kirillov, head of the Orenburg

Board (*Ekspeditsiya*) and founder of the first town of Orenburg (later Orsk), reported that with the establishment of the new outpost he had conquered a 'New Russia', 'rich in metals and in minerals';[1] while the town itself was 'very necessary not only to restrain the Kirgiz, but for the opening of a free route for goods to Bukhara, to Vodokshan, to Balkh and to India'.[2]

The settlement of Bashkiria is notorious for the ruthless thoroughness with which local resistance to Russian domination was crushed.[3] In the eighteenth century this process reached its climax. The Bashkir revolt of 1735–40, bloodily suppressed, coincided with the introduction of a more active Russian policy; Orsk was founded in 1735, Orenburg in 1742. The revolt also introduced the final stages of the conflict: the last serious outbreak of Bashkir dissidence, after a flare-up in 1755, arose in the 1770s out of the Pugachev rebellion.

The period following the revolt was one of construction and consolidation; it fell to Nepluyev to carry out reforms planned in the late 1730s. As one account puts it,

the time had now come – and finally the Russian authorities realized this – to pay more serious attention to the region, in order to ensure its peaceful development after nearly two hundred years of ruinous struggle. The further development of the military settlements, which was now made into a system, and the proper ordering of the civil administration: these were the two principles which now began to be applied to the region.[4]

Establishment of a sound administration was expected to foster both economic development and population growth in the area.

Despite the new departure which his work represented, Nepluyev was able to build on foundations laid by his predecessors earlier in the century. In particular, in developing the commercial potential of Orenburg, he had to his advantage the sweeping privileges granted to the town a few years before. The official Instruction given to Kirillov at that time had emphatically stressed the desirability of developing both commerce and industry. Kirillov was to build a jetty on the Aral Sea, survey the routes to Khiva, Bukhara and Tashkent, and to use every possible means to attract Asian trade. 'To obtain the return of the Indian Company which was in Bukhara and has returned to India', the Indian merchant Maravgi Barayev from Astrakhan was sent back to India, with a copy of Orenburg's charter and a loan of 1,000 roubles for trading purposes.[5]

In view of the scarcity of merchants, Asians were later permitted to sell goods retail as well as wholesale, a right usually reserved to Russian subjects,[6] and Nepluyev welcomed such settlers as the 'trading Tatars' from Kazan who established the Seyt Suburb (*Seytovskaya Sloboda*) near Orenburg, bringing both capital and population into the area.[7] The grant of privileges to new towns was a routine procedure, especially where commercial prospects were good, and in the case of Orenburg they very soon began to achieve the effect desired.[8]

For commercial operations security was essential, and Nepluyev devoted much energy to military organization and settlement. Previous settlement of both military and civilians had involved a great variety of social and national groups. From an early date Russian official and unofficial immigrants – peasants and townsfolk, soldiers, exiles and fugitives – alternated with peoples of non-Russian stock from the Volga.[9] In the seventeenth century, Polish servicemen and prisoners of war from areas conquered by Aleksey Mikhaylovich were transferred to military service on the Trans-Kama Line.[10] Units of the 'land militia' set up in 1731–2 served there, as did other 'serving foreigners', and local Tatars. Nepluyev's development of the system of military fortification was very successful; by the end of his administration the region was enveloped in a network of fortified lines, manned by six regiments and the recently-formed Orenburg Cossack Force, with a total altogether in 1760 of over 20,000 men.[11]

Almost the entire population of the region was engaged in or concerned with agricultural pursuits. The non-peasant population combined these with military service or work in mines and industrial enterprises, and the town population was minute. The Bashkirs themselves were a semi-nomadic people, stock-breeders, and for a long time official policy upheld the inviolacy of their vast land-holdings. But from the late seventeenth century onwards considerable settlement took place on Bashkir lands, involving non-Russian nationalities as well as Russian peasantry.[12] The manner of settlement varied, but the usual result in the long term was the partial or even total expropriation of the Bashkirs. Many of the non-Russian elements settled as labourers or tenants of the Bashkir owners. They remained loyal to the Russian authorities during the troubles and were rewarded with the lands they occupied. Other groups simply squatted on suitable land, or made short-term agreements with the Bashkirs on expiry of which they refused to leave. Later, large-scale land-purchase and transfer of serfs by Russian *pomeshchiki* became common, like that vividly described in S. T. Aksakov's 'Family Chronicle'. Land was plentiful, good and cheap. With the area fully and finally pacified, landlord colonization became a significant element in its development.

The government continued to assign service elements to Orenburg, and to send exiles there as well as to Siberia.[13] Such settlers received the treatment customary for authorized migrants: tax exemptions for the first years and material assistance in various forms. The great majority of peasants in the region, however, were unofficial immigrants, fugitives of one sort or another. A principal refuge for such people in the eighteenth century was Poland: one report in the middle of the century estimated their numbers there to be as high as one million.[14] But they also made their way in large numbers to all the Russian border regions, finding a welcome from landowners and industrialists and from most of the Cossack Forces, or forming their own villages and settlements. The official attitude to the problem was severe, though from time to time the government was forced to recognize that its measures against flight remained largely a dead letter. Exceptionally, local needs could deliberately be put first. In 1736, for example, to meet a need for labourers and craftsmen in the newly-established towns and strong points of the region, Kirillov received official instructions to 'let it be known discreetly' (*razglashat' pod rukoy*) that fugitives who came in from the Yaik would be registered for work in Orenburg. When sufficient numbers assembled in answer to this offer, they were divided into groups and sent off to their allotted place of work, and recruit receipts were sent to former owners.[15]

For administrators charged with developing frontier regions – in Orenburg Province as elsewhere – such people were invaluable, and they sought as far as possible to retain them. The second revision, in 1744, brought Nepluyev face to face with the problem. The Senate ordered all local authorities to ensure the return of fugitives to their place of origin. Nepluyev protested:

All peasants in Isetsk County (*provintsiya*), in number 5,154 [male revision souls], are not native to the province but are immigrants (*skhodtsy*) from different places, who settled here earlier, and have been placed under the poll tax. If they are sent back, the settlements (*slobody*) will be emptied, there will be no-one to carry out state services so necessary in Orenburg Province, since these are largely performed. . .by fugitives.

Furthermore,

it is only by the provisions supplied by these settlers as tithe quit-rent that the garrisons are maintained in the fortresses newly constructed from the Siberian end of the line along the Orenburg tract, and the regular troops who are used for all military requirements. In addition, these peasants are used when necessary for military purposes as well, in place of Cossacks, which happened quite often during the last Bashkir disturbances.[16]

The figure of 5,154 included 2,779 *odnodvortsy*; 591 'synodal and monastery peasants'; 308 landowners' serfs; and 54 members of the merchantry. (The rest were simply designated *raznochintsy*: people of various – that is, non-noble – rank.) Nepluyev further stressed that by returning them to their former domicile, the state would lose not only much of the population of the region but also the money and provisions given to help the settlers.[17] The Senate finally agreed that those, at least, who had settled before 1719 (the first revision) should be allowed to stay where they were. Nepluyev successfully defended illegal settlers in other counties of the Province; and much the same situation prevailed in border regions elsewhere in the Empire.[18]

Besides the general settlement of military and civilian elements, successive administrators of the Orenburg region had to organize the establishment there of specific groups of settlers of very varied character. In 1736 a system was devised for the settlement of discharged soldiers on the Trans-Kama Line and elsewhere in Kazan Province, parts of which were included in Orenburg Province in 1744.[19] The decree announcing the new measures linked them explicitly with military settlements in the seventeenth century, adding that they were intended to give livelihood and status to old soldiers, whose helpless, poverty-stricken condition lowered the morale of those still serving and fostered desertion.[20] Elsewhere their value to the region itself was stressed.[21] The decree promised land 'as was given to former servicemen and is given to the land militia, from twenty to thirty chetverts for each family', to be held in perpetuity and inalienable to other social groups. Grants in cash and kind were specified, and a director designated to take charge of the new colonies. Churches and schools were to be built when the villages reached a sufficient size.[22] The following year another decree appointed what Vitevsky calls a 'chancellery for migration' (*pereselencheskaya kantselyariya*) to direct the settlement. It comprised two senior officers and a civil servant, to be supported by 'three worthy men of the rank of Major' and 'a Secretary and the necessary number of clerical staff; also, for the apportionment of land, . . .four land surveyors'.[23] This system of settlement created a position for the discharged soldiers similar to that of the *odnodvortsy* and the land militia. In the long run, the authorities found it very successful; the system was adopted for other areas of the Empire and used throughout the century.[24]

Another project in Orenburg Province on a similar scale was the settlement of converted Kalmyk in a special colony on the Volga, which had, however, a more chequered history. Russian policy towards non-Christian subjects held traditionally to the dual principles of toleration and proselytism. The latter in particular was approved, since adoption of Orthodoxy implied acceptance of Russian hegemony and the Russian way of life. As a result, conversion was encouraged by the offer of material incentives, release from obligations to native rulers, even remission of sentence for crimes committed. Coercion, too, was not uncommon. Naturally, while such methods had some success, they also influenced the quality of the converts.

Early efforts to settle baptized Kalmyk, first in Kiev and other Ukrainian towns, then in towns on the Volga, were unsatisfactory.[25] Those sent to the Ukraine objected to separation from their relatives; those scattered on the Volga were too close to their unconverted kinsfolk for the peace of mind of the Kalmyk rulers. The solution was found in the creation of a new town and fortress, Stavropol, on the Volga above Samara, which was to give the converts a community of their own. Building started in 1738 under the supervision of V. Tatishchev, then in charge of the region. Some Kalmyk settled in Stavropol itself, others in small settlements nearby along the river.[26]

Exact conditions of settlement were published the following year. They offered generous land grants, according to rank. Poorer Kalmyk could receive additional help in kind, while for those most in need a small cash fund was placed at the disposal of the head of the colony, the Kalmyk Princess Tayshina. The garrison of the fort on which the new township centred was to instruct the hitherto nomadic settlers in agriculture, and subsequently schools and churches were established.[27] Tatishchev's nineteenth-century biographer, Popov, notes grudgingly:

This was the way they colonized the Volga region in the eighteenth century with aliens (*inorodtsami*), maintaining them at the cost of the Russian population. Tatishchev in this respect simply did his duty as he understood it. He considered himself obliged to care for migrants who, having accepted Orthodoxy, lost the former distinction of their nationality. At least, such views were shared by the whole of ancient Russia. Tatishchev's care for the Stavropol Kalmyk even went so far that he requested for them a physician, under-physician and necessary medicaments, things in which Russian society of his time was not rich.[28]

Stavropol was later used as a centre for the settlement of other Asiatics who became Russian subjects. In 1757 the Senate accepted Nepluyev's suggestion that Dzhungars (*Zyungortsy*), who as a result of war and internal dissension were seeking Russian protection, should be settled there on a military basis. By 1760 the number of male Dzhungars sent to settle, together with prisoners of various nationalities escaped from the Kirgiz, had reached 1,765, so that further special settlement areas had to be allocated.[29]

The problem of slaves who escaped from the Kirgiz and wished to receive baptism had first become serious with the construction of the Orenburg and Siberian Lines. It presented a number of difficulties. The Russian authorities simply sent back those refusing conversion, but those accepting Christianity were harboured and protected. The Kirgiz became so incensed at this that in 1759 they decided to move away from the areas of Russian settlement; so to placate them, the College of Foreign Affairs proposed to the Senate that compensation, in the form of a present of twenty or twenty-five roubles, should be given for any escaper pursued to the Lines. In addition, the reception of converts should in future be kept secret. To recoup the expenditure, the College proposed sending able-bodied men to enlist in the Baltic regiments, and all others for settlement to areas away from the frontier.[30]

The Senate accepted the suggestion of gifts in cases of pursuit; but instead of the Baltic regiments, it decreed that all such escaped slaves should be sent to the Senate Office (*Senatskaya Kontora*) in Moscow. From there they should go to the Moscow Provincial Chancellery, to be placed in service with any private person who might wish to take them. That person would pay the state's expenses for their release and journey to Moscow: further than this the Senate minutes do not specify the terms of the transaction. This system became law and now converts were given to anyone interested, in return for the amount expended plus ten roubles. Under the new procedure a total of 521 escaped slaves of both sexes – apparently including some Dzhungars – were sent to Moscow between 1759 and 1763; though evidently, at least initially, some slaves were settled in Stavropol.[31]

In 1739, at about the same time as the foundation of the Kalmyk colony, the Senate approved a project to recruit and settle Little Russians in Orenburg Province. In the event this proved a fiasco. Two hundred and nine families came, from whom 849 men were registered as Cossacks; but the settlers were quite unequal to their task. They failed to establish themselves economically despite considerable assistance, and became a liability rather than a reinforcement to the security of the region: several times they were surprised by the Kirgiz, and had to be protected by government forces. Most of them returned to Little Russia in 1744.[32] The point of interest in this case is the method by which the project was carried out. The initiative came from the authorities and had nothing to do with the original situation of the settlers themselves. An officer was sent on special mission from Orenburg to the Ukraine, with powers of recruitment and lavish promises to those who should accept. His propaganda caused much excitement among both peasants and Cossacks, and aroused the hostility of the Little Russian senior officers and landowners (*Malorossiyskiye starshiny i vladel'tsy*) who succeeded in limiting the number who left despite Senate support for the scheme.[33] The Orenburg envoy, Captain Kalachov, is a good example of the official recruiting agent familiar from the Serbian military immigration into the southern Ukraine during the first two-thirds of the century; and, as we shall see, this military immigration gave rise to one further, foreign, settlement in Orenburg Province in the 1750s.

These illustrations of official methods and policy on border settlement are typical for the eighteenth century in Russia. Vitevsky's summary of the manner of official, government-sponsored colonization can be extended to all the instances considered:

And so we see that the *government itself moved to the assistance of Nepluyev in the colonization of the Orenburg region*, sending various elements there from other places. Seeking to populate the 'empty lands' of this spacious area, it distributed grain and money for the journey and initial establishment of the migrants 'to the new places'. Giving them land in abundance, the government also endowed them with various privileges, and in order better to organize their internal regime, set up special offices and authorities. Concerned for the material well-being of the new settlers, it did not forget their spiritual needs, contributing to the construction of churches in their settlements, and to the building of schools for their children.[34]

The summary is worth quoting at length particularly since it typifies the official view, which emphasized formal rather than actual achievement, and the requirements of the state rather than the interests of the migrants. Until the beginning of the nineteenth century, settlers were sent to new areas usually because these needed population, rarely because the settlers themselves wanted or needed to be moved.[35] In Russia as elsewhere in both the Old World and the New, migration and settlement on new lands faced the pioneer with relentless labour, with the problems of acclimatization and adjustment to a new environment, and often with physical danger. And despite measures to facilitate and assist new settlement, Russian official 'inner colonization' had its full share of the hardship and difficulties which characterized most colonial enterprises in their early stages.[36]

Map 1. European Russia ca. 1800. Insets show the locations of Maps 2–4.

*Foreigners in Russia and foreign immigration in the eighteenth century
before 1762: policy, practice and projects*

By the mid-eighteenth century, the role of Western Europeans in the
policies of the Russian government had become almost as much an
established tradition as had the methods of frontier settlement.
Westerners were used, essentially, to furnish commercial capacity,
technical and other skills which the native Russian population was
unable to provide. The deliberate policy of reliance on the West in
these fields had reached its climax under Peter I. His Manifesto of
1702, addressed in the first instance to those wishing to take military
service, and secondly to merchants and artisans, attracted immigrants
from all over Europe.[37]

In the majority of cases, whether European or not, such foreigners
could rely for definition of their status, rights and duties on specific
enactments governing the position of particular categories or nationalities. Foreign merchants, for instance, might be protected by bi-
lateral trade agreements; the rights of foreign entrepreneurs were set
out in broad terms in the *Manufaktur-Reglament* of 1723.[38] The
charters granted to Greeks and Armenians are mentioned below.
Certain basic rights were (in theory) secured to all – freedom of con-
science, for example, and relative freedom of entry and exit, at least
during most of the century.[39]

The successors of Peter I continued his policies towards European
personnel. The Western communities in the capitals became increasingly numerous, variegated, and prosperous, and by the end of the
century Westerners were to be found in all corners at least of European
Russia. On the whole the government, unlike a large proportion of the
population, approved of such immigration whether state-sponsored or
not, and itself recruited Westerners for government service throughout
the century.[40]

Workers were also recruited for state factories, or for enterprises
enjoying highly-placed support. In 1761 the French Ambassador in
Petersburg reported that 'there arrive here daily French manufacturers
and workers of all sorts', engaged by his Russian opposite number in
Paris for a projected textile mill which, he claimed, was a venture of
the Empress and some leading courtiers.[41]

The Russian authorities were less willing to take action in obtaining
skilled labour for ordinary private Russian enterprises, the no-man's
land between government service and the independent foreign artisan

or entrepreneur. Yet, in many branches of industry, levels of native expertise remained low and skilled personnel had to be sought abroad if they were to be improved. Where individual entrepreneurs were unable or unwilling to do this, the Colleges which acted as supervisory authorities had a certain obligation to assist. In 1753, for example, the College of Manufactures reported to the Senate deficiencies in the design of patterns for silk-printing. 'The designers at those [private] factories only make patterns from imported models, and without a model are incapable of producing a pattern by themselves.' The College proposed to bring in foreign specialists to teach them.[42]

The Senate, however, adhered to the policy of non-intervention. If Russian factory owners wanted foreign specialists, they must hire them themselves with only a minimum of assistance from Russian diplomatic representatives abroad. The reasons for this attitude were fully set out in a decree on a similar case in 1761. The terms offered by the Russian side were usually so low, and the conditions made by any Westerner of skill and experience so high, that agreement could be reached only with difficulty.[43] As a result, many foreigners who did accept contracts were poorly qualified, or adventurers.

Furthermore, when the government itself did undertake to recruit foreign labour, it could not be sure of finding jobs for the men it engaged. This was demonstrated in 1759, when the Senate decided to turn to advantage the Russian occupation of East Prussia. Senate Secretary Sukin was sent to Königsberg 'for the collection of all information concerning the commerce of the Kingdom of Prussia', and for the 'transfer from Königsberg to Russia of any factories useful to Russia which may be found there, by blandishments offered (*prilaskivaniyem*) to the entrepreneurs and workmen'.[44] A small number of workers was recruited. On arrival in Petersburg, some registered in guilds as independent craftsmen, or took employment in government departments; but it proved extremely difficult to place the remainder. In the end, several were 'given passports' to find their own livelihood, and one at least returned home.[45] The policy of non-intervention in private labour needs remained in force throughout the later eighteenth century, and official agencies did not recruit skilled labour as such for private purposes.

If Russian policy towards the West in the fields mentioned was closely concerned with questions of commercial and technical capacity, relations with foreigners in the south and east were governed by rather different considerations. Only the commercial interest remained the same. Within the Empire, the Kalmyk, Kirgiz-Kaysak and similar nationalities of the eastern border areas were factually and legally foreigners. While they recognized Russian suzerainty, relations with them were conducted through the College of Foreign Affairs: although the designation 'people of other birth or stock' (*inorodtsy*) clearly defined the distinction drawn between them and foreign nationals in the exact sense – 'of other lands' (*inostrantsy, inozemtsy*).

In Russian relations with the latter – peoples of Asian and Balkan countries – religious and commercial factors were paramount, both intertwined with the politics of the Eastern Question. Much of the Eastern trade through the Caspian in the eighteenth century was in the hands of Armenians, Indians and other foreigners settled in Astrakhan. The Armenian community especially was large and well established. Immigration had been greatly encouraged by Peter I following his Persian campaign, and during the first half of the century his successors granted further privileges.[46] All Asians, particularly those taking Russian citizenship, enjoyed considerable advantages and immunities as well as civic autonomy. By the middle of the century the Armenian colony exceeded 1,500 in number and was a major force in the economic life of Astrakhan.[47]

The efforts made to develop commerce through Orenburg in the 1730s and 1740s accorded with Russian experience in Astrakhan, and policy regarding both trade routes was very similar. Conversely, when new privileges were being drawn up for Astrakhan in 1762 (already after Catherine's accession), a postscript to the Senate decree on the subject specified that the Orenburg charter of 1734 should be used as a model.[48] The same decree offered concessions for a thirty-year period to foreigners settling round Astrakhan, adding specifically that they should have freedom to 'set up factories and works and to follow crafts unhindered' (§ 16).

The most important activity in this respect in Astrakhan was the processing of raw silk. But the decree was basically concerned with commerce. The next clause extended the same privileges to foreigners settling near Temernik on the lower reaches of the Don, the only 'port' with access to the Black Sea then fully under Russian control. Clause 17 envisaged the settlement here of 'relatives and correspondents of the subjects of both Turkey and the Venetian Republic'.

This decree, and others amplifying it,[49] demonstrate the unity of commercial interests in all areas open to trade with the East. They express, of course, the Russian government view and reflect the specific hopes placed in foreign elements by official circles. In the same context, finally, should be mentioned a decree of 1744 which had defined the position of Persian – effectively Persian Armenian – merchants in the south-east at large. Under this enactment, any such people wishing to settle in Russia for commercial purposes were to be well treated and to receive help in establishing themselves. But the concessions offered should not be publicized, to avoid offending Persia; and for the same reason such immigrants were to be directed to Astrakhan, and not allowed to join the young Armenian community in the new town of Kizlyar.[50]

The commercial role of foreigners in the south-east was paralleled by their importance in overland trade to the west and north-west of the Black Sea. Armenian communities had long existed in towns of the Western Ukraine, and Greek merchants likewise had a well-established association with its principal trading centres. Orthodox belief and commercial acumen ensured the acceptability to the Ukrainian authorities of such Greeks settling there for trading purposes. The most significant community was the famous Greek Brotherhood of Nezhin, which evolved in the 1680s. At the height of the Greeks' prosperity, in the middle of the eighteenth century, Nezhin had the largest fair in the Ukraine, and the Brotherhood numbered among its members merchants whose capital compared not unfavourably with that of the wealthiest of the region.[51] Like the Armenians, the Greek communities of Nezhin and elsewhere enjoyed considerable privileges and civic autonomy, playing in return a major part in trade both locally and abroad.[52]

In Russian relations with the Southern Slavs, and with other Balkan nationalities which looked to Russia for support against their overlord or oppressor Turkey, religious and political factors naturally played a larger role. Contacts in this field were also of long standing, and immigration of a variety of nationalities – individuals and small groups – was a commonplace feature of border movement in the south. Southern Slavs had early served in the Russian armies, and in the eighteenth century Peter I renewed this tradition. One of the principal contacts was with Serbs living in Austrian territory. A small number of these served under Peter in the Pruth campaign of 1711 and those remaining were settled in the Ukraine in 1715, on lands which later became the military colony of Slavyanoserbia. Attempts at the end of Peter's reign to form a hussar regiment by recruiting further Serbs from Austria foundered on Austrian opposition, and the proposed regiment's strength had to be made up by transferring to it several hundred Ukrainian

Cossacks. But 'Serbs' – in fact a variety of nationalities – continued to trickle into Southern Russia to enlist. In the 1740s three other regiments were formed on the pattern of the Serbian Hussar Regiment (Moldavian, Hungarian, Georgian) and during the Seven Years' War two more (Bulgarian and Macedonian). As before, the names of the regiments did not accurately reflect their national composition.[53]

The stationing of these elements in the Southern Ukraine was part of the wider, traditional, Russian system of border security. The foreigners made little impact on the country until the 1750s. Then the founding of the Serbian colonies of New Serbia and Slavyanoserbia, in 1752 and 1754 respectively, placed a considerable area under the almost autonomous control of the Serbian commanders Khorvat (New Serbia) and Shevich and Preradovich. The initiative in the founding of these colonies came from the Serbs themselves, Austrian subjects placed in difficulties by the reorganization of the border militia in which they served. They approached M. P. Bestuzhev-Ryumin, the Russian Minister in Vienna. Petersburg reacted favourably to his report and gave the Serbs very considerable concessions, including a large land grant, on condition that they should form border regiments of agreed type and composition. Genuine Serbs were always in a minority among the foreigners who joined the units; and the small numbers of the initial settlements necessitated constant recruitment, which was carried out in Austrian and Turkish territory throughout the 1750s, on the previous pattern. Officers and men could win promotion proportionate to the number of new recruits they obtained. Fifty made the recruiter an ensign, seventy-five a lieutenant, one hundred a captain.[54]

The Serbian colonies were not a success from the official point of view. Militarily they were an almost complete failure, and Khorvat in particular proved so lawless and self-seeking that within ten years he had been exiled and the autonomy of the colonies abolished (1763–4). In the 1750s, however, their creation caused considerable stir among the Orthodox subjects of Turkey and Austria.[55] Whether because of this, or because of the general unrest of which it was itself a symptom, similar proposals came in from other would-be immigrant leaders. Among others, in 1752 a Montenegrin Bishop, and in 1759 a 'Dalmatian' one, requested official assistance in bringing large numbers of their countrymen into Russia.

In the first case, the Russian authorities not only accepted the Bishop's offer, but set up a special 'Montenegrin Commission' to deal with the migration. It had four members, Russians and Slavs, with a staff of NCOs, and considerable funds. Between 1754 and 1758 some

1,500 Montenegrins (and other nationalities) entered Russia. Most of them were recruited, however, not by the Commission, which proved singularly ineffective, but by a lone Herzegovinian, one Yakov Ezdemirovich. Ezdemirovich later made a career in the Russian army; the immigration was halted in 1758 for political reasons and because of the poor quality of the immigrants.[56]

The political situation in the Balkans decided the Senate to settle these newcomers in an area remote from possible contact with the Turks. Orenburg Province, where Nepluyev was actively engaged in colonization, was a fairly natural choice, and orders were given in 1756 to survey territory between Orenburg and Stavropol, close to the Volga. (Shevich and Preradovich had also originally been offered land in this area.)[57] The Senate specified that the Montenegrins should not settle together, but be scattered among Russian dwellings; accordingly, Nepluyev proposed that some should be allocated to the fortresses of the region, and others given land in the Samara steppe on the river Irgiz.[58] A settlement was made along these lines, but numbers were much fewer than expected: many immigrants entered the Russian army or went elsewhere, and only 257 Montenegrins and Albanians came to Orenburg Province, late in 1756. And after three years these settlers decided that they, too, wished to join the army, or in some cases Khorvat in New Serbia. They were released, and their lands were later reassigned for the new settlement programmes of the 1760s.[59]

The projects of the Dalmatian Bishop Semeon Kontsarevich and his son, Lt Ignaty Kontsarevich, put forward in 1759 and again in new proposals in 1763, were very similar in their aims. But they met with a cool reception from the Russian authorities, chastened by experience with the Montenegrin immigration. In 1763 the Senate offered Ignaty Kontsarevich no more than travel expenses and limited diplomatic assistance. His recruits were to make their own way to the Russian border and on no account to give offence to other powers.[60] The numbers brought in by the Kontsareviches in 1759 (to New Serbia) were small, and there is no evidence of large-scale immigration resulting from the later plan.

Thus foreign immigration into the Ukraine in the 1750s came exclusively from the Balkans. But the decade also produced a number of projects involving Westerners, as a settlement area for whom the southern border region was likewise envisaged. In 1758, for example, during the Seven Years' War, the Saxon General Weissbach suggested the formation in the Ukraine of settlements of Prussian deserters and refugees. His plan – which in the event was not adopted – was intended both to encourage flight and desertion from Prussia, and to use the immigrants to strengthen Russia's border defences.[61]

An earlier and more important proposal had come from a French Protestant in the Russian army, a Brigadier de Lafont. In 1752 he presented a memorandum drawing attention to the advantages to be gained from the immigration into Russia of French Huguenots, who could set up silk and wool industries in the Ukraine. The project was prompted by reports of continuing persecution of Protestants in France. Knowledge of the brilliant success of Huguenot settlements elsewhere ensured Russian interest in the scheme; and Prussian recruiting methods provided a model. A powerful commission, under the Chancellor, A. P. Bestuzhev-Ryumin, began immediate discussion of the question, and Lafont was shortly transferred from his station in the Ukraine to the College of Foreign Affairs in Moscow, to help in the deliberations.[62]

In several respects, Lafont's proposals represented a new departure. It was the first time that recruitment abroad had been considered for the establishment of rural colonies as a means purely to economic development rather than border defence. There had, of course, been earlier cases of government intervention to control non-Russian settlement which had no military purpose: for example, that of Karelian immigrants at the end of the seventeenth century. But this and similar cases presented the question of regulating rather than instigating immigration, and there was no intention of using it for specialized economic purposes.[63] Furthermore, Lafont's plan presupposed effectively a complete government programme, more complex, and depending much more on government initiative, than the measures required – for instance – for the Serbian settlement in progress at the same time. Its scope was comparable at least to that of the abortive Montenegrin Commission.

The government commission prepared a thorough study of Western experience in settling Huguenots and other immigrants. Russian Ministers in Western capitals were asked in October 1752 for information, and Korff in Copenhagen was specifically ordered in addition to report on a Danish manifesto inviting foreign immigration, which had been published in 1749. The commission debated the most favourable location for the intended colony. The Ukraine was first proposed, but the Chancellor favoured a site on the Volga near Astrakhan. Any failure of the projected silk plantations could then be made good by raw silk imports from Persia. Lafont took an active part in the commission's work, and the conditions finally decided upon for the future immigrants essentially reproduced further proposals which he had made during November 1752. The conditions were in many respects similar to those of the Danish manifesto, and offered a wide range of inducements and privileges.[64]

The College of Foreign Affairs decided to place Lafont in charge of recruitment. He was to be based in Northern Germany and to follow the recruiting methods used by other powers, notably Prussia and Denmark. Detailed instructions were drawn up concerning the size of financial grants and means of transportation, while a circular was prepared to Ministers in the West enjoining co-operation with Lafont. Those in London, Copenhagen and Warsaw, beyond his range, could recruit colonists on their own initiative.[65] The operation had now grown in scope far beyond the persecuted Frenchmen.

However, this thorough beginning was doomed to frustration. A full report sent to the Empress for final approval in 1753 remained unanswered.[66] Over a year later (April 1754), the College of Foreign Affairs received a verbal order to send the whole matter to the Senate for discussion and implementation, and accordingly forwarded copies of the preliminary materials – the Danish Manifesto and the reports from Ministers abroad – without, however, mentioning Lafont and his proposals at all. But the Senate also gave no decision, or even a reply; and the Seven Years' War soon made the plan to recruit from France and central Europe temporarily impracticable.[67]

Nonetheless, conditions in Europe were potentially so favourable for an enterprise of this type that the idea did not die out. The Senate itself initiated the mission to Königsberg in 1759 whose results have already been mentioned; and there are reports, based on admittedly unreliable sources, of some emigration from there during Apraksin's occupation of the area in 1757.[68] One other incident from the late 1750s is recorded by Pisarevsky. A Russian officer, another Frenchman by the name of Larivière, sent to Germany in 1756 to buy horses for the army, was approached on behalf of large numbers of German families wishing to emigrate to Russia. The Russian Minister in Vienna, to whom Larivière took the matter, refused to act without orders from Petersburg; and Larivière's attempts to gain the attention of the government for the migration succeeded only three years later, after his return to Russia. In 1759 he at last received an answer: any new applicants should be promised a good reception, but no financial help could be given 'because of the present burdensome war'. The question was, however, being studied 'with due diligence', and he would be informed as soon as a decision was taken.[69]

The decision had still not been reached by the end of 1761 and the death of Elizabeth. Nothing was done about it under Peter III. But Peter did receive, and on his own terms accept, one proposal concerning the settlement of foreigners in Russia. This was the project of J. G. Eisen von Schwarzenberg. A German settled in Livonia as a Lutheran pastor, Eisen was a true child of the Enlightenment, a 'projector', and above all a dedicated opponent of serfdom. The plans which he presented at Court early in 1762 aimed at the emancipation of the serfs in Livonia, as a prelude to emancipation throughout the Empire. Eisen proposed the settlement of foreigners in this context primarily as a means of creating free peasant communities which would demonstrate the superiority of free men over serfs, and of a free over a serf economy.[70] Peter III found the idea interesting from another point of view, however, and Eisen 'received the order to make a plan as to how Livonia could be peopled with Germans, in order in the future to have a reserve for the twenty German regiments which are to be created'.[71]

The Livonian land-owning lobby in the Russian capital mounted an intrigue against Eisen, and finally he had to leave Petersburg empty-handed, even before the fall of Peter III.[72] Catherine's early aspirations gave him another chance: he will reappear in 1763. Eisen's projects add a new dimension to the question of foreign settlement in Russia, and in addition form, as it were, a connecting link between the plans and activities of the 1750s, and the broader, more theoretically based measures of Catherine's reign.

Population policy and practice in Europe and Russia in the eighteenth century

Despite his passionate advocacy of freedom for the Livonian peasants, Eisen's interest in foreign settlement was not in fact limited to its possible uses in his campaign against serfdom. He considered it also in the wider context of the question of population and its fluctuations, which by the mid-eighteenth century had become a general preoccupation of political economy.[73] Similar interest and concern can be found in almost every country in Europe. The question exercised academics and theoreticians, and found its way further into the 'conventional wisdom' of the day. The dominant theme was a demand for the highest possible levels of population. This formed the central idea of the elder Mirabeau's work, *L'Ami des Hommes*, which went through twenty editions in France between 1756 and 1760.[74] In Britain in 1763, the

Wilkite *North Briton* used the idea to attack Britain's vast American acquisitions from France on the grounds that they could cause ruinous depopulation. 'I believe it is a point which even none of the Scottish writers will deny, that the richness of any country does not proceed from the greatness of its extent, but the number of its inhabitants.'[75] This writer, had he but known it, was repeating a proposition affirmed in similar terms by Lomonosov in Russia two years previously; while Lomonosov was conversant with the work of earlier European writers on the subject.[76]

The view that the strength of a country depends upon the size of its population – or, as it was often formulated, that the glory of a monarch is proportionate to the number of his subjects – stemmed from mercantilist theory, and was most fully developed by the cameralists and subsequent writers in Prussia and Austria. The Austrian Joseph von Sonnenfels, for instance, a prominent representative of this view whose chief work was later translated into Russian, described population growth as a dominant principle of statecraft. Population levels were crucial for political affairs (defence); for 'police' (dense population facilitates internal control); for commerce (consumption and circulation); and for finance (taxation). In short, they affected decisively all the major areas of government activity.[77] Frederick II of Prussia, in his *Political Testament* of 1768, advanced the same thesis, contrasting vast, empty Russian Siberia unfavourably with small, densely-populated Holland from the point of view of revenues and military strength.[78] French writers in the mid-eighteenth century, on the other hand, for example Montesquieu and the later Physiocrat Mirabeau, were more aware of the necessary balance between population growth and means of subsistence. But they still linked population increase with agriculture as a true basis of national wealth.[79]

These doctrines both fostered and reflected an unprecedented interest in means of maintaining and increasing population. They were prominent especially in the absolutist states of Europe, where they had considerable influence on contemporary social policies.[80] From the middle of the seventeenth century onwards, a whole 'populationist' literature grew up. The type and scope of measures advocated varied considerably. They included medical reforms, and social and fiscal measures designed to make marriage easier, more attractive, and more fruitful. Some writers found marriage and monogamy constricting and rejected them altogether.[81] Among other measures, foreign colonization was generally approved, though often with reservations. Eisen was one of many who objected to the cost involved; while some writers stressed the difficulty of integrating large numbers of foreigners into an alien society.[82]

Most of the ideas advanced in the eighteenth century were not new. They originated with the writers of seventeenth-century France, Britain, Germany; and Colbert, for example, had put many of them into practice under Louis XIV. Furthermore, much writing merely reflected or systematized ideas current in government circles.[83] The 'populationist' school was in any case not entirely dominant in contemporary thought: Malthus had a number of precursors in different parts of Europe.[84] But where 'populationist' theory matched the needs of a specific situation or the ambitions of a ruler, theory and practice went closely together. In the period in question, their unity was most complete in Austria and Prussia. These states at once accounted for the larger part of contemporary writing on population and had the most active and long-established population policy.

In Russia, the concept of population increase as a principle of political economy found acceptance more gradually. The problem to which it related was a perennial one: in Solov'yov's words, 'that perpetual evil of the Russian land, the physical lack of people, the disproportion of the population to the area of the enormous state'.[85] And in the eighteenth century this disproportion was accentuated by a notable increase in the state's manpower requirements, both direct and indirect. New undertakings – Peter I's expansion of the armed forces, for example – demanded immediate large resources. Policies with less immediate physical impact, such as Peter's ultimately highly successful efforts to increase the tax revenues, likewise logically required the highest possible population levels. More generally, Russia's overall economic development during the century increased the need for labour, and for supporting population at large, despite the natural population growth of the time. As we saw in discussing Orenburg Province, a significant factor in such economic development was territorial expansion, which continued throughout the period; economic aims as much as strategic or defensive considerations formed its driving force, and expansion itself often created a need for population to settle newly-acquired areas. Catherine II herself made the connection between aggrandizement and economic growth succinctly, if perhaps rather too grandly, in a note written while she was still Grand Duchess:

To join the Caspian to the Black Sea, and both to the seas of the North; to make the commerce of China and the East Indies pass through Tartary: this would be to raise this Empire to a degree of might above that of the other empires of Asia and Europe. And who could resist the limitless power of an absolute prince who rules over a warlike people?[86]

But such acquisitions only became really useful after they had been pacified, rendered defensible, and given a population sufficient to control and develop them. Catherine had already observed, in another somewhat contrary note: 'Peace is necessary to this vast empire, we need throngs of people, but not devastations; let's make our enormous deserts swarm with them, if possible. . .'[87] These statements foreshadow very exactly some lines of her later policies, and indicate equally the role that population policy had to play in them.

Another factor which has sometimes been cited[88] as a principal cause of under-population in Russia's border regions, and one which became increasingly effective in the first half of the eighteenth century, was serfdom, which immobilized large numbers of peasants on landlords' estates in the older settled lands of the centre. Clearly the general attitude of the state towards the mobility of all peasants inhibited free outward movement of population; but the relative importance of this should not be over-estimated. Apart from the prevalence of illegal movement, and the increasing interest of the eighteenth-century land-owning class itself in border lands, these areas had a particularly high birth rate and also received many native immigrants of different kinds.[89] Serfdom may have slowed, but it did not prevent, the rapid growth of population in newly-opened areas; the increase in the Southern Ukraine, to take a fresh example, was very large indeed during the century.[90] Overall, mobility would seem to have been less important than absolute numbers in a state which 'supports twenty million inhabitants and could support two hundred million'[91] – and which thought it could make use of them as well.

But despite the obvious applicability of 'populationist' ideas to eighteenth-century Russian circumstances, the connection between state aims and high population levels was not immediately made specific, and there is little sign of 'populationism' as such before the middle decades of the century. Concern for the plight of the common people expressed in the reign of Peter I was couched in different terms, though sometimes deriving from similar ideas; and even measures which may have been 'populationist' in inspiration were officially motivated in other ways. A decree of 1712 on foundling houses, for example, stated that their purpose was to prevent unmarried mothers 'from doing a still greater sin (that is, murder)'.[92]

In the second quarter of the eighteenth century, however, specific

references appeared to the desirability of population increase, and by
the middle of the century it had passed into the generally accepted
canon of political theory. Tatishchev had named 'the increase of the
people' as first among the sources of national wealth,[93] and in 1754
(four years after his death), the question reached the Senate, which
considered projects 'concerning the preservation of the people'.[94]
Population growth is one of the blessings of Elizabeth's reign enumer-
ated by Lomonosov in his eulogy of Peter I composed in 1755, and
its necessity is axiomatic in the same writer's work 'On the Preservation and Increase of the Russian People' (1761).[95] This was the first
attempt in Russia at a comprehensive treatment of the subject; and
the ideas it expresses are in most respects typical of this school of
thought.

Set out in the form of a letter to Count I. I. Shuvalov on the occasion
of his birthday, the work represents, according to the introduction, 'old
notes of my thoughts relating to the increase of the general good'.
Lomonosov proposed to expound these thoughts under eight general
headings which, taken together, would have formed a complete treatise
on political economy. The first heading, and the only one in fact discussed in the letter, was that concerning population.

I consider as the starting point of this [sc. the general good] the most
important matter of all: that preservation and increase of the Russian
people, in which consists the greatness, might and wealth of the entire
state, and not in its great area (*obshirnosti*), useless without inhabitants.

Lomonosov subdivides this topic into thirteen points, of which the
first ten are all social and medical measures fully within the 'populationist' tradition: four items are concerned with increasing ease and
fertility of marriage, three with curbing infant mortality, two with the
need for moderate living and better medical services, and one with
investigation of the causes of epidemics. The eleventh deals with violent
deaths, which in Lomonosov's view were largely caused by brawls and
brigandage. 'Harmful brawls occur between neighbours, and especially
between landowners, which can be obviated by nothing but land
surveys.' The main reason for the persistence of brigandage was the
lack of efficient civil policing and administration, which was aggravated in many areas by lack of towns and of an official presence. 'There
are many obscure places in Russia, five hundred versts and more without towns, direct refuges for brigands and all sorts of fugitives and
passportless people', who find unquestioning hospitality from the local
peasantry; in such places 'it is necessary to found and situate towns,

giving large villages civic rights to set up administrative offices (*ratushi i voevodstvy*) and protecting them with reliable fortifications and precautions against the brigands'.

Thus under-population led not only to low productivity but to social disorder. These troubles were always more noticeable on the periphery, and one additional factor in the steady outward expansion of government authority was the need to establish control and order. At the same time, Lomonosov was aware that the 'fugitives and passportless people' were not all evil-doers. The next section (12), on the fugitive problem, adopts a liberal attitude, blaming flight 'mostly on landlord oppressions and on military conscriptions' and adding that 'it is better to act with gentleness' in the matter. The problems and purposes of regaining fugitives were obviously similar to those of foreign immigration. The two questions were interwoven in the Russian practice of the 1760s; and Lomonosov makes a direct connection between them in section 13:

The place of fugitives abroad can conveniently be filled by the reception of foreigners, if suitable measures are taken to that end. The present unhappy time of war in Europe forces not only single people, but whole ruined families to leave their fatherland and seek places distant from the violence of war. The broad dominion of our great monarch is capable of containing whole peoples secure in its interior, and of supplying them with all things needful, which require only the ordinary labour of men for their valuable production...

Thus for Lomonosov, as for the great majority of theorists and of practitioners in the field of population policy, the settlement of foreigners was merely one among many possible courses of action, alternative or complementary. Lomonosov's plans, however, at least as formulated here, were limited and even cautious, approaching foreign colonization in terms of the fugitive question and of the existing, temporary situation in Europe. This view stops short of the optimism of Russian official policy in the early sixties, which shared with that of other countries the implicit assumption that foreign colonization was something to be pursued for its own sake, not merely when immediate conditions were especially favourable. Lomonosov's caution accords with his well-known lack of enthusiasm for the didactic function so widely attributed to foreigners in Russia in the eighteenth century, a role cast also for Russia's projected immigrants by some, though by no means all, of those concerned in planning the immigration. The same scepticism finds expression in Lomonosov's strictures on the way in which foreign apothecaries neglected the training of their Russian apprentices: a neglect which he rightly saw as detrimental to both medical services and the nation's health at large (section 9).

In the question of colonization, practical difficulties were at first often either overlooked or underestimated. This was the case in Russia. Other governments, after similar bitter experience, accepted them as inevitable. Frederick the Great once damned all his immigrants with the remark that 'the first generation of colonists is usually not much use'.[96] But Frederick found his profit in the second and later generations, and he was most assiduous, and most successful, in encouraging immigration into Prussia.

Ever since the Treaty of Westphalia (1648), the rulers of Brandenburg–Prussia had actively colonized their territories with foreigners (usually Germans), and on Frederick's accession in 1740 the number of new subjects thus acquired was already some 150,000.[97] Prussia had welcomed Huguenot refugees after the revocation of the Edict of Nantes. The Potsdam Edict of 1685 attracted 20,000; subsequently it became the basis of all foreign settlement in Prussia throughout the eighteenth century. The consistent policy of religious toleration practised by the Prussian rulers contributed largely to their success in this field.[98] Frederick II made colonization a central part of state policy, under a special government department whose task it was 'to attract as many foreigners into the country as it is at all possible to do'.[99] Beheim-Schwarzbach lists eighty-eight major ordinances on colonization during the forty-six year reign, not to mention minor decrees.[100] The influx of colonists over the same period is estimated at 350,000; and by Frederick's death in 1786 nearly 20% of his subjects were immigrants or their descendants.[101]

This reservoir of new population proved invaluable to Frederick, particularly during the Seven Years' War, and his successes then were one of the factors influencing Austrian policy in the same field after 1762.[102] Austria also had a tradition of foreign colonization, though not on the same scale as that of Prussia, nor was immigration into Austria–Hungary in the eighteenth century so considerable. Schünemann puts the total for the period 1740–90 at 150–200,000, or one half to two thirds of the Prussian figure.[103]

Besides Prussia and Austria, other nations were active in the field of recruitment and colonization. France and Britain sought to populate overseas colonies; Britain had earlier 'planted' Germans in Ireland.[104] Germans settled too in Andalusia, in the Sierra Morena, where the colonies were intended by their creators to be a social experiment, 'to create at one stroke an ideal society, free from those blemishes inherited from the past which affect. . .contemporary Spanish society'.[105] And Denmark had been trying to obtain foreign settlers since the end of the seventeenth century.

Danish offers of asylum to the French Huguenots met with little response. A further attempt in 1723 was likewise unsuccessful; and the Manifesto of 1748–9 already mentioned attracted just three immigrants. However, the Seven Years' War created conditions more favourable to recruitment, and a new Danish attempt in 1759 finally brought over 8,000 colonists to Jutland and Schleswig between 1761 and 1763. But the colonies proved difficult to establish. The land was poor, the colonists unfamiliar with local conditions, the native population unfriendly. Some colonists returned home, others went on to Russia. Those who remained accustomed themselves only gradually to their new environment, though ultimately they prospered.[106]

The middle of the eighteenth century, especially the period immediately following the Seven Years' War when peace had freed governmental energy and resources for things other than military, was the heyday of 'populationism' and of foreign colonization in Europe. The Russian immigration programme started in 1762, that of Spain in 1766. Austria renewed her efforts while the war was still in progress; those of Prussia and Britain continued as before. Already by the 1750s the theory and the reality of foreign settlement in the West were well known in Russia, as the work of the Lafont commission and the writings of Lomonosov show. The *coup d'état* of June 1762 gave the Empire a ruler who had both the opportunity and the inclination to engage in it herself.

2

Catherine II and the Manifestos of
1762 and 1763

The immediate context: Catherine and public opinion

Catherine II was a confirmed adherent of 'populationist' views and well aware of their applicability to Russia. 'No prince in modern times has ever made the subject of population so intimate a concern of government as the late empress', claimed William Tooke.[1] Even before her accession, Catherine had expressed herself in favour of measures to increase population. In the notes previously quoted she followed up her proposal, 'let's make our enormous deserts swarm', with the practical suggestion that conversion of Russia's non-Christian subjects was in general to be avoided, since 'polygamy is more useful for the population'. Another note deplored the high rate of death in infancy in Russia: 'what a loss to the State!'[2] The *Instruction*, Catherine's most explicit political credo, has a whole chapter (Chapter xii) devoted to population, written in the same spirit, and much of it taken directly from Montesquieu.[3]

The Empress's personal interest and initiatives led to the execution during the 1760s of various 'populationist' measures apart from the scheme of foreign settlement: the creation of a Medical College, for example, and the establishment of Foundling Houses.[4] Her reign was in fact the first in Russia to show systematic concern with population; and the historian of her population policies, M. M. Shpilevsky, regarded this preoccupation as the driving force behind all her social legislation.[5] Catherine's policies in this field cannot, of course, be considered in isolation from her other preoccupations. In common with the principal theorists of the subject, she regarded population increase essentially as a means to increase the wealth and power of the state – and with them her own 'glory'. As Schlözer put it: 'Russia is rich, fertile, and powerful. What does she lack to become yet richer, more fertile, more powerful? People.'[6]

The most frequent justification given for encouraging immigration was the huge extent of untouched land in the Empire awaiting exploitation. Natural resources which could expand both agricultural and industrial production would lie dormant so long as labour was not available to work them. 'Empty lands', 'empty places' – such phrases recur as a leitmotif through discussion and legislation on foreign settlement. One of the most forthright statements of the problem appears in the preamble to the 1763 Manifesto itself. Noting that 'a great many... Places for the settlement and Habitation of Mankind...remaine yet uncultivated', the Manifesto stressed the presence of mineral resources, and then the potential for trade and industry: 'and they having Woods, Rivers, Lakes, and Seas belonging to Commerce, enough, are very convenient for the increase and augmentation of many Manufactures, Fabricks and other Works'.[7]

Thus immigration was viewed primarily as a means to further the general development of the economy. As we shall see, it also had a place in other concerns of Catherine and her government, such as the control of outlying parts of the Empire; and it became intertwined, too, with areas of social policy – from the outset, for example, with the problem of fugitives and how to reclaim them; later, with Catherine's treatment of the Jews, and her interest in relations between landlords and their peasants. But her overriding, or underlying, concern throughout was economic.

Outside the government itself, Catherine's concern with population found wide support from public opinion at Court, among the educated classes, and in academic circles. The second half of the eighteenth century witnessed an unprecedented vogue in Russia for political economy and all fields of economics. K. Lodyzhensky records numerous 'extensive' memoranda dating from this period, composed by writers of various social classes and dealing with multifarious problems.[8] There was a rapid growth of publications on such topics, both journals and books. Foreign works were translated and reproduced; the first Russian statistical surveys now appeared, the first history of commerce, new works on agronomy. And awareness of the West and Western ideas, stimulated by contacts during the Seven Years' War, spread steadily further through society.

Writers and commentators on the Russian economy at this time generally took under-population for granted: a basic fact of Russian life.[9] In the field of population policy, both the activities of other European powers and the doctrines of the 'populationists' were well known. In France, whose intellectual life was closely followed, 'populationism' was at its height.[10] The work of a German writer on the subject, Bell, was among books in the library of Lomonosov. Others of the school, the Prussians Justi and Bielfield, as well as Sonnenfels, whose views have already been discussed, were translated into Russian – Bielfield at the instigation of Catherine herself. Following Lomonosov, other members of the Academy of Sciences, both Russian and foreign, wrote on the question.[11] The populationist viewpoint remained dominant in official and upper-class circles for much of Catherine's reign; and although before the end of the century it was under attack in Russia as elsewhere, even its opponents were prompt to acknowledge the general acceptance which it had enjoyed for so long.[12] Particularly in Catherine's early years, her more dramatic measures in this field caught the public imagination. The development of the Saratov colonies themselves was closely followed in contemporary works of geography, and in calendars and almanacs such as the *Khronologiya veschey dostopamyatnykh* published annually by the Academy of Sciences from the 1770s.[13]

The Foundling Houses in Moscow and Petersburg also became a focus of public attention. They were initiated with Catherine's full approval by a highly-placed member of the aristocracy, I. I. Betskoy, under the slogan: 'Care for the poor and concern for the increase of people useful to society are two supreme duties of every pious ruler.'[14] They called forth generous donations, and a large number of imitative institutions were created throughout the Empire, many of them founded by private individuals. Some philanthropists turned their own houses into centres for orphans. Even members of the highest aristocracy took foundling children into their personal care. Catherine wrote to a correspondent from Petersburg in 1763: 'Many have voluntarily agreed among themselves, while waiting for the opening of the Foundling House, to feed some [children]. Stroganov has taken two and the Countess Bruce one. Let me know if any good souls are doing the same where you are. They have all taken one or two each, some even more.'[15]

Some highly-placed individuals were eager to find foreign settlers for their own private purposes. At the end of Elizabeth's reign Count Ivan Chernyshev, and later his brother Zakhar, had tried to establish on their estates a colony of Moravian Brethren from Herrnhut in Saxony. Early negotiations failed, because of persecution of previous Herrnhut missionary activities in the Empire, but on the personal intervention of the new Empress, the discussions were renewed in 1763 as part of the government programme: and finally they led to the conspicuously successful Herrnhut colony of Sarepta.[16] Count Peter Rumyantsev also established a religious colony on his lands, in 1770.[17]

The government's immigration scheme attracted interest for yet another reason. Some saw European immigrants as carriers of a superior Western culture. In continuing their traditional policy with regard to Western specialists, the Russian authorities tended to over-value foreigners and their possible contribution. Where native skills were lacking, the use of outsiders was natural, and normal practice; but many such people were poorly qualified, and reliance on them could also lead to a vicious circle, the replacement of foreigners with more foreigners, or a neglect of existing native talent. These attitudes, with their attendant dangers, were equally common among the Western-orientated Petersburg society from which the ruling elite largely came: here it was normal practice to hire Westerners for private requirements both economic and cultural, especially as the way of life now almost obligatory in the capital was impossible without Western merchandise and Western skills.

The same attitudes carried over easily onto foreign settlement. The Russian Minister in Hamburg, Musin-Pushkin, went so far as to suggest that foreign settlers

can by the skills they have acquired, by their handiwork, crafts and various machines hitherto unknown in Russia, reveal to [Russian] subjects the best and quickest means of working the land, of increasing domestic livestock, of afforestation, of the useful application of all possible sorts of products, of setting up their own factories, of conducting the entire husbandry.[18]

These sentiments were later echoed by the head of the colonist administration, G. G. Orlov himself;[19] and they explain the interest in private colonies of the Chernyshev brothers.

Thus in her population policy Catherine found a ready understanding among the upper ranks of Russian society. Furthermore, this was an area in which no important vested interests were threatened. With the end of the Seven Years' War, the accession to the throne of a convinced 'populationist' and enthusiast for the West whose ideas were largely echoed by public opinion, and with the existence of extensive official documentation on foreign settlement elsewhere, the stage was finally set for realization of the idea in Russia. A start was made within four months.

The formulation of policy: evolution of the Manifestos of 1762 and 1763

On 14 October 1762, the Senate received an Imperial decree which stated:

> As there are in Russia many empty places not settled, and many foreigners petition Us to allow them to settle in such empty places, therefore We once and for all time permit Our Senate by this decree, in accordance with the law and in consultation with the College of Foreign Affairs, for this is a political matter, to receive henceforth into Russia without further report to Us all persons wishing to settle, except Jews. We hope in time by this means to increase the glory of God and his Orthodox faith, and the well-being of Our Empire.[20]

This was the first step towards a systematic policy of foreign settlement. The source of the particular initial impulse which set things in motion cannot be established with certainty. French diplomats in Petersburg at the time reported confidently that the initiator of the whole scheme was François Pictet, one of Catherine's secretaries and later a 'director' of private colonies on the Volga.[21] This seems unlikely; but even if their information was correct, Catherine can have needed little persuading, and she remained closely involved right through the preparatory stages.

On receiving the Empress's decree, the Senate ordered all its departments to present at once any unresolved cases concerning the settling of 'foreign people' in Russia. This enquiry produced no immediate results. Of seven departments which replied, only the Military Board (*Voinskaya Ekspeditsiya*) had papers – on the New Serbia colony and Ukrainian Cossack settlement.[22] Another order, eleven days later, to check whether there existed any surveys of 'empty and unpopulated places, both on the River Don and generally throughout Russia', was equally fruitless,[23] despite the fact that a general order for such information had been sent out the year before.[24] While replies were still coming in to the Senate's queries, Catherine added to her instructions of 14 October: 'Do the same also with Russian migrants of all kinds.'[25]

The Senate already had before it, as a legacy from Peter III, the case of fugitive Old Believers living in Poland who wished to return to Russia but were unwilling to do so under existing conditions.[26] It had been intended to place this question before the Empress for her decision; but in view of the new order the Senators decided (12 November 1762) to press forward with a declaration on the schismatics which they had previously prepared. At the same time the Senate sent word to the

College of Foreign Affairs that it should 'use the utmost efforts in the matter of the recruitment (*vyzov*) of foreign people, except Jews, for settlement in Russia, and especially manufacturers and artisans'. The College was also to inform the Senate whether it had information about any such would-be immigrants, and to give its opinion as to the basis on which they should in future be settled.[27]

The College of Foreign Affairs was in no hurry to reply. But the Senate soon received a final list of the cases which had previously been sent in for its own consideration and which were still held unresolved, in some cases after several years, in its departments.[28] They numbered six, including as item number one the Lafont project. The case of the Old Believers in Poland, which was not yet finally dealt with, also found its way on to the list. Of the other four, one was a note that a certain Court Counsellor Sheliga had given N. I. Panin a secret project for the settlement of foreigners on empty land in Orenburg Province. The Senate found that it had no copy of this memorandum, and no idea of Sheliga's whereabouts; and there is no further mention of him in the Senate's minutes.[29] But Sheliga was in fact a magnificent specimen of the species of 'projector' so plentiful around the Russian court at this time.[30] He was persistent. He had followed the Senate to Moscow after the Court moved there for Catherine's coronation in September, and reported his presence and his business to the Senate Office;[31] and he was not to be got rid of merely with a snub. In August of the following year (1763), Catherine wrote in exasperation to the Procurator-General, A. Glebov: 'Inform the Senate that they are to take a signed undertaking from Court Counsellor Sheliga, on pain of loss of all rank, that he will no longer bother us with petitions and the presentation of projects.' Sheliga was claiming at this stage to be involved in litigation over estates in Poland, and over a large sum of money in Sweden. Catherine ordered him to be given his certification of release from service (*abshid*) and a gift of 250 roubles for travel expenses, '*on condition that he go abroad immediately to pursue his claims*'.[32]

Another item of unfinished business on the Senate's list was a report which had come in from Hamburg, in 1758, of 'manufacturers' who wished to set up production of fine-quality textiles in Russia, with state or private assistance. The question had been examined in the College of Manufactures. No Russian factory owner had wished to employ them or set up a factory on the terms they proposed; they had no capital of their own, and the College, 'on the suspicion that they are simply weavers', had given a negative opinion. But no final decision had been reached.[33]

In the same year the Senate had received a report from the Provincial Chancellery of Astrakhan, forwarding a petition from the Astrakhan *politseymeyster*, Prince Melkhisedek Baratayev, a Georgian. Baratayev set forth the wish of his 'brothers and relatives' to become Russian subjects and to settle in Russian territory. The Georgians had been driven to this step by constant harassment from mountain tribes of the Caucasus, 'Mountain Tatars, Lezghins and Tablins'. They were prepared to take service in the Hussar regiments on the border, and asked accordingly for a grant of land near Kizlyar 'on which up to one thousand families, and above, might settle without interference (*utesneniye*)'. The Astrakhan Provincial Chancellery quoted the 1744 decree on the settlement of Persian subjects[34] in support of Baratayev's request, and another from the College of Foreign Affairs in 1747 permitting Georgians and Armenians escaping from captivity in the Caucasus to settle where they wished in the same area. It added that 'around Kizlyar, as a frontier area, full settlement with people is very necessary'. The petition had not been considered at all by the Senate, which now did not know whether the Astrakhan authorities had done anything about it.[35]

Finally, there was a very recent item involving a wealthy Jewish merchant, Kalmar, from The Hague. Having heard of Russian measures to foster trade in the Empire, he had expressed the wish to set up an office in Russia under the management of his own sons, and indicated that many prosperous Jews would do likewise if permission were granted. The Russian Minister at The Hague, Gross, had written for instructions to the College of Foreign Affairs, which had sent the matter on to the Senate on 26 July 1762. After a check of previous decrees on the subject, the Senate had reported on it to Catherine on 31 July.[36]

Although the dates given do not coincide, this episode must be the one recorded by Catherine herself as having taken place 'not eight days' after her accession, and reproduced from her notes by Solov'yov. The latter found no trace of it himself in the Senate records: possibly the original was removed to the files used here when the Senate made its enquiries. Solov'yov also records that Catherine attended fifteen Senate meetings between 1 July and 1 September, so it is perhaps permissible to think that when she afterwards recalled the events of the first difficult and exciting weeks of her reign, she may have confused one session with another.

However that may be, the incident clearly made an impression on her, emphasizing the delicacy of her position. When the Senate presented the question to her, she was faced with a dilemma. She had been brought to the throne, she realized, amid popular discontent and under the banner of the defence of Orthodoxy. 'To begin the reign with a decree permitting free entry to Jews would be a bad means of allaying public excitement; but to declare the free entry of Jews harmful was impossible.' The Senate, seeing her embarrassment, offered for her consideration the extracts already prepared from previous laws. The last was Elizabeth Petrovna's celebrated declaration: 'I wish no mercenary profit from the enemies of Christ.'[37] In Catherine's view, so categoric a statement necessitated and justified a cautious decision: she ordered the question to be postponed.[38] The Senate recorded no resolution in the case of the Dutch Jew, and the file is marked – in fact incorrectly in view of the decree of 14 October – 'decided by the Manifesto following'.[39] But this was by no means the end of the matter. Pursuing in public an anti-Jewish policy, Catherine took steps in 1764 to ensure that Jews would be admitted unofficially to New Russia; and her chosen instrument in this connection was the administration by then set up for the immigration programme.[40]

On the basis of the available documentation, and without waiting for further information from the College of Foreign Affairs, a Manifesto was drawn up and published on 4 December 1762.[41] It would seem to have been composed in some haste: short, and couched in general terms, it repeats the phrasing of the decree of 14 October, promising kind reception and protection to foreign immigrants and forgiveness to returning Russian fugitives. The Senate, says the decree, has been instructed to draw up detailed plans and instructions. On publication of the Manifesto Catherine at once ordered that it should be translated into 'all foreign languages' and printed in all foreign newspapers.[42] The Manifesto did not come before the Senate before publication, and the subject does not reappear in the Senate records until after 4 December.

At the next Senate meeting, of 12 December, Catherine gave further instructions. 'For the acquisition of great advantage to the state', the Senate was to

recruit for settlement in Russia foreign craftsmen and skilled workers of different types, who are to be allowed to settle not only in the places assigned, but may also according to their wishes live in all Russian towns and earn a living by their skills; and as to what concessions should be given to them over and above this, for their greater encouragement and consonant with the national interest, the Senate is to compose a draft for a Manifesto and present it for Her Highness's approval.[43]

The Senate ordered extracts to be made from all previous decrees bearing on the subject, and a draft proclamation to be drawn up. But for the moment the question of the Old Believers remained in the forefront of its attention. On 13 December the Senators approved the final details of the manner of return, registration and settlement of such fugitives, and the following day, together with the declaration already prepared, these were published as a Senate decree. The preamble referred specifically to the Manifesto of 4 December, and gave a short résumé of legislation on fugitives since the time of Peter the Great. An appendix listed areas in which those returning could settle as state peasants.[44]

Meanwhile the Senate staff was busy with the translation and printing of the Manifesto itself. Copies to local authorities within the Empire were finally dispatched at the end of December.[45] The Manifesto was accompanied by a Senate decree of 31 December ordering all authorities to report back on the availability of empty land under their jurisdiction, if any, and whether its settlement would adversely affect the present local inhabitants.[46] Soon afterwards the College of Foreign Affairs reported the dispatch of the Manifesto on 7 January 1763 to Russian Ministers abroad. A covering circular enjoined the use of all possible means to obtain publicity, and prompt assistance to all foreigners who might respond. Any Russian fugitives who came forward were to be dealt with at Ministers' discretion, pains being taken to dispel the least doubts or hesitations.[47]

The terms of the Manifesto were bound to arouse hostility in some quarters abroad. The College of Foreign Affairs was particularly fearful of this in the case of Turkey, traditionally sensitive to any signs of Russian activity on her borders and usually thought by the Russian government – not always justifiably[48] – to be similarly resentful of any loss of her subjects. The Russian Minister in Constantinople, Obreskov, was instructed to make known the contents of the Manifesto secretly to such people as might be inclined to take advantage of it, but on no account to publish it openly in Turkish territory;[49] and the College of Foreign Affairs even set about recalling manuscript copies of the Manifesto in Tatar and Turkish which in the general dispatch had gone out to Kiev, Astrakhan and the fortress of St Dmitry (later Rostov-on-Don). But the Senate countermanded this: not only had the original order come from the Empress herself, but the only reason for not printing the proclamation was lack of type for the languages involved. In any case, anyone knowing the language would have no difficulty in translating from a Russian copy. It was only necessary to ensure caution on the part of the local authorities concerned.[50]

The efforts of the Senate to attract the Old Believers back into the country had considerable success, and in May 1763 the privileges offered were extended to fugitives of all kinds.[51] As far as foreigners were concerned, initial reactions to the Manifesto from Ministers in the West were concerned principally to criticize its lack of precision. Vorontsov from London (18 February/1 March 1763), Ostermann from Stockholm (21 February/4 March), Gross from The Hague (11/22 February)[52] all requested further details of what Ministers could offer, and where and how foreigners would be settled. On 10 April the College of Foreign Affairs forwarded these requests to the Senate, together with copies of the papers of 1754. The latter included the 1749 Danish Manifesto, the reports gathered at the time from Russian Ministers abroad and, as a separate item, the proposals of the Lafont commission. The College remarked in its report that although circumstances had changed somewhat since the commission drew up its proposals, these 'can however give no little relief in the consideration of this matter in the present case'.[53]

This communication was in fact the long-awaited answer to the Senate's enquiry of 12 November 1762 as to information held by the College. In the meantime another enquiry had been sent on 30 December in almost identical terms, and when that too remained unanswered, a reminder which almost amounted to a rebuke.[54] But now it was the College's turn to be delayed. Further dispatches came from abroad, pressing for an answer. The Russian Minister in Danzig, Rehbinder, who on publishing the Manifesto had received many enquiries from local artisans, had already taken matters into his own hands and made cash advances to some of those wishing to emigrate. In his report (1/12 April) he justified himself on the grounds that this would encourage others. On 20 April Catherine herself gave a ruling, approving Rehbinder's action but stressing that only those in real need should receive financial help. At the same time she ordered the Senate to be reminded of the matter, and of her interest in it.[55]

The intervention of the Empress prodded the Senate into action; at least, a month later they devoted an entire session to the problem of immigration and the representations of the College of Foreign Affairs. The minutes of the meeting give a detailed picture of what these contained. The College reported that it had received no requests from Europeans, but that petitions 'have been coming in for a long time from Serbs, Montenegrins, Vlachs and such-like', whom, however, it was difficult to accept because of Turkish susceptibilities; so that on the last request, from Moldavians and Vlachs, the College had been able to reach no decision.[56]

The Senate also had to consider the question of settling on the southeastern frontier near Kizlyar 'Persians' (largely Armenians) and mountain tribesmen who wished to become Russian subjects: a question already decided in principle by an Imperial order to found a new settlement for the immigrants. The order was given effect with the creation in the same year of the town of Mozdok.[57]

The Senate first turned its attention to the problems of the Ministers in Europe. All the relevant documents before it were presented once more, starting with the December Manifesto and Catherine's subsequent order on the recruitment of artisans. The Senators were content, finally, merely to repeat their instruction of 12 December: the new Manifesto already demanded by the Empress was to be composed 'as quickly as possible, . . .on the basis of the law, and with consideration of the interests not only of those immigrant peoples but more of the state'.

The question of the Moldavians and Vlachs, civilians who wished to settle on the rivers Bug and Sinyukha, was more difficult and received more direct treatment. The area named was right on the Turkish border, and the College of Foreign Affairs felt that Turkish subjects could not be settled there without risk of 'unpleasant consequences'. The Senate agreed, and decided as the only alternative that

if among Moldavians, Vlachs and other peoples of the Greek faith, Turkish subjects, large numbers have conceived an ardent desire to migrate to Russia, reliable people should secretly be sent to explain to them the unsuitability of their settlement near the border and persuade them to settle inside Russia; they need have no doubts as to land and amenities, of which the best and the most fertile, and not at the greatest distance, shall be given to them, and in accordance with their request both in their husbandry and in trades and commerce and in other things proper measures will be instituted. And, more precisely, land should be assigned to them in Orenburg Province on the Volga and in other free places there.[58]

As far as the Mozdok settlement was concerned, the commandant at Kizlyar had already been ordered to draw up an Instruction for the officer in charge, and a charter (*privilegiya*) for the settlers. These documents had not yet been presented to the Senate, which therefore decided to inform the new Governor of Astrakhan, Beketov, that he and the commandant should compose a charter 'not only for the places around Kizlyar already designated. . .but also, on the basis of the law of 31 July 1762 on trade,[59] for the whole of the Astrakhan Province'. This was to go with the Instruction for consideration by the College of Foreign Affairs and the Senate.[60]

On the question of immigration from Europe, a resolution merely to hasten the new manifesto, even 'as quickly as possible', could not satisfy the College of Foreign Affairs and the diplomats abroad. After receiving approval for his action in making small cash advances, Rehbinder in Danzig had already proceeded with the dispatch of his recruits to Russia. His report of this (16/27 May), received at the beginning of June, underlined the urgency of advance planning. The Vice-Chancellor, Prince A. Golitsyn, insisted to the Empress on the need to know beforehand what terms and conditions were to be offered to the immigrants, and Catherine directed the College of Foreign Affairs yet again to the Senate for clarification.[61]

But that very same day (7 June) the Office of the College reported the arrival of Rehbinder's recruits: a party of forty-five, nineteen Russian subjects and the remainder foreign artisans with their families. The Russian fugitives and deserters among them were sent straight to the Military College, but the Office requested instructions from the Senate on the foreigners, since they were pressing for information and action.[62] A week later the College of Foreign Affairs itself, following the Empress's resolution, sent a similar request in order to be able to inform Ministers abroad.[63] On 25 June the Senate gave a ruling. The remaining three Russians were to be dealt with by the Petersburg Provincial Chancellery; the foreigners were to go to the office of the Petersburg Magistrature, which would administer the oath of loyalty and place them in appropriate craft guilds. In view of the Danzigers' voluntary immigration, and to avoid hardship to them 'because of their foreignness', the Senate added: 'until the future promulgation of the general statute concerning foreigners, to give further encouragement to immigration by others, give out now ten roubles for each person'.[64] The idea that potential immigration must not be discouraged by adverse measures, but rather promoted by special treatment of those already involved, becomes from this point a recurrent, at times almost obsessive, theme in official settlement policy.

Events were catching up with the authorities. Even now, however, it was Catherine who put forward the idea, first mentioned at this time, of a special government agency to look after the interests of the foreigners and to which they could turn in case of need. The concept was not entirely new. The Prussian colonization programme was run by just such a body, a fully-fledged government department. In Russia,

P. I. Panin in a speech to the Senate had already urged the need of such an institution both for Russian fugitives and for foreign colonists:

It has been widely spread abroad in neighbouring states that in Russian judicial offices the doors are closed to those who come empty-handed; therefore to attract settlers it is necessary to place them in the special care of some one of the Ministers or Senators, one for the foreigners, one for the schismatics, and to publish this in foreign countries.[65]

But, as far as the records go, it was Catherine who first used the term 'tutelary offices' (*opekunstvennyye mesta*), a term and concept which took final shape in the Chancellery of Guardianship of Foreigners (*Kantselyariya Opekunstva Inostrannykh*).[66] On 26 June the Empress wrote to Glebov that the Senate should consider this matter, and on 4 July she personally instructed the Senate to prepare terms of reference for a 'special office' for foreigners, 'and not only one to which they can all apply, but which should further have permanent care and guardianship (*opekunstvo*) over them, and therefore this office shall be called tutelary for immigrating foreign peoples'.[67]

Faced with this command, the Senators at last bestirred themselves to make a personal contribution: the Senate officially recorded an invitation to its members to present their own proposals ('opinions').[68] Three such memoranda have been preserved: one by Count A. Buturlin, a joint submission by Senators N. Korff and A. Zherebtsov, and one anonymous script. Buturlin's, the first in order,[69] is dated 9 July – on which day the Senate also recorded a decree from the Empress giving foreign immigrants the right to two weeks' free lodging in Petersburg on first arrival.[70]

Buturlin was exclusively concerned with trades and commerce; agriculture is not even mentioned in his memorandum. Merchants, he said, who wished to establish themselves in Russia, who brought in with them 'sufficient' capital and took Russian citizenship, should be made members of Russian merchant guilds. Within prescribed limits, they should receive all the privileges they might ask. They could be allocated buildings at present vacant, 'of which there are sufficient in many towns' (§ 4). Foreign artisans likewise should be registered in the appropriate guild (*tsekh*) and given free quarters in the houses of their Russian counterparts, free board for one year and tax freedom for ten (§ 5). Buturlin thought mainly in terms of immigration from Europe and of settlement in north-western Russia, considering that a chief centre should be in 'spacious and great Nov Gorod' which, he said, was underpopulated. Settlers there should receive 'stone' houses at state expense, repayable over thirty years, and promises of monopoly in their product once they were established (§§ 6, 7). The main type of immigrant envisaged was the small, German artisan ruined by the recent wars (§ 1); but groups suffering religious persecution should also be encouraged to settle in Russia, if necessary by the dispatch of special envoys for this purpose, 'not going into the question of their spiritual harmfulness, but simply trying to increase the number of people in the Empire'; examples were given from Saxony (the Herrnhut community) and from Poland. The most appropriate area of settlement for these heretics would be the towns and fortresses of the Baltic (Dorpat, Pernau and elsewhere), and Pskov and Velikiye Luki (§ 9).

These two towns, with Smolensk, could also form reception points for foreigners entering Russia overland (§ 2); but water offered the best and cheapest method of transport, to all Russian Baltic ports, which thus became the principal points of entry. Help for the journey, which would not be costly, could be given by the Russian Ministers in Hamburg and Danzig (§ 1).

Buturlin's project also takes some cognizance of other regions: § 2, on points of entry, ends – almost as an afterthought – 'and Kiev especially for Greeks and Vlachs'. Military immigrants were to be sent to New Serbia (§ 8); and another example of religious persecution given is the Armenian church, particularly the Armenians of New Julfa near Isfahan;[71] ruined by taxation, they could be attracted to Astrakhan. If these blandishments failed, the former Indian Company at Astrakhan should be re-established, with all its previous privileges (§ 10).

Foreigners falling ill on the journey to their place of settlement should receive free hospital treatment (§ 11); and responsibility for the settlers should rest with local military commanders or specially-appointed officers, who could demand assistance from the civil authorities under the general supervision of the Senate (§ 12). All these measures, wrote Buturlin, should be published abroad (§ 3).

The scheme outlined by Buturlin is unsatisfactory, giving scant consideration to the specific mechanisms required to organize migration and settlement (the problem in fact posed by Catherine), and showing a merely parochial conception of the needs and potentialities of foreign colonization at large. Altogether more thorough and realistic was the joint memorandum of Korff and Zherebtsov.[72] They divided their submission into two parts: a discussion of the 'tutelary authority', and a consideration of concrete measures governing the recruitment, reception and distribution of foreign colonists. Without specifying sources or areas of settlement, or going into all the minutiae of administration, their memorandum states the main organizational problems to be considered and makes suggestions on the most important. The general outline is in many respects similar to the final provisions of the published legislation.

Korff and Zherebtsov approach the practical problems of large-scale immigration imaginatively and comprehensively, and evidently have a clear understanding of the type of immigrant who was likely to respond to Russian invitations. They stress, for instance, in the first part of their proposals, the need to fix in advance exact personnel requirements, and to appoint to the 'authority' staff with a command of relevant foreign languages (I, §§ 1–2); the desirability of detailing beforehand places of settlement, and of appointing to these areas paid officials to take charge of the newcomers (I, §§ 4–5); and the necessity, besides long-term financing which can be adjusted in the light of experience, of assured financial resources for immediate needs such as the maintenance of indigent immigrants (I, § 6). The 'authority' in their view should have sole jurisdiction over the foreigners and be subordinate directly to the Senate, so that it can obtain immediate action when necessary (I, § 3).

In the second part of the memorandum, proposals on the wider questions show a similar grasp of basic factors and an attempt to plan on a large scale. The broad range of privileges offered to immigrants is motivated explicitly by the consideration of attracting prosperous foreigners and property-owners ('which is very much to be desired'), and which could be achieved only with the prospect of 'direct profit and specific advantages' (II, preamble). At the same time the authors felt that needy artisans should also receive help (II, § 5). Privileged conditions are suggested for those 'who may wish to set up and teach [sic] woollen, linen, copper, iron and other types of factory, viticultural and sericultural undertakings (*stroitel'stva*)' (II, § 7); and husbandmen, besides a land grant, are promised farm animals and a year's grain supply (II, § 7).

One important point mentioned for the first time here concerns serfdom. No immigrant may be enserfed, even if he himself wishes it (II, § 12). This was reiterated in subsequent legislation, though occasionally ignored in practice.[73] Other suggestions include the possibility of making contracts with foreigners in their place of origin (II, § 8), and separate conditions for wealthy temporary immigrants (II, § 9). Otherwise foreigners should be required beforehand to take an oath of loyalty on arrival (II, § 10). These points, and all the other privileges offered

(II, §§ 1–4, 6), should be embodied in an instruction to the 'tutelary authority' (II, § 10).

Besides these two memoranda, the only other proposals preserved in the Senate records are a set of seven points entitled 'An approximate plan for consideration concerning immigrants into Russia', without date or signature.[74] Another copy of this exists among the personal papers of Catherine, and was published by Pekarsky in the Collection of the Imperial Historical Society, together with brief notes by Catherine herself.[75] The first three clauses of this document specify the nature of the 'tutelary authority' and the means of reception of immigrants, and in effect are the prototypes of the following legislation; clauses four to seven share the preoccupations reflected in the previous memoranda: while agriculture is considered, merchants and artisans remain at the focus of attention (§§ 4, 6, 7). Tax exemptions are recommended for the former of up to fifty years, if they will settle in closed colonies (§ 7), while for the latter 'less than thirty years is not possible' (§ 6). In particular, 'if, as is desirable, some company of merchants, and with artisans, should wish to settle in Russia: there are places especially suitable for such on the Volga below Saratov down to Astrakhan, where as non-farmers they can build fortified points, live safely and trade in Russia and in Persia and where they wish' (§ 4). As for agriculture: any husbandmen should receive the same exemptions as those stipulated for artisans (§ 6), and an allocation of empty land such as was made to the Montenegrins in Orenburg Province, 'of which the plan, and an approximate calculation of how many thousand households (*dvorov*) can be settled, are kept in the Governing Senate and those places remain empty to the present time' (§ 5).

Once members of the Senate had had an opportunity to express their views, further discussion of the scheme was transferred to circles closer to the Empress. Simultaneously with the presentation of the Senators' memoranda, Catherine held consultations with her immediate advisers[76] in which the 'Approximate Plan', judging by its terse formulations, its similarity to the subsequent legislation, and by the presence of the annotated copy among the papers of the Empress, played a part. By 18 July, Catherine could write to Glebov:

Aleksander Ivanovich! I return to you herewith the draft of the Manifesto and the Instruction, with the remarks of the future Guardians, from which a fair copy should be drawn up for signature. It seems to me that they have omitted several necessary points from your draft, which can be written in again; but what they have added gives great hopes of their industry. As people as yet unaccustomed [to their work], they have been rather slow in writing, but it may be hoped that in future they will act more nimbly.[77]

These texts in their final form were published on 22 July. Three decrees of that date announced the creation of the Chancellery of Guardianship of Foreigners, defined its powers and duties, and set forth the conditions and privileges to be offered to foreign immigrants. The brief decree on the Chancellery of Guardianship[78] stressed that it was to provide the 'special and specific office' envisaged by P. I. Panin and by Catherine, and made public the appointment as its President of G. G. Orlov, then at the height of his favour – a clear indication of the importance attached to the post by Catherine. By the terms of its 'Instruction',[79] the Chancellery held equal status with government Colleges, had the right to correspond directly with Russian Ministers abroad, and in all matters except accountancy was responsible directly and solely to the Empress. As a preliminary measure, until the scope of operations became clear, 200,000 roubles per annum were allocated to meet requirements: both the running costs of the Chancellery itself and all expenditure on the immigrants.[80]

Conditions for the foreigners of whom the Chancellery was to have charge were given in a second Manifesto.[81] This document formed the basis for foreign immigration into the Empire over the next forty years, and became effectively the 'civil constitution' of the immigrants.[82] It offered freedom of entry into Russia to all foreigners (I) – this time without exclusions: Jews are not mentioned in the 1763 Manifesto. Foreigners could enter the country at any border point (II), with assistance from Russian Ministers abroad for those unable to make the journey at their own expense (III), and were to receive a wide range of rights and privileges. They were free to choose a domicile anywhere in the Empire (IV), to practise their own religion and – if forming separate colonies – to build their own churches. These rights did not extend to the foundation of monasteries, or to proselytism; only Muslims might be converted, and also enserfed (VI, § 1). All dues and taxes were remitted for a fixed number of years, depending on the place of settlement: least in the capitals, most for rural colonies. Six months' free lodging on arrival was promised, as well as all necessary assistance to establish newcomers in their chosen livelihood. Such assistance could include grants of land, and a cash loan, interest-free for ten years and repayable thereafter in three equal yearly instalments (VI, §§ 2–4).

Those forming separate colonies received the right to internal self-government and to military protection (if they wished) during the initial period of their establishment (VI, § 5). They could also hold fairs and markets without toll (vi, § 11). All immigrants could claim duty-free import of personal effects, and of goods for sale to a value of three hundred roubles per family (vi, § 6). Exemption from military and civil service was promised, though those who wished to enter the armed forces as volunteers could do so, and would receive a bounty of thirty roubles (vi, § 7). Free transport and living expenses would be provided for the journey from the Russian border to the place of settlement (vi, § 8). Entrepreneurs introducing new industries into the country were offered a special concession: ten-year exemption from duty on imports (vi, § 9). And all independent entrepreneurs had the right to buy serfs for their labour force (vi, § 10).

All these privileges were guaranteed to both immigrants and their descendants (vii). On first arrival all immigrants had to take an oath of loyalty to the Crown (v), but the right of exit was guaranteed at any time on payment to the Treasury of a set proportion of the emigrant's wealth (ix). Anyone, finally, who should be dissatisfied with the conditions offered could negotiate other terms through the Chancellery of Guardianship (x).

An appendix to the Manifesto gave a register of lands available for settlement, though with the qualification (iv) that it was by no means exhaustive. The register in fact repeated almost exactly that given with the decree of 14 December 1762 on the Old Believers, and gave pride of place to the 'meadow' (eastern or left) bank of the Volga around Saratov, where their settlements were already growing up. Most alterations were slight, usually deletions of references to native Russian settlement authorized or effected in the areas named. What might be an incentive to Russian fugitives, who would be pleased to join fellow-countrymen already settled, was evidently considered a disincentive for foreigners who would expect lands unsettled and unencumbered. The most significant change was the alteration of 'Siberian Province' to 'Tobolsk Province' (§ 1). This was made only in the printed version, and at the insistence of Orlov, 'in order by the first designation not to give foreigners any unnecessary ideas (*istolkovaniya*) or doubts'.[83]

The similarity of the two registers is particularly interesting in view of the fact that by this time (July 1763) answers had come in to the Senate's enquiry of 31 December 1762, concerning the availability of land for settlement.[84] In fact, the first register had been prepared thoroughly, and the new returns added little. The majority of replies were negative. Orenburg Provincial Chancellery said it had none save that formerly allocated to the Albanians and Montenegrins, 'on which now. . .schismatics from over the Polish border are to be settled' and of which the Senate had the plans.[85] These were actually in the register already. Stavropol reported that all free land there was pre-empted for Kalmyk converts, and that it would probably be insufficient even for them.[86] The Tsaritsyn and Chorny Yar authorities lower down the Volga, while noting an abundance of free land, emphasized its general infertility, lack of timber, and especially the physical danger of attack.[87] There were a few additions, notably in parts of Voronezh Province and the North Caucasus, able to accommodate five thousand families.[88] But in view of the explicit statement that the existing register was not exhaustive, further changes in it were presumably considered un-necessary.

The content of the legislation of 1763

A factor frequently stressed in discussion of the 1763 legislation is the indebtedness of its provisions to earlier models and precedents. The organization created and the conditions offered by the 1763 decrees show points of similarity and contact in several respects with previous Russian practice in regard to migration and immigration. Among the papers considered by the Senate was a rather selective list of previous legislation regarding foreigners, made at the time of the 1750s investi-gation of the subject, and going back to the late seventeenth century.[89] The conditions offered in the 1763 Manifesto to foreign entrepreneurs and artisans continued and extended rights and facilities already guaranteed to these groups, and the same was largely true for mer-chants: although commerce was mentioned only in the preamble to the Manifesto, the terms offered to all foreigners encouraged immigration by merchants as well.[90] In the ongoing question of government policy on fugitives, the connection established between them and foreign immigrants was not confined to theory and to the initial drafting of legislation. Similarity of treatment extended both to recruitment abroad and to the choice of areas for settlement. The new Chancellery of Guardianship may be seen, similarly, as a development of the type of administrative structure set up to deal with the Montenegrins under Elizabeth Petrovna, or with the earlier old soldier settlements; and the Chancellery's recruiting methods had much in common with those used in the Southern Ukraine since the 1750s and before.

Nevertheless, despite these similarities and continuities, there is no indication that precedent at home had decisive importance in the actual formulation of policy and of the final legislation; in some cases similarities indicate as much the identity of the problems to be solved, as imitation or common inspiration. A more striking model was the known practice of foreign powers; and most writers on the immigration programme have emphasized the influence of foreign example.

The preparatory studies of foreign practice which were made at the time of the Lafont project certainly seem to have borne fruit. The general structure of Catherine's Russian scheme follows closely the pattern of colonization in other countries, notably Prussia, and in individual points direct parallels with foreign models can be traced. There are material and even textual similarities, for example, between the 1763 Manifesto and the Prussian Potsdam Edict.[91] To give another, more specific example, section x of the Manifesto, permitting negotiation of special terms, is identical with a provision of the Danish Manifesto of 1749 which had figured so largely in earlier Russian plans, and which shows other points of similarity with the later ones. M. L. Vorontsov specifically recommended the Danish edict to Catherine in 1763 as a source for her legislation.[92]

Foreign precedent was, therefore, important. There were, however, still other, and more immediate, factors. Section x could also be seen, for instance, in the light of negotiations proceeding with the Herrnhut community in Saxony, which has already been mentioned. Catherine herself showed warm interest in the Herrnhuter Brethren, and discussions with them took place on her express orders. The relevance of section x to the Herrnhuters' case is obvious; and according to their historian Hafa, their negotiations had a direct influence on another clause, that guaranteeing religious freedom (vi, § 1). The Herrnhut intermediary even claimed that the Brethren were to have been mentioned by name in the Manifesto, had he not prevented it for lack of authority to commit Herrnhut so positively to settlement in Russia. This is possible, though seems unlikely. Although in Hafa's account Catherine appears most anxious to secure a Herrnhut colony,[93] religious toleration was a feature common to almost all the European colonization programmes, and it was by now traditional as well in Russian dealings with most foreign nationals, so that it would have been surprising had it not appeared in the Manifesto in some form in any case.

There is no reason in fact to suppose that either section x or clause vi, § 1 was included specifically in response to the requests of the Brethren; nor yet to assume that section x owed its existence exclusively to Danish precedent – the obvious need for flexibility in attracting and dealing with disparate types of immigrant made that provision self-evidently desirable. In the last analysis, the most important considera-

tions were the requirements and immediate pressures of the current
Russian situation, and all the factors discussed so far were necessarily
weighed against these criteria. Thus the question of religious freedom
raised by the Herrnhut negotiation formed part of a wider issue which
had to be settled for the immigration scheme as a whole. Toleration,
already largely traditional, was essential if Catherine's aim of attracting
non-Orthodox settlers was to be achieved. But Russian religious
sensibilities had also to be conciliated. So the normal freedoms of belief
and worship were guaranteed to ordinary settlers; the Herrnhuters, as
a specifically religious, Protestant, and proselytising community, had
to pass the scrutiny of the Holy Synod before they were admitted, and
they were not allowed to proselytise among Orthodox Christians; and
although Jews were not mentioned in the 1763 Manifesto, reference
back in the preamble to its predecessor, and Catherine's caution the
following year in dealing with the settlement of Jews in New Russia,
suggest that the authorities still considered Jewish immigration to be
unacceptable to public opinion. In short, just as the general demographic and economic needs of the country initially gave validity and
scope to Catherine's populationist ideas, so in many cases (including
section x and clause vi, § 1), it was the specific pressures of individual
Russian circumstances, and the government's perception of these,
which determined the use made of precedent whether native or foreign,
and which shaped the conditions offered and the categories of settler
sought.

Another area in which present concerns were reflected was the matter
of tax exemptions. These were offered for varying periods to immigrants settling in different places. The shortest period of exemption,
five years, applied to the Baltic provinces and to the two capitals,
Moscow and Petersburg, and represented in effect a disincentive to
settle there. Apart from the fact that these were areas of high population density, this must be seen in the light of recent decrees prohibiting
new industrial development in the two capitals, on the grounds that
their resources were under strain.[94] Conversely, the longest period of
exemption was offered to those forming compact rural settlements; and
this reflected a general shift in official thinking on immigration, away
from the towns and towards the countryside.

This change of emphasis is the most striking feature of the 1763
Manifesto compared with the discussions which had preceded it; it has
raised questions both as to the government's immediate intentions, and
as to the exact theoretical springs of the new policy. Most earlier

measures, and even much of the preliminary discussion of 1762 and 1763, as far as it is recorded, stressed primarily urban settlement. They looked to artisan and entrepreneurial elements as the most probable and desirable categories of immigrant. The new stress on non-urban settlement reflected contemporary Russian concern with 'empty spaces', at the expense of the traditional emphasis on foreign skills and their didactic function. Musin-Pushkin's *Kulturträger* conception is in fact remarkably absent from both the discussions on the subject and the finished legislation. The 1763 Manifesto was not even intended exclusively for the West; it was dispatched in all directions, wherever there was any prospect of recruitment. The emphasis at this stage is on quantity rather than quality, on the emptiness of the country and the overall dearth of population, rather than on lack of skills, as a cause of economic backwardness.

Accordingly, the new Manifesto offered the most attractive terms to immigrants who would form separate rural settlements – to those who would 'come over by many Familys and by whole Colony's and settle themselves on the open Fields or uncultivated Grounds' (vi, § 2). Such people would realize both objectives: population increase *per se*, and the occupation of otherwise deserted areas. This preference, only implicit in the Manifesto, is stated explicitly in § 2 of the Instruction to the Chancellery of Guardianship. In receiving and helping foreign immigrants, the Chancellery is 'especially to persuade them, but without coercion, to settle in empty places'. The extreme lengths to which the representatives of the Chancellery went to fulfil this particular point of the Instruction led subsequently to the establishment as peasants of many quite unsuitable colonists. The inevitable consequence of the Chancellery's actions was a settlement largely agricultural in character. And this has given rise to the view that the immigration policy under the influence of Physiocratic ideas was primarily concerned with agriculture.[95]

This conception has rightly been rejected.[96] Certainly, the ideas of mercantilism were steadily being displaced in Russia by others which placed greater stress on agriculture and were closer to Physiocratic views. Both trends can be found side by side in Russian writings and legislation of the time. 'Populationism' was a product of the mercantilist school; the Physiocrats also considered a high population level desirable, provided the economy could support it. Population and agriculture are linked in contemporary writings, including Catherine's 'Instruction', and in some of the recruiting propaganda of the immigration programme.[97] But in 1763 they were not obviously, and certainly not exclusively, connected in the minds of the authors of the Manifesto: the preamble already quoted is hardly a picture of the farming life. The Manifesto made specific provision for entrepreneurs, and a certain amount of entrepreneurial settlement later took place.[98]

Furthermore, there was no suggestion that the rural settlements were necessarily to be agricultural, even though this was in the nature of things probable for the majority. The single most successful colony, Sarepta, deliberately based its economy on crafts and small-scale industry. And in 1765 Catherine herself applied the relevant clause of the Manifesto to the almost exclusively urban Armenian community of Astrakhan.[99]

The Manifesto, with its promise of free choice of domicile and its relative silence regarding different immigrant categories, clearly envisaged that immigrants should engage in all and any forms of activity; the key to the immigration policy in its formulation at this stage is to be sought in the overall demographic situation in Russia at the time, and in the then prevailing (basically mercantilist) theories of population.[100] At the same time it is also clear that the Chancellery of Guardianship, once it had taken active charge of immigration, adopted a somewhat different position.[101] As will be seen, it came down firmly in favour of peasants as opposed to other classes of immigrants, at least from the West, and sought deliberately to create compact agricultural colonies rather than allowing free choice of domicile. Orlov in some of his reports stressed the potential didactic function of such settlement, and the technical skills which Russia might gain with these immigrants.

Thus it seems necessary to distinguish two trends, or even perhaps two periods, in Russian government policy on immigration at this time, of which the second or later one – expressed in the actions of the Chancellery of Guardianship – was concerned to a greater extent with agricultural settlement. But even now, grounds for arguing a specific Physiocrat influence are few. The extent to which the Physiocrats' ideas were current in Russia in 1763 is debatable, and in any case interest in agriculture in the economic context was by no means a Physiocrat monopoly.[102] And the Chancellery seems in fact to have been guided to a large extent by practical considerations. It regarded peasant immigration as the best way to achieve maximum possible settlement of 'empty places', a view quite in keeping with the original aims of the policy. Although it restricted its activities in the industrial sphere, there were practical reasons for this too, and the decision did not necessarily reflect any basic change in its thinking. Altogether, the theoretical inspiration for the new immigration policy as a whole is most plausibly to be found in the older ideas of the cameralists and mercantilism.

The drafting and promulgation of the 1763 Manifesto did not finally determine the exact scope, focus, and boundaries of the new scheme. The change of emphasis away from the earlier stress on urban settlement and towards preoccupation with rural colonies can be attributed only to Catherine and her entourage; nothing in the record offers a detailed explanation. But apart from this, several suggestions were considered for expanding the jurisdiction of the Chancellery of Guardianship into other areas: in mid-1763 neither Catherine herself nor the Senate was sure how far the new programme could or should be extended.

The Senate wondered whether, besides foreigners, the Chancellery should not have 'guardianship' also over 'Russian subjects remaining without care in infancy, and widows'.[103] There had been one or two attempts to deal with some aspects of these problems in the previous decade,[104] but the proposal was presumably prompted by the discussion in progress at the same time of Betskoy's project for the Foundling House.[105] The Senate's suggestion met with a favourable reaction from the Empress. She ordered the postponement of any official report, but added, nonetheless: 'meanwhile compose the Instruction necessary for this and present it for HIH approval'.[106] On 1 September 1763 a Manifesto announced the creation of the Foundling House, under the sign already noted of popular welfare and population increase. While the General Plan for the scheme included provisions to be made for widows and, by extension, orphans,[107] its central feature was an institution designed to save unwanted infants and to provide a maternity home for indigent and unmarried mothers. The Senate evidently wished to remove other functions from the Foundling House, perhaps to combine all forms of adult 'guardianship' under one authority. But the obvious suitability of keeping all branches of social security as far as possible under the same organization must have precluded adoption of the Senate's proposal. The jurisdiction of the colonist administration was extended to include Russian nationals only at the beginning of the nineteenth century.

Catherine herself wished the Chancellery of Guardianship to bear at least partial responsibility for foreign immigration already in progress in the south-east and east, areas which as sources of immigration had received little consideration in the preceding deliberations. In 1763, the Kizlyar commandant requested instructions on how to finance the

Mozdok settlement. He received an initial grant of five hundred roubles from the College of Foreign Affairs, which usually controlled relations with these border peoples, and was told to address himself in future to the Chancellery of Guardianship,[108] although there is no indication that the Chancellery was ever intended to take over the immediate administration of the new town, which from the outset remained under the jurisdiction of the local authority.

A similar situation obtained in the question of slaves escaping from the Kirgiz-Kaysak, and other immigrants from the same area. Some two months before the Senate's discussion on widows and orphans, it had received a note from the Empress demanding to know why 'Dzhungars who have come over and been sent here from Tobolsk are being sold here'.[109] Enquiry showed that existing practice was based, as we have seen, on Senate decrees; and that of the 521 converts sent to Moscow, at the time of the enquiry sixteen were still there awaiting distribution, and held meanwhile in custody (*v ostroge*). The list makes interesting reading: a motley collection of both sexes, ranging in age from 15 to 70, and of varied nationality. Their cost per head to the state had been from 21 to 24 roubles. Catherine immediately ordered that in future such new converts should not be sold to private individuals, but settled in Imperial estates (*dvortsovyye volosti*) of their own choice: their expenses were to be written off and they themselves to receive material help and education to fit them for life in Russia.[110]

It soon became clear that the ex-prisoners had no conception of any of the areas open to them for settlement, and the Senate decided in the following year to give them open passports to live where and as they wished within Russia. Those unwilling to accept this free choice could settle in Stavropol. Confirming these decisions on 12 March 1764, Catherine ordered the Chancellery of Guardianship together with the then Orenburg Governor, Volkov, to draw up regulations governing the position of these people, 'according to the jurisdiction given in its Instruction';[111] and the following year the Senate sent further papers on the same question to the Chancellery for an opinion.[112] But, once again, responsibility remained not with the Chancellery of Guardianship but with the Principal Chancellery for Imperial Estates (*Glavnaya Dvortsovaya Kantselyariya*).

An even more obvious case of this type, at first sight, was the immigration continuing from the south. But although the Chancellery engaged in recruiting activities in Turkish, Venetian and Austrian territories, it did not and was not intended to have control, except in a few cases, over foreigners emigrating from these countries. (The second

Kontsarevich project for recruitment to New Serbia was exactly contemporary with the publication of the July legislation.) The question received little attention, since a relevant administrative structure already existed in the shape of the Serbian settlements; and the transformation of these in 1764 into the Province of New Russia precluded any direct intervention by the Chancellery in that area.[113]

In short, the Chancellery of Guardianship was intended to initiate, control, and administer a type of mass immigration for which there was no direct precedent in Russia, but not to have charge of related fields in which a procedure already existed. In fields where such procedures were being simultaneously created, the line of demarcation – after some hesitation – was drawn firmly. For the tasks assigned to it the Chancellery had very considerable powers: the terms of the legislation of 1763 and of the following two years which amplified it represent an attempt, in the admiring words of Klaus, to create 'a complete and finished system of rural–colonial establishment', covering all aspects of the problem under a strong central authority.[114] However, Klaus's admiration was naive. It was typical of Catherine's style of government to do things – particularly to begin things – on a grand scale and with inadequate preparation: 'the principle', in the words of a contemporary already quoted, 'which ruined so many excellent schemes'.[115] Catherine's energy ensured a fairly rapid start to the project of foreign settlement. But the special government department and the large funds allocated could not compensate, in the working out of the programme, for the defects of the Russian bureaucracy, for the confusion in subsequent thinking on the colonists' designation, and for the lack of foresight which called for immigration before any concrete steps had been taken to receive or deal with it.

3

The response: settlement 1763-1775

Recruitment

Although criticized by Russian ministers abroad for its vagueness, the 1762 Manifesto did produce some response. It brought Rehbinder's Danzig artisans into Russia; and at the other end of the country the Armenians of Astrakhan used the new proclamation to increase their own numbers. In 1767 they reported that they had translated the 1762 Manifesto into their own language and sent it to 'our reliable friends' in Persia, a step which they claimed had been very effective.[1] But it was the second Manifesto, of 1763, distributed in the same way as the first, which marked the serious beginning of recruitment; and the Russian recruiting campaign grew steadily in intensity over the next two and a half years.[2]

However, although Russian representatives abroad now had full instructions, and set actively about the work of finding and engaging emigrants, there were many difficulties. At a time when concern with population was a dominant feature of political theory in Europe, no European state wished to lose its subjects, or to have competition in recruiting new ones. In Turkish territories the considerations which had prevented open publication of the first Manifesto were reinforced by the clause of the second which envisaged the enserfment of Muslims. Austria, in her role both of Balkan and European power, took a hostile view of Russian competition for her Hungarian settlement programme: she not only forbade the publication of the second Manifesto, but in 1762 and 1763 issued decrees renewing an existing ban on emigration from Hungary.[3] Prussia took similar steps.[4] France at this time had reduced her recruitment, following the cession of North American territories to Britain and the failure of a projected settlement in Cayenne; but she still wanted settlers for Corsica.[5] Publication of the Manifesto was banned, severe penalties were imposed on French subjects trying to emigrate, and several foreign recruiting agents found their way to the Bastille.[6] Spain was equally hostile; Sweden, which had accepted the first Manifesto, rejected the second, and took measures to hinder and discourage emigration[7] – although Denmark allowed the proclamation to appear. Of the larger powers, only Britain and Holland (according to Pisarevsky) permitted free publication, and here the existence of relatively high living standards at home, and national colonies overseas, made prospects of large-scale recruiting remote.[8] In Central Europe, the main hunting ground, many smaller states also forbade emigration: Switzerland, and, in the Holy Roman Empire, Bavaria, Bayreuth, Hessen-Kassel, the Palatinate, Saxony, Trier and Worms all had such legislation.[9]

As a result, the field for effective legal recruitment in Europe was limited largely to the free cities and the states, particularly of southern and western Germany, where such laws did not exist. Elsewhere agents could, of course, enlist openly such elements as foreigners living in the states where they operated; and it was taken for granted that unofficial encouragement was to be given to local subjects in evading the law.[10] In any case the smaller principalities of the Empire, whether or not they forbade emigration by their subjects, were least able of all European states to withstand the actions of larger powers, either administratively or politically. Official prohibitions were extremely difficult for such states to enforce. Their frequency underlines their ineffectiveness: Hessen-Kassel, for example, issued four decrees of this nature between 1727 and 1754, and three more in 1762, 1764 and 1766.[11] Small states had also to balance their own interests against the need to remain on good terms with their neighbours and the big powers: with Russia, seeking colonists, or with Austria, hostile to Russian recruitment and conducting her own.[12]

Additional factors pointed to the Empire as a source of immigrants. It had by now become a traditional recruiting ground for those states with longer experience in the field, notably Austria, Britain and Prussia; and social and economic conditions, particularly in the aftermath of the Seven Years' War, predisposed many people to emigrate. But the main reason for the general success of recruitment in the area seems to have been the fact that state authorities lacked the power, and in some cases the legal right, to prevent it.[13] Consequently, the great majority of immigrants into Russia at this time were German.

The predominance of Germans over other nationalities has resulted in stubbornly persistent claims that the Russian government was concerned to recruit Germans in preference to colonists from other countries. The reasons alleged by proponents of this view have been that Germans were known (or thought) to be particularly valuable colonist material; or that Catherine, the German princess, favoured her countrymen above all others.[14] Other historians on the contrary have rightly been at pains to point out that the Russian authorities at this time were not especially seeking Germans, or even Western Europeans.[15] The Russian proclamations were sent out to places as far apart as London and Constantinople, Stockholm and Vienna. Copies dispatched to the Austrian capital included translations into Greek, Serbian, and Rumanian;[16] while in 1764 Catherine warmly welcomed the prospect of immigration from Persia.[17] Although Russian diplomats occasionally showed prejudice against particular nationalities,[18] the predominance of Germans among the early colonists was overwhelmingly the result of conditions and circumstances in Europe, rather than of the predilections or policies of Catherine and her ministers.

Despite economic and political conditions in Central Europe, however, hostility or non-co-operation from local governments could complicate the work of gathering recruits, and such difficulties were aggravated by the limited means of publicity available to diplomats – largely newspaper advertisements and separate handbills.[19] As a result, initial numbers were small. But the diligence of the Russian diplomats did establish a steady trickle of foreigners from Europe towards Petersburg.

Ministers recruited as and where they were able, and it soon became necessary to define more exactly the types of immigrant desired. Circular rescripts sent out from Petersburg in October and November 1763 insisted that *fabrikany i manufakturshchiki* should not be engaged without prior submission to Russia of detailed conditions, and would be accepted only if likely to be 'useful'.[20] The Chancellery of Guardianship added, faithful to its emphasis on agriculture:

At the same time you are to note that for the peopling of empty places in our Empire husbandmen and agricultural workers (*zemledel'tsy i pakhatnyye lyudi*) are especially needed, of whom no matter how many apply to you, desirous of coming here, you are to dispatch them to our frontiers without the least hindrance, on the basis of the published Manifesto.[21]

On the other hand, people wishing to enter 'any sort of service' were by no means to be encouraged, but should be left to find their own way to Russia if they persisted.[22] These stipulations came just in time. It was natural that Ministerial propaganda should have its most immediate effect in the towns, and first arrivals were largely urban in character: Rehbinder's Danzig artisans were followed in October by a handful of workers from Korff in Copenhagen, who had promised them jobs in state factories.[23] However, immigrants of other types were already arriving: at the end of the same month Musin-Pushkin sent a group including 'real husbandmen' from Hamburg.[24]

A further difficulty besetting recruitment was the unreliability of the people enlisted. Apart from those who absconded immediately on receipt of the maintenance and travel grants distributed by the Russian Ministers, many emigrants were lost on the journey through flight or the blandishments of other agents, especially where the route lay over-land. Vorontsov, in London, collected over two hundred recruits. But he lost the majority before departure to British Government agents and a private company engaging settlers for Carolina, and the remaining sixty-eight following shipwreck and mutiny on the Dutch coast.[25] Simolin in Regensburg, and even Musin-Pushkin, though both more successful than Vorontsov in their recruiting, had similar trouble in retaining those engaged.[26] In any case, total numbers were small, and the inefficacy of operations conducted by the diplomats alone became increasingly clear. So it was not surprising that other methods were proposed. In September 1763 Simolin had suggested the appointment of a special commissioner to administer the embarkation of emigrants in Lübeck, the main exit port for Petersburg,[27] and at about the same time several Ministers independently recommended the use in recruit-ing of special private agents.

Employment of recruiting agents, for both military and colonial needs, was by this time a traditional method used by all European powers, and there existed in Central Europe a great many people experienced and even specializing in the supply of 'human goods' to whoever would pay for them.[28] Almost as soon as the Russian Mani-festo became known, Russian diplomats in Europe were approached by such individuals wishing to make contracts, of course on suitably advantageous terms. At the same time, the Russian authorities in Petersburg also were besieged by similar applicants, of whom Sheliga was one of the first.

These were of varied nationality and status; and at first, like Sheliga, most of them were rejected, in accordance with the initial policy of using exclusively diplomatic channels. Thus one item noted, but not included, in the Senate's file for the Chancellery of Guardianship under 5 May 1763 is entitled: 'Following the report of Valenir Sauleski, a Vlach of the Turkish territories, requesting the return by N. I. Panin of the project presented by him Sauleski on emigration to Russia of volunteers from various nations.' This had been unceremoniously 'sent to the public archive' with documents relating to the College of Foreign Affairs.[29] Another applicant was an official of the Livonian College of Justice, J. von Canitz, who presented to G. G. Orlov a detailed memorandum setting forth a complete theory of recruitment of foreigners from Europe, which he himself was of course to direct.[30] Bernardin de Saint-Pierre, who was seeking his fortune in Russia at the time, his novel *Paul et Virginie* and attendant literary reputation still in the future, offered a project to set up 'a little republic of Europeans' on the Aral Sea;[31] while a converted Persian serving in the Serbian Hussar Regiment, Yakov Grigor'yev syn Shirvanov, wished to establish new military colonies in Orenburg Province.[32] Other proposals for military colonization, like those of the Persian, were rejected, since this was not the purpose of the programme.[33]

Some offers had a more favourable reception, however. The Serbian priest Philip Trebukhovich, sent to Venice in January 1764 'to persuade and bring out hither for settlement people of his own Serbian nation', had first approached the Chancellery of Guardianship in November 1763 on his own initiative. At that time the Chancellery possessed no instructions on the use of non-diplomatic personnel, and had to ask Imperial approval. This was the more necessary, it said in its report, as 'besides him there are many applicants eager to undertake such recruitment; and it seems that the greatest success may be achieved by such missions'. Catherine replied: 'This is permitted, according to circumstances and necessity, but all must act cautiously in respect both of [national] interest and of policy.'[34] Simultaneously with Trebukhovich, the Chancellery sent out 'Oriental-languages interpreter Vasily Mirolyub(ov)' into Austrian territory.[35]

Once the principle of private recruitment was admitted, the Chancellery, with the help of Ministers abroad, soon had contracts with agents covering central Europe and operating into the Balkans. They were largely of two types.[36] The first collected settlers directly for the Crown, receiving in return a cash payment usually directly proportionate to the numbers sent in. The second received no *per capita* payment, but instead the right to an area of land proportionate to the number of settlers they recruited, and a loan to cover expenses. Their profit lay in exploiting the land to be settled by those they enlisted. To ensure their advantage, these agents obliged potential settlers to sign contracts, including such stipulations as the right of tithe for the 'directors' of the colony (i.e. the agents themselves). The agreements created in effect a dependent relationship between director and settler, disadvantageous to the latter, and full of trouble for the future: particularly as those recruited by Crown agents, and who were free of such obligations, were to be settled nearby under direct state administration.[37]

These agents were usually called *vyzyvateli*. During 1764 and 1765 the Chancellery signed at least twelve contracts, of both sorts,[38] and Ministers abroad were able to make contracts on their own initiative, at least with Crown agents.

Besides Trebukhovich and Mirolyub, other *vyzyvateli* contracted with the Chancellery to operate in the south. Gian Batista Vandini promised to recruit Italians; while the Hungarian Ivan Filipovich, Major (retired) of Serbian Hussars, was to bring 'into Russia for three years, through Kiev, foreigners from Europe, except Poles, Jews and Asian peoples'.[39] Immigration through Kiev, the main southern gathering point, was in the charge of A. P. Mel'gunov, who was commander-in-chief of the Serbian settlements and, after the creation of the new province, Governor-General of New Russia. Mel'gunov used a variety of agents for the work. Besides Mirolyub and Filipovich, who evidently came within his sphere of control, the names are recorded of Major Bashkovich, and Lieutenants Roste, Stefanov, Chechuliy, Ratmet, Nikolayev, and Fyodorov; and there were others. These men recruited Moldavians, Vlachs, Bulgarians, Greeks, Prussians, and 'Austrian subjects'.[40] In December 1764 Mel'gunov had already written to the Senate from Kremenchug requesting further printed copies of the 1763 Manifesto. The seventy copies he had received in August 1763 'have almost all been distributed, and although people now sent out are given copies of the printed sheets, no-one abroad believes them, and people are afraid to emigrate...' Mel'gunov wanted more copies 'in all foreign languages, and especially in Polish, Latin and Russian', which the Senate hastened to print and dispatch to him, adding French and German versions for good measure.[41]

Mel'gunov also made clandestine use of Jewish emissaries to recruit Jewish settlers for New Russia from Prussia and Poland.[42] The head of this operation, the merchant Levi Wulff, had as assistants 'the New Russian merchants David Levi Bamberg, Moisey Aron, Ber Beynamin, with their servants'.[43] And it was evidently in this connection that the Chancellery sent out the following circular to southern border authorities in 1764: 'People of any nationality and [religious] observance crossing the border with the intention of entering service or settling in the New Russian province shall immediately be admitted into the afore-mentioned province. They shall not be asked their nationality or observance, or required to produce passports.'[44]

The settlers recruited by Mel'gunov's own agents were not the concern of the Chancellery of Guardianship. Only those engaged by Mirolyub and Filipovich came under its jurisdiction, and they, as we shall see, were handed on for settlement to the Little Russian College. The majority of *vyzyvateli* who contracted with the Chancellery operated in North and Central Europe.

Most of these latter recruiters and their agents worked in the German states of the Empire. But other countries were also visited. In 1764 the Swedish authorities were alerted to the activities of three Swedes who had taken Russian citizenship and were recruiting in Finland: Lieutenant Paul Friedrich Eschner, Cornet Johann Peter Beckman, and Cavalry Captain Johann Wenander.[45] Three agents named in Switzerland, one Schnorff operating in Baden, Fassbind in Zug, and Mottet-Petitmermet in Murten, all working for the major *vyzyvatel'* Beauregard, sent more than one thousand Swiss emigrants to a collecting point in Basel in the years 1766–72, despite government countermeasures.[46] A host of recruiters, real or suspected, appears in the correspondence of French diplomats and in the archives of the Bastille, although many of those named, if they recruited at all, did so outside France.[47] Holland and the states of Northern Germany were also involved since they provided the emigrant routes to the sea and embarkation for Russia.

The most ambitious *vyzyvateli*, and the most successful, were those who were to establish their own colonies. These men ran their own operations on a considerable scale, and were in fact the employers of many of the lesser agents of whom we hear. There were three main groups, largely French or Swiss, and headed respectively by Francois Pierre Pictet and Jean Baptiste Le Roy; Antoine Meusnier de Precourt, Jean de Boffe, Quentin Benjamin Coulhette d'Hauterive; and Baron Caneau de Beauregard. Another group, Ludwig Paul D'Haucourt and associates, could not find sufficient security for the advances they requested, and had to withdraw.[48] These agents were a mixed bunch. Pictet, for a time personal French secretary to Catherine II, was a Genevan, a protégé of Voltaire. His guarantor for the contract was Orlov himself; Pictet then stood security for the Parisian Le Roy, who proved the more energetic partner.[49] The second group initially approached the Russian Ambassador in France; its leading personality was Meusnier de Precourt, who had been among other things a victualler and a police official in Paris.[50] Beauregard, owner of an estate in Holland, but apparently of French or Alsacian origin, insinuated himself into the favour of Count A. R. Vorontsov following the latter's transfer from London to The Hague, and came to Russia almost as the personal friend of Vorontsov and his uncle the Chancellor.[51] He had also sought to enlist the aid of Jacob von Stählin.[52]

The type of person engaged in the recruiting can be seen in Vinsky's description of a man known to him, in keeping whose acquaintance he describes himself as 'incautious':

In the summer of 1777, in the Riga Inn, I stumbled by chance on a certain foreigner, whom I had once seen equally fortuitously some five years before. This strange person, of German Israelite stock, took up provisioning in Prussia during the presence of our army there, and on this business came to St Petersburg when the army returned to Russia, in order to settle his accounts and – so he assured everyone – to receive from the Treasury the large sums due to him.

At my first meeting with him, I saw him dressed from head to foot in velvet and gold, scattering gold pieces in the inn and pouring champagne on every side. That he had money, one could gather also from the fact that he was taken on as a partner by the recruiting agents gathering colonists for settlement in Russia, and that he was for a time contractor in the Saratov *uyezd* for the building of houses for the settlers, where however, oppressed by Ryazanov, then in charge of the colonies, he came to St Petersburg to take him to court. As a foreigner and a wastrel he did not lead his merry life for long; his cash, such as he had, and his claims soon went to the four winds, and at my meeting with him now, instead of velvet, he was dressed in a greyish, tattered frieze-coat, and had lodging with a middle-aged German lady, Kuhlengrüben...

Wandering continuously through all Petersburg, forcing his acquaintance on all he met or who crossed his path, it would positively be said that he was known to people of all stations, from Senators and Generals to pancake-makers.[53]

Almost all the *vyzyvateli* had in common the qualities of greed, enterprise, imagination, and a more or less total lack of scruple. Vandini, a confidence trickster, apparently never even began recruiting;[54] the others assumed false noble titles, claimed excessive expenses, recruited forbidden categories of immigrants, gained settlers by false pretences. They also stole recruits from one another. Of those on whom full records are available, only Mirolyub and the Crown agent Florentin completely satisfied the Chancellery.[55] But in part precisely because of their unscrupulousness, the *vyzyvateli* were extremely successful.

The self-styled 'directors', those who were organizing their own colonies,[56] engaged numbers of secondary agents – far more, according to Simolin, than could be usefully employed.[57] At the same time the Russian diplomats continued their efforts, usually working through Crown agents whom they sometimes hired themselves. Some of these were former sub-contractors to the principal *vyzyvateli*. Florentin changed his status in this way; while the Strasburger Jean Frederic Rollwagen, who had first himself approached Musin-Pushkin in 1764, made a contract with Meusnier de Precourt, but corresponded simultaneously direct with Musin-Pushkin in Hamburg and A. R. Vorontsov (now transferred to The Hague).[58]

In addition Simolin, who had been instrumental in the appointment of the commissioner Schmidt at Lübeck, proposed that similar official Russian representatives should be placed in charge of the enrolment and transmission of emigrants at other important points. In 1765, with approval from Petersburg, he personally accredited two further commissioners, Karl Friedrich Meixner in Ulm, and Johann Facius, who after some difficulties established himself near Frankfurt am Main. They acted as salaried officials of the Crown, under a special Instruction drawn up by Simolin.[59]

The recruiting operation in Europe succeeded beyond expectation. The *vyzyvateli* and their minions scattered propaganda and brilliant promises[60] on all sides, and their activities caused a real emigration fever, particularly in many parts of the Holy Roman Empire, such as the recruiting of no other state had aroused. The year 1766 in particular produced an overwhelming response. Those enrolled flooded into Lübeck, swamping the barracks and private accommodation arranged for their use before embarkation, so that they had to be diverted in considerable numbers to Hamburg. Lack of ships and adverse winds aggravated the problem. In April the Russian government dispatched a naval frigate and several transports in an attempt to alleviate the situation, and it also took steps to accommodate emigrant overspill in Holstein.[61] But meanwhile the Russian interpreter Vikhlyayev wrote from Hamburg on 15 May (N.S.) 1766:

There are over two thousand colonists here who are nearly lying on top of each other and who have absolutely no room; and in Lübeck there are thirteen thousand and, as here, it is impossible to accommodate anyone else; and both here and there the turbulent influx of colonists is producing a shortage of accommodation and money.[62]

Lembke, the successor in Lübeck to Commissioner Schmidt, who had died of tuberculosis, dispatched in the year 1766 alone, 17,886 people.[63]

The authorities in Petersburg were also hard put to it to cope with such numbers; moreover, they had to take into account the growing European opposition to the recruiting campaign. The pervasive hostility of Austria created numerous difficulties, and the exodus of 1765 and 1766 provoked other states of the Holy Roman Empire into protest and counter-measures. The culmination of this movement was an Imperial edict promulgated by Joseph II in 1768, forbidding emigration from any part of the Empire.[64] But already in 1766 the Russian authorities had called a halt. A decree of 9 November announced the suspension of enrolment, until such time as those already accepted should be properly established. The public decree stressed the difficulties created by the unexpectedly large response; dispatches to Ministers laid more weight on the increasingly unfavourable political situation.[65] Although the measure was said to be temporary, it in fact marked the end of mass recruitment for a decade.

The great majority of the immigrants in this period arrived during 1766; but the influx did not stop immediately after the November suspension. Recruits accepted before the decree, but after the closure of the shipping season, were sent on during the following year; while some *vyzyvateli* for a time continued to recruit in defiance of the ban. Immigration after 1767, however, was negligible, even though small numbers continued to arrive until 1774.

By the standards of eighteenth-century Europe, the results of the Russian recruiting campaign were impressive. The official figure for registered arrivals between 1762 and 1775 is 30,623.[66] For the Chancellery of Guardianship, it remained to settle the foreigners which it had thus gathered.

Immigration and registration

For most immigrants from Central Europe – the great majority of all those enlisted – the way to Russia was by sea, from Hamburg or (usually) Lübeck. The commissioners in Lübeck had a permanent office with clerical staff which looked after colonists sent in by Crown and private agents, and normally arranged their dispatch on specially chartered vessels, mostly British or Hanseatic. The Russian diplomat most directly responsible was Vikhlyayev, placed in charge by Musin-Pushkin and based in Hamburg. Vikhlyayev carried on correspondence on recruiting operations with Ministers throughout Europe, and was also instrumental in finding Lembke as assistant, then successor, to the ailing Schmidt.[67]

The earliest arrivals in Petersburg, however, as we have seen, came direct from Danzig in June 1763. Rehbinder had addressed his people to the Office of the College of Foreign Affairs; and by Senate decision they were sent on from there to the Office of the Petersburg Chief Magistrature (*Glavnaya Magistratskaya Kontora*), for registration in the Petersburg craft guilds.[68] Most immigrants who were specifically enrolled as craftsmen or industrial workers were recruited early, before limitations on non-agricultural elements were enjoined, and before Ministers abroad had become more selective. Several of Rehbinder's people had expected to be given work in Russian factories, with accommodation supplied.[69] Korff's recruits, announced in a dispatch of 1/12 October 1763, and consisting of 'silk manufacturers', two Frenchmen, Lacombe and Vandier, and a Dane, Schönfeld, had similar hopes, and proved quite unsuited to the Chancellery's requirements. They 'claimed that [they came] after repeated urgings from Korff [and] with the assurance that on arrival in Russia they would be given work in factories according to their skills, and with a sufficient annual salary...' Their demands to the Chancellery were quite inconsistent with the Manifesto, and the Chancellery found it

impossible to satisfy them, especially as there are no state silk factories in Russia, and they do not wish to go and settle with the other foreigners, nor to be placed in private factories, like several such workmen [who] have gone to Astrakhan; and they demand solely that they should be given work in state factories with a salary of six hundred roubles per annum, or that they should be permitted to establish near St Petersburg at state expense a factory for silk tissues and brocades: but since... HIH was not pleased to grant approval for the construction of such a factory, Lacombe and his associates were refused; and they have finally asked...permission to return to Copenhagen.

The request was granted, and the petitioners were even let off the debts which they had incurred to the Chancellery.[70]

While the position of immigrants wishing to remain in Petersburg was being clarified, settlement had already begun in the areas stipulated by the Manifesto. A Chancellery of Guardianship report to the Senate of 21 October 1763 stated that while 'empty places have been designated to foreigners for settlement in Astrakhan, Belgorod, Tobolsk and Orenburg Provinces,...those of the foreigners who have so far reported have wished to settle in Astrakhan Province, whither over twenty families have already been sent'.[71] To what extent this 'wish' was inspired by the Chancellery, it is impossible to say. Some of these people were evidently those silk weavers just mentioned, for whom Astrakhan would certainly offer good opportunities of employment. At all events, from this point onwards preparations for large-scale settlement were increasingly focussed on Astrakhan Province.

The 'twenty families' were closely followed by other arrivals in Petersburg, and as numbers rose, the house allocated in the city became quite inadequate. In 1764 a new procedure was evolved. On leaving their ships at Kronstadt, immigrants were now taken to a reception centre at Oranienbaum, outside the city. One contemporary German account records: 'Then came the Russians with their beards and their Russian carts, loaded us up and took us to Oranienbaum. There we stayed six weeks, and everybody had to build themselves a hut, for which wood and brushwood were distributed to us.'[72] It was, however, only the first arrivals there who had to build their own huts; later groups were accommodated in barracks left by Peter III's Holstein regiments. Nor was six weeks the norm for transit; most groups went through more quickly.[73] In general, under the eye of nearby authority, conditions remained fair. Catherine herself, it was reported, visited the immigrants, in order to inspect her new subjects.[74]

In paragraph VI, § 8 of the 1763 Manifesto, the Empress had promised her colonists 'Diet-money' from the time of their registration, whether abroad or in Russia. But the nature and levels of such payments were at first left undefined, and the Chancellery of Guardianship simply took over the rates fixed by Musin-Pushkin in Hamburg, which reflected the Hamburg cost of living: fifteen kopecks per day for a man, ten for a woman, six for a child between 2 and 15, and two kopecks for one younger. By 1766 the Chancellery was finding this system very unsatisfactory. Orlov reported that despite lower costs in Petersburg, the colonists were wasting their money, 'squander it more on drink and other superfluous items', and were even falling into debt. Consequently the system was regularized with a new, lower official tariff of ten kopecks for both men and women, and three children's grades of six kopecks (10–17 years), four kopecks (2–10) and two kopecks (under 2). Catherine noted on the report that maintenance should be given in cash or kind, whichever was more appropriate.[75]

At Oranienbaum in 1764 a special commissioner was placed in charge of the foreigners, one Adam Assendelft;[76] and in 1766 a Chancellery interpreter, Ivan Kuhlberg, and four clerical staff were appointed to work with him. Kuhlberg in particular was to record the wishes of the immigrants, as prescribed in § 4 of the Manifesto, and to ensure their establishment accordingly.[77] His instructions from the Chancellery included the injunction to persuade foreigners, '(but without coercion)', to settle in 'empty places': a repetition, in fact, of § 2 of the Chancellery's own Instruction. Kuhlberg interpreted this to mean that all, if possible, should take up agriculture; and he proceeded to apply it to the arrivals of 1766 – including such as book-binders, bell-founders, army officers and chimney sweeps – without exception. Those who proved obdurate, 'despite much exhortation to them on my part that they should at least agree to pursue their trade together with agriculture', as Kuhlberg reported, found themselves simply overruled: everyone who passed through Kuhlberg's hands had to settle on the land.[78] This violation of the Manifesto was evidently condoned by the Chancellery, since not only did Kuhlberg continue his work, but there was no redress for those thus coerced. The result was the dispatch of the overwhelming majority to rural settlement near Saratov, and much trouble subsequently for the authorities from an ill-assorted colonist population in part quite ignorant of agriculture.

Preparation for settlement: Saratov

Following the promulgation of the 1763 Manifesto, the Chancellery of Guardianship sent out decrees in September, and again in October, of that year to the authorities of areas scheduled for foreign settlement, instructing them to welcome and protect immigrants, and to shield them from the usual abuses of Russian bureaucratic procedure.[79] But with people already leaving for Astrakhan, more concrete measures were needed; and on 17 October a decree was issued to the Astrakhan Provincial Chancellery, requiring the latter to meet without delay all legitimate financial demands which the foreigners might make upon it. Such money was, however, a loan, to be collected in due course by the Provincial Chancellery itself, and strict watch was to be kept to ensure its use only for the prescribed purposes.[80]

In practice, the Provincial Chancellery found this procedure most unsatisfactory. It reported back in February 1764 that each amount given to the foreigners brought requests for more; and that loans were used largely for daily maintenance, rather than to establish a home and work. The safest method was to buy for the newcomers, in their presence, the things they needed: which saved both them and the Treasury from their ignorance of local prices. Furthermore, there was little security for these grants, 'since many of [the foreigners] are extremely poor, and not only are unable to set themselves up quickly in their craft, but have not even sufficient clothing...' – while up to the time of the report over two thousand roubles had already been paid out. The Provincial Chancellery wanted fixed amounts set for grants, and an escort to convoy immigrants on their journey,

so that those ignorant of Russian usage suffer no misuse (*obid*) from coachmen on the way, or from the harshness (*surovosti*) of their hosts in village quarters; and others not of very sober condition may better keep the money given them for their journey, rather than, having spent it, borrow at a loss from their carters, who, as is now the case. . .have to be repaid here.

In the view of the Provincial Chancellery, the carriers should receive half-payment in Petersburg and the other half on arrival, to stop loans and cheating both by them and by the settlers.[81]

With the exception of fixed grants, for which no provision was made in the Manifesto, the Chancellery of Guardianship approved all the actions and proposals of the Astrakhan authority (reply of 1 March 1764). But the Astrakhan Provincial Chancellery had in fact to deal only with a small number of early arrivals, many of whom settled actually in Astrakhan town.[82] Still in October 1763, the Chancellery of Guardianship had taken steps to remove from Astrakhan's jurisdiction the immediate administration of the whole settlement scheme, by placing in charge a special representative of its own. This step was motivated by fears that pressure of routine work would prevent the Provincial Chancellery from dealing thoroughly with the project, and by the need to conduct special surveys and make plans of the lands involved. Accordingly, Captain Ivan Reuss was appointed to the Chancellery of Guardianship for these purposes, with transfer to the civilian rank of Collegiate Assessor. He had good qualifications: a Baltic German, he knew French and Russian, and was a trained engineer. Two subalterns and three clerical staff were appointed to serve under him.[83]

Reuss did not leave Petersburg immediately to take up his appointment, although the same report which announced it to the Senate noted the arrival of Musin-Pushkin's 'real husbandmen', 240 Germans, adding that they should be sent on at once. There were evidently arrangements to be made in the capital; and the number of immigrants gathered was at this stage still small enough not to make departure essential. Reuss left Petersburg only in January 1764, in the middle of winter. With him went his staff and a party of settlers, travelling in three 'columns', two or three days apart. The journey – unlike that of later larger, and slower, groups in winter – went well, and they all reached their destination of Saratov within two days of each other, 13–15 February.[84]

On arrival, Reuss based himself for administrative purposes on the local state authority, the town's *Voyevodskaya Kantselyariya*, and accommodated his charges with the local population. This procedure – quartering in private houses on first arrival – continued until December 1764, when the Chancellery of Guardianship decided to build barracks instead, 'in consideration of the burden to the local inhabitants' of this quartering.[85] Some of the newcomers wished to settle in Saratov town: on 3 March, Reuss reported that 'the foreigners Soulier, a baker, and the Italian Palgari' had enrolled themselves as townsmen (*meshchane*).[86] On the basis of § 4 of the Manifesto, others followed suit. The Saratov Voyevoda's Chancellery was very unwilling to allocate town land to these people, who naturally wished to receive plots for their personal use, like their fellow burgesses. The question finally went as far as the Senate, which not only ordered the Voyevoda's Chancellery to give the foreigners equal rights with other townsfolk, but warned it explicitly to abandon such obstructive attitudes for the future.[87] The final total of those settling in Saratov town was 137 of both sexes.[88]

Meanwhile, after much preparation, the Chancellery of Guardianship's blueprint for the Saratov settlement was finally published on 19 March 1764: the general provisions of the 1763 Manifesto at last received concrete form.[89] The document addressed itself primarily to the question of land allocation, tenure, and survey: the implications of §§ 2 and 6 (ii) of the Chancellery's Instruction.

First of all, it defined the area of settlement. Although the Manifesto had specified complete freedom of choice for those wishing to settle, and the Register appended to it had listed lands in a variety of places, the prominence given in the Register to the Volga region about Saratov gives a strong indication (as G. Bonwetsch points out[90]) of the direction of official thinking as early as the summer of 1763. In fact the Register of December 1762 and the encouragement of the Irgiz Old Believer communities were previous pointers in the same direction; and the territory chosen for the colonist programme made it effectively an extension of the Old Believer scheme. At what point the final colonist area was determined, is not clear. Although the lands listed in the Register were all on the left or 'meadow' bank of the river, the authorities were already specifying in November 1763 that the immigrants would settle 'not on that side of the Volga on which the nomadic Tatar and Kalmyk roam', but on the right bank, 'near places already inhabited'.[91] The decree of 19 March defined just such an area, a broad sweep of territory on the right bank above and below Saratov, and stretching west along the Don well towards Voronezh.[92] The choice was explicitly based on three factors: the area was wholly surrounded by existing settlements, so that even when the colonies expanded, 'there will not be the slightest danger of any harmful undertakings'; it was very suitable for future expansion; and the establishment here of villages fairly close together would encourage trade between them, helping to accustom the foreigners to their new home: 'and thereby. . . Russia will no longer appear [to them] so strange and wild, as at present' (§ 1). In the event, colonies were established on both sides of the river.

The basic administrative division within the colonists' territory was to be the district (*okrug*), containing some 40,000 desyatinas, and not more than 1,000 families (§ 5). The only criterion suggested for dividing families among districts was religious, to avoid confessional disputes: this principle was largely, but not always, observed in practice. In the villages each family, irrespective of size, was to receive a grant of thirty desyatinas, 'the same as *odnodvortsy* (of whom there are about four male souls in each household)';[93] this would avoid disputes and later awkward adjustments, and any additional labour could find employment with other families or as craftsmen. Each married man, childless or not, was to be given his own holding; but since 'an unmarried man cannot be an efficient peasant', bachelors were to receive holdings only in exceptional circumstances, and on condition of marrying within the year (§ 3). In each colony, empty house plots and land, one sixth of the total, were to be set aside for future new families, and the same proportion allocated for craftsmen (§ 5).[94] The fairs promised by the Manifesto were reserved to the main settlements of each district. The local government of the latter was to be codified and systematized in conjunction with the colonists themselves (§§ 4 (vii), 5).[95]

The most detailed provisions were those concerning property-ownership and inheritance (§ 4). The land allocated to the colonists was vested not in the individual households but in the village as a whole. It could not be sold, mortgaged or divided, and the holdings of anyone leaving the colony reverted to the community. The same applied to grants which might be made for special purposes, 'such as for the erection of churches, factories, works, vineyards, etc.'. The individual family holding was, however, to be hereditary, and here the Chancellery introduced the principle of ultimogeniture,[96] hoping that this would force elder sons to learn a trade. If, however, the youngest son should for any reason prove unfit, the father could make his own choice of heir. Movable property was left to the disposal of the parents. Should a household be left without any male members, the first man entering it by marriage became the legal owner, on condition of supporting the remaining women until their death or marriage. All other land belonged to the village in common, except that any deposits of precious metals which might be found were automatically excluded from the village's holdings.

Thus careful provision was made for the basic constitutional needs of the colonies, in so far as they depended on the Chancellery. In practice much of the plan remained on paper. Ultimogeniture, completely opposed to the settlers' customs, rapidly became a dead letter; and even the hereditary principle by the end of the century had given way to repartition, which was then increasing among the Russian peasantry. It was only later in the settlements of the south, particularly those of the Mennonites, that the individual farm was accepted as the unit, indivisible and hereditary, of land ownership.

The closest parallel to the system proposed for the new colonies was the position and development of the *odnodvortsy* at this time, not only with regard to land-tenure, but also from the point of view of local administration and social status. We have already seen that the size of the colonist land-holding was taken directly from that of the *odnodvortsy*. Conversely, Catherine shortly afterwards considered the possibility of using the judicial system planned in the Saratov colonies as a model for the *odnodvortsy* of Voronezh. Furthermore, according to the 1763 Manifesto the colonists had the right – purely theoretical and never exercised – to own serfs. The two categories had in common also a certain ambiguity of position in the Russian social hierarchy: only in the nineteenth century were they both unequivocally seen as (separate) divisions of the state peasantry.[97]

Besides defining the system of property rights in the colonies, the decree of 19 March 1764 made full provision for surveying the areas assigned for colonist settlement (§§ 6, 7). In April survey teams were accordingly sent out, first to the Saratov area, later to most of the places named in the Register.[98] They were largely under the charge of three specially-appointed 'supervisors';[99] Reuss directed the work around Saratov itself.[100] The survey revealed the full extent of the legal chaos which characterized land tenure at the time, particularly in border areas: especially where land was plentiful and settlement preceded the establishment of sound administration, legal forms were often neglected. Equally characteristically, the Chancellery of Guardianship was very imperfectly informed concerning the distribution of population and the amount of free land in the territory it had chosen. Although it protested to the Senate in pained astonishment at the extent of illegal *pomeshchik* land occupation, and at the number of illegal residents in Saratov, it had in fact rather under- than over-estimated the area available.[101]

Reuss, who bore direct responsibility for the colonists waiting to be

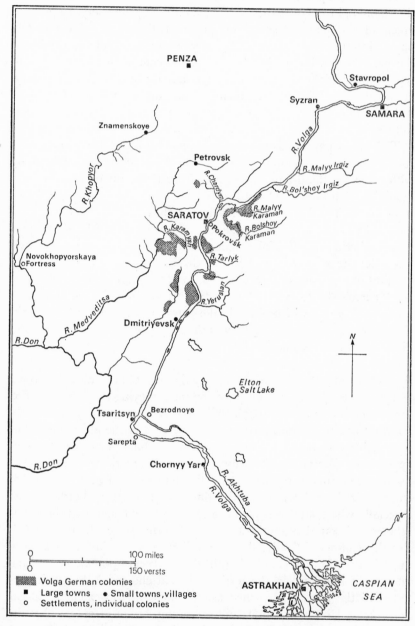

Map 2.   The Lower Volga Region in the 1760s.

settled, and for the conduct of the survey, had his hands full, so much so that the Chancellery feared he would be unable to cope without more staff at his disposal. In June 1764 the proposal was therefore put to the Senate that a special office should be created, under Reuss's direction, to ensure adequate administrative capacity. The Senate rejected the idea on the grounds that the Saratov Voyevoda's Office was quite able to cover the additional work involved; but the Chancellery would agree to this only on condition that 'reliable and capable' people were placed in the posts of Saratov Voyevoda and his Assistant. The Senate allowed the Chancellery to propose its own candidates, and these were duly appointed in October 1764: Major Nikita Stroyev as Voyevoda, and Captain Brandt as his Deputy.[102]

But even so, separate administration soon became essential; and in April 1766 a general reappraisal of the Chancellery staff took place. One consequence was the appointment of Kuhlberg to work with Assendelft in Oranienbaum. In Moscow an official of the Treasury Department (*Kamer-Kollegiya*), Captain Tikhmenev, had been acting since 1763 as Commissioner for the Chancellery. In view of the 'no small difficulties' involved in carrying both jobs, he was now transferred entirely to the Chancellery's work, and his zeal rewarded with promotion.[103] The previous temporary secondment of a Chancellery interpreter to the Astrakhan Provincial Chancellery was also made permanent, since that office was to hold special responsibility for the Herrnhut settlement (Sarepta) near Tsaritsyn.[104] But most important of all, a separate Guardianship Office (*Opekunstvennaya Kontora*) was set up in Saratov, subordinated to the central Chancellery. It had four senior staff, headed by a Chief Judge (*Glavnyy Sud'ya*), Lieutenant-Colonel Rezanov, and twenty-seven clerical and other personnel. Reuss joined it at its inception. A command of regular soldiers and Cossacks was also attached to the Office. It was envisaged as a temporary institution, to function until such time as the colonists should become accustomed to Russian life and could be returned to the jurisdiction of the local state authorities.[105]

The first Saratov colony, Nizhnaya Dobrinka, was established on 29 June 1764. Between 1764 and 1768, while the survey and the gradual building of the first villages continued, 104 colonies were founded on both sides of the Volga.[106] This was one of the largest and most compact of all foreign settlements in Russia; but it was by no means the only one at this time.

Settlement elsewhere in Russia: settlement by contract

The arrangements made by the Chancellery of Guardianship tended to channel all colonists to the Saratov area, for settlement on the basis of the 1763 Manifesto and of any special agreements entered into with recruiting agents in Europe. But two groups of the immigrants arriving through Petersburg escaped Kuhlberg's impressment. Those who did not pass through Oranienbaum, or who could approach the Chancellery direct, were able to choose their own livelihood. A very few joined the army, thereby earning the 30 rouble bounty promised: by 1774 the Chancellery had paid out 102 roubles 80¾ kopecks under this heading.[107] Entrepreneurs made their own agreements with the Chancellery, as did artisans settling in Petersburg. The second group were those who, under contracts with private individuals or other government bodies, agreed to settle elsewhere than Saratov.

In 1765 – well after the initial establishment of the Saratov settlement, but before the largest (1766) influx of immigrants – the foreigners waiting at Oranienbaum were told of 'HIH pleasure' that some colonies should be established near Petersburg. A decree of 30 September gave overall responsibility for the new project to 'our Jägermeister Pohlmann' and immediate charge to the director (*upravitel'*) of Tsarskoye Selo, F. Udalov, with whom the new colonists signed special contracts.[108] On the basis of these arrangements, three colonies were established: 60 German families formed the Novo-Saratovskaya colony on the right bank of the Neva 13 versts from Petersburg; Srednyaya Rogatka, 12 versts from the capital on the Tsarskoye Selo road, housed 22 families; and a further 28 settled 14 versts from Tsarskoye Selo on the right bank of the Izhora river, in the Izhora or Kolpino colony. These settlements acquired the colloquial German names of Sechziger, Zweiundzwanziger, and Achtundzwanziger Colonie respectively, after the number of their founding families.[109]

The new colonies remained under the direction of the Tsarskoye Selo administration; the colonists fairly soon achieved a reasonable standard of living, also some reputation for German thoroughness and honesty. They likewise soon became one of the standard objects of comment in travellers' and other accounts of the Russian capital. In one such work published towards the end of Catherine's reign, J. Georgi remarked of them: 'The German colonists who inhabit villages in various districts have indeed established themselves after the manner of the German countryside; but with the passage of time they are gradually adopting more and more from Russian agriculture. The Russian country folk on the other hand copy them in almost nothing.'[110] The hope of a model farming establishment which evidently underlay the creation of the Petersburg colonies was very imperfectly realized, at least under Catherine, although they were noted for their potatoes and – according to Reimers – for their *Colonisten-Butter*, which found a ready market in the city.[111]

At the beginning of the nineteenth century several new colonies were added to the original Petersburg group. But in 1767 a further settlement had appeared in Ingermanland (the Petersburg Province), on the same special contractual basis: 67 German families founded the villages of Lutsk, Porkhov, and Frankfurt outside Yamburg, near Narva. These were part of a comprehensive restoration and development of the whole town of Yamburg, undertaken at this time by I. P. Yelagin. The project involved the rebuilding of the town itself, and the establishment there of textile mills, for which the colonies might supply a labour force.[112]

Although clear evidence is lacking, a similar special or model function may have underlain the two other foreign colonies established on the same basis in the north of the Empire at this time, the German settlements of Hirschenhof and Helfreichsdorf, set up by Governor Browne of Livonia on Catherine's instructions in 1766, and occupying an estate between Riga and Daugavpils (Dünaburg). Their history has been told at length by W. Conze.[113] Interest in agricultural improvement was however an explicit motive in the 1765 initiative of the Governor-General of the newly-created Slobodskaya Province of the Ukraine, Major-General Shcherbinin, to acquire colonists for his domain. In August 1765 the Chancellery of Guardianship agreed to invite colonists to settle there; and altogether 81 families set out for Ostrogozhsk, near Voronezh, in January 1766.[114] The originator of this scheme was Colonel S. Tevyashov, representative of a prominent local family.[115] Instructions to Ostrogozhsk on the first party of 60 families demanded that 20 of them should be sent on to Khar'kov, and the remainder found quarters in Ostrogozhsk until a site for the colony could be determined. But the search for suitable lands for the Germans ran up against the hostility of the local population: summoned by the authorities for questioning as to land available in the vicinity, the inhabitants roundly declared that they knew of none. Tevyashov had to take up the search himself; and it was finally he who took responsibility for the colony.[116]

The site eventually allocated to the immigrants lay on the river

Sosna, directly across the water from the house of Tevyashov and his carefully-landscaped park.[117] In fact, the colony's land actually belonged to him; and according to one account his interest in using the newcomers as model farmers led him initially to propose settling them in scattered groups on different parts of his estates – a suggestion the colonists successfully resisted.[118] In 1781 the official reply to an Academy of Sciences questionnaire on the region described the colony as situated 'in a most advantageous place near the river Sosna' and as having

one large street along its length, and another across its width leading to the water and into the fields; in it is one house belonging to the pastor, 52 colonist houses, in their midst one wooden church, the houses are built in one line, at some distance one from the other, which gives an agreeable prospect and correct symmetry, all the houses are also partly wood, partly half-timbered (*faferkovye*), covered with shingle, and with large windows looking out onto the street.

The number of colonists reaches 72 families and they have a pastor of the Augsburg confession.[119]

The report was equally specific on the colonists' occupations:

...they...exercise themselves in arable farming (*khlebopashestvo*), and having ploughs of the Württemberg and Brandenburg type they work the soil much better than the local farmers. However their principal commerce (*promysel*) lies in good tobacco of various sorts, which they carry round for sale through the Khar'kov and Voronezh viceroyalties, sometimes sell in their houses, and sometimes even take to Moscow, and from that they earn an income incomparably more lavish than from arable farming, recently they have begun to grow madder needful in the dyeing of broadcloth, but not yet with the desired success. On market days they bring into Ostrogozhsk considerable quantities of potatoes, white and red cabbage, celery, and other good garden greens and root crops of different sorts, and their women make excellent...butter, cheese similar to the Dutch, and thereby provide mutual advantage and satisfaction, in Riebensdorf there are people able to weave and dye broadcloth skilfully, who live all the time in...Voronezh at the cloth mills.

In this same colony they make pipes in the Dutch manner from local clay; there are, besides, gardeners and weavers able to weave broadloom linens, the women knit stockings and make straw hats.[120]

If Riebensdorf remained an isolated enclave, the only foreign settlement in the new Slobodskaya province, P. Rumyantsev, the Governor-General of Little Russia (the former Hetman Ukraine), had to oversee several rather various settlements. The first was the Belovezh group of German colonies near Nezhin, dating likewise from 1766. Here, as the following year at Yamburg, immigrants were expected to revitalize a former – if much older – existing settlement. The land involved was transferred specially to the jurisdiction of the Little Russian College, and Rumyantsev received instructions to establish one hundred colonist families there 'and to renew the empty township called "in Belyye Vezhi", by settlement in it...of foreign townsfolk up to fifty families...'. Rumyantsev had complete charge over the organization of the colonies, and a special sum of 77,500 roubles was allocated for the project out of local revenues.[121] One hundred and sixty-seven colonists signed two contracts to settle in the district and town of 'Catharinen Pohl' (Yekaterinenpol)[122] and altogether six settlements were founded in the same year.

The *Topographical Description of the Chernigov Viceroyalty* compiled in 1786 gives an extensive account of these colonies some twenty years on. Yekaterinenpol, founded on the remains of an ancient city mentioned in the Nestor Chronicle, had been settled according to plan by 51 colonists designated as urban artisans and *meshchane*. 'However, lacking sufficient occasion to sell their goods to anyone on the spot, some have scattered among the Little Russian towns; others have settled down and taken up petty commerce with the sale of horses and spirits, and have not yet attained the status of townsmen and *meshchane*.' The Director of the colonies lived in the fifth village, Kalchinovka; their internal life was regulated by a statute, written in German, which had been supplied specially by Rumyantsev.[123]

The Little Russian College had likewise to take charge of the settlement of the southern immigrants recruited by Filipovich and Mirolyub, as well as others arriving independently. (The terms of their appointment restricted both the latter agents merely to recruiting abroad.) A special board (*ekspeditsiya*) was created within the College, under the charge of Senior Auditor Bashilov, 'to take in all points the measures necessary, and for all supervision (*nablyudeniye*) concerning these colonists, especially the Germans coming in through Kiev'. Another stated purpose of the new department was to encourage immigration by *romunskiy narod*: Moldavians, Vlachs and Transylvanians.[124]

The suggestion for the separate board originated with the Chancellery of Guardianship, and was part of comprehensive proposals which it made for the recruits of both agents. The Chancellery suggested that the new authority under Bashilov should draw up a statute covering all aspects of the settlement and send a copy of it to the Chancellery; 'or, following the example of the contracts made with colonists by various private people,...the original itself of that Statute for confirmation'.[125]

Mirolyub's mission had brought in 150 foreign settlers, and representations from deputies of many more who wished to form a nationally exclusive ('Rumanian') community.[126] Not all of Filipovich's recruits, who numbered 579, were of the same origin; and the Chancellery therefore had to make provision for two separate groups. The lands initially assigned to Filipovich's group, and then others substituted near Tula, proved unsuitable, and finally no specific allocation was made for them.[127] They were encouraged to enter military service, to settle in New Russia, or to enrol as merchants and craftsmen in existing towns and villages. The 'Rumanians' among them were free to join the other group if both sides so wished; all others were to be settled at Rumyantsev's discretion.[128] One party of these people, Bulgarians, subsequently formed the village of Borshchagovka, near Kiev. Some of the Germans joined the Belovezh colony and a small group of German artisans settled at Kiev, 'near the Kievo-Pecherskiy fortress'.[129]

The second group had made ambitious proposals, most of which were nonetheless formally accepted. They wished to settle near Kiev and to form a large colony, with its own civic authority (*magistrat*) and guilds, and with considerable trading rights within Russia and abroad. They also wanted to build a monastery (refused), and to set up a printing press, 'to print various divine church and secular books in our tongue, for the instruction of our children and for sale within and outside the state'. Mirolyub, in fact the brother of one of the deputies, was to become typographical corrector, civic secretary, and school teacher in the new colony.[130]

Subsequent reality did not correspond to these rather grandiose plans. In 1767 fifty-six families, 133 people, of Mirolyub's party settled in a new 'town' near Velikiy Khutor, by Pereyaslavl (Poltava Province), with an initial annual allocation of 12,300 roubles. More immigrants were expected to join them; but two years later numbers in the colony were still insufficient in Rumyantsev's eyes even to warrant a separate church, and they received permission to hold Greek-language services in the church of Velikiy Khutor.[131] Ruban's *Curious Almanack* for 1775 shows 67 families; in 1785 the whole settlement, 'Vlachs, Bulgarians and other foreigners', moved to the Crimea.[132] Besides this group, and the Kiev Germans, Ruban also lists one other, larger settlement of some 100 unidentified families at Bakhmut, in the east of New Russia.[133]

The southern groups of colonists formed part of the larger stream of New Russian immigration to be described in Chapter 4. One other colony was set up at this time on a contractual basis: the Herrnhut foundation of Sarepta[134] near Tsaritsyn, some little way south of the main Volga settlements. Sarepta was perhaps the most important, and certainly the best known, of all the individual colonies; its antecedents have been described. The Herrnhut representatives pursued their negotiations with skill and caution and, after the Synod had finally accepted their theological doctrine as permissible, the Moravians concluded an advantageous agreement in 1765.[135] In particular, the Brethren were to be dependent solely on the central Chancellery of Guardianship: which gave them in practice almost complete autonomy, although a measure of practical responsibility resided with the Astrakhan Provincial Chancellery.[136]

The text of the agreement held out vague but dazzling promises on the part of the Brethren, such as the building of towns and establishment of trade with Asia; although the Brotherhood later claimed that the former item had been introduced by their intermediary, an outsider, to increase his own importance.[137] (Neither promise was realized.) But one important point was left unsettled. The Synod, while accepting the Brotherhood's doctrines, proved obdurate in the matter of permitting non-Orthodox missionary activity, despite the reference to the conversion of Muslims in the Manifesto; and in the agreement this question, cardinal for the Brethren, was passed over in silence.[138]

Besides the sound material and constitutional basis secured through the negotiations, Sarepta enjoyed continuous support from Herrnhut; and furthermore, the morale and professional stature of the Sarepta Brethren was superior to that of the average colonist. These factors were instrumental in the colony's rapid success.

Besides the six separate groups of German colonists, and the further settlements by contract in the south, which were all essentially state foundations, the Chancellery of Guardianship also arranged for foreigners to settle on private land. On 1 November 1765 it had produced a new legal procedure, avowedly relating to the contractual agreements made by Udalov for the new Petersburg colonies, but extending the right of 'hiring' colonists to private persons as well, 'both the gentry, and to merchants and free foreigners living here'.[139]

Initially the plan was restricted to Ingermanland, and its intention was explicitly to spread and equally to improve agriculture there (§ 1). It provided for two types of settlement. Firstly, anyone who wished could receive a grant of empty Crown land, free, on condition of peopling it at his own expense from among the immigrants then arriving, or with 'free people already living here' (§§ 3–4). Ten years were allowed to complete the settlement, failing which the land reverted to the Crown and the defaulter had to pay rent retrospectively for its use (§ 7). If after two or more years the land was still unsettled, it could be given to any new applicant who could show a contract of settlement with a number of foreigners sufficient to people the plot (§ 8).

In fact, this system was not new in the area. Since the early days of Russian rule in Ingria, the government had made land grants there, on the condition of their settlement with native peasants. A succession of decrees had regulated the procedure.[140] But the new law made no mention of these precedents.

The decree regulated very carefully the relationship between the settlers and the *poselitel'*, as the recipient of such a grant was called. Great emphasis was laid on the personal freedom of the former, the contractual obligations on both sides, and the duty of the Chancellery to guarantee and enforce their agreement (§§ 2, 4, 6). Contracts – 'as with private people, so with the Chancellery of Imperial Estates or other official offices' – were to be submitted to the Chancellery of Guardianship for safe-keeping. The land-grant could not be divided, mortgaged or sold unless the third party acknowledged the settlers' rights without alteration (§ 4). The *poselitel'* was responsible for collecting from his settlers the money due from them to the Chancellery, according to the terms of the 1763 Manifesto. Otherwise neither he nor they were liable to taxes during the ten-year exemption period; relations after that time would be governed by the contract (§§ 6, 9).

A second type of settlement envisaged under the scheme was the establishment of foreigners on land-owners' estates. This was altogether a simpler matter. On completion of the contract, the estate owner was to pay the Chancellery at once the full sum owing for each immigrant; 'and otherwise, apart from protecting them from attacks by those engaging them (*soderzhateley*) and from infringements, by either side, of the agreement concluded, the Chancellery of Guardianship for Foreigners should be in no way concerned with such foreigners either during or after the years of exemption' (§ 11). Sale and inheritance of any land involved were governed by § 4; the only other limitation concerned criminal cases deserving corporal punishment, where the landlord could not act by himself but had to inform the Chancellery (§ 13). Landlords in this category also received the designation *poselitel'*. A final note in the decree stressed the financial saving to be obtained from the scheme, as well as its agricultural value.

The plan was sufficiently successful to be extended, within eighteen months, to cover all parts of the country.[141] It was noted that many of the foreigners themselves desired particularly to settle like this, 'that is, partly with owners of villages, partly with merchants, and especially with factory-owners, who...wish to take them for work in all sorts of crafts'. The new decree permitted all colonists bound for Saratov, both those of the Crown and – providing they would release them – those of the *vyzyvateli*, to settle elsewhere in this manner; and it emphasized the need for close supervision of contracts by the Chancellery, since terms of contract could now be very varied.

In his report to the Empress from which this decree evolved, Orlov again referred to the cultural and economic advantages of the system, especially that of free land grants.

Not only may YIH native subjects in various places learn various crafts hitherto unknown to them, the fertilizing (*odobreniye*) of plough-land and particular aspects of agriculture itself; but lands now...lying waste will be cultivated, for it is impossible for anyone not having an abundance of land to attempt such a settlement, except of a few craftsmen or workers.[142]

The great emphasis placed on the rights and freedom of colonists entering into such agreements was necessary in the circumstances. Detractors of the settlement programme and agents of other powers in Europe often played upon natural fears of enserfment among the emigrants. This concern also recalls, however, the later activities of Pastor Eisen (which are discussed below), particularly in view of the cultural significance attached to the system by Orlov. The cultural advantages were equally calculated to appeal to those among the upper classes who were concerned over agriculture and estate management. An outstanding case was Count Zakhar Chernyshev, who had already demonstrated his interest in his earlier negotiations with Herrnhut. Chernyshev had now sought foreigners once again for his estates; and the fact that he had persuaded 'a considerable number of families from among the colonists travelling to Saratov' to settle on his lands 'in the interior' of Russia was one of the immediate reasons given by Orlov for extending the *poselitel'* scheme from Ingermanland to the Empire as a whole.[143]

The subsequent development of the *poselitel'* system is not entirely clear. In 1768, during the debates in the Legislative Commission on the rights of nobles to establish 'free' villages, a deputy cited the recent colonist laws as a precedent; G. Orlov intervened to say that 'the old laws were being revoked and others newly established', so that the colonist example could not be used.[144] Much land available under the scheme remained vacant: in the 1770s considerable areas assigned to the Chancellery of Guardianship in Ingermanland were leased out on *obrok*.[145] And in 1772 it required a special decree for one Prince Izenburg to recruit and settle foreign colonists on an estate newly-purchased in the Vyborg area.[146] But cases of *poselitel'* settlement can be documented during and after the 1760s; and a decree of 1803 refers to the law of May 1767 as still in force.[147] The known cases are varied, both in their location and in the character of the settlers involved. Some thirty Bulgarians, for example, made contracts with the Monastery of the Brethren in Kiev;[148] a group of 12 German families who joined the southern Crown colony of Josephstal in the 1790s had originally 'been recruited by various landowners, but then had gone to live [on the estate of] *pomeshchik* Naumann near the river Oryol';[149] while Field-Marshal Peter Rumyantsev gave shelter in 1770 to a community of Hutterite refugees from the trans-Danubian principalities, who formed a colony on his estate of Vishenki in Chernigov Province.[150]

The first variant of the scheme – the granting of land on condition of its population within a certain period – followed in any case a pattern already established, not only for native settlers in Ingermanland, but also in contemporary settlement in the south. The working of the system in the north is exemplified by the case of the German George Trappe, whom we shall meet later as a recruiting agent for Potemkin. In 1776 Trappe received a grant of two *pustoshi* (empty plots) near Narva, on condition of settling on them 60 foreign families which he himself was to bring in within 10 years. He failed to fulfil his quota, recruiting only 28 families. This was noted in 1787, but he was not immediately dispossessed. However, in 1792 another applicant for the estate appeared; in Trappe's absence, his property was auctioned to recoup the rent prescribed in such cases and the estate was confiscated.[151]

In a letter to Prince A. B. Kurakin complaining of the treatment he had received, Trappe described the conditions facing an entrepreneur of this kind:

During fifteen years I expended infinite care, trouble, and money, having built there a factory for which I obtained the materials from Holland...Having constructed in addition forty and four buildings great and small intended for 28 German families whom I had brought over at great expense and who have been cruelly expelled, and having cleared and reclaimed land with great difficulty – since I found nothing there but woods and marshes which I drained to make meadows – I have suffered a loss of over Sixteen Thousand roubles.[152]

Not surprisingly, many of those who took land grants were not so

energetic as Trappe, and at the end of the century the widespread
failure to develop estates granted in this way in the south became
something of a scandal.[153]

Livonian connections

The new system of settling colonists on private estates provides a close
parallel (as we shall see) with another interest of G. G. Orlov, the
further activities of Pastor J. G. Eisen, and so suggests a link with
Catherine's actions over the peasant question in Livonia in the 1760s.
In the early months and years of her reign the Baltic provinces presented the Empress with problems of policy in diverse but often inter-
related areas. The newly-established export of grain through the Baltic
ports, for example, led on to the whole question of Baltic commerce at
large, and to the creation in April 1763 of a special Commission on
trade through Riga.[154] Part of this complex matter was the admission of
Jews to trade in the Russian Empire, something the native Riga merchants had been hankering after ever since Elizabeth Petrovna banned
it in 1742: although the Jewish community was kept within strictly
limited bounds in Riga, it had played a valued role in the commercial
and financial affairs of the city. Another larger aspect of the same
question of commerce was the rights and status of Riga's trading
classes. Commerce and crafts were essentially in the hands of the city's
German population, whose guild organization and privileges went back
to medieval times. They had provided models for Peter I's Russian
guild and urban legislation in the 1720s, but in the later eighteenth
century they came increasingly under criticism. The Statute on the
Riga trade worked out in 1765 by the new Commission circumscribed
the power of the city authorities to regulate commerce, and tended to
challenge their entrenched position.

Catherine also wished to assert Imperial over local authority in her
dealings with the Livonian landed nobility. Her initial declaration of
willingness, in September 1763, to defend their chartered rights soon
turned out to be at odds with her wishes for the use of Crown estates in
Livonia and her views on the status of the peasantry there; and Ya.
Zutis sees most of her actions in these areas in the mid-1760s as an
increasingly systematic attack on the manifestations of a local separat-
ism which she found intolerable.[155] It was from the beginning of
Catherine's reign, he suggests, that the 'Baltic question', the problem
of Baltic privileged status, emerged in its full form.[156] But Catherine
was building on existing foundations: the basis for change had been

laid in preceding decades.¹⁵⁷ And, as with the peasant question, in several areas such change and the problems it involved had points of contact in the 1760s with the immigration programme.

In the sphere of Baltic commercial affairs, the 1763 Manifesto fitted smoothly into the new line of policy already being pursued by the central authorities, which aimed at the encouragement and development of Livonian commerce and whose clearest expression was the new Commission on the Riga trade. The former Swedish territories conquered by Peter I formed (with the addition of Moscow) one unit for the Manifesto's tax exemption regulations: 'those, which desire to abide in the City's, as also to list themselves for Handy-Crafts or Trade in Our Residence in St Petersburg or in the adjacent places, in the Citys of Livonia and Estonia, Ingermanlandia, Corelia, and Finland, or in Our Capital City of Moscow' were offered exemption for five years (§ VI (2)). Zutis notes that the Manifesto did stimulate the settlement of foreign merchants in the Baltic provinces: though he offers no details or supporting evidence.¹⁵⁸ But besides the general stimulation which the invitation of foreigners could give to Baltic commerce, the new immigration system also provided a mechanism for central intervention in more specific areas. One of these was the question of the Jews.

Jewish merchants in Riga had traditionally played a notable part in the city's commercial activities. Their position there had been governed – and restricted – by special regulations; but the city authorities, while jealously enforcing these rules, fully appreciated the value of the Jewish presence, and the expulsion of Jews from the Empire in 1742 had been a considerable blow. As we have seen, Catherine was faced with the problem of re-admitting the Jews very early in her reign; and at that time she chose deliberately to postpone dealing with it. But in February 1764 further representations were made by Jews, asking to be allowed to live 'in Russia and the conquered provinces' – probably Little Russia and the Baltic lands¹⁵⁹ – and offering in return to pay accounts still standing from the date of their expulsion in 1742. This new initiative was supported a month later by the official representative of the Riga Magistrature (City Council) in St Petersburg.¹⁶⁰

Little had happened to change the considerations which had originally led Catherine to exclude Jews from the provisions of her immigration programme. But now she adopted a subterfuge, in order both to realize her own wishes in the matter and to further her immigration plans, without having to go back on her public position. At the end of April 1764 Governor-General Browne in Riga received the following rescript by special courier:

If some merchant people of the New Russian province are recommended by the Chancellery of Guardianship of Foreigners, permit them to reside in Riga and carry on commerce, on the same basis as the laws allow in Riga to the merchantry of other Russian provinces. In addition, if these people send their managers (*prikazchiki*), representatives and work-people to New Russia, also for settlement there, then give them a suitable escort and passports from you for their dispatch and security, without regard to their confession and belief; and in addition, if three or four persons come from Mitau who wish to travel to Petersburg for certain claims they have with the Crown, give them passports, not mentioning their nationality and without enquiring into their confession, but write. . .only their names; and so that you should know them, they should have a letter from the merchant Levi Wulff, who is here, which they are to show you.

On the formal Russian text Catherine had written a personal postscript in German: 'If you don't understand me, it will not be my fault, the President of the Guardianship Chancellery wrote this letter himself, keep all this secret.'[161] Browne at once sent on the courier, Major Rtishchev, to Mitau, with a letter to the Russian Resident there, who sent back with him seven Jews. Fulfilling the orders contained at the end of Catherine's rescript, Browne dispatched them to Petersburg; and in the capital the Mitau Jews joined with Levi Wulff in negotiations with A. Mel′gunov, Governor-General of New Russia.

This episode has been described at length by Yu. Gessen.[162] Essentially Mel′gunov – with the active approval of Catherine and G. G. Orlov – wished to use Wulff's services to settle Jews in New Russia. The Jews on the other hand were primarily concerned to secure trading rights in Riga. Both sides got what they wanted. Wulff and three others, including two of the Mitau Jews, went back to Riga with a Chancellery recommendation, as Browne had been given to expect by the opening lines of Catherine's rescript, and at once began recruiting Jews from Polish and Prussian territory, while the Chancellery wrote to Browne that they were to have trading rights in the city on the basis of the conditions offered to all foreigners by the immigration laws. Although the 1763 Manifesto, unlike its 1762 predecessor, had not explicitly excluded Jews, nor indeed mentioned them at all, throughout the whole transaction any reference to Jewishness was scrupulously avoided.

The Jewish migrants recruited by Wulff and his assistants gathered in Riga to await dispatch to New Russia. Gessen has no figures for the numbers engaged, but they were enough to cause comment, and resentment when they broke the old rules governing the length of stay and residential limits allowed to Jews in the town. Browne had further correspondence with Catherine and the Chancellery before an ambiguous *modus vivendi* was established – 'our will is', wrote Catherine, 'not to publish permission to live in Russia specially for those persons of whom you wrote to the Chancellery of Guardianship, however, also not to have a strict prohibition either. . .'

The net result of this secret operation was evidently not very significant in terms of settlers for New Russia; though the government continued to encourage Jews to settle there. Jews sent in 1769 with prisoners of war from the Danubian principalities were directed to the province, as a result of which Jewish immigration into New Russia was formally legalized;[163] and in the mid-1770s, under the regime of Prince G. A. Potemkin, several communities of Polish Jews were accepted for settlement there as foreigners.[164]

In Riga, Mel'gunov's activities led on to the re-establishment of a permanent Jewish population, and the issue in 1766 of new rules governing their position. As before, length of stay and place of residence were restricted, as were the occupations they could engage in. These limitations did not apply to the recruiting agents under Wulff, however, and while they retained this exceptional status their privileged position and rather arrogant attitude to their less-favoured co-religionists caused considerable friction within the community.[165]

So in the matter of the Jews, Mel'gunov and the Chancellery in their search for immigrants helped the city fathers of Riga, and the Jewish merchants themselves, to realize quite different aims. But in another sphere, that of relations between the essentially German city authorities and the Latvian inhabitants of Riga, the provisions of the 1763 Manifesto operated against the wishes of the Magistrature. In 1767 the Senate issued a decree 'concerning the registering of foreigners as townsmen in Riga, on the basis of the Manifesto of 1763'.[166] The occasion was the case of a bookkeeper, Tobias Georg Eflein, who was seeking membership in the Riga Great Guild, which its members and the Magistrature denied him. In support of their refusal they put forward various arguments, notably that Eflein had given no proofs of his standing as a bookkeeper, and that his wife, as a Latvian, had no right to guild membership – indeed her father had been refused it in a special case heard in 1752.[167]

The case of Steinhauer versus the guild and the Magistrature (1747– 53) was a significant event in the history of race relations in Riga. The Steinhauers were Latvian; Matis Steinhauer and his son Jan, possibly runaway serfs, but sailors by profession with long experience of the sea, settled in Riga from Courland in the late seventeenth century.

Matis possessed an exceptional talent for judging the quality of timber, and built an international reputation as an assessor of ships' masts: Peter I gave him the office and title of official inspector of masts. His sons followed in his footsteps. The Steinhauers' expertise, and their own commercial operations, greatly expanded the timber trade through Riga, and also made them wealthy men. In the course of time the family set up or acquired saw-mills and other enterprises, and bought land and several houses within the city boundaries.[168]

However, all this had to be done under someone else's name. Only members of the city's Great Guild had full rights to trade and own property in Riga and the Guild, composed of Germans, refused the Steinhauers membership on grounds of nationality. The Magistrature, likewise German in composition, took a similar view. In 1747 Matis's sons took their case to the highest court of appeal, the Senate; but although – according to Zutis – the city had no legal leg to stand on, it dug deeply into its purse and bought a favourable judgement, so that the final Senate verdict in 1753 went against the appellants.[169]

This success encouraged the city authorities to push discrimination against Latvians in Riga still further. In the same year the Guild put forward a project suggesting among other things the confiscation of all immovable property in the city belonging to Latvians; Latvians, even free men, were to wear peasant dress, not to engage in any commercial activity, and were to be obliged to clean the city's drains and clear its refuse, 'so that they should not forget their origins, nor seek the privileges assured to citizens, and should remember eternally that they are slaves'.[170] In face of this threat the Latvians in their turn managed to find highly-placed patrons. The then Governor-General of Livonia, Prince Dolgoruky, supported them, and in 1754 one of the Steinhauers, Daniel, was created 'commissar of commerce' for Schleswig and Holstein by no less a person than the heir to the throne, Grand Duke Peter. This promotion saved all his property from confiscation.[171]

But it was only in 1767 that the effects of the original Senate judgement were reversed, by the Senate itself. Eflein was Daniel Steinhauer's son-in-law; and after hearing from both sides in the case, and from the Chancellery of Guardianship, the Senate found in his favour. The new judgement not only refuted the specific arguments advanced by the Guild and the Magistrature, which the Senate considered either unfounded or specious; it rejected the whole stance of the city authorities. In particular, the Senate declared that 'the acceptance and increase of suitable and worthy townsfolk of any and every loyal city does not depend upon the will of the townsfolk themselves, nor upon that of the

Riga Magistrature. It is indisputably the right of the Monarch. . .' It ordered Eflein to be enrolled in the Great Guild on the terms laid down in the 1763 Manifesto, which were to be the basis for dealing with any future applications as well.[172]

This assertion of national over local authority was fully in keeping with Catherine's policy in the wider question of the autonomy of the western border regions (the Baltic provinces and the Ukraine). And as the restrictive attitude of the Riga Great Guild towards outsiders' trading rights had only recently been denounced by Governor Browne as an obstacle to the growth of trade,[173] the Senate's decision can also be seen as consistent with government intentions on commercial expansion. Catherine's declared policy at this particular time was to expand the Riga trade without infringing existing privileges;[174] the Senate's verdict was aimed at an abuse, not a defence, of privilege, which was also commercially restrictive. In this case too, therefore, the immigration legislation was used to break down barriers created by ethnic and national divisions, and to widen commercial opportunity within the city.

One of the earliest formulations of Catherine's policy on the Riga trade, that it should be expanded without infringing existing privileges, appears in her comments on a report presented to her in 1763 by Kammerherr Godofred von Linke.[175] Linke was a civil servant, and worked for many years in the treasury department (*Kamer-kontora*) of the provincial administration in Riga. Under Elizabeth he had enjoyed considerable standing with the government, and he was one of the officials involved in a cadastral survey in Livonia between 1757 and 1760.[176] In 1763 Linke presented information to Catherine on means of raising greater revenues in Livonia. The Soviet historian H. Strods refers to a report (*donosheniye*);[177] Linke's contemporary Baron Schoultz von Ascheraden, the representative of the Baltic nobility at Petersburg, spoke of a project. But whatever the exact form and status of Linke's proposals, he dealt both with the Riga trade and with the agrarian situation in Livonia, and the government was sufficiently interested to set up a special committee under Z. Chernyshev to examine his ideas.[178]

The Baltic landed establishment was wary of Linke, suspecting him of advocating the curtailment of their rights in estate tenure and control over their peasants. Schoultz received instructions to keep an eye on him, and could soon report back to Riga the main contents of the 'project': Z. Chernyshev, he said, had personally given him extracts to read. Schoultz's account deals only with matters affecting the Livonian landed interest. According to his report, Linke wished to increase the Livonian revenues by increasing agricultural production. But the seventeenth-century Swedish methods of increasing productivity and revenues, by carrying out a new cadastre and then increasing peasant dues, had proved disastrous (Linke said) for the peasantry. Consequently an additional labour force had to be found elsewhere, and it could in fact be provided through immigration: 200,000 people should be brought across from Prussia and Lithuania to settle the Baltic provinces and bring the population up to the necessary levels. Linke also proposed other, less radical measures to the same end.[179]

The idea that the Baltic provinces were underpopulated was not in itself a novelty. But such a proposal, involving large-scale redistribution of land, could not appeal to the Baltic nobility, and certainly the numbers proposed (if Schoultz's figure is correct) were unrealistic. Linke's grandiose immigration plan came to nothing. Late in 1763 Schoultz (again according to his own account in reports back to Riga)[180] even persuaded G. Orlov and the Chancellery of Guardianship to send into the interior of the Empire a group of German immigrants who wished to settle in the Baltic provinces. Schoultz named Eisen as the instigator of the request from the colonists, though M. Stepermanis in his account of the episode notes that supporting evidence is tenuous.[181] There is also no evidence as to connections between these events and the founding of the Livonian colonies of Hirschenhof and Helfreichsdorf in 1766: the latter settlements were established on the basis of an Imperial decree to Governor Browne, but the origins of the project remain obscure.

Schoultz also had to face a threat which he considered more serious than that posed by Linke: the renewed activities of Eisen in Petersburg. Eisen reappeared in court circles in the autumn of 1763, and caused Schoultz considerable concern.[182] This time, as before, Eisen came in response to an Imperial summons: the Orlov brothers had suggested his recall to Catherine, and the message was sent to him through G. Orlov's own office, the Chancellery of Guardianship.[183] In October 1763 Eisen had a personal audience with the Empress, who accepted copies of his writings and authorized publication of part of one of them, devoted to a denunciation of serfdom in Livonia.[184] She also gave him facilities to put his ideas into practice on a small scale. Eisen favoured a gradual, not an immediate abolition of serfdom, and as a first step proposed the introduction of contractual relationships between landlord and serf, and hereditary tenancy for the peasants of private estates. Catherine placed her own estate of Bronnaya, near Oranienbaum, at his disposal for this purpose. 'In preparing the plan, however', wrote Eisen, 'I found that that [estate] was much too small for a trial which was intended as a model for the whole Empire; and until the return of Her Majesty from Livonia I was given leave to go home.'[185] Catherine set out on her official visit to Livonia on 20 June, and returned on 25 July, 1764.[186] 'Thereupon', continues Eisen, 'Her Majesty gave the Count Orlov the estates of Ropsha. . .Kipin [Kipen'], Skvoritz, Schungerhof [Shungorovo] and Liguva, near Petersburg, in order through me to get rid of serfdom and establish colonies.'[187]

Eisen spent a year and a half in Ropsha on this work. The intention behind it was apparently to establish contractual relationships for peasants on newly-distributed estates, who were threatened with enserf-ment by their transfer to a private owner.[188] Eisen prepared contracts for each estate. But the final issue of the contracts hung fire and he gradually found himself being squeezed out of his position. Eventually he was relieved of his task at his own request; and in 1766, with compensation from Orlov, he withdrew from Petersburg for the second time.[189]

In the absence of hard evidence, the explanation of this episode offered by Ya. Zutis, that Eisen fell victim to a clash of parties at court over the policy to be adopted *vis-à-vis* the peasantry, seems quite plausible.[190] In his immediate aims, therefore, Eisen was unsuccessful. But his views and writings are significant in the general context of Catherine's early interest in agrarian matters and in the peasant question, and they do seem to have had some impact. Official policy in this area has been much discussed and the subject remains controversial.[191] The problem as a whole lies outside our present concerns, but there are some immediate points of contact with Eisen's ideas.[192] Eisen's activities may possibly have had a bearing on the well-known but rather mysterious proposals on 'free villages' which were debated in the Legislative Commission summoned by Catherine in 1767. In the official draft on the rights and prerogatives of the nobility, the thirteenth article proposed that nobles should have the positive right to change the status of villages in their possession from serf to free, in other words to emancipate their peasants. The idea was strongly attacked by Prince M. Shcherbatov, the principal spokesman of the conservative nobility; whether or not the main proponent of the measure, Grigorii Korob'in, was acting as Catherine's mouthpiece, is a matter of dis-pute.[193] But whatever Korob'in's role, the actual concept of such villages is close to the system envisaged by Eisen. And in preceding discussion one deputy to the Commission, Ursinus of Dorpat, pointed out that non-nobles might also own villages, 'especially in the present circumstances, when colonists will be settled': a reference to the contractual settlement provided for in the *poselitel'* laws of 1765 and 1767.[194]

These laws appear to be a direct result of Eisen's work. They represent in fact an exact implementation, for foreign colonists, of the system Eisen was trying to establish for Russian peasants at Ropsha.[195] Where Eisen found no acceptance for his project concerning the native peasantry – in the Commission, indeed, Shcherbatov in 1768 rejected any such idea on principle – Grigory Orlov and the Chancellery had no need to fear opposition to the settlement of foreigners. On the contrary, as Orlov's reports and the example of Z. Chernyshev show, the Russian upper classes were eager to engage such people, usually in the hope of obtaining skilled labour, and noble *poseliteli* were quite prepared to accept the contractual limitations which the nobility at large rejected in the case of native serfs.

Apart from its application to the peasant question, we have seen that Eisen was also concerned with foreign colonization in its more general role as a mechanism for national population increase and economic development. On his second visit to Petersburg, in 1763, he pursued this idea together with his emancipation project. In 1766 he recalled:

In St Petersburg I made a suggestion that colonies should be established at Awwinorm, Flemmingshof and Lais-Schloss, and the village Mastwet made into a town. This town could have communication by water with Dorpat, Pskov, and Narva, and that not merely with small vessels... Perhaps it may come about, for they seem already to be taking notice of my suggestion concerning Yamburg.[196]

Eisen's plans for Awwinorm, a Crown property where he had lived on first arrival in Livonia, and for the other Livonian estates, had no discernible results; and the historian of the colonies Hirschenhof and Helfreichsdorf, W. Conze, denies him any part in their creation either.[197] An influence on the Yamburg settlement, however, is quite possible. Yelagin's plans envisaged just such a transformation as Eisen proposed for Mastwet, and the settlement of the Yamburg colonists in 1767 was only part of a comprehensive development scheme for what had been till then an insignificant village. The colonists both increased the population and provided a reservoir of labour for Yelagin's new industrial ventures in the town.[198]

Eisen was widely regarded, both in his own time and later, as an eccentric, a projector of the worst sort. His opponents fostered this reputation, which he himself bitterly resented. 'I went back to [my parish of] Torma', he wrote of the debacle of 1766, 'and the name of a dangerous project-maker and enemy of the nation was the pillow on which I, the truest friend of the Livonians, had to lay my head.'[199] If A. Schlözer's account of Eisen is to be believed – and Schlözer claimed to have been Eisen's confidant during the latter's stay in Petersburg – the reputation for project-making had some foundation: according to Schlözer, for example, Eisen offered Catherine a special plan to ensure the loyalty of her guard.[200] But in many of his ideas and writings, and particularly in those concerning the peasant question, Eisen was within limits both sane and practical. His views were not even exceptionally radical. It was in the political sphere that he failed, having no status of his own and relying excessively, and somewhat naively, upon support and understanding from the ruling power. This attitude also character-ized the other several and varied public activities in which he engaged during the remaining years of his life.[201] He spent his last days as steward to one of the Chernyshev brothers, who engaged him in 1778 to supervise estates near Moscow. One wonders whether Eisen found German colonists among his new charges. He died at Chernyshev's estate in February 1779.

The development of the first colonies

As we have seen, the region to which the foreign settlers had been assigned was the frontier zone of the time, fertile and spacious, but sparsely populated and poorly controlled. Through the eighteenth century Russian settlers and others of local stock had been spreading down the Volga, particularly on the right bank, and especially since the creation in 1718–20 of the Tsaritsyn fortified line, which put an end to Tatar incursions up the river. The first noticeable wave of settle-ment in the area began under Peter I and lasted till about 1740. A second began in the 1760s.[202] As part of this process, landlord settle-ment was also reaching down the Volga in the direction of Saratov. In 1767 Catherine II, on her voyage to Simbirsk higher up the river, was able to stay at an estate above the town belonging to Count Ivan G. Orlov; and Count P. I. Panin owned property not far away.[203]

The Empress was struck by the beauty and abundance of the Volga lands: 'in a word', she wrote to N. I. Panin, 'these people are spoiled by God...everything that you can imagine is here in plenty and I do not know what else they could need: everything is available and every-thing is cheap'.[204] And not only the Empress was impressed. Two other Orlov brothers travelling with her, Grigory and Vladimir, were capti-vated by lands to the south of I. Orlov's village, on the Samara Bow. A local nobleman of their acquaintance had pointed out the vast potential of the area; and in 1768 the five Orlov brothers swapped extensive estates on the upper reaches of the Volga for a huge stretch of land which became the Orlov family estate of Usol'ye.[205]

The exchange of accessible, well-populated and well-established estates near the two Russian capitals for stretches of land on the distant lower Volga was an act of faith, or rather a calculated risk. As Vladimir Orlov's biographer remarked, it promised the Orlov family 'only a future, distant, advantage; but this advantage, on condition of firm and watchful management, was certain'.[206] The same was true for the new colonies downstream; but there the immediate problems were greater, and so correspondingly was the need for good management. Below Saratov the country was even less developed; there was little settled population, especially on the left bank. The further south, the emptier the land.[207]

The colonists, it will be recalled, had been envisaged by some planners as replacements for the Montenegrins of the 1750s. But they were only one of several elements which the government was now beginning to establish on the Volga: the second wave of settlement was actively directed and encouraged by the authorities. In 1765 the government began selling land in Astrakhan Province to members of the nobility; local officials were among the first applicants, including the Astrakhan Governor, Beketov.[208] And besides the Old Believers who responded to the proclamations of 1762–3 and settled on the Irgiz, from 1765 Cossacks and Kalmyk were settled on the Volga to strengthen the security of the river between Tsaritsyn and Astrakhan.[209] These were significant steps; but a great deal remained to be done. The situation in the area and its gradual development can be judged from the fact that the town of Tsaritsyn, together with several other points of settlement and defence in the south, received a civil administration only in 1769.[210]

The Saratov colonies got off to a bad start: preparations on the spot were quite inadequate. It should have been clear from the outset that large-scale settlement would be considerably complicated by the conditions of the area; and the Chancellery was soon brought up against this fact. Not only did the survey work require careful checking, and the issue of new decrees to clear the tangle of property relationships;[211] the supply problems soon became intractable. An important factor aggravating the situation was the unexpectedly large response abroad, especially in 1766; no prior provision was made for anything like the numbers which arrived. Although, for example, little timber was available in the immediate vicinity of Saratov, the first timber contracts

were made by Reuss only on his arrival, and covered only 250 houses.[212]
Already by early 1766 the authorities were in difficulties. Emergency
financial arrangements had to be made;[213] and in October of that year
a further Commissioner was appointed, Guards Captain Durnovo,
with a small staff and a very wide geographical field of action. He was
to organize 'supplies necessary for the construction next summer of
houses for the colonists, and...their swiftest provision with horses and
other stock, agricultural implements and household appurtenances'.[214]
His task was formidable. In September 1766 the Senate reported to
the Empress that 1,300,000 planks were needed; in April 1767 the
Chancellery of Guardianship lamented its continuing inability, despite
the searches of Durnovo, to find sufficient carpenters to build the 2,000
houses then outstanding. Even by 1769, only 4,560 had been built for
the 6,433 families settled.[215] The others shared houses, or lived in dug-
outs or the barracks.

Contemporary accounts – memoirs, visitors' descriptions, official
records – paint a grim picture of the first years of the settlement. Transport from St Petersburg was ill-organized. Parties unexpectedly forced
to winter en route could not find sufficient quarters, and fell victim to
epidemics.[216] Of 26,509 colonists dispatched from Petersburg, according to official figures, 3,293 were lost by death or flight on the journey.[217] Nor were conditions on the spot encouraging. One colonist,
C. G. Züge, recalled the arrival of his party on the site of their village
on the Medveditsa, one of those for which no preparation had been
made: 'We stared at each other, shocked to see ourselves here in a
wilderness which, apart from a small wood, showed nothing but three-
feet-high, largely withered grass as far as the eye could see.'[218]

Besides the difficult task of establishing themselves more or less from
nothing, the colonists had to withstand the depredations of robbers, of
the Kirgiz and the Kalmyk, and to contend with unfriendly Russian
neighbours, with whom because of inadequate surveying they clashed
on land allocation. The colonist administration was more advantageous
to the foreigners than would have been subordination to the Voyevoda's
Chancellery, even after the appointment to it of Chancellery of
Guardianship nominees; and in the first years of the settlement the
material support and assistance given by the authorities was crucial to
the colonies' survival. But this support itself was frequently delayed,
inadequate, or inappropriate; and the staff of the colonist Office was
by no means exempt from the usual vices of Russian officialdom.

Nor was any significant support in hardship and illness forthcoming
from clergy or medical personnel. These, it is true, were allowed for in

the provisions made by the Chancellery of Guardianship, which in this respect, too, improved on the usual conditions of the Russian country-side.[219] On the other hand, the colonists, unused to the new environment, were more vulnerable than the native population. In the early years at least, religious, educational and medical care left much to be desired: a gap only partly filled by the Brethren of Sarepta.

Another important factor was the activity of the *vyzyvateli* and their representatives. Most were already in trouble with the Chancellery of Guardianship for various offences: Pictet and Le Roy for attempted smuggling, Le Roy and Precourt for abuses committed in Hamburg, whence they had been brought back to Petersburg under arrest.[220] Beauregard had infringed his contract in several ways.[221] The chief sources of trouble, however, were the pretensions of the *vyzyvateli* – or 'directors', as they were called in this context – within the colonies, and the additional obligations of their recruits. The terms of the latter's contracts were vague and at odds with the 1763 Manifesto; and the colonists soon sought to repudiate them. The private colonies began to pass in fact (though not officially) under the control of the Saratov Office. The Chancellery of Guardianship, at fault in having omitted at the outset to regulate the relations between the two sides, at first took no decisive action. But in 1775 a commission of enquiry was instituted, as a result of which in 1778 the 'directors' were removed completely, and all colonists placed on an equal footing. However, the commission felt it had a primary duty 'to preserve the dignity and credit of YIH court in Europe, from any damaging revelations on the part of the *vyzyvateli*, and thereby to preserve for the future a ready means to the renewal of such recruiting operations'; and the 'directors' were given ample compensation.[222]

All this formed the background to another serious defect of the colonies: the character of the colonists themselves. This question has occasioned a great deal of controversy, German and colonist writers seeking to refute the common Russian view of the immigrants as 'the scum of Germany'.[223] In the first years, the development of the colonies certainly left much to be desired. And while difficult conditions and maladministration played a large part in this, there were undoubtedly among the immigrants – particularly among the early arrivals – some who were failures at home, or adventurers hoping for an easy life. On the other hand, many sound people, ruined or driven abroad by the upheavals of the time, had also joined the emigration; and it seems likely that these formed the great majority. Perhaps most importantly, Kuhlberg's activities brought into the colonies a large number of settlers lacking any knowledge or skill in agriculture. Several individual cases of this type are recorded at the upper end of the social scale. Klaus published in 1869 the memoirs in verse of the German officer von Platen, of noble family, forced by stark poverty to emigrate to Russia in hope of entering military service there, and sent on to Saratov against his wishes.[224] He became a school teacher in one of the colonies. Züge recalls the feckless Freiherr von Hollstein, who ended as a shepherd, still delighted if any passer-by greeted him as Herr Baron.[225] But the great majority of agriculturally unskilled settlers were naturally of a much more lowly social origin; and the proportion of these unsuitable people to the whole has been one of the main points of contention. One official source put the population figures for 1767 as follows: in a male working population of 7,186, 4,440 were peasant farmers (61.8%), 2,550 artisans (35.5%), 60 merchants and 136 *raznochintsy* (together 2.7%).[226] The crafts represented were largely those required in a rural community; but the distribution of the artisans was unbalanced, so that there were often too many craftsmen in one village, and in general their numbers overall were too high for the needs or the then economic capacity of the colonies. As a result, many were forced to turn to agriculture, while others left the colonies (with or without permission). In 1769 an attempt was made to separate settlers capable from those incapable of farming, and 579 families (in a total of 6,433) were officially registered as unfit for agricultural work. But this figure should probably be regarded as an absolute minimum, rather than as an accurate reflection of the real desires and abilities of the colonists.[227]

These problems were aggravated by the settlers' unfamiliarity with the climatic and agricultural conditions of the Volga area, which led to persistent harvest failures in the first years of the settlement. It later turned out, too, that some of the villages had been established in unsuitable places, with poor land and unhealthy water supplies.[228] As if to complete the confusion, in 1774 the colonies found themselves directly in the path of Pugachev and his peasant army. Saratov surrendered to the insurgents, its defences weakened by a dispute over seniority and tactics involving the town's commandant Boshnyak, the head of the Guardianship Office Lodyzhensky, and the poet G. Derzhavin, then a young officer on special assignment.[229] The Office itself had already been evacuated to Astrakhan, but money and records were left behind or lost on the way, and grain and flour stores in Saratov were plundered and burnt.[230] The colonists' attitude to the rebellion has been variously described. Several hundred, at least, joined

Pugachev's forces; after his defeat 432 were 'returned to the colonies'.[231] Downstream, Sarepta was plundered, although its inhabitants all escaped safely to Astrakhan; damage amounted to 67,545 roubles.[232] In the same year, the Saratov colonies were also raided twice by the Kirgiz. They carried off large numbers, on the second occasion over 800 colonists, together with some 700 Russian peasants. Most were quickly released by pursuing troops, some later ransomed; but 370 were never recovered.[233]

The events of 1774 were disastrous for the colonies, destroying what economic stability had been achieved. Much stock and property was destroyed, and the little grain sown in the autumn failed. A report by Orlov late that year reckoned the total necessary to redeem the situation at 266,000 roubles.[234] This new allocation was to be counted as part of the colonists' debt. But the sums owed by the colonists, after repeated additional subsidies since settlement, had by now reached huge proportions; and for the earliest settlers, 1775 was the last of the ten years of grace before repayment of the advances made to them by the Crown. In the circumstances, payment was obviously impossible; and in a final attempt to set the colonies on a sound footing, the authorities drew up a set of sweeping new proposals.

The first reaction of the Chancellery of Guardianship to the difficulties which it encountered with its new charges, had been to lay the blame at the colonists' door. In a letter to them of 28 April 1765 Orlov accused them of drunkenness, laziness, improvidence, arrogance, and insubordination.[235] Nonetheless, as we have seen, the colonists had genuine grounds for complaint. Furthermore, despite his special appointment, Voyevoda Stroyev had no great success either with the settlers or with his superiors. The first were dissatisfied with him, according to C. G. Züge, because he treated them 'too much in the Russian manner'; the second found him careless (again according to Züge) in his distribution and supervision of monies advanced to the colonists.[236] The Voyevoda's Chancellery was also accused of negligence in not controlling the *vyzyvateli* and their direction of the colonies.[237] In May 1765 the Chancellery ruled for the colonists against the Voyevoda when deputies came to Petersburg to protest over the taxation of colonist houses in Saratov;[238] and at just the same time it dispatched Johann Reinhold Forster to the Volga to inspect the colonies.[239]

J. R. Forster subsequently became famous in his own time as a member of Captain James Cook's second South Seas expedition, and as a naturalist and scholar; later his reputation was eclipsed by that of his eldest son George. In the early 1760s Johann Reinhold was the reluctant incumbent of a Lutheran pastorate near Danzig. Late in 1764, or in January 1765, he made an agreement with Rehbinder to visit the Volga, in order as an eye-witness to refute malevolent rumours current in the West concerning the new colonies. In April 1765 the two Forsters, father and son, reached Petersburg, where Johann Reinhold was well received by Orlov, and in May they journeyed on to Saratov. During the next five months they travelled widely in the region. Johann Reinhold collected specimens and made surveys; he also carried out commissions for the Academy of Sciences and – according to a later account from the Chancellery of Guardianship – for the *vyzyvatel'* Beauregard as well.[240]

His inspection of the colonies, however, convinced him that the colonists had justifiable grievances; and he brought back with him to Petersburg a colonist deputation. The report that he presented in the autumn of 1765 was highly critical, particularly of Stroyev; while waiting for a response from the Chancellery, Forster worked with another Lutheran Minister who was also his host in the capital, Pastor Dilthey, on a legal code for the Volga colonies.

But Forster had reckoned without either the nature or the style of operations within the Russian civil service. His report was entirely contrary to the original intentions of his mission, and to the obvious expectations of the Chancellery and Orlov. Stroyev intrigued against his accuser; and Forster's arrogant and self-righteous outspokenness proved counter-productive. The report was not made public, and its exact contents still remain unknown; neither was the legal code adopted. Hopes of reward and a post in the Russian service proved illusory – money offered in recompense of his work and travels he rejected as inadequate. And in 1766 he left Russia, an embittered man, to seek better fortune with George in Britain.

The effect of Forster's intervention in the affairs of the colonies is difficult to gauge. In December 1765 Orlov sent a second letter to the colonists; it refers to petitions which may well have been those of Forster's colonist deputation. Orlov still took the tone he had used in his April letter, and now threatened to resign his post as President of the Chancellery if the colonists did not reform themselves.[241] Within six months, however, with the number of immigrants growing rapidly, there followed radical reorganization of the local colonist administration: in April 1766 Catherine approved the establishment of the Saratov Guardianship Office, a development which Orlov, in his report to the Senate, declared to have been requested by a common petition of all the colonists.[242] And in the following year the Empress embarked on her voyage down the Volga, which some observers expected would take her as far as Astrakhan.[243]

From her letters to Panin written on the way, there is little sign that Catherine herself at this stage ever intended to go beyond Simbirsk, where she in fact turned back; but several of her party, including G. Orlov and Z. Chernyshev, had planned to continue at least as far as Tsaritsyn.[244] In the event only Orlov's younger brother, Vladimir, travelled on to Astrakhan, accompanied by members of the Chancellery of Guardianship, with whom he inspected colonies and colonists on the way.[245] The colonists at the time bitterly regretted that Catherine never saw her colonies personally – surely the Empress would have understood and righted her settlers' wrongs?[246] But this was not a safe assumption to make. Orlov's inspection was rather superficial, to judge by available evidence, and it brought no relief. On the contrary, if contemporary colonist memoirs are to be believed, it was followed in September 1767 by a new prescription that all colonists should devote themselves solely to agriculture – a more extreme measure than anything that had gone before.[247]

The new Guardianship Office was set up, as we have seen, as a temporary institution, to take care of the colonists until such time as they could be returned to the charge of the local state authority. In a memorandum to the 'director' de Boffe, the Office declared that the immediate duties defined for it by the Chancellery were: 'to govern all colonists without exception, and to have charge of all measures and to exercise the principal supervision in all settlements, until the [regulations governing] internal jurisdiction shall be composed and the powers of the *vyzyvateli* determined'.[248] The right of internal self-government had been promised in the 1763 Manifesto, and this was the object of the legal code which had occupied Forster. In 1767 the 'director' Le Roy presented to the Chancellery for its approval a code which he had drawn up to regulate the administration of his own colonies. The Chancellery rejected this draft, firstly because it was unsuitable and because Le Roy in any case was exceeding his rights, but also on the grounds that composition of a colonist code at this time would be premature: too little was yet known 'of the moeurs, customs and conditions of the colonists'. The Chancellery also asserted that the settlers themselves had proved incapable of producing a code of their own, and had happily left the task 'to the will of the authorities established over them'.[249] By 1769, however, the task was completed. In drawing up its regulations for the colonies' internal administration, the Chancellery sought information from Herrnhut on *Polizei-Ordnung* in Britain's

American colonies, in Saxony, the Palatinate, and other German states;[250] whether or not Forster's ideas were also used is unknown – the Chancellery later declared them to have been inappropriate.[251]

The final document, or 'Instruction', followed the lines of Orlov's letters of 1765: it embodied the view that the colonists must be compelled to work, and it was buttressed with a system of supervision by district commissioners (*okruzhnyye komissary*), to be recruited from among retired army officers. Pisarevsky compares the Instruction to 'rules governing a home or agricultural colony for delinquent minors';[252] it made a mockery of the promise of internal autonomy. With this new system of supervision and control, and the weeding-out of those unsuited to farming which was undertaken in the same year, the authorities hoped to make possible both good order and economic prosperity.

Yet this system, too, had little success, since it failed to meet the basic problems of the colonies' situation. Nonetheless, after the disasters of 1774 the Chancellery still adopted, initially, a similar approach. In March 1775 it put forward proposals to abolish the elective status of colonist local officials, making them dependent on appointment by the Office, and to increase the number of *okruzhnyye komissary* from six to thirteen, one for each colonist district. A second division of the colonists was also to be undertaken, more radical than that of 1769, to weed out those incapable of earning a livelihood by farming. The latter were to be compulsorily enrolled in the army, or sent to forced labour, preferably in Astrakhan: 'where, because of their nearness to their homes, by the heavy burden of their labours they will inspire no little terror in those remaining [and stimulate them] to excellent zeal in their work'.[253] Those considered suited to farming would be given one final grant to set them on their feet. But they were to be placed under a two-rouble poll tax, to ensure a start to debt repayment, and this was to be enforced by the introduction of collective responsibility (*krugovaya poruka*).

These proposals, which abrogated several privileges granted in the Manifesto and brought the colonists much closer to the position of the Russian peasantry, were approved both by Orlov and by the Senate. Before they could be implemented, however, Orlov was replaced as head of the Chancellery by the Procurator-General, Vyazemsky. This was the result of Orlov's fall from favour, though the change was made ostensibly to allow him to travel abroad. Vyazemsky remained in charge until the Chancellery's abolition in 1782, even though the Empress officially appointed him 'only until such time as We shall choose another reliable person for the period of the absence of its President'.[254]

From the time of Vyazemsky's appointment, a new direction of policy is discernible. The harshest of the Chancellery's proposals – the poll tax, abolition of the elective principle, forcible enlistment and public works – were rejected as infringements of the promises of 1763. Debt repayment was postponed for a further five years. Those found unsuitable for farming, and who did not wish to remain or were not accepted by their communities as labourers, could choose either to join the army or to seek a living elsewhere; while a system of voluntary public works, the erection of an earthwork around Saratov, was instituted for those remaining who could not otherwise support themselves.[255] At last the provision of the 1763 Manifesto granting free choice of domicile was effectively realized.

The new turn in government policy represented a lessening of emphasis on supervision and state support, and an attempt to make the colonists stand on their own feet.[256] It was not entirely successful; and accounts from the later years of the century suggest continuing detailed control of colonist life.[257] But the removal of the worst farmers, and above all the growth of a new generation accustomed and adapted to life on the Volga, brought in time a large measure of prosperity.[258] In 1782, on the implementation of Catherine's provincial reform, the Chancellery and its Saratov Office were abolished; the colonies came under the administration of the local authority and the particular charge of the Saratov Director of Husbandry (*Direktor Domovodstva*).[259] Fifteen years later, with the creation of a new supervisory government body, the Board of State Economy, Guardianship of Foreigners and Rural Husbandry, and with the restoration of the Saratov Office, the colonies became once more an object of particular government concern and attention.[260]

Although some difficulties experienced by the Saratov colonies had specifically Russian causes, others were intrinsic in this type of settlement. They represented the 'first act of a common and inevitable process in the evolution of isolated linguistic enclaves, which occurred in more or less sharply-defined form in isolated German settlements (*Streusiedlungen*) everywhere'.[261] Problems of adjustment to a new life, under alien and often harsh conditions, tended to prevent all such first-generation settlers from achieving any great prosperity. Russia's experience here in fact followed that of Frederick II.[262] The other Russian colonies underwent the same process to a greater or lesser extent, and likewise encountered specific local difficulties. Riebensdorf and Belovezh, for instance, although formed of better farmers than were on average the Saratov colonists, suffered from unsuitability or insufficiency of land. And besides the isolation of the Belovezh site, the Russo-Turkish war was a major obstacle to the proper establishment of the Belovezh artisans; many of those who left the colony moved to Nezhin, where a considerable number succumbed to plague in 1771.[263]

However, drastic measures like those applied on the Volga in 1775 were required only in the Livonian settlements. Here the removal of colonists unable to develop their holdings was ordered in 1781, on the Saratov pattern;[264] and this was followed, as in Saratov, by a gradual but definite improvement in the colonies' fortunes. Of all the colonies only Sarepta, more carefully organized, dedicated to a specific purpose, and helped with resources and personnel from Herrnhut, was able to establish itself well and quickly.

The small labour force available and the bad quality of much of Sarepta's land, which turned out to be impregnated with salt, encouraged the Brethren to turn their energies primarily to trades and industry; and in this they conformed to the wishes both of the Russian Government and of Herrnhut. In 1768 a tobacco factory was set up, to process local and imported leaf; but the most successful development was weaving. Cotton fabric produced in the colony, and called after it Sarpinka, rapidly made a name for itself far beyond the Volga region.[265] The colony also had a variety of flourishing crafts. Even the damage caused by the Pugachev rebellion was less serious than it might have been, and it had the advantage of forcing a valuable reappraisal of the colony's economy after it had passed the initial stages.[266] A mineral spring discovered nearby in 1773 attracted an increasing number of visitors and helped considerably in the colony's growth. Sarepta's vogue as a spa reached a peak with 300 guests in 1796: thereafter it fell away rapidly, as new, more potent springs in the Caucasus gave rise to resorts of greater luxury than Sarepta could provide.[267]

Still the colony flourished. It had an important influence on the Saratov colonies, supplying them not only with technical skills, but also with medical and educational aid and personnel. The Saratov colonies also became the main theatre for Sarepta's missionary activities. No durable agreement was ever reached with the authorities under which Sarepta could fulfil its original function, and although some work was done among the Kalmyk, this was of little account; the main effort thus came to be diverted to the colonies upstream, and ministers from Sarepta or sent directly by Herrnhut exercised a considerable and beneficial influence there. Schools were also set up (the first in 1772) to cater for Sarepta's children. They maintained a high standard: even the Russian Orthodox bishop of Astrakhan wished to send his relatives to them.[268]

The prosperity, and the fame, of Sarepta grew steadily from the 1770s and according to Klaus, nineteenth-century travellers would make detours of several hundred versts simply in order to be able to answer in the affirmative the question: 'And did you visit Sarepta?'[269]

The sudden influx of some 25,000 people into a sparsely-populated border region was bound even in the short term to have considerable impact on local life. Saratov, at this time a garrison town of less than 9,000 male population,[270] felt the effect at once. Although local re-action was initially somewhat hostile, Falk found in 1769 that 'the colonies contribute greatly to the prosperity of the town'. The colonists among the townsfolk were 'saddlers, painters, engravers (*reshchiki*), goldsmiths, sculptors, hat-makers, weavers, gunsmiths, and so on'.[271] These first artisans were not themselves particularly successful, but they were nonetheless an important addition to the citizenry.[272] Movement between the town and the colonies increased with time, and in the nineteenth century the German community in Saratov, centred on the *Nemetskaya Ulitsa* in the middle of the town, played an important part in its development.

However, Saratov was not the only place to receive colonists. Some had remained in Astrakhan. In 1765 the Astrakhan Provincial Chancellery, reporting on the availability of land for settlement near the town, said there was none suitable, and that 'although a few foreigners have come to settle in Astrakhan, even they live in the town among the local residents in houses bought for them by the Treasury, and others in hired houses'.[273] Other towns, as well as local estates, took up some of those who fled from the colonies in the early stages, or were able to acquire passports. The French colony Rossoshi in parti-cular was depleted in this way. Falk wrote that it 'is half empty, as its inhabitants have scattered throughout the Province to teach children or to look after them'.[274] Nationality, of course, played an important part here, as well as the notoriously low demands made on such 'peda-gogues'. Vinsky met one such Frenchman in Orenburg:

I went to the house of the Prince [Khvabulov, the Vice-Governor], having learnt that he had a teacher for his children, a Frenchman. Here I was received in friendly fashion. The teacher, a native of the Garonne, re-cruited for settlement in Russia but unable to come to terms with our land, had decided rather to cultivate the minds and hearts of young gentlefolk; decided and succeeded; for he had a position bringing him in a yearly salary of 500 roubles and all found. And how did he educate them? What did he teach? Ah, that matter was quite foreign to him. A Frenchman was needed in this house for the children; he was a Frenchman – and everyone was happy.[275]

Attempts at flight were quite common in the early years. The authorities were much concerned, and used all available means to prevent them, including the Cossacks attached to the Guardianship Office.[276] Nonetheless, some escapers were successful: for example the handful of Rhinelanders whom the French diplomat de Tott rescued – according to his own story – from the Nogay Tatars in the Crimea in 1767,[277] or the more fortunate fugitive Züge, whose account of his life as a colonist gives an immediate and vivid picture of the early years of the settlement.[278]

It was not only the loss of their settlers which angered the Russian authorities, but particularly the resulting adverse publicity. De Tott's story was later used to undermine Russian recruitment;[279] and diplomats in the capitals ill-disposed to the colonization scheme seized upon any unfavourable report. The French Minister and his staff, in particular, were outspokenly critical; they were only too pleased to help French colonists who turned to them,[280] and to pass on to their government anything discreditable. In June 1766 for example, the Ambassador, de Bausset, wrote to Paris:

I have heard that the Empress has been very annoyed with me over what the *Gazette de France*, no. 38, said about the colonies on the Volga. She attributes to me the truths in these reports which offend her *amour propre*. She should however be so just as to allow other rulers to keep their subjects by using the same weapons She employs to steal them away...[281]

Catherine certainly made use of similar channels to put her own case; and she, of course, had valuable personal contacts. Three years later, à propos of other hostile reports, she was writing to Voltaire:

...you must know, since it gives you pleasure, that my fine colony of Saratov has some 25,000 souls, that in spite of the editor of the Cologne *Gazette* it has nothing to fear from the incursions of Tatars, Turks, etc., that each canton has churches of its confession, that the settlers cultivate their fields in peace, and that they pay no taxes for thirty years.[282]

And it was ostensibly unfavourable foreign publicity which had inclined the Russian authorities to accept the initial overtures of J. R. Forster.

Legal departure from the Saratov colonies became easier, and more widespread, following the review of 1775. Those declared unsuitable for farming totalled 1,755 (of both sexes). The majority decided to remain in the colonies as labourers or artisans. Military service attracted a dozen others, with their dependants. The remainder, 529 in all, received passports to go 'to various places to seek a living'.[283] From this time dates the appearance of German colonists in Orenburg, where they engaged in petty trade. The nineteenth-century traveller Basiner found the small colonist group there in a prosperous condition, trading in tobacco and also following 'handicrafts and some agriculture, although more for their own needs than for trade. The qualities most peculiar to Germans. . .have acquired them a good reputation here as well, and assured them a good income. . .'[284]

However, although many individuals settled in the Volga region, the largest single group appears to have made its way back to the capitals, where it joined the communities of Western artisans and tradesmen. In 1782 the Chancellery of Guardianship reported to the Senate in Petersburg that of 'over three hundred families' released on passports from Saratov since 1775, 'a great part. . .live here and in Moscow'.[285]

The capitals were also the preferred location of many of the foreign entrepreneurs who contracted with the Chancellery of Guardianship under § VI of the 1763 Manifesto. Compared with the thousands of 'colonists' proper, these individuals were a mere handful; and the enterprises which they set up proved largely ephemeral. As will be seen in chapter 5, they represented one aspect of deliberate government policy, and they were not entirely unimportant. But the main emphasis in operations under the Manifesto in the early years up to 1775 fell on mass immigration and rural settlement, and this was to be the pattern of settlement in other places and later periods as well.

However, the operation of Catherine's policy in the creation of the Volga colonies had had serious defects. The new, active policy on immigration embodied in the decrees of 22 July 1763 owed its emergence at that particular time essentially to the convictions and the initiative of the new Empress. Catherine and her advisers sought to formulate and implement her ideas as state policy at a high level; but neither she nor they seem to have had a fully realistic conception of the problems involved, nor in fact of what the policy itself was actually designed to achieve. The confusion between quality and quantity, between specialized (agricultural) and indiscriminate recruitment, was never properly resolved, and left behind it the legacy of disillusionment and hardship described. Above all, the scope of the operation was misjudged. The numbers of those who came bore no relation to the numbers expected. The splendid beginning – the creation of a new government organ at collegiate level – gave way to repeated *ad hoc* measures. The lack of mechanisms to regulate recruitment abroad, and the lack of detailed advance planning in the area of settlement, was to say the least short-sighted; and traditional bureaucratic procedures were inadequate to remedy the shortcomings. The government found itself swamped by events which it had set in motion and which it could no longer control; the result was the – once more *ad hoc* – suspension of recruitment in 1766, the improvisations of Durnovo, and all the difficulties which followed.

A further crucial misjudgement was made on the financial side. By eighteenth-century standards the annual allocation of 200,000 roubles was substantial; but it fell considerably short of the actual cost of the operation. The accounts of the Chancellery of Guardianship show an outlay to 1 January 1770 alone of some 4,897,200 roubles; and while over three million of this was in the form of recoverable loans, these were neither interest-bearing, nor redeemable for several years to come.[286] The final cost of the immigration programme in this period was well in excess of five and a half million roubles;[287] and this, coming at a time when the state finances were in chronic deficit, was a powerful restraint on further activity.

Besides the difficulties resulting from the immigration policy itself, external factors also militated against any extension of recruitment on the pattern of the Volga settlement system. The attention of the Empress and the government was increasingly absorbed with Polish affairs, while from 1768 onwards – the year also of Joseph II's ban – all resources and energy were devoted to the war against Turkey. But the treaty of Kuchuk-Kaynardji, which ended the war in 1774, gave Russia large new territories, under-populated and exposed, in the south, and *ipso facto* created an imperious need for settlers to fill them. These were sought wherever they could be found, at home or abroad. It is striking that after this time foreign immigration was only rarely encouraged on a doctrinaire basis as a general policy; while welcoming it as an instrument of internal development, future administrators approached it in the context of highly specific, and usually geographically limited, economic and political needs.

This was pre-eminently G. A. Potemkin's view in the development of the new southern territories after 1775. However, the methods and principles which he adopted were also closely connected with those previously prescribed for the settlement of New Russia, in the Plan worked out for that region in 1764.

4

Southern Russia 1764–1796

The Plan of Settlement of New Russia, 1764: the formulation of settlement policy in the south

The administrative re-organization of the Serbian settlements in 1763–4 represented a rationalization of their position in accordance both with internal developments and with broader state policy. Khorvat's ill-doings, reports of which had been coming in for several years, formed the immediate object of an investigation of New Serbia, which resulted in the banishment of Khorvat to Vologda. The enquiry exposed the very unsatisfactory condition of the settlement, and focussed attention on its anomalous status; and a parallel examination of Slavyanoserbia produced similar results.

However, the actual condition of the Serbian colonies at this time was only one cause of government interest in them. The official investigations formed part of a wider concern with the Ukraine, stemming from preoccupation with the Black Sea question on the one hand, and on the other from the Empress's determination to suppress what remained of Ukrainian autonomy. The latter trend expressed itself in the abolition of the Hetmanate and the subordination of the Zaporozhian Sech' to the Little Russian College, in 1764, and in the introduction in the rest of the Ukraine of an administrative structure similar to that elsewhere in the Empire.[1]

The solution adopted for the Serbian settlements accorded both with these centralizing tendencies of the beginning of the reign, and with the aim of strengthening Russia's position on her southern boundaries. The special status of the colonies was abolished, and they were transformed into border regiments under the overall command of the Governor-General of Kiev, I. F. Glebov. In 1764 the Province of New Russia[2] was created, absorbing the two Serbian enclaves and most of the territory between them. Stretching from the domain of the Don Cossacks

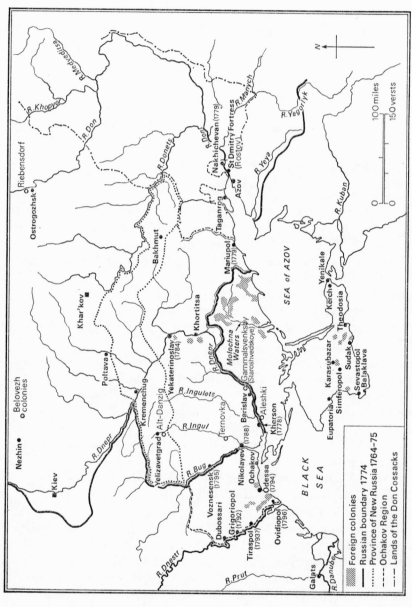

Map 3. The Southern Ukraine, 1764–1804.

to the Polish border, the new Province formed a single unit in the centre of the southern boundary region, and jutted ominously into the 'free lands' of the Zaporozhian Cossacks.[3]

The task of formulating detailed proposals for the re-organization of New Serbia had fallen to Lieutenant-General A. P. Mel'gunov, already known to us for his subsequent work on immigration. By a decree of 11 June 1763, he was appointed to succeed Khorvat; and at the same time he was ordered, under the guidance of Glebov, with the assistance of his Serbian deputy, and of

the best staff officers of that corps, to draw up a plan, in conformity with the privileges and decrees concerning New Serbia, for the reform of that New Serbian corps and its restoration to the best condition, growth and orderly life, with due regard for factors conducive to the increase of settlement in the New Slobodskiy regiment,[4] and of schismatic villages; and for the summoning from Poland of fugitives, both Little Russians, and also schismatics and others of Our subjects.

The last stipulation went in fact well beyond the limits originally prescribed for Khorvat, and the decree stressed this point:

Although according to the privileges and the obligations of Khorvat it was forbidden to receive into service and to settle in New Serbia any save those nationalities prescribed, which were Serbian, Bulgarian, Wallachian and Macedonian; however, as still to the present time insufficient numbers of these people have come in, therefore, in order as far as possible to settle and increase the steppe regions there with a real cordon, they being essential in view of their border position: We graciously order that together with the peoples named shall be received fugitives coming in from Poland, not only Little Russians, but also Great Russians and all nationalities, in accordance with our personal decrees and Manifestos concerning the immigration of fugitives and foreigners.[5]

The result of Mel'gunov's work (revised by the brothers Panin) was a 'Plan, concerning the distribution of state lands in the New Russian Province for their settlement', which was published in March 1764.[6] The same decree set out and confirmed the structure of the new Province. In June a commission, of which Mel'gunov was also a member, presented a plan for Slavyanoserbia, joining it to the New Russian Province just formed.[7]

Mel'gunov's Plan of Settlement has attracted much attention in recent works on the Southern Ukraine, in particular that of Polons'ka-Vasylenko.[8] She points out the strongly 'populationist' features of the document, and its subordination of the entire life of the province to the needs of colonization. She stresses, too, the disregard of existing social patterns implicit in the Plan: she sees underlying its provisions the assumption that New Russia was virgin territory, *tabula rasa* for the planner's pen – an assumption, in Polons'ka-Vasylenko's eyes, which was unprecedented.[9]

This is perhaps an overstatement of the case. A similar attitude can be found in the official approach to the Saratov area of settlement; and Polons'ka-Vasylenko herself noted the same approach in the first establishment of the Serbian colonies.[10] The 1764 Plan in any case preserved several important features of New Serbia's organization. It also had obvious points in common with the Saratov 'blueprint' published at about the same time, given their different circumstances. And while it is true that the attempt to organize an entire province on these lines was unique, this too requires qualification. Firstly, the Plan initially covered only New Serbia and the New Slobodskiy Regiment, an existing exclusive area of settlement which was now to be made into the Province of New Russia. Secondly, its provisions in fact envisaged a social structure closer than hitherto to that of the rest of the Ukraine.[11]

Mel'gunov included within the single framework of the Plan most of the elements to be found in the various separate decrees relating to the general immigration programme, to which in fact he had been referred in his original drafting instructions. The overriding concern, however, was military effectiveness: the new Province retained the border role of its predecessor and military requirements largely determined priorities of settlement.

The Plan consists of eight chapters: On Privileges; On the Division of Land, and Principles of Tenure; On Regimental Recruitings (*O komplektovanii*); On Revenues; On Forests; On Commerce, Merchants, Factories, and Enterprises; On Boundaries; and On Schools.[12] The first chapter set the general scene. Settlement was open to anybody – 'people of any status, who have come and in the future may come in from all places': anybody, that is, moving legally. Every settler, military or civilian, would receive land in permanent hereditary ownership (§ 2). Civilian settlers were lured with promises of freedom from compulsory military service and the prospect of unrestricted and duty-free trade across the border, as well as the free sale of salt and spirits (§ 3) – the latter especially a considerable concession for the period. There were also cash incentives for settlement: 30 roubles for all foreigners entering military service in the province (§ 4), and 12 for Zaporozhians and Russian fugitives doing likewise (§ 5). Civilian settlers, Russian or foreign, could all claim the same amount, 12 roubles (§ 6).

As regards recruitment abroad, recruiting agents (*verbovshchiki*) were offered a set rate of 3 roubles 'for recruiting, travel and provisions' for each foreigner engaged for military service, and 2 roubles for each foreign civilian settler. 'Russians and Poles' in both categories were worth one and a half roubles per head (§ 7). Anyone receiving a land grant in New Russia was obliged to people it at his own expense with settlers from abroad (§ 8). Servicemen were exempt from service for their first year of settlement, to enable them to set up their home properly; but they would receive no pay during this time, merely 'what is given for establishment' (§ 9).

There are several interesting features here. The offer of land to all comers abrogated the usual restrictions on its ownership. The introduction of civilian settlers was a departure from the New Serbian pattern, but fully in accord with Mel′gunov's instructions; while the peculiar circumstances of New Russia dictated the priority of foreign over Russian, and military over civilian settlement, as well as the use envisaged of recruiters abroad.

The second chapter, governing land distribution and tenure, formed the crucial part of the Plan. It divided the territory of New Serbia into 70 districts (okrugi). Of these, 52 were reserved for servicemen, 2 for town-dwellers, and 16 for foreigners, Old Believers and other returning native subjects 'who shall wish to settle in separate settlements (poselit′- sya osobymi slobodami)'.[13] Each district was to have from six to sixteen years' tax exemption, according to the quality of its land and the ease of its settlement. The districts were subdivided into 'lots' (zhereb′ya) each containing 24 plots (uchastki), of which there should be up to 700 in each district. The plot was to remain indivisible and always of the same size, 'so that it will be always easy to serve from it without any new adjustments, and for civilian settlers to pay the usual direct tax' (§ 1).

In 32 districts the size of the plot was set at 26 desyatinas, in the remainder, which lacked timber, at 30 desyatinas (§ 1). Land would be given in accordance with rank, but no-one might own more than 48 plots under any circumstances (§ 4, iv, v), and owners were bound to live within the Province (§ 4, vi). All land was divided into three categories: land of state peasantry, who were to pay a land- (not a poll-) tax; that of landowners, also liable to a land-tax; and servicemen's land, which was not taxable (§ 3). In return for this tax freedom, each military plot had to provide one soldier for service, and special provisions, including substitution by civilian settlers, were made to ensure continuity in the event of death (§ 5).[14] Chapter III prescribed the same use of substitutes in the case of retirement, resignation or flight (§§ 1–3), and required that households should be kept as large as possible, even extended to include outsiders, and that division of them should be avoided, to ensure a sufficient pool of labour and service.

Chapters II and III also dealt more specifically with the question of the recruitment of settlers. All civilian land-grants of more than one plot were conditional on settlement of the land with foreign immigrants;[15] but extra land could be claimed specifically for this purpose, and by people of any status (II, § 4). Such recruiters, on settling a norm of one household per plot, would be confirmed in hereditary possession of the land. Anyone not making a start within one year, or failing to fulfil the norm within three years, would lose his grant, unless he had good grounds for his failure.

These rules covered civilian settlement, the second category of land; and the new owners, having brought in new inhabitants at their own expense, were to pay only half the tax levied on the peasants of the first category (II, § 4, ii). The relation between the new owner and his settlers was not mentioned, being left to the agreement of the two sides. Although officially before 1775 such settlers were supposed to be recruited from abroad, there was from the outset a native element among those brought in for this purpose.[16] Military rank – and so land – could also be acquired by the recruitment of settlers, however, although the norms set were high, and the grant of a rank was intended primarily for those bringing in military recruits.

People recruiting military settlers were required merely to enlist them, and to present them to the authorities. On completion of this task the recruiter was assigned to a regiment and would receive a military land-grant in accordance with the rank earned. (The Plan also provided specially for recruiters in this category who were unfit for service.) The recruitment norms for receipt of a rank were rather higher than in New Serbia under Khorvat: for the rank of Major – 300 servicemen; for Captain – 150; for Lieutenant – 80; Ensign – 60; and Sergeant (*Vakhmistr*) – 30. For those seeking military rank by bringing in civilian settlers, the norms were doubled (III, § 4). Thus, while for military purposes the New Serbian system was retained, with the additional requirement of civilian settlement an adapted and developed form of it was evolved which foreshadowed the *poselitel'* system shortly introduced by the Chancellery of Guardianship.

Chapter VI of the Plan, on commerce and industry, took full account of New Russia's border position and military character. Trade was to be fostered with the Crimea and with Turkey (§ 1). Merchants and craftsmen, both native and foreign, were invited to settle in the main towns of the province (§ 2), though native merchants got rather less favourable terms (§ 3). The establishment of commercial and industrial enterprises received every encouragement, 'especially such...whose products are necessary for the equipment of the regiments, that is, cloth mills, tanneries, hat or Hussar cap factories, button and canvas production, sheep-farms, studs and other useful undertakings'. Enterprises in these categories qualified for subsidies in the form of loans at 6% per annum (§ 4). Foreign artisans could also claim help in equipping themselves, depending on the value of their craft to the community (§ 6). The most extensive privilege, however, went to 'those who will set up a silk farm, vineyard, tobacco factory, and other such undertakings of which there are very few, or none at all, in the state' (§ 5).

The last chapter, and in some ways the most interesting, is that 'On Schools'. Druzhinina and Polons'ka-Vasylenko rightly stress the difference of its tone and style from what had gone before. Side by side with specific directives stand lofty generalizations on the role of education in society and on the civilizing influence of 'virtuous women'. Education should be free and universal, and the poor and orphans were to receive maintenance from the state (§ 1). Hospitals and foundling houses were also envisaged on this basis (§ 3). The tone is that of enlightened absolutism, of Catherine's Instruction and Betskoy's report on the Foundling House. According to Polons'ka-Vasylenko, the programme outlined remained on paper; but some of its provisions reappeared in the administrative structure devised for the state peasantry of New Russia in 1787.[17]

The similarities are clear between the Plan, and the terms of the 1763 Manifesto and subsequent connected decrees on immigration. The differences were dictated by the requirements of Mel'gunov's drafting instructions. Suspension of tax on salt and spirits, for example, was a means to minimize the attraction in this respect of neighbouring Poland; the same applied to freedom from recruitment.[18] The complete silence on serfdom and the explicit rejection of the poll-tax also point in this direction. At the same time, military needs determined forms of land-tenures and inheritance. They, too, decided the highly-differentiated rewards offered for settlement and the subordination of economic development to regimental requirements; while the excellent commercial potential of the area was also considered.

Settlement in the new Province proceeded apace after 1764.[19] The rate of population expansion in New Russia between the third and fourth revisions (1763–82) was greater than at any time before or after. In the one year 1764, for example, immigration into Yelizavetgrad

County alone (*Yelizavetgradskaya Provintsiya*, the western half of New Russia comprising the territory of New Serbia and the New Slobodskiy Regiment) was 5,787 male souls, which brought the male population to 32,571. The newcomers were 2,311 Ukrainians, 2,904 Russians, 462 Vlachs, and 110 Serbs and other foreigners. The total male population of the County rose to 48,119 in 1769, and to 62,299 in 1772.[20] The different elements involved in the immigration into New Russia at this time, under the provisions of the Plan, are described in the works of Druzhinina, Kabuzan, and Polon'ska-Vasylenko already quoted, and will not be detailed here. While the Plan set a particular pattern on population growth, and undoubtedly stimulated immigration from abroad, the majority of newcomers to New Russia were Ukrainians, followed in order of numbers by Great Russians, and landlord colonization played a considerable part. Figures given by Kabuzan show that in 1769 landlords' peasants formed 14.5% of the population, and by 1774 those of Ukrainian landlords alone 20%.[21]

Rapid immigration, with a predominance of native elements, continued on the original territory of New Russia after 1774. In this year the boundaries of the Province were extended and the new Azov Province created, to take in the lands ceded to Russia under the treaty of Kuchuk-Kaynardji. The new population which settled in these territories included a high proportion of state peasantry of different categories in the south of the region, while returning fugitives and foreigners (from Bessarabia) were most numerous towards the west. The principles of the Plan of Settlement were applied to the acquisitions of Kuchuk-Kaynardji, as they were to all the new southern territories which were annexed to Russia during the last decades of the century.

The Plan itself suffered various changes during this time, most serving the interests of the upper classes and tending to equate New Russia with the rest of the Empire. An increasingly narrow interpretation was given to the clause defining rights of land-ownership. The maximum size of holdings was considerably increased,[22] the time limit for settlement extended, and penalties for failure in this respect diminished. Land-owners were permitted to live outside the Province; and alterations in the taxation system worked to their advantage. Most of the basic principles of the Plan remained in force, however, in some form, and strongly influenced settlement patterns until the end of the century.[23]

The treaty of Kuchuk-Kaynardji provided the basis for the meteoric development of Russia's southern borderlands in the last quarter of the eighteenth century. Throughout and beyond that period, the central fact upon which policy in the south immediately turned was, as before, the confrontation with Turkey. Official planning took into account the requirements both of defence and offence, and the primary aim was to create a military and economic strength capable of withstanding and overthrowing any force which Turkey might pit against Russia. From this point of view it is important to bear in mind the unity, for the purposes of policy-making, of the whole region of southern Russia, including New Russia, the North Caucasus, and the Province of Astrakhan. For a number of years after 1774 this huge territory, reaching from the Bug to the Caspian, formed the unofficial principality of Prince G. A. Potemkin; and it is in the light of his personal control that the projects and achievements of the 1770s and 1780s, especially, should be regarded.

Potemkin's position as favourite was confirmed during the latter stages of the Russo-Turkish war of 1768–74. On the conclusion of peace, he rapidly attained a commanding position in the territories over which the war had been fought and which, together with the lands of the Zaporozhian Cossacks in 1775, now passed under Russian rule. Between February 1774 and the end of 1775, he became first General, then Vice-President of the Military College (President in 1784); Governor-General of New Russia and Commander-in-Chief of New Russian regiments, Commander-in-Chief of all light cavalry and irregular troops (and thus of all Cossack forces), Governor-General of the new Azov Province, and Governor-General of Astrakhan Province.[24] The latter position he retained until 1781, when with the opening of the Saratov Viceroyalty (*Namestnichestvo*) he became Viceroy, relinquishing this post to his cousin, P. S. Potemkin, in 1783.

Even after 1783 Potemkin remained in charge of Caucasian affairs; and Russian policy in this area, although largely within the executive control of P. S. Potemkin, who in 1785 became also Viceroy of the Caucasus, stood under his overall direction. G. A. Potemkin was thus a prime mover both in the celebrated 'Greek Project', and in contemporary Russian plans for similar advance in Transcaucasia. The last third of the eighteenth century was marked by an active Armenian 'national liberation movement', which pinned its hopes on the creation of an autonomous Armenian state under Russian protection. If the Greek Project was a maximum programme, a grandiose vision whose ultimate realization proved impossible,[25] the Armenian plan was much more a product of the immediate political situation, and offered for a time fair prospects of success.[26] Both projects underline the trend of Imperial policy in the south; they also emphasize Russia's attitude to those nations on her southern borders who provided the largest contingents of foreign immigrants at this period. Our account will look first at the eastern end of Potemkin's domain, before returning to the main arena of his and his successors' activities, New Russia.

The North Caucasus after 1774

The most pressing question in the south immediately after 1774 was consolidation. Potemkin wrote in 1776:

Following the present extension of the state boundaries in the directions of Turkey, Poland and the Crimea, and equally on the occasion of the destruction of the former Zaporozhian Force, it is essential to strengthen the defence of [the boundaries] by the addition of such a number of troops as not only should provide protection for the settlement of Azov and New Russia Provinces by people of different nations, against raids by neighbours from these directions. . .but [these troops] should be in a position, with reinforcement by the Ukrainian division nearest them, to make the requisite resistance to any sudden attack on the frontier they defend, and to contain for a time the pressure of the enemy, until the necessary military measures can be taken.[27]

Defence on the southern borders, in other words, should be in the hands of troops based locally; and, equally important, it was specifically a prerequisite for the continuing civilian settlement of the region 'by people of various nations'.

The same intention lay behind the plan, put forward by Potemkin and approved by the Empress in April 1777, to build a new fortified line from Mozdok to Azov. It was to replace the long obsolete Tsaritsyn line, and to provide a continuous cordon between the Caspian and the Black Seas. But in this project, economic considerations were much more to the fore. The official 'description' of the proposed line explained:

The line protects from raids by neighbours the border between Astrakhan and the Don, and the pasture-lands (*kochev'ye*) of our Kalmyk and Tatars; it gives the latter a means to expand right to the Black Forest and the river Yegorlyk, giving them thereby a better livelihood, and will cut off various mountain peoples, in the feeding of their horses and cattle, from those places which our subjects by right should use. By its position, [the line] gives the opportunity to set up vineyards, silk and cotton plantations, to increase stock-breeding, stud-farms, orchards and grain production.

It will join the Azov with the Astrakhan Province, and in time of war with the neighbouring peoples, may restrain their pressure on our lands, reinforce the action of our forces in the Crimea and elsewhere. Besides this, it gives a means of entry into the mountains there and into the homeland of the Ossetians, and a means of exploiting in time their ores and minerals. It will stop the secret transport of forbidden goods into Russia, thereby increasing customs revenues.[28]

Besides the general prospects of economic development so described, Potemkin made it clear in another part of the same report to the Empress that he intended to rely at least to some extent on foreign settlement to populate the northern Caucasus, as well as New Russia:

The foreign newspapers are full of praises for the new settlements set up in the New Russia and Azov Provinces. Reading them, and especially the privileges, most attractive to all, granted by YIH to the newly emigrated Armenians and Greeks, and which are referred to in those prints, the public will realize the full value of the communities established by You.

To encourage this, I consider it essential to communicate personally with our Ministers at various [foreign] Courts, so that they should try to attract useful inhabitants of any status, not excluding even Jews, such as possess, however, large capital, for migration to the new Mozdok line, which abounds in everything needful for life.[29]

In response to this, Catherine ordered the Senate to consider the settlement of the line, in consultation with both the Military College and the Chancellery of Guardianship, and 'especially' with Potemkin himself. Vyazemsky discussed the matter with Potemkin, and as a result, in October 1778, a scheme was put forward for the transfer to the south of some of the Saratov colonists: for several years a number of villages on the left bank had been complaining of bad land and conditions and requesting, through the Saratov Office, permission to move.[30] But nothing came of this project until seven years later, when Potemkin's proposal to seek foreign settlers for the Caucasus was taken up as a whole.

Failure to implement the scheme was probably due principally to the unpreparedness of the region to be settled. The building of the new line itself (variously called Caucasus, Mozdok, or Azov Line) began in the summer of 1777; and it provoked a strong reaction among the mountain peoples of neighbouring Kabarda whose lands were affected. The Kabardians were subdued only in 1779, after considerable military operations. Potemkin pressed his advantage home: one clause of the Kabardian deed of submission gave Kabardian slaves the right to leave their owners and settle on the Russian side of the line.[31] Construction continued into the first years of the following decade, the additional labour force needed for the work being supplied by two regiments of Cossacks brought in from the Khopyor and the Volga.[32] Some considerable land-grants were made in the area, and old soldiers were settled to reinforce the Cossacks. Initially, however, the region remained insecure, and population inflow at this time was very small.[33]

In December 1782, when most of the work on the line was completed, an Imperial decree was issued, regulating the question of land-grants there. It offered land to 'all those desiring it for settlement'; distribution of grants was to be under G. A. Potemkin's sole supervision, and the decree envisaged serfs from central provinces as a major colonizing element.[34] But really vigorous measures were taken only after the annexation of the Crimea in 1783, which brought much of the Kuban under Russian rule and greatly facilitated control of the northern Caucasus. In 1784, P. S. Potemkin planned an extensive migration of *odnodvortsy*, 'economic' – former monastery – peasants, and of state peasants from Kursk, Tambov and other Provinces. The response was very considerable – although the migration was stopped in 1788 because of the Turkish war.[35] The Senate in 1784 was at pains to clarify the decree on land of 1782. Since that decree had ordered land to be given for settlement to all applicants 'without distinction of birth or status', *odnodvortsy* were to be included under it. It also applied to all other categories of state peasantry.[36]

The resumption of colonization was part of activities connected with the creation of the Caucasus Viceroyalty, which was formally inaugurated by the Viceroy, P. S. Potemkin, on 18 January 1786. The Viceroyalty had been officially formed from the previous Caucasus and Astrakhan Provinces by a decree of 5 May 1785; and almost simultaneously a development plan for the area, presented by P. S. Potemkin, had received Imperial approval.[37] The thirty-three points of this document, while leaving some matters to be decided in detail in the future, represented a complete programme of settlement and of administrative organization. They provided, too, a logical extension of the process of assimilation of the Volga and the northern Caucasus, continuing throughout the eighteenth century, some aspects of which we have already noticed. Thus post-roads were to be built and settlements established along them, between Tsaritsyn, the new Mozdok line, and Cherkassk, capital of the Don Cossacks (§ 10). Settlers along the roads were to receive a free grant of 20 roubles per household, and the same sum was to be given to old soldier settlers (§ 12), and to the inhabitants of a new town to be built between Cherkassk and the line (§ 11).

Not surprisingly in view of the nature of the new Viceroyalty, and of the very recent promulgation of Catherine's Charter to the Towns of the Empire,[38] considerable attention was paid to urban development. The document called for the 'unobtrusive' construction of towns near the mountain tribes subject to Russia, as instruments both of defence and of assimilation (§ 2). Kizlyar, Mozdok 'and other such towns' received a civil administration for the first time (§ 3); and of twelve clauses dealing with Astrakhan Province, seven were devoted to various aspects of the civic and economic development of Astrakhan town itself. Most interestingly from our point of view, the three articles dealing specifically with foreigners considered them also in an urban context. The Urban Statute (*Gorodovoye Polozheniye*) of the Charter to the Towns was prescribed as the legal framework for the activities of foreign and non-local merchants in Astrakhan (§ 32); and it was to be the basis likewise for resettlement in the new Viceroyalty of any Saratov colonists who wished to pursue urban trades there (§ 4). The Charter also announced the impending promulgation of a Manifesto which was to invite 'Transcaucasian immigrants' (*vykhodtsy iz-za kavkazskikh gor*) to settle in the Caucasus Province: it would be 'useful' to found a special town for Armenians, provided sufficient numbers answered the proclamation (§ 5).

This Manifesto duly appeared on 14 July 1785.[39] Despite the previous official characterization of it, it was addressed to all foreigners, without national limitation (even of Jews), 'who may wish to establish their residence in the towns and settlements of this Province'. It offered rather less than its predecessors: religious and civic freedom, equality of rights with native inhabitants, freedom from taxes for six years, and freedom of departure, on the usual terms, from the Empire. Not only was the Manifesto not confined to Transcaucasian nationalities, but the Russian government, finally implementing Potemkin's ideas of 1777, had it published in the West. The ban on emigration from the German Empire, imposed in 1768 by Joseph II, was still operative, and closed most of central Europe to this type of propaganda; but the Manifesto appeared in the newspapers of towns as far apart as Leghorn and Danzig.[40] Among its Western readers it appears to have aroused no significant interest in the Caucasus. In Danzig, however, it directly fostered an interest in emigration to Russia which led to the German and Mennonite settlements in New Russia of the late 1780s and the 1790s.[41]

The plan to settle Saratov colonists in the Caucasus Province proved equally abortive. When it was announced in the colonies, it started a migration fever which Ogaryov, the Director of Husbandry, had great difficulty in calming. But of the seventy-four families who went to the south, many died, and the remainder scattered through the towns of the region or returned to the Volga with their tails between their legs. Despite the declared intentions of the government, the Germans had been settled in a village on their own – Bol'shiye Madzhary, on the Kuma. Pallas found it in 1793 'completely abandoned. These settlers lived here upwards of a twelve-month in subterraneous huts; but from the unwholesomeness of their situation they lost part of their numbers, which originally amounted to 183 [male] persons.'[42] Only ten families stayed on, and shortly even they were 'sent away by the authorities there against their will', for an unspecified reason, back to the Volga.[43]

More realistic, and more fruitful, were the hopes placed on immigration from Transcaucasia. The 1780s were a period of rapid Russian penetration into the Caucasus, marked by negotiations with local potentates, by a treaty of protection and suzerainty with the Georgian Tsar Heraklius,[44] and by plans for a military expedition against Persia, closely connected with the Armenian project already mentioned.[45] Armenians in particular continued to enter Russia, swelling the existing communities in the northern Caucasus region. The town of Grigoriopol, founded on the western border of New Russia in 1792, originated in negotiations with the Transcaucasian Armenians in 1784.[46] And when a Transcaucasian expedition was finally undertaken, at the end of Catherine's reign, it brought back with it on its recall by Paul a considerable body of Armenians, who received a variety of privileges, and 15,000 desyatinas of land on the Kuma, where they built the Town of the Holy Cross.[47]

In general, however, conditions in the North Caucasus at this time were not favourable to foreign settlement on a large scale, and made even native Russian settlement difficult. Landlord settlement proceeded slowly: noble recipients of the large land grants made after the opening of the Viceroyalty used them principally for stock-breeding, because of lack of labour, and peasants transferred to the area found the journey exhausting and the conditions of the new region very difficult. In 1790 61% of the rural population of the Caucasus Province were *odnodvortsy*, a high proportion of the remainder Cossacks.[48] The region was never fully secure. The pro-Turkish, religiously-inspired movement of Mansur in the mountains,[49] starting in 1785, preceded the Russo-Turkish war of 1787–91, itself only one further episode in the continuing Russian confrontation with Turkey and Persia. As a result, the population of the forward areas of the Viceroyalty remained

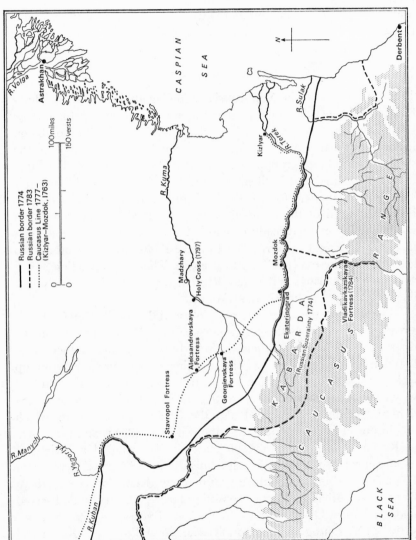

Map 4. The Caucasus in the later eighteenth century.

Russian border 1774
Russian border 1783
Caucasus Line 1777–
(Kizlyar–Mozdok, 1763)

100 miles
150 versts

R.Volga
Astrakhan
CASPIAN SEA
Derbent
R.Sulak
R.Terek
Kizlyar
R.Kuma
Mozdok
Madzhary
HolyCross (1797)
Aleksandrovskaya Fortress
Georgievskaya Fortress
Ekaterinograd
Stavropol Fortress
KABARDA
(Russian Suzerainty 1774)
Vladikavkazskaya Fortress (1784)
CAUCASUS
RANGE
R.Manych
R.Yegorlyk
R.Kuban
BLACK SEA
N

overwhelmingly military (Cossack) in character; and if, altogether, the region north of the Caucasus had by 1800 become 'included in the sphere of contemporary civilization for the first time since the Mongol invasion',[50] the progress of civilization and development there was less than in the neighbouring but more favourably disposed territory round the Black Sea.

New Russia after 1774

The state of affairs in New Russia following the Peace of Kuchuk-Kaynardji demanded more rapid and incisive measures than those adopted for the Caucasus. The immediate political aim of consolidation had to be pursued first and foremost through radical changes in the structure of military groupings in the area. One such change Potemkin himself explained and justified in the report of 1776 already quoted.[51] This policy statement formed the background to Potemkin's re-organization in 1776 of the irregular regiments settled in New Russia, to which the report specifically related. The number of troops and regiments was increased, steps taken to make them more efficient and to keep them more effectively up to strength. The re-organization aimed deliberately at bringing the New Russian regiments more closely into line with those elsewhere in the Ukraine.[52]

The reform of the irregular troops followed that of the Don Cossacks, already carried out with similar purpose in February 1775; and the destruction of the Zaporozhian Sech' in June 1775 was another manifestation of the same policy, the crushing of an autonomous group which resisted subordination to central Russian authority and so weakened Russian control.[53] Into this process of military re-organization and centralization fitted also the foreign military units which fought on the Russian side during the war of 1768–74, and came over to Russia on the conclusion of peace. They included a variety of nationalities: Moldavians, Vlachs, Bulgarians, Albanians, Greeks and Poles. Two regiments of these troops received land on the southern Bug.[54] The 'Albanian Force', consisting largely of Greeks, had served under Aleksey Orlov in the Archipelago Expedition; its members settled in Taganrog and the now Russian coastal towns of Kerch and Yenikale, where they took up cordon duties.[55] In the same period of war with Turkey, in 1770, large numbers of Nogay Tatars, nomads subject to the Ottoman Empire, were persuaded to accept Russian 'eternal friendship and alliance', and moved in October 1770 from their lands on the west of the Black Sea to the steppes near Azov.[56]

However, as Potemkin's administration took a firmer grip on the new territories, and local authorities became operative, the emphasis turned to civilian settlement. The fields from which new material was sought increased rapidly in variety and number. Potemkin, like his predecessors, continued to view foreign immigration as a major means to increase population, and offered foreigners more considerable privileges and inducements than were normally extended to Russian and Ukrainian settlers. Foreigners were no longer, however, the primary object of policy; and unless favoured for special reasons – agricultural or other expertise, military value, or the political purposes of the government – they became simply one source among others to be tapped for the urgent task of peopling the new territories.

The scope of the measures adopted for this purpose can best be seen in the variety of groups brought into the new Taurian Province after the annexation of the Crimea in 1783. The population of the Crimean peninsula had been severely depleted in the preceding decade by war and disease, by the emigration of much of its Christian community in 1778 and by the departure to Turkish territory of many Nogay and Crimean Tatars after the annexation. The following years were a period of intensive and systematic settlement activity. Potemkin's approach emerges clearly in one of his reports to the Empress, of 10 August 1785:

I am using all my powers to bring this land into the most flourishing condition. From various places I have summoned colonists knowledgeable in all spheres of economy, to serve as examples to the native inhabitants. But this spacious and most abundant of lands in Russia has not yet a tenth part of the population proportionate to its size, and therefore I presume most humbly to request the following means of peopling it.

For large-scale settlement, the 'humble request' grouped the Stavropol Kalmyk from the Volga with unemployed clergy, schismatic Old Believers living in the Ukraine with their fugitive fellows across the border in Poland. It also proposed the removal of internal customs barriers in the Crimea, since 'if it pleased YIH to remove the duty entirely from the Taurian peninsula, the [Customs] guard would thereby be reduced, and many inhabitants would be attracted from abroad'.[57]

These proposals were put into effect.[58] Four thousand spare clergy were gathered from all over central Russia and the Ukraine; Old Believers of all classes were offered privileges and material assistance for settlement in the new areas, as were also all categories of state peasantry – for whose migration to the south permission had already been given four years earlier. But this was only part of the picture. Land was distributed as before, on condition of its settlement, with serfs or from other 'permitted' sources. The authorities condoned the harbouring of fugitive peasants; measures had already been taken, very successfully, to encourage the return of fugitives from abroad.[59] Convicts were sent to penal work in the region. A previous decree, of 14 January 1785, had ordered the dispatch to the south of 4,425 recruits' wives, to join their husbands there;[60] while in view of the predominance of men in the population, special measures were adopted to bring in single women. Authorization was given for payment to recruiters of five roubles per female head, on the basis of the Plan of 1764. Soldiers stationed in the province who agreed to marry and settle there could qualify for immediate release from military service. Attempts were made to woo the Old Believer 'Nekrasovtsy', former Cossacks living across the border under Turkish rule, and to settle the Volga Kalmyk already mentioned.[61]

Few of these measures were new. What was remarkable was their extent, the breadth and intensity of colonizing activity. Material was to be taken wherever it could be found; and the same approach characterized much of the foreign immigration of the time in New Russia. Apart from the Nogay and the Crimean Christians, who moved as unified groups, numerically by far the most important immigrants were the Moldavians and Vlachs, who had been strongly represented ever since the founding of the Serbian colonies. Moldavians entered Russia continuously until the late 1780s. Between 1763 and 1782 some 23,000 arrived in New Russia, the influx being particularly great during the Russo-Turkish war. They settled principally in the west of the region (Yelizavetgrad County[62]), where in 1782 they easily outnumbered the Great Russian settlers (though not the Ukrainians); but the Moldavian population further to the east also increased considerably.[63]

Potemkin valued these settlers highly; significantly, however, he gave them no better terms than those which he offered to the native state peasantry. An order to the Governor of Yekaterinoslav Province, of 1 July 1784, stated:

Considering as a very important object [of policy] the settlement of the land, and the attraction from abroad of a number of people sufficient for that purpose, I prescribe for your exact and careful implementation the good treatment of such foreigners. This means will stimulate many [more] to follow them. I propose to satisfy in Aleshki the requirements of all sufficiently useful immigrants, and, specifically, to give each a pair of oxen, a horse, cow, and all the equipment necessary for their work, to assign land, eight desyatinas per head, not including non-farming land.

Potemkin added:

A further forty families are now coming in down [the Dnieper]; do not fail to receive them yourself and to establish them on equal terms with the previous arrivals, after which it will be possible to send (*otpustit'*) some of them to invite other immigrants.

A further order of 1 July makes it clear that the foreigners are Moldavians.[64] These conditions of settlement were identical with the terms on which Potemkin had already settled two groups of native state peasantry in Aleshki, on the Dnieper near Kherson.[65] At about the same time, the offer of a Moldavian captain in the Russian army, to recruit among his fellow-countrymen for the Taurian District, was accepted by Potemkin – but with reserve: the operation was not to cause trouble with Turkey.[66] Moldavians also settled in the Crimean peninsula at this time; and a group of Bulgarians numbering some five hundred formed the village of Mangush in Simferopol uyezd.[67]

In the case of the Moldavians, Potemkin simply encouraged and exploited an already existing situation. But he was quick to take advantage of almost any possible new source of settlers from abroad, even when the numbers involved were small, and his efforts during the 1780s brought the most varied immigrants into the region under his administration. Swedish peasants on an estate about to change hands; Greeks and Corsicans in Minorca driven from their homes by the Spanish; Danzigers facing economic decline; English convicts offered for deportation – all were considered suitable.

If the offers of a few would-be recruiters or settlers were rejected, this was because the conditions asked were exorbitant, or because the prospective colonist material appeared exceptionally inappropriate. American Loyalists, for example, who reportedly approached Potemkin in the aftermath of the American revolution, were 'very particular in the terms they require', so that the Prince was 'afraid that they may be descendants of those people who migrated from England during the civil wars in the last century, and who may be supposed to entertain opinions by no means compatible with the spirit of such a government as this'.[68] In the other cases mentioned, however, Potemkin and his agents pursued their object with energy and perseverance: 880 Swedes duly settled in Yekaterinoslav Province, forming the village of Starosh-vedskoye (Gammalsvenskby); Danzig, scene of the recruiting activities of George Trappe, who acted as Potemkin's private agent, furnished nearly one thousand settlers ('Danzig colonists') in 1786; and from the same area the following year Trappe engaged a considerable contingent of Mennonites, subsequently the best and most successful of all the peasant farmers of southern Russia; 228 Mennonite families settled on lands belonging to Potemkin on the Dnieper at Khortitsa, the site of the former Zaporozhian Sech'.[69] Others followed in the 1790s. The Greeks and Corsicans, 1,010 in number, were recruited by the Russian 'general naval commissioner' in Leghorn, Count D. Mochenigo, whose activities caused quite a stir in Italy. They included in their company a variety of other nationalities from Italian coastal towns; and they proved very poor settler material. The final shipload of about 200 – a motley crew consisting of 180 Italians with a sprinkling of Greeks, Slavs, Swedes, Germans, Maltese, French and Spaniards – mutinied, tried to seize their ship, and were brought into Kherson in irons. They were quite unsuited to agriculture, to which they were first assigned, and finally dispersed among the coastal towns of the Black Sea.[70] Hopes of an English penal colony foundered on the opposition of the Russian Ambassador in London, S. R. Vorontsov. The latter's subsequent account of the incident, somewhat flattering to himself and very hostile to Potemkin, throws light on the attitude of those elements in the highest circles who opposed Potemkin's activities in the south.

Prince Potemkin, erratic in all his desires, ashamed of having expelled from the Crimea the peaceable Tatar farmers, wished at all costs to repopulate this peninsula with inhabitants of any sort whatsoever, be they even dangerous, no matter; and having learnt through the newspapers that the authorities here [sc. Britain] did not know what to do with several thousand malefactors, who had not committed sufficient crimes to be hanged, but who were such rogues that it was dangerous to keep them in society (since the establishment of Botany Bay did not then exist), he took the Empress unawares and gained from her an order to me to request that the British Government place these malefactors in my charge for transportation to the Crimea.

Vorontsov was appalled:

Surprised and ashamed for my Country at a project as dishonouring as it was harmful, I wrote to Count Bezborodko that the Empress's confidence had been abused in this affair.

The Ambassador's arguments against the project carried the day – although, he said, Potemkin never forgave him.[71]

Vorontsov also states that Catherine had at this time (1785) 'published in all the papers of Europe an invitation to farmers, viticulturists, artisans of all trades and merchants of all religions to establish themselves in the Crimea'.[72] There seems to be no further evidence of an official proclamation in exactly these terms. A Manifesto concerning New Russia was, however, promulgated in 1784, opening Kherson, Sebastopol and Theodosia to foreigners for commercial purposes; it followed directly upon a Russo-Turkish trade treaty concluded the previous year. The citizens of 'all nations maintaining friendly relations with the Russian Empire' were invited to trade in these ports, which were given the same rights as Petersburg and Archangel in commercial matters. Furthermore, 'if any foreigner conceives the wish to settle in those or in others of Our towns and settlements, and to take Our citizenship', he was free to do so; and he was promised in addition freedom of worship, the right to leave the country at will, and 'limitless freedom to set up factories, handicrafts, and all else permitted for his own and the common advantage, and he shall enjoy all these benefits and privileges granted to Our other subjects of equal status with him'.[73]

Thus this Manifesto, like that on the Caucasus, gave pride of place to urban, commercial and industrial pursuits. And Potemkin sought to use exactly the same means to attract foreigners to his new town of Nikolayev in 1789.[74] His methods in these spheres were as direct and comprehensive as in those of agriculture and military settlement. He sought out, both at home and abroad, the skills particularly needed for specific projects, and at the same time encouraged the establishment of all other crafts and industries in which ordinary immigrants, native and foreign, were proficient. When a Greek from Constantinople set up a 'factory of golden Turkish brocade' in Taganrog in 1781, he received not only a subsidy, but a salary as well. Potemkin justified the award with the statement that 'every new enterprise, especially in a region possessing as yet no craftsmen whatsoever, demands help and encouragement from the State'.[75]

The Danzig colonists were used in a similar way to further urban development; they had been recruited with an eye to Kherson. Of 910 recruits, a mixture of peasantry and artisans, 755 reached the south. Fourteen families settled in the Swedish colony, much depleted by death and desertion; 21 formed a new colony of their own, Alt-Danzig. All the rest were placed either in Kherson, or in the Crimea, where the administration was engaged in the construction of several palaces. Thirteen families went to Sebastopol. The inn-keeper Witte went to Kherson (on Trappe's original suggestion), with a free house for a year and a subsidy of 800 roubles: Potemkin considered that 'the establishment of an inn in Kherson is extremely necessary'.[76] Another agent of

Potemkin's, a Saxon named Hermann, was recruiting urban settlers for Kherson in central and southern Europe at about the same time.[77]

Thus Potemkin drew on an extremely wide range of settler material, both native and foreign, in his efforts to populate and develop New Russia. And apart from his readiness to seize any chance opportunity which might present itself for recruitment abroad, he followed his predecessors in exploiting military and political situations to the same end, by deliberate incitement of various foreign groups to migrate to Russia and to settle there. The Albanian Force was one case in point. It had been recruited by A. Orlov at the beginning of the Russo-Turkish war of 1768–74 for immediate military purposes, in accordance with the traditional Russian policy of rousing Turkey's Christian subjects against her. But from the outset the possibility of subsequent settlement was held in view, and following the establishment of the Force on the Sea of Azov in 1775, its members were given the option of civilian or military status. Their military organization was retained, and Potemkin – now in charge of New Russia – obtained an annual requisition of 72,000 roubles for the maintenance of both 'serving and non-serving Albanians'.[78] A list among his papers, dating from 1775 to 1776, gives their total numbers as 1,236 in Kerch and Yenikale, and 545 in Taganrog.[79] In 1784, following the annexation of the Crimea, the Greek units moved to take up cordon duties at Balaklava, within the peninsula.[80]

On the other hand, the conditions set for the Greeks' settlement deliberately offered considerable incentives to merchants and entrepreneurs, as well as extending the right of settlement to several other categories of foreigner, and many 'Albanians', and other Greek immigrants who later joined them, took advantage of this. Those in Taganrog created a flourishing community with its own civic organs and a considerable foreign trade, even attracting some members from the older Nezhin fraternity.[81] Like the other Greek civilians, they did not move in 1784. By that year the community, with about one hundred merchants, owned at least 15 merchant ships (one source shows 30), and possessed trading capital of over 80,000 roubles.[82] The smaller groups in Kerch and Yenikale also found their feet. In 1788 these two ports had between them 59 Greek merchants and 199 Greek *meshchane*, and numbers rose in the following years.[83]

Of a comparable, though somewhat different, nature was the migration in 1778 of some two thirds of the Christian population of the Crimea to the northern shore of the Sea of Azov. The Crimean Christians were predominantly Greeks and Armenians; the former founded the town of Mariupol, the latter that of Nakhichevan.[84] Catholic (Uniat) Armenians formed a small separate colony in Yekaterinoslav.[85] In the case of the Christian migration, Russian hopes of cultural gain for the new area of settlement were allied with an essentially political question, Catherine's designs on the Crimea. The migrants formed the most cultured and prosperous section of the Crimean population and their departure from the peninsula, organized at Potemkin's instigation in 1778 during the Russian occupation, had the specific aim of weakening the Khanate. This procedure, like the recruitment of the 'Albanians', has been seen as a continuation of a traditional Russian policy, the wooing and winning of allies or collaborators within an enemy area.[86] A further explicit, though secondary, consideration lay in the fact that the Christian community had been an important supplier of foodstuffs for Constantinople: Suvorov, largely in charge of the operation, saw the removal of the migrants as an immediate blow against Turkey.[87] The loss of the Khan's Christian subjects, to the number of 31,386,[88] was a serious setback to the economy of the Crimea, though it is doubtful whether it influenced at all deeply the course of events in 1783.

Another category of immigration pertained to cultural and technical matters, where the object was the development of particular branches of the New Russian economy. Here Potemkin relied principally on individual specialists. Like his agricultural and military settlers, he took them wherever he could find them. Historians have frequently stressed the huge scale of Potemkin's resources; as D. Bagaley put it: 'one might say that the whole of Russia performed special services for the benefit of the enterprises of His Serene Highness' in New Russia.[89] Potemkin could command from the rest of the country native or resident specialists of the most varied kinds: carpenters from Petersburg and Olonets for his shipbuilding programme, German smiths from Moscow, textile workers from the Baltic, doctors, agronomists, painters, engineers.[90] But he also sought many specialists from abroad; and for the same purpose Catherine turned to her own foreign correspondents. One of these was Dr J. G. Zimmermann of Hanover, whose exchanges with Catherine are full of such matters. In a letter of 10/21 January 1786 she set out Potemkin's particular requirements: her present reply, she said, was

according to the personal note of Prince Potemkin, Governor-General of the former Crimea: 'In Tauria the principal matter must without question be the cultivation of the land and the nurture of silk worms, and consequently also mulberry plantations. Cloth could be made there, but the wool is not of the best sort; cheese-making would also be very desirable (N.B. scarcely any cheese is made in the whole of Russia). Another of the principal objects of attention in Tauria could be gardens, above all botanical gardens. For all these developments we inevitably need sensible, knowledgeable people. The Crown has no need to undertake the engagement of other workers apart from these, but if any wished to come at their own expense, they would be well received and would enjoy the various advantages stipulated in the published manifestos.'[91]

To develop viticulture the Frenchman Joseph Banq was engaged; for silk production the Italians Notara and Parma. While the English gardener Gould fully justified his long employment with Potemkin, his fellow-horticulturist and countryman Henderson turned out to be a 'shameless deceiver'.[92] The German von Falkenburg was taken into service as a mining expert;[93] and despite Potemkin's doubts about the quality of Crimean wool, he sent for thoroughbred rams from abroad, and for foreign labour to work in a new textile mill.[94]

These last plans, like many others, were interrupted by the second Turkish war of 1787–91. But the textile mill, first projected in 1783 for the Crimea, and based initially on workers and machinery from the state factory at Yamburg, near Narva, had already begun functioning on Potemkin's own estate of Dubrovna, with specialist labour both Russian and from abroad.[95] This was a temporary location pending its transfer to the south. In 1794, together with a silk mill of similar type, it was finally removed to Yekaterinoslav. The two mills were large-scale state enterprises, the first of their kind in the Southern Ukraine. In 1794, the cloth mill had 659 workers of both sexes, including 56 foreign craftsmen.[96]

Of equal significance was the iron foundry established in 1795 on the Lugan, a tributary of the Donets, by the Scot Charles Gascoigne, whom we shall meet again in Chapter 5. The idea for this enterprise originated likewise, in 1781, with Potemkin, who hoped to make good New Russia's lack of wood fuel by exploiting the coalfields of the Donets basin. Gascoigne used British specialists as well as native labour from other foundries.[97] The works acquired considerable importance for the equipment of the Black Sea fleet, a task which it shared with a munitions factory and another foundry set up earlier in Kremenchug and Kherson respectively.

Potemkin's use of foreign specialists extended also to the realms of medicine and education. At the end of 1785, still greatly preoccupied with the organization of the Crimea, he was seeking medical staff for his new province, a task in which Zimmermann proved very helpful.[98] The most notable of the latter's recruits was the Hamburg physician Dr Meyer, who received the title of 'official physiologist or Chief Doctor of Tauria', with the rank of Court Counsellor (eighth class), a salary of 1,500 roubles, travel expenses of 1,500–2,000 roubles and pension rights for his family in case of his death. Meyer in fact proposed to bring in a whole 'colony' with him. He wrote to Zimmermann from Hamburg in December 1785:

I myself hope to take with me to Tauria a splendid colony of selected good people, when the conditions in my memorandum are honoured with Imperial approval. A good start has already been made in recruitment; however, I cannot speak of this either publicly, or in definite terms, and indeed it would be inappropriate to mention it in the Memorandum when the latter has still not been approved. Yesterday my colony, which is to accompany me, received a new addition. It was joined by an expert dyer of cloth, and of wool in general, who is here in Hamburg, and with whom will travel his two sons...

There is one, too, among my recruits, a young and skilful painter, who knows gilding, lacquering and interior decorating (*odevat' pokoi*). His father was the personal physician of the Prince of Waldeck, and he spent a long time in Italy.

A young merchant of good family, who has already served in the offices of merchant houses, several joiners and other people have also enlisted. Only the search for doctors is proving somewhat difficult.

I still hope to learn Russian in the course of this winter.[99]

Still more ambitious than this search for physicians were Potemkin's plans for a university in Yekaterinoslav, which, with its cathedral, designed to outshine St Peter's in Rome, was intended to become a monument to Catherine on a European scale. In this case, too, Potemkin looked to the West to find staff for his new institution. Even before it had been organized, several professors were engaged, and began to receive salaries.[100] But the bubble soon burst. With Potemkin's death in 1791, not only the university, but the cathedral and his own magnificent palace were abandoned, unfinished. As late as 1815 a government official found the town 'more like some Dutch colony than a provincial administrative centre'.[101]

Yekaterinoslav was perhaps the most signal and symbolic example of visionary fantasy in Potemkin's work in New Russia, of that vein of unchecked imagination and showmanship which was caught and held in the stories of 'Potemkin's villages'. Potemkin, like Catherine, loved grandiose projects, which he could by no means always bring to completion. But his work, completed or not, contributed greatly to the development of New Russia; under his administration the essential foundations were laid for the subsequent growth of the Southern Ukraine.

In the five years between Potemkin's death and the end of the reign, government policy and activity in the south continued on the same lines as before, though with changing emphases. Under the administration of Platon Zubov (1793–6), who aspired to equal Potemkin as administrator and statesman, the latter's favourite projects – Yekaterinoslav, Nikolayev – fell from the limelight, and attention focussed on the new Ochakov District. Here in 1795 Zubov set up the ephemeral Voznesensk Viceroyalty, centred on his own creation, the town of Voznesensk. But this new town had little economic or military importance, and after Zubov's fall in 1796 it remained insignificant.

However, Zubov's ambitions were by no means the determining factor in the development of the Ochakov District. As a new province, an acquisition of the Treaty of Iasi, and possessing obvious commercial potential, the region naturally required special treatment to assure its security and rapid assimilation into the Empire. The first such measure was a short decree of 26 January 1792 to the Senate (before Zubov's assumption of administrative control over New Russia):

We most graciously order that the land lying between the Bug and the Dniester, newly acquired to the Russian Empire from the Ottoman Porte, be joined to Yekaterinoslav Province, entrusting care for its settlement by inhabitants coming from abroad, according to their condition and on the basis of the Plan concerning the Yekaterinoslav Province, to the administrator of that Province, Major-General Kakhovsky.

Kakhovsky was to report back as soon as he had decided how to organize the new region;[102] the 'Plan' referred to was that of 1764. Another decree of the same date gave Kakhovsky more detailed guidelines; among other points, it again demanded close adherence to the Plan, and the utmost possible speed.[103]

Settlement of empty land with elements from abroad thus remained a cardinal point of policy in the Ochakov District. It was very appropriate to the circumstances. The area had been heavily settled by migrants from neighbouring Moldavia since the early 1770s, and although these had scattered during the war, immigration resumed at a very heavy rate in 1792, and persisted. At the end of that year, Moldavians represented 49% of a population of 23,743; in 1799, with a total population of 46,700, they formed 39% of the whole. (The proportional drop reflected heavy settlement by landowners of Russian and Ukrainian elements).[104]

Most specific policy measures concerning foreign immigration in this period, however, linked it with urban and commercial development, thus continuing the trend visible in the Manifestos of 1784 and 1785. A decree of 27 July 1792 extended the six-year tax exemption, promised in the 1764 Plan to rural settlers only, to townspeople and merchants.[105] But the most important enactments related to Odessa and to Voznesensk.

Odessa, formed on the site of the old Turkish fortress of Khadzhibey, received its proper foundation only in 1794. The previous year, the number of inhabitants officially recorded there was 8 male and 2 female; and numbers began to rise only with the start of work on a military and civilian harbour.[106] On 19 April 1795, Catherine confirmed proposals by Zubov 'concerning the establishment of a settlement of co-religionist peoples in the town of Odessa and its environs'.[107] These consisted of two 'statutes' (*polozheniya*), 'one concerning the settlement there of the Greeks and Albanians who served Us with excellent zeal in the last war with the Turks, and the other relating to those co-religionists, who may conceive the wish to migrate there from various foreign places'.

For the latter, Zubov proposed to build, 'initially', 53 stone houses, of two sorts, 'with small shops and other outbuildings according to Asiatic custom', at a total cost of 22,000 roubles. The immigrants could live in them for up to one year, while building for themselves; or they could buy the houses, at cost, to be repaid over five years – their payments, it was suggested, would be used to build further houses for following arrivals (§ 1). Poor immigrants should have grants 'to help them in the initial move, for travelling and maintenance costs, for one year's subsistence on arrival, and to equip themselves during their settlement'. Grants should be of 100–150 roubles, repayable after ten years in three equal annual parts (§ 2); the ten years were to be tax-free, and the government also promised exemption from quartering (§ 5). Freedom of worship went without saying, but when the number of immigrants reached 57, they were to have their own church, built with state funds: 2,000 roubles were allocated for this (§ 3). Immigrants were also free to bring in goods for sale duty-free to the value of 300 roubles; this clause was based explicitly – unlike clauses 2 and 5 – on the 1763 Manifesto. A final provision established the office of Guardian (*Popechitel'*) of the new settlers 'according to the example of the institution of Marshals in Societies of the Nobility', to assist and protect the newcomers in their initial settlement and to ensure the observance among them of 'peace, tranquillity and friendly agreement' (§ 6). The military settlement was exactly analogous with that of 1775 on the Sea of Azov.

The number of Greeks and Albanians who have arrived in Russia, and who in large part are wandering homeless in the southern regions, is now – as far as is known – between two hundred and three hundred; and, as the Deputies sent by them have shown, without doubt will increase still more if firm measures are taken concerning them, and means are given for their settlement.

Their suitability to naval service, their devotion to Russia, and indeed simple justice demanded a favourable solution to their difficult position.[108] A Greek division was therefore to be formed, 'after the example of the [Balaklava] Greek Regiment', with three hundred privates and a corresponding number of officers. It would be financed from the surplus of the sum paid out for the Balaklava force, and would be settled near Odessa. Fifteen thousand desyatinas of good land, near the sea, would be provided for present and future servicemen, and plots given in hereditary ownership: to lower ranks – 25 desyatinas, to officers – 50, to staff officers – 120. Ten thousand roubles for house-building, 500 roubles for a church formed a non-returnable grant, while a further 20,000 roubles to be administered by the Chief Director of Construction in Odessa, Admiral de Ribas,[109] would be returned, as usual, in three annual payments after ten years.

The two schemes were put into effect immediately. By November of the same year, 1795, Zubov could report that the Odessa Division had been formed to full strength, and a temporary Committee set up to guide its settlement.[110] In fact, the Division was not a great success. The land allocated became in the following years the object of pretension and counter-pretension; and pending proper use the divisional funds were diverted to a scheme for providing bullock carts for the construction works in Odessa. This was supposed to work to the profit of the Division and the benefit of the town, and initially it was successful. Before actual settlement could be undertaken, however, or accounts extorted from the divisional treasurer, Colonel Kes-Oglu, a Greek, who was also Guardian of the civilian community, the Emperor Paul disbanded the Division. It was reconstituted in 1803, but had a very chequered career until finally transformed in 1810, together with the Balaklava Regiment, into a military settlement.[111]

The civilian project fared rather better. The same report of November 1795 said that 32 of the proposed houses had already been constructed, and that in them were living those settlers 'who at present are not yet able to build their own houses'. The list of civilian immigrants sent to Zubov by Kes-Oglu was somewhat ambiguous: it showed '62 settler families of this sort already arrived, and in addition, second-guild merchants – 5, third-guild merchants – 22, and people of various status – 14, of whom those desiring them have received sites for houses, which they have already begun to build'. Kes-Oglu, although zealous in his duties, was finding it impossible to fulfil all the obligations of his Guardianship, and had already suggested the formation of a special panel of 'a few merchants who are Greeks', to deal with the affairs of the Greek civilians.[112]

Zubov concluded that the rapid general increase of population in Odessa augured well for the future of the port, but that it necessitated the creation of a town Magistrature on the basis of the 1775 Provincial Statute, 'both for the benefit of all citizens in general...and also especially for those co-religionist peoples'. The new office, besides its ordinary legal and administrative functions, should administer the funds for Greek civilian settlement in the town, and 'have special care in everything concerning the recruitment of people from abroad and their actual settlement'. In these matters only, it would work with Kes-Oglu and be subject to the supervision of de Ribas.[113] The formation of a Magistrature was approved on the lines suggested, although its personnel allocation was based on that of the Grigoriopol Magistrature created the year before, to which we shall return. In 1796 the new office was duly established, as a Russian Magistrature (intended to represent all Odessan citizens, not specially the foreigners): it opened on 14 January, and an international body of office-holders was at once elected. The mayor (*gorodskaya golova*) was merchant of the second guild Andrey Zheleztsov, the deputy mayors (*burgomistry*) one Migunov, and the Greek Floganti. Other members of the offices were also Greeks.[114] The specific needs of the foreign community, especially the Greeks, were however met shortly after, through the adoption of Kes-Oglu's suggestion of a special panel: in 1797 a separate 'Magistrature for Foreigners' was formally created, with Kes-Oglu as one of the deputy mayors.[115]

Almost simultaneously with his Odessa schemes, Zubov was occupied in drawing up plans for Voznesensk, which was to be his personal contribution and monument in the extension of Russian dominion in the south. He planned to use every available sort of settler. Bulgarians, first, met with his approval because they 'are industrious people, careful in their husbandry, and have a particular inclination to arable farming and horticulture'. Then 'all new colonists from Prussian and other territories' were to be directed to the environs of the town, while craftsmen, especially stone-masons and plasterers, were to be sought 'from among the Greeks and Armenians of Mariupol, and those who have come from Anapa and other Turkish fortresses, our co-religionists. . .now settled in Yekaterinoslav Province'. Native Russians from interior provinces could also provide skills: market gardeners from Rostov, masons and plasterers from Yaroslavl, carpenters from Kostroma, stone-cutters from Olonets; and side by side with these, 'good farmers, and people knowing other crafts simple but of prime necessity, from other well-populated Provinces where lack of land is making itself felt, as for instance: from Tula, Kaluga, Oryol, Kursk Provinces. . ., up to 1,000 peasants from each'.[116]

One particularly desirable category were Old Believers. Native migrants were promised: four-year tax exemption, free maintenance en route and on arrival; free seed for sowing; 15 desyatinas of land per male soul; free housing; and a 50 rouble establishment grant, to be repaid over ten years after the expiry of the exemption period. The total estimate for the construction of Voznesensk was a round 3,000,000 roubles; one item specified was 7,500 roubles for the erection of 'a Moldavian Church in the Bulgarian suburb'.[117]

It is clear from the settlement plans of both Odessa and Voznesensk that much foreign immigration at this time was a result of the second Russo-Turkish war. This was true not only of the Archipelago Greek troops – whom Potemkin before his death had already destined for settlement in the Ochakov District[118] – but also of the Voznesensk Bulgarians, and of various refugee groups, among them the small colony of Turks which settled in Kherson Province in 1792. It applied also to the Nogay Tatars who settled on the Molochna River in 1790, and to some extent too, to the Grigoriopol Armenians; and besides particular groups, the Russian authorities were always on the look-out for stray individuals in the areas occupied by the Russian armies.

The Bulgarians formed part of a larger body of 831 families which had been gathered together at Potemkin's behest 'from various places' on the Danube, and settled on the left bank of the Dniester. This appears to have been done with scant concern for their wishes, and 58 families fled back into Moldavia. The remainder were consequently felt to be unreliable, and 287 families (976 individuals) were moved further away from the border area and re-established on the Bug, on land of their own choice. In 1792 a retired army captain was appointed to supervise the settlement and in 1794 the settlers received a grant of over 13,000 roubles, interest-free for ten years, to provide houses, stock and implements.[119]

The Turks created the colony of Ternovka, outside Nikolayev, with a ten-year grant of 20,000 roubles, and on conditions similar to those of the 1763 Manifesto. They stood initially under the charge of Admiral N. Mordvinov, and in 1795 numbered 64 males and 13 females.[120] The same year Maria Guthrie visited the colony during her tour of the south:

I went today with Lady Mordwinoff and family. . .to see a little Turkish colony a few versts from hence [sc. Nikolayev], consisting of about a hundred souls, with a Turkish naval officer at their head. This gentleman, called Salih Aga, was sent by the famous Captain Bashaw, Hasan Pasha, to transact some business with the Field-Marshal Prince Potemkin, then commanding the Russian armies; during which time he had the misfortune to lose his protector, then Grand Vizier; and, as he was sure that on his return he should be persecuted by the numerous enemies of the deceased minister, as well as those of the Hospodar of Wallachia, Prince Nicolas Marvoine, just beheaded, who had equally protected him, he took the wise resolution to keep his own head on his shoulders by remaining in Russia, and was made a Brigadier-General in the naval service of her Imperial Majesty.

This little colony is pleasantly situated on the Ingul, and well lodged in snug stone houses, with the free exercise of their religion, customs etc.; as we soon perceived by their manner of living, and by a handsome little mosque; in short, they seem to be in a very comfortable thriving state, and the Turks are much better cultivators than I expected to find them.[121]

In 1799, at their own wish, the Turks moved to the town of Karasu-Bazar.[122] Ternovka was later re-occupied by Bulgarians.

The Nogay Tatars who settled on the Molochna river, to the north-east of the Crimean peninsula, in 1790, were sent there by order of Potemkin from the eastern end of the Sea of Azov (Yey steppe). They formed part of the Budzhak and Yedisan hordes which had come over to Russia during the first Turkish war;[123] and since then they had had mixed fortunes, since the authorities never really trusted them, and they were twice moved to different areas, with very harmful economic results. In December 1790 Potemkin again wished to remove them from proximity with the Turks, in case they should turn against the Russians during their Caucasian operations; so he ordered that some should be sent eastwards, and the rest westwards to the Molochna.[124]

The progressive trans-settlement of Nogay to the Molochna continued for a number of years – one particularly large group, of some

1,000 families, came in 1795. An order to the Russian commanders in the Caucasus and on the Kuban of March 1792, dealing with these people, is striking for the careful tone it adopts towards them: they are to be given 'all necessary advantages and tranquillity' in order to encourage them to take up a settled way of life, but the transformation is to be achieved strictly on a voluntary basis, 'persuading them by the example of mildness and justice...and by urging those extensive privileges accorded to all peoples moving to settle under Our sceptre (*derzhava*) by the Manifesto of 14 July 1785'.[125] Thus the Nogay were explicitly included within the framework of the immigration policy; and the government seems at this stage to have been trying to make up for some of the hardships which its previous policy had inflicted on them. Like other foreign colonists, but without the 'colonist' title and under a separate administration, they became the object of particular government concern: a special Board (*Ekspeditsiya Nogayskikh Ord*) was set up to administer their settlement.[126] By the end of the eighteenth century the Molochna Nogay numbered about 16,000 (of both sexes).[127]

The Armenian founders of the town of Grigoriopol likewise came from areas affected by the war of 1787–91: the towns in the south – Izmail, Kilia, Bendery – occupied by the Russian forces. The first stages of the settlement were carried out by arrangement between Potemkin and the Armenian Archbishop Joseph Argutinsky, an ardent nationalist and outstanding member of the Armenian community in Russia. Grigoriopol was designed as a completely Armenian town on the lines of Nakhichevan (although subsequently the local provincial administration and non-Armenian settlers soon encroached on the privileges granted to the community). Together, Kakhovsky and Argutinsky solmenly laid the foundation stone on 15 July 1792. Proper construction began only in 1794, when the town's Magistrature was also set up. Despite difficult beginnings, Grigoriopol became one of the most important of the frontier towns established on the new eastern border. In 1793–4 it had a population of 4,052.[128]

Although the Armenians of Grigoriopol came principally from the towns of Bessarabia, the colony, as we have seen, had its roots in the previous decade. It shared this feature with the Mennonite immigrants of the 1790s: between the years 1793 and 1796, 118 families came from Prussia to join their compatriots in the Khortitsa colonies.[129] The same applied to the Moldavian settlers of the Ochakov District, who, however, as before, were not considered 'colonists', but settled under the terms of the Plan for the Yekaterinoslav Province. And a number of other foreign or alien groups settled in New Russia at this time, with the consent and encouragement of the New Russian administration, but not on its initiative: land-hungry Germans from the Petersburg colonies,[130] French royalists hoping to restore their fortunes,[131] Greeks from the Ionian island of Zante.[132]

Thus in a number of cases, foreign settlement in New Russia in the last years of Catherine's reign did not depend on the initiative of the administration, but had external or prior causes. In this sense, the historian Ye. Zagorovsky is correct in speaking of foreign immigration at the time as 'a series of separate episodes, not connected by a common conception, and not producing in their results such a quantity of colonizing material as we saw under Potemkin'. He is also correct in attributing this in part to 'the lack of energy and talents in Zubov himself and his assistants' – though it should be added that Zubov had much less time at his disposal than did his predecessor. Quite unacceptable, however, is Zagorovsky's claim to see a 'general cooling towards colonizing questions...in the last years of Catherine's reign, in the Empress herself and her collaborators'.[133] A coherent policy aimed at encouraging foreign immigration is clearly evident in this period, and it equally clearly emanated quite as much from the circle of the Empress as from the New Russian administration.

Another aspect of policy in the 1790s draws attention: the obvious return to reliance on the 1763 Manifesto as the basis of immigration for individual groups. The provisions of the Manifesto had not been entirely superseded under Potemkin. His papers on the Taganrog Greeks, for example, contain relevant extracts from sub-clauses of section VI, and the conditions of migration 'requested' by the Crimean Christians were in fact a point-by-point restatement of the Manifesto.[134] But in general, Potemkin preferred to offer or negotiate separate conditions with each contingent, according to circumstances (a procedure and right itself of course guaranteed to immigrants by the 1763 proclamation). In the later period, the actual provisions of the Manifesto were taken as the foundation in a majority of cases mentioned – explicitly for the Zante Greeks and those settling in Odessa; implicitly and not in all points, in the case of the Turks and the Bulgarians. This, too, suggests a lessening of self-sufficiency and flexibility in the administration after 1791.

One other factor deserves mention at this point: the importance of precedent in the acquisition of foreign settlers. Perhaps the best example was the Greek Brotherhood of Nezhin. Their privileges are cited or referred to in the petitions of almost every southern Greek community from Yelizavetgrad in 1754[135] to Odessa in 1797.[136] The Crimean, and later the Grigoriopol, Armenians also served as points of reference for subsequent arrivals;[137] the second contingent of Khortitsa Mennonites, as well as subsequent settlers in Khortitsa and the later Molochna settlement, followed as a direct result of the establishment of the first. Thus the extreme concern for reputation and precedent so frequently found in almost all stages of Catherine's immigration policy[138] was to some extent justified.

So the active policy adopted in New Russia from 1775 to 1796 with regard to foreign immigration enjoyed a considerable measure of success. It brought in a numerous and varied body of foreign settlers, who contributed in general to the population of the region, and in particular cases to its economic development, especially in the new towns. But in relation to the general tempo and character of colonization and mass settlement in New Russia, the policy was somewhat misconceived. The rulers of Southern Russia never made foreign immigration the exclusive object of policy which it had been in the 1760s; but they certainly expended on it very considerable resources of money and personnel. Yet throughout the south foreign immigrants – even including Moldavians and Vlachs – were always outnumbered by settlers of Great Russian and Ukrainian stock; and the relative importance of foreigners in the population figures shrank steadily as time went by. As Soviet writers have emphasized,[139] in numerical terms foreigners were of secondary importance in the settlement and assimilation of New Russia in the eighteenth century. Their contribution in the economic sphere was more important than their numbers, but still not a crucial factor in the overall picture, although they played a very important role in some areas of industry and commerce, or in such spheres as the politics of Russo-Turkish relations. And even when they were of good quality, foreigners cost the state far more than did native settlers, in terms both of cash and of administration, and they were usually slower to adapt themselves to local conditions. Realization of these facts became increasingly widespread at the close of the century, and found partial expression in the new Rules on immigration of 1804.

5

Urban and entrepreneurial settlement under the 1763 Manifesto

Context and policy

According to the Manifesto of 1763, foreigners settling in towns were free to choose their own occupations, and received certain exemptions and concessions; but they were offered no exclusive rights which would set them apart socially from their fellow-townsmen. The majority, as was natural in a group consisting predominantly of artisans, appear to have become members of the craft guilds. The entrepreneurs, however, were usually placed directly under the Chancellery of Guardianship, instead of being subject to the College of Manufactures (*Manufaktur-Kollegiya*) and its Office (*Manufaktur-Kontora*).

Throughout most of the eighteenth century the College, in accordance with the rights and duties set out in its founding Statute (*Manufaktur-Reglament*),[1] exercised control over all Russian manufacturing industry. Only heavy industry – mining and metallurgy – was controlled by the College of Mines (*Berg-Kollegiya*). Officially, all other enterprises set up in Russia had to receive the consent of the College of Manufactures and accept its supervision. Such licensed (*ukaznyye*) enterprises and entrepreneurs enjoyed considerable privileges and exemptions; and the College was always on the lookout for unlicensed operators, whom it pursued with great vigour, but little success. This situation lasted until 1775, when Catherine finally abolished all restrictions on manufacturing enterprise.[2] The abolition of the system led directly to the abolition of the College itself in 1779.[3]

In the later period of its existence, the College of Manufactures was located in Moscow and had under its jurisdiction the industry of almost the whole of Russia; the exceptions were the Petersburg area, with a small part of the Baltic region and of the then Novgorod Province, which were controlled by the College's Office, located in the new capital.[4]

The College of Manufactures dealt equally with native and with foreign manufacturers, and the latter often took advantage of the College's power to provide loans to entrepreneurs.[5] In general, foreign enterprise and expertise had a large part to play in the early stages of Russian industrial development. We cannot go further into this question here.[6] Suffice it to note that, in the later eighteenth and early nineteenth centuries, foreign entrepreneurs played a pioneering role in several important branches of industry, for instance the Dane, Christian Lieman, in cotton printing,[7] or the Scot Charles Baird in metallurgy and machine construction;[8] while the foreign expert in government service is a recurring phenomenon from the beginnings right up to 1917, and beyond. A third category deserving mention consisted of foreigners who entered into association with Russians who could supply essential capital. Silk stocking manufacturer Benjamin Müller, for instance, set up a factory in 1758, then sold it three years later to Count S. P. Yaguzhinsky. Müller stayed on as director. Yaguzhinsky, rich and well-connected, provided capital and serf labour; and in 1762 he even secured an increase in import duties on foreign stockings together with a five-year ban on new stocking factories, on condition that he meet all Russian demands, at stated prices. The factory did well, and developed a considerable volume and variety of production in silken goods; though by the mid-1780s it had accumulated debt and had to be sold off.[9]

The 'factories', or manufacturing enterprises, set up in Petersburg and elsewhere under the immigration programme were subject to the control of the College of Manufactures and its Office only in certain cases. The College demanded, and received from the Chancellery of Guardianship, details of all new establishments, and sometimes applications were considered by both it and the Chancellery, jointly, or even apparently separately. But immediate control and responsibility normally rested with the Chancellery or an appointed representative (for instance, the Office in Saratov).

Compared with the scope of a Yaguzhinsky or the success of a Lieman, the achievements of the Chancellery's entrepreneurs were rather modest. Despite the welcome promised in the 1763 Manifesto, the Chancellery was in general disinclined to accept anyone in this category under its own jurisdiction unless they fulfilled a particular need, or appeared likely to make a clear contribution to the nation's industrial development. And this attitude was soon reflected in the circulars sent out to diplomats abroad.

Initially, instructions on the matter bore a fairly positive tone. In May 1763, Gross from The Hague reported that a bankrupt silk master from Lyons, Dumont, wished to come and establish himself in Russia at state expense, bringing with him three companions, including 'one of the best Lyons silk designers'. Catherine wrote on the report:

Write to Musin-Pushkin [in Hamburg, where Dumont was waiting] that he should make an agreement with him on the cost of his journey here; and to all Ministers that if they are approached by *fabrikanty* and *manu-fakturshchiki*, they should first assure themselves as to these people's skill, and then finance them at my expense, if they ask help for the journey to Russia.

As for Dumont himself, whose proposals had evidently found favour, 'Kronstadt, Tsarskoye Selo, Peterhof, the Strelna estate, Oranienbaum are open to him for setting up his factory, and all help will be given'.[10] Five months later, however, in the same October rescript which called for maximization of peasant immigration, orders were going out that utmost care should be exercised, and only 'useful' entrepreneurs accepted, after careful consultation with Petersburg. There is no necessary contradiction here: no material promises were made to Dumont beyond 'all assistance', which did not necessarily mean anything more than the conditions promised by the *Manufaktur-Reglament*. But the attitude expressed in the later instructions was quite different. This rethinking apparently resulted from such cases as those of Lacombe and Vandier:[11] for these two were neither the first nor the last. Silk seems to have been popular with such early entrepreneurial applicants; the October rescript speaks of 'silk and other manufacturers', while the decision on principle to refuse permission for new silk production in Petersburg itself had been taken on earlier proposals from a 'silk manufacturer Richard'.[12]

In August of the following year, the government felt constrained to explain its position at length. Most foreigners who had so far applied (Ministers abroad were told) had an inaccurate idea both of the nature and of the level of development of Russian industry: they were unaware of the highly-centralized organization of production in many enterprises, and they imagined that even a mediocre technician from the West would be welcomed with open arms. The result was a waste of time and money, and disillusionment on all sides. Consequently (the circular continued) money would not normally be made available to set up factories at state expense; but all assistance (including loans as opposed to grants) would be given to foreign entrepreneurs who could establish themselves at their own expense, and prove their reliability.

Any arrangement in these cases should therefore adhere closely to the provisions of the 1763 Manifesto, to avoid both loss to the Treasury and 'complaint by those foreigners who have been deceived by their own imaginings'.[13]

This more restrictive approach, which contrasted favourably with official optimism regarding agricultural settlement, reflected thinking in some official circles on industrialization in general, and accorded with the policy of the College of Manufactures. Catherine herself expressed doubts, at this time and later, as to the wisdom of introducing advanced techniques in the then economic and social context of Russia.[14] The College, even when favourably impressed by a foreign project, felt that traditional Russian organizational forms and methods were more appropriate. This was its reaction in 1764 to proposals received from one Franz Joseph Lindemann, 'Director of the Manufactures and Factories of His Highness the Elector of Bavaria', for the establishment of large-scale woollen cloth and silk production in Russia. The project included a sheep farm, textile mill, and dyeing plant, all to be set up at state expense and run (allegedly very profitably) by Lindemann, with foreign technicians and Russian labour. The College admitted the usefulness of this type and scale of production; but it doubted Lindemann's arithmetic, and felt that in any case it would be extremely difficult to find workers and a site to fulfil his requirements. Furthermore, Lindemann's promise to employ local labour was in fact a disadvantage,

for if, as he proposes, such a multitude of people were taken from the land and the villages and appointed to the factory, then – in addition to the great cost involved – their removal from agriculture is itself harmful in the condition of this State, and on the contrary, the increase of such factories in the villages...is not only easier and more readily to be achieved, but also those peasants engaged in the industrial work, and especially in the preparation and spinning of wool...can continue their agriculture un-abated and carry out factory work in time free from labour in the fields.

Lindemann could therefore come to Russia on the basis of the *Manufaktur-Reglament*, or apply to the Chancellery of Guardianship; but a state undertaking could not be contemplated.[15]

The only normal exceptions to this ruling were completely new types of production. Thus the College, shortly before rejecting Lindemann, had shown itself ready to finance two Englishmen, Kelly and Bury, who proposed to introduce 'semi-silk and woollen English materials' not then manufactured in Russia. After established native textile producers had proved unwilling to take up the Englishmen's offer on their

own mills, the College decided to set up the foreigners itself, adding that
when the new venture was properly under way, 'in accordance with the
above-mentioned decrees of the College's statute, it will be necessary to
give that factory, for its greatest increase, to the glory and benefit of the
state, to reliable private persons wishing to conduct it'.[16] The one state
enterprise known to the present writer which was set up within the
colonist context was the textile mill at Yamburg, established in the
1760s under the Frenchman Levallier. This mill, whose history is discussed at greater length below,[17] was designed precisely to make fine
cloths not otherwise produced in Russia, and it was in fact offered for
sale to private buyers. But the development of Yamburg represented
altogether something of a special case.

Besides the loan system administered by the College, and governed
by § 23 of the *Reglament*, financial backing was also available from the
Chancellery of Guardianship, which could and did make advances
from its own funds to all the entrepreneurs whom it engaged. But the
authorities' cautious approach, the favouring of traditional forms or
existing native industry, and the soaring costs of the Saratov and other
settlements, all militated against the acceptance of large numbers of
foreign entrepreneurs under the immigration programme.

Immigrant artisans experienced no such difficulties with the Chancellery; they could at once take membership in the craft guilds of the
town in which they settled. Western artisans in Saratov and Astrakhan
as well as in the capitals stood on the same footing as their Russian (and
other Western) neighbours; while immigrants such as the Armenians in
Astrakhan also joined institutions already created for their nationality.[18]

Merchant and craft guilds (*gildii* and *tsekhi*) had been introduced
into Russia by Peter I in an attempt to encourage crafts and commerce,
and to improve technical skills.[19] The three merchant guilds, ranked
according to the capital possessed by members, included not only
merchants and traders in the strict commercial meaning of these terms,
but also (among others) non-noble entrepreneurs. In the eighteenth and
nineteenth centuries, 'merchant' (*kupets*) was an elastic, not to say
elusive, term; and the same was true to some extent of 'craftsman' or
'artisan' (*remeslennik*). The guilds were placed under the overall jurisdiction of the Chief Magistrature (*Glavnyy Magistrat*) in Petersburg,
and locally under the Magistrature of their own town.

During the eighteenth century, the strength and status of the craft
guilds varied considerably. Like their merchant counterparts, they were
artificial creations of the state, not in keeping with the tradition of

crafts in Russia; and guild membership, while conferring certain advantages, carried with it a liability to perform work on contract for the state whenever this might be necessary. Russian craft guilds did not have the complete monopoly enjoyed by their Western counterparts and models, and had to bear competition from itinerant outsiders, largely peasants, or from anyone who wished and was able to set up on his own. Membership was only obligatory for those who wished to take apprentices and exhibit a sign, while craftsmen working by themselves for private sale could remain outside.

Worse still, there were insufficient powers to enforce the official regulations. It was difficult to ensure full registration of those obliged to register, and then to control those who did. When in 1761, for example, the Senate tried to direct the Petersburg joiners' guild to carry out work in the Winter Palace, the order met with a poor response: the Guildhall (*Gil'dyanskiy* or *Gil'deyskiy Dom*), the headquarters of guild administration in Petersburg, reported that so many Russian joiners had been taken into the Construction Office of Tsarskoye Selo and other bodies carrying out official work, that none were paying dues to the Guildhall, and not one was now available to meet the Senate's requisition;

and as to whether there are any master-joiners available in the German guild, the Guildhall does not know; since these craftsmen have stubbornly refused hitherto to pay any taxes for civic needs, and as a result of their disobedience, they do not stand in the jurisdiction of the Guildhall.[20]

This incident illustrates two further points. Firstly, government bodies which used skilled workmen had their own permanent employees; and although these should legally have been guild members, in practice they rarely were, since each official body wished to maintain exclusive control over its own men.[21] Secondly, foreign craftsmen had from the outset the right, frequently used, to form their own separate guilds, called German or foreign, instead of joining the Russian organizations. Both types existed in many towns with a foreign population.

The condition of the craft guilds in Russia was a matter for constant criticism throughout the eighteenth century. Those, and there were many, who saw in them a socially and economically valuable institution, repeatedly emphasized the need for closer control of handicrafts, and more efficient organization.[22] In 1760 Elizabeth Petrovna's Conference cited the bad state of the guilds as a major obstacle to the recruitment of much-needed foreign artisans.[23] Several instructions to deputies to the Legislative Commission of 1767 stressed the point.[24] Successive administrative changes did not make a great deal of difference to the situation in practice, and it remained much the same throughout the period under consideration.

The guilds themselves were in any case very unevenly spread over the country, being in general better organized and developed in towns on the periphery of European Russia than in the central provinces. Petersburg, as the capital, the city in which guild organization was first introduced in 1721, and the domicile of a large number of foreign artisans accustomed to and benefiting from guild membership, had by far the most numerous and most prosperous craft guilds in the Empire. In the towns of the Volga region, too, guild organization was well developed, and here also the foreign elements had a definite part to play.

The Volga region: the Astrakhan Armenians

Astrakhan had a very mixed population, lying as it did in an ethnically complex region, and attracting numerous foreigners by reason of its commerce. Figures for the male population in 1783 show 16,724 Russians, 5,116 Tatars, some 2,000 Armenians, 179 Ukrainians, 103 Kalmyk, 89 Indians, 86 Georgians, 84 Germans and 79 Persians.[25] The 'Asians' (the term was used loosely) enjoyed special status and their own administrative structure: privileges often resented by other townspeople and by the local authorities. The Armenians, for example, had repeatedly to struggle to maintain their independent status.[26] Ultimately, however, these struggles were successful: the central government, and also the more perceptive of the administrators on the spot, fully appreciated the value to Russia of the immigrants and, with some vacilliations, official policy remained favourable to them throughout the century. Fully in this spirit were the proposals for the area made by V. N. Tatishchev during his Governorship of Astrakhan (1741–5), which stressed among other things the desirability of foreign immigration. His representations led to decrees of 1744 and 1746 which specified at length the exemptions and privileges to be given to Eastern immigrants, and laid the foundation for the subsequent prosperity of the foreign communities.[27]

Together with the Armenians, the Indians were the most important of Astrakhan's foreign inhabitants. In view of their significance in the town, their numbers appear small; but this derived from the way of life which they adopted, described here by Academician Ozeretskovsky, who visited the town in the 1780s:

The Indian bazaar (*gostinniy dvor*) is built like a stone barricade such as one finds around old monasteries. In it live and trade the Indians, of whom there are some one hundred persons. Their little rooms have no windows on to the street, but only openings in the ceiling, through which light enters. They come out from India through Persia at an early age with very small means, which they then increase in Astrakhan by trade, and living there continuously for ten, twenty or thirty years, become extremely wealthy, so that some among them have now one or more hundred thousand roubles in their possession.

They register themselves neither in the merchantry, nor in the Asian urban community (*meshchanstvo*), and therefore hold no civic posts. They merely pay an annual quit-rent of twelve roubles per shop. They have commercial contacts with Persia, Khiva and Bukhara, neither do they neglect to trade also with the Russian inhabitants and especially with the Astrakhan Tatars.

They give the Tatars goods on credit at terrible rates of interest, so that these poor people are eternally in their debt, and frequently pay off their creditors by handing over their wives. This is the origin of the Agryzhan Tatars in Astrakhan, whom the Indians (none of whom have wives of their own here) have begotten with the Tatar women, the wives of their debtors.[28]

The Armenians, by contrast, brought their wives and families with them; the majority, while maintaining contacts with their homeland, took Russian citizenship and regarded Russia as their permanent domicile. Whereas the growth of their community in the first half of the century came largely from immigration, the spectacular expansion of the second half – from about 1,500 to over 5,000 – was more the result of natural increase, although immigration continued at a significant level.[29]

In the 1750s and 1760s government policy on Astrakhan favoured Asian, and particularly Armenian, settlement as before, both by general measures to promote Russia's Eastern trade,[30] and by steps aimed at maintaining or improving the settlers' position.[31] In particular, a decree of 1763, coinciding with the final deliberations on the second immigration Manifesto, gave the Astrakhan Armenians the right to build additional churches, which had become necessary with the growth in numbers – a right granted explicitly to encourage immigration.[32]

The following year, when the Governor of Astrakhan proposed changes in the town's administration which would virtually abolish the special status of Asians, his plans were completely rejected. First, an Imperial decree ordered him to base all further measures strictly on the 1763 Manifesto, article VI, § 5 of which, on internal self-government it was said, could quite correctly be applied to these groups. A second decree pointed out that the facts given in the Governor's own report proved the value of these foreigners; that they paid for their privileges by a special tax; and that, consequently, any 'improvements' which the Governor wished to make in administration should be effected gradually, proceeding by consent and not by force:

for to give them greater inclination to live here, some freedom according to their status must of course be allowed them, since by the Manifesto concerning foreigners and those settling in separate colonies and hamlets, internal jurisdiction is left to their discretion.[33]

Government protection of the Armenians in Astrakhan was paralleled by efforts to facilitate their migration to the town. Most Armenian immigrants came to Astrakhan from, or through, Persian territory. Neither Persia nor Turkey, as dominant powers in Transcaucasia, could favour such migration; and therefore, both in general regulations and in practice, the Russian authorities sought to avoid giving offence.[34] The prize was worth having. The Armenians brought large capital investment to the Eastern trade, and in the middle decades of the century outstripped other nationalities engaged in it. In 1764 they accounted for 53% by value of all imports, and 40% of all exports, through Astrakhan. They were dominant besides in the silk and cotton industries of the area, also objects of special government interest, which reached the height of their development in the second half of the eighteenth century. In 1787, one of the peak years of the silk industry, there were 38 silk-weaving enterprises operating 298 looms in Astrakhan, of which 32, with 268 looms, were owned by Armenians. Figures for cotton cloth production from the same period show 250 enterprises: 209 Armenian, 27 Tatar and 14 Russian. Silk production in the town fell into decline at the end of the century, partly from a fall in general demand, partly under increasing competition from other textile producers, notably Sarepta and the Volga German colonies. Cotton production was maintained and increased, however, into the nineteenth century.[35]

The average number of looms in the Astrakhan 'factories' indicates the general small scale of production; in fact many of these entrepreneurs were considered not as merchants but as craftsmen. Figures for the Astrakhan craft guilds in the 1750s show 322 Armenian members, together with 173 Russians and 48 Tatars, a total of 543 in 26 guilds. Of the Armenians, 115 were listed as manufacturers (*fabrikanty*) and their workers. The largest of these producers owned 19 looms, none of the others more than 8.[36]

Since Asians were exempt from obligatory civil and military service, there were few Armenian civil servants in Astrakhan. The only exception was the staff of the local Customs authority, in which they held most of the senior posts.[37] There were, however, a considerable number of clergy; and as the eparchial centre for all Armenians in Russia, Astrakhan was the seat (from the early 1770s) of Archbishop Joseph Argutinsky. Argutinsky's passionate concern for the fate of his native country was shared by other members of the Armenian community and – rather like Odessa for the Greek independence movement in the nineteenth century – Astrakhan became a centre of Armenian nationalist sentiment and activity.[38]

The Russo-Turkish war of 1768–74 naturally raised the hopes of the Armenian patriots in Astrakhan. One of these, Moysey Sarafov, put his hopes into writing, and in July 1769 sent to the College of Foreign Affairs proposals for joint Russian–Armenian action to free Armenia from Turkish domination. Armenian troops, raised from the expatriates living in Moscow and the southern border towns, were to march with a Russian expeditionary force to join the Georgian Tsar against the common enemy. The aim was the restoration of a national Armenian dynasty under the protection and suzerainty of Russia. In presenting his proposals, Sarafov styled himself 'Astrakhan silk farm owner'. The Armenian historian Academician A. R. Ioannisyan, in his account of this episode, describes him as a 'rich and influential Armenian entrepreneur and merchant, who had connections in government circles and even at the Court itself'. In the matter of the project, Sarafov was acting not simply in his own name, but on behalf of a whole group of the Armenian *haute bourgeoisie* then living in Russia, including the Court jeweller Ivan Lazarev.[39]

Nothing came of Sarafov's proposals. N. I. Panin, to whom they were relayed, found them 'not worthy of consideration'; he merely had enquiries made in Georgia about the possibility of using Armenians against the Turks. And although Tsar Heraklius of Georgia gave a favourable judgement on this question and a Russian expeditionary force did cross the Caucasus in 1769, the expedition's aim was only to support Heraklius, and no further action was undertaken.[40]

If Sarafov was unsuccessful in the political field, however, he had better fortune elsewhere. It would seem that he could indeed rely on influential connections in Petersburg; and the value of these contacts became apparent in dealings which he conducted over a number of years with the Chancellery of Guardianship for Foreigners, and in the unusually strong support which he received from it. He approached the Chancellery almost immediately after its creation, seeking permission and assistance to set up a silk farm near Astrakhan. 'In consideration of the fact that this enterprise is very useful for the Russian state', the Chancellery agreed, and obtained authorization for a grant of as much land as should be needed and a loan of ten thousand roubles (later increased to fifteen thousand). Permission was also given for the purchase of up to three hundred male souls.[41]

Sarafov set to work; but there were delays and difficulties. His guarantor died in the following year, and most of the loan had to be returned. Yet cash was essential; 'for the transfer to the farm of the peasants he is buying, and for the establishment of arable farming there, it is essential in this settling of peasants to make a dam covering a wide area, in view of the flooding in those parts'. The Chancellery finally relented, and Sarafov was able to proceed.[42] Even now, however, he had difficulty in finding sufficient serfs to buy from private owners: there were relatively few serfs at this time in the lower Volga region, the immediate environs of Astrakhan. In 1769 the Governor of Astrakhan proposed the sale to private buyers of the labour force at the unsuccessful Akhtuba state silk farm, near Tsaritsyn. One bidder had already appeared. But the Chancellery intervened strongly in favour of Sarafov, whose farm was suffering from the lack of labour, and who in any case was ready to offer a higher price: competition between two bidders would bring more profit to the Crown.[43]

The sale did not in fact take place. Sarafov did succeed in establishing his farm, but, like other similar enterprises to be mentioned shortly, it achieved no great importance in the long run. We have a glimpse of it from the diary kept by V. G. Orlov during his journey down the Volga to Astrakhan in 1767. On 27 June he dined with Sarafov, and visited his plantation. The number of mulberries was not yet very great. Sarafov was also trying to grow cotton; and Orlov noted three mills used to irrigate the farm.[44]

Raw silk production was not the only area in which Sarafov enjoyed the Chancellery's support. In 1763 the latter ordered the Astrakhan authorities to allow him to build merchant ships on the Caspian, a privilege claimed by the Russian merchants of Astrakhan as theirs alone.[45] And when, on a voyage to Persia in 1765, a vessel belonging to Sarafov suffered the loss of essential tackle, forcibly appropriated in a crisis by a Russian government official, interpreter Shubin, the Chancellery took the matter to the Senate, defeated the College of Foreign Affairs which tried to defend the culprit, and at long last – ten years later – won restitution to Sarafov for damage and lost profits to the sum of 830 roubles 96 kopeks.[46]

The permission granted to Sarafov to build ships led to a clash between the Governor, Beketov, and the Armenian community at large. The Russian merchants in Astrakhan protested to Beketov, who took up their cause. His arguments were that only townsmen of Astrakhan (*meshchane*), not foreigners, had the right to own ships, and that in any case Armenians were unreliable and gave information treacherously to Persia. The Chancellery insisted, nonetheless, that Sarafov should go ahead, and should be given every assistance in his undertaking; whereupon another prominent Armenian merchant, Grigoriy Kampanyan, or Kampanov, petitioned the Senate for the same right to be extended to all his countrymen in Astrakhan. The Chancellery's evidence supported him.

After due deliberation, the Senate decided that Armenians who had taken the oath of loyalty to the Crown were as much true citizens, and had the same rights, as anyone else in Astrakhan. As far as the accusation of treachery was concerned, the Senate considered it quite unfounded: the only evidence offered was in fact the case not of an Armenian at all, but of a Russian, 'the Astrakhan *posadskiy chelovek* Ivan Stolarev, who converted to Islam in Persia and to please Gedayem Khan of Ryashcha built a regular sea-going ship and several sloops'. Permission was given for all Armenians to operate merchant vessels, and the Governor was called upon to justify his actions in the matter.[47] In other contexts, Beketov appears as an energetic official interested in the development of the area under his control.[48] In his dealings with the Armenian community in Astrakhan, his attitude seems to have been very similar to that of the Saratov Voyevoda's Chancellery towards the Saratov urban settlers in 1764: and it provoked the same angry response from the Senate.[49]

The Volga region:
Western and other entrepreneurs in Astrakhan and Saratov

Moisey Sarafov was perhaps the most considerable, but he was by no means the only entrepreneur whom the Chancellery of Guardianship helped to establish in the Volga region in the first years after its creation. A number of French and German immigrants applied to the Chancellery for money, land and assistance for similar purposes; and the majority, like Sarafov, were concerned with the production of silk in some form. Astrakhan, as has already been noted, attracted a few

Western silk weavers, who probably made up the bulk of those Westerners mentioned as living in the town in 1763 and later. Other colonists found their way to Astrakhan on the same basis: the two Greek brothers Kumanov, who joined the Russian navy in 1769, had originally gone there in 1764 under the immigration legislation to set up a silk farm and vineyard.[50] Most of these people were hired workers or single weavers, but one man at least, Johann Svenson, who went to Astrakhan in 1763 in company with 'silk manufacturer Lumberg', obtained a grant of over five thousand roubles to make silks and semi-silks, and succeeded in establishing himself on a somewhat larger scale.[51] He was the only Westerner among seven Astrakhan entrepreneurs visited by V. G. Orlov. Svenson was then producing woven silk on ten German looms; he boasted to Orlov of the much greater efficiency of the German, as compared with the Persian, type.[52]

The general impact of the immigrants on the town of Saratov has already been noted. They represented a variety of trades and constituted a considerable addition to the town's artisan population; and the entrepreneurs among them contributed to a general, if slight and brief, rise in industrial activity there. Ye. Kusheva, in her study of the town at this time, notes that the 1760s and early 1770s 'are marked by a certain expansion' in the industrial field, although 'not so much in the results achieved, as in the variety and number of attempts to establish factory production'; and colonist enterprise played a clear role in this.[53]

Immigrants' projects were certainly varied. Three stand out particularly among them. Two were run by Frenchmen, Antoine Verdier and François Palisse, and the third by a German, Erich Vorsprecher. Verdier received a grant of 6,000 roubles for sericulture and silk weaving; with his associate Jean Roux, he had come to Petersburg from Hamburg in 1764, and negotiated a contract with the Chancellery of Guardianship giving them money and 60 desyatinas of land to develop a mulberry plantation outside Saratov and to breed silkworms. Verdier's obligations included the training of 12 apprentices from local garrison schools, in both sericulture and the manufacture of silk stockings, for 5 years.[54] He made a successful start, and by 1769 he had over 50,000 mulberries.[55] He later sold the plantation to a local merchant and devoted himself to running his stocking factory in the town.[56] Under its new owner, the plantation languished; in 1767 the stocking factory was producing silk stockings, but on only three looms, and taffeta, both of 'excellent quality'; also satin, 'much inferior'.[57]

The other Frenchman, François Palisse, perhaps the most successful colonist manufacturer in Saratov, set himself up as a hatter. Like Verdier, Palisse came from Hamburg with an associate, Antoine Socier, and their families, and the two concluded a contract with the Chancellery of Guardianship in 1764. They travelled at their own cost, promised to bring in skilled workers from abroad (at government expense), to train three Russian apprentices, and to repay within 10 years a loan of 4,000 roubles and the cost of the factory which was to be built for them. In return, they received all the personal concessions promised to immigrants; free land for the factory, which the Chancellery agreed to erect in view of their initial inexperience of Russian conditions; and grants of land for themselves personally, as well as 60 desyatina plots for each of their workers. Socier on reaching Moscow refused to go any further; but Palisse went on to Saratov and duly started production. Most of his goods were bought by the army, but 'feather-down and new woollen hats' from his factory, 'cleanly made', sold in Saratov at from 2 to 5 roubles, and were exported as far afield as Moscow.[58]

The third more notable figure, the German Erich Vorsprecher, received an advance of 2,400 roubles and was also to set up a factory, for the production of 'silk, semi-silk and cotton materials'.[59] References to cotton and woollen production in Saratov, quoted by Kusheva,[60] most probably relate to this undertaking. All three enterprises were under the control of the local authority, at first the Voyevoda's Chancellery, then the Guardianship Office. The scanty and sometimes unclear details on Vorsprecher's factory supplied by Shafranov and Kusheva can be supplemented from the memoirs of Christian Züge, who worked for Vorsprecher in Saratov, and whose personal account of the Saratov entrepreneurs and their operations is best allowed to speak for itself:

There existed [in Saratov] three factories set up by foreigners. In one silk stockings were manufactured, in another hats, in both the directors were Frenchmen. The third, in which cotton cloths and scarves were produced, had been set up by a German named Vorsprecher, who with his wife was a native of Leipzig, and who had had a factory in Poland before he came to Saratov. Each of these three manufacturers had received a house and a considerable cash advance from the government. Vorsprecher got four thousand, the hatter seven thousand roubles, which however did not seem very secure in the hands of either of these people. In particular the hatter quite obviously spent far more money than the profit from his factory could warrant, as it only employed a few people. Nevertheless he kept four horses, which were used almost exclusively for his pleasure, as he seldom had need of them in his business. He never drove or rode out without servants in attendance, and in general his lifestyle was as magnificent as that of the greatest houses in Saratov.

Things did not look much better in the case of the cloth manufacturer. It is true that when I came to Saratov he had four people working for him, of whom two were Germans, and the other two Mordvinian Tatars who had learnt the trade previously in the factory of an Armenian in Astrakhan...; but when one looked a little closer, one soon saw that things were going backwards rather than forwards for Mr Vorsprecher. The reason for this was partly his ignorance of the Russian language, which he made no effort to learn, but a more immediate cause lay in the dissatisfactions of his relationship with his wife. She was nearing sixty, and could no longer meet the demands and wishes of a man in his prime. So Vorsprecher sought consolation with the Russian women, which had the double disadvantage that he neglected his business affairs, and also spent many a rouble on these excursions which would have been much better invested in his enterprise and trade.

... These two manufacturers had received advances without being able to provide testimonials to show that the money was well spent on them. Their poor success soon proved the contrary...Nevertheless no closer investigation was made, and nobody thought of saving what could still be salvaged before it was too late.[61]

Besides the three principal colonist manufacturers, one Jean Robinot set up a soap works in the town; and early in 1766 a German colonist, Silberstrom, joined with three local Russian merchants, who stood surety for him, to start a vitriol works just outside it. Silberstrom received 500 roubles from the Voyevoda's Chancellery; production began, but the Russian partners deceived and finally robbed Silberstrom, leaving him in 'total poverty'. By 1768 the enterprise had completely collapsed.[62]

One or two colonist undertakings in the Saratov region were less closely connected with the main towns. The project of a Greek, named as Papa Dmitriu, to 'raise livestock for the making of tallow candles and various edible dairy products', seems to have required a rural setting; and the conditions attached to the Empress's consent suggest that she envisaged his settling in the Volga area.[63] The French merchant Bousserole, an associate of the unsuccessful *vyzyvatel'* d'Haucourt and the jeweller Ador, set up a considerable silk farm near the Novokhopyorskaya fortress on the western side of the territory defined in the decree of March 1764. He received a loan of 20,000 roubles, other grants and expense allowances, and undertook to train 30 apprentices. Bousserole died in 1774, and the farm passed to his guarantor Prince Paul Shcherbatov; but in the long term its success proved no greater than that of Verdier.[64] The exact location of one other project mooted for the Volga region was never made specific: Voltaire's desire to transfer his Ferney watch factory to Saratov or Astrakhan, repeatedly expressed in his correspondence with Catherine, was always qualified with the regret that old age made the project impossible.[65]

This seems to have been the sum of colonist enterprise in Astrakhan Province in the 1760s and 1770s. It amounted to relatively little, despite the fact that some of the subsidies given were considerable. Although V. G. Orlov may not have been a very expert inspector,[66] his comments on the Saratov enterprises were dismissive: he considered the hat and stocking factories 'unimportant, especially the stocking factory, where there are both few workers and few goods produced'.[67] Both of these in any case burned down in the big fire of April 1774, and were not restored; Palisse managed to struggle on until 1779, but then his property was sold to meet his debts, and he himself was placed on a state salary.[68]

Petersburg: the foreign artisan community

Petersburg in the later eighteenth century was already a thoroughly cosmopolitan city, both in the composition of its population and the tastes of the Russian upper classes which formed its higher society. Schlözer, looking back on the capital as he had known it in the 1760s, recalled his astonishment on first arrival: 'Generally speaking, Russia is a great world, and Petersburg is a little world – in miniature...I came, saw and – was amazed; and I was no bumpkin up from the country.' Nowhere else could he have found 'such a striking variety, so many instructive subjects, broadening the mind, as in Petersburg... Asiatic luxury, extending even to spend-thrift extravagance, is here united with pure, European taste. No Stoic can remain faithful here to his principle *nil admirari.*' The population was equally colourful:

> What a variety of people, as regards race and language! – far more than in Cadiz. Here Asia meets Europe: Armenians, Kalmyk, Bukharans (there were no Chinese in my time), in a word, people from almost all parts of the world without exception...Religious services are now[69] held here in fourteen languages.

Many of the arrivals from abroad came seeking their fortune, and the majority were German:

> a constant influx of foreigners, especially Germans (at least, they were the majority of those I saw) of whom the half had been thrown up on the

shores of Russia by the storms of ill-fortune, strange adventures and sharp-witted projects. At that time anyone was admitted who could show a passport from some unknown little town or other, and no questions asked.[70]

Another observer, Diderot, writing during his stay in the following decade (1773–4), echoed Schlözer's comments in much less favourable terms: for him, Petersburg 'will never be anything but a confused accumulation of all the worthless nations of the world'.[71]

A number of Western immigrants came to Russia, as we have seen, on the invitation of the government. Most, however, travelled on their own initiative. A great many arrived completely without means – some such people received state assistance on grounds of destitution.[72] Those fared better who brought letters of recommendation to countrymen already established or to well-placed Russians.[73] The Germans formed the largest group of foreign nationals in Petersburg; their flourishing commercial community, centring on St Basil's Island (*Vasil'evsky Ostrov*), had soon overshadowed other nationalities, and the name of the French Quarter (*frantsuzskaya sloboda*) set up on the island under Peter I to house immigrant craftsmen, did not survive long.[74] German traders and craftsmen, together however with French and other Western counterparts in certain fields, supplied most of the home-produced luxury articles in demand among the upper classes. Russian craftsmen tended to work for the mass market, selling lower quality goods at lower prices. Such occupations could provide an ample livelihood:

As everywhere, so here some professions and crafts are more advantageous than others, and some give only scanty profit; but in general the class of artisans in St Petersburg is more prosperous, has a better way of life and better tone than in many other capitals, both on account of the size of the place, the brilliant Court, the flourishing commerce, the wealth and the luxury which predominates, and because it also receives orders from the provinces on account of better taste.[75]

The German artisans rubbed along fairly comfortably with their Russian neighbours, though the latent and overt friction to be found in the relations of any such cultural minority with its hosts were also present here. Vinsky, marrying into a 'poor but honourable German family', found a friendly welcome side by side with bitter hostility from his new relatives.[76] On the other hand, Pushkin's tale of Moscow craftsmen, 'The Coffin-Maker', illustrates from a slightly later period (after 1812) the Russian religious and national animosity towards foreigners which lay not far beneath the surface.[77]

160   *Human capital: the settlement of foreigners in Russia*

In general, however, relations were cordial enough, as the following description of a prosperous Petersburg artisan family at the beginning of the nineteenth century suggests.

I have passed many pleasant hours in the house of my shoe-maker, a worthy elderly Lübecker. His eldest son... had spent several years in France and England, spoke both languages fluently and well, was not unversed in the literature of these nations, and played in addition a splendid flute. The sixteen-year-old daughter was a highly cultured girl, who in Germany would have surpassed many a young lady of high rank...

This degree of education is not to be found in the children of every German artisan, but they all have more education than their parents... There are, it is true, thorough-going philistines who can never rid themselves of the 'cousin tailor and shoe-maker', but these are largely avoided...

The interior ordering of a prosperous German craftsman['s home] is in no way inferior to the most elegant households in Germany. His furnishing is very tasteful, usually in mahogany..., beautiful bronzes, mirrors, chandeliers, excellent pianos, carpets, etc. His cuisine is among the best in St Petersburg; is it then surprising that many a gentleman with star and title condescends to frequent such houses, in order – besides acquiring an ample credit – to eat his fill for once of something better than his scanty kitchen can furnish him at home?[78]

However, this rosy picture, reflecting in any case the cultural levels of Alexander's, not Catherine's, reign, by no means represented the life style of all German artisans in Petersburg. The same writer attributed the low standards of the city's German theatre in large measure to the fact that the audience consisted principally of uneducated German craftsmen;[79] and in the year in which he began his book (1810), the same foreign handworkers sought relief from a new tax on the grounds that 'in all guilds there is a multitude of poor craftsmen'.[80] This would seem to reflect a reality quite as significant as the affluence of the Lübeck shoemaker; and it was to this end of the social scale that the foreign immigrants belonged who joined the guilds of Petersburg under the 1763 Manifesto.

The Petersburg craft-guild community, in which Rehbinder's immigrants and those following them took membership, had in 1761 1,127 members. In 1766, this figure stood at 1,339: 562 Russian and 777 German master craftsmen (*mastera*) in 35 and 53 guilds respectively.[81] Rehbinder's recruits were duly enrolled as guild members by the Office of the Chief Magistrature; but with the creation of the Chancellery of Guardianship, problems of jurisdiction arose which took more than a year, and Senate arbitration, to settle.

In October 1763 the Chancellery requested the Office to supervise its new charges, and be responsible for their debts to the Chancellery. But the Office refused; and it claimed further that the guild officials (*altermany*) on whom the responsibility would devolve, should not undertake this burden either. Their office did not oblige them to do so, and in any case they were fully occupied with their own business. The Chancellery should itself ensure adequate supervision or security. The Chancellery countered these arguments with references to the statutory duties of the Office and pointed out that, while no-one would stand surety for poor and unknown foreigners, 'because of their poverty it is impossible to give them no loan at all'.[82]

The Senate took the side of the Chancellery, and ordered the Office to be responsible for the foreigners and their debt repayment. The Chancellery, it decided, was to inform the Office how much money was allowed to each individual for the purchase of instruments and materials, and to send it the required amount. The Office would then forward this sum to the Guildhall, to be administered by the guild officials, who would give out money as required against a receipt, and ensure its proper use. The *altermany* were also to be responsible, when the time came, for collecting repayment instalments, which would be sent back to the Chancellery through the Office.[83] The publication of this decision on 9 December 1763 established a standard procedure for foreigners joining the Petersburg craft guilds under the Manifesto.[84] (And besides the case of Eflein in Riga, a case in Moscow also came before the Senate.[85])

As the overall figures for guild membership suggest, the number of colonists registering with the Petersburg Office as artisans was not very large; this was probably the result of the change of emphasis in the policy of the Chancellery of Guardianship from the autumn of 1763, favouring agricultural rather than urban settlers. The two groups sent by Rehbinder in June and July 1763 totalled 14 craftsmen and 41 people. Their cost to Rehbinder was 6,132 guilders, and as we have seen, these early arrivals received a special gratuity of 10 roubles, both to avoid hardship to them and 'for the further encouragement of other similar people to emigrate and settle likewise'.[86] Details of these people, and other passing references, indicate a variety of trades.[87]

Some data are also available on a number of foreigners who for various reasons remained in Petersburg, but did not join guilds; these were cases notably where the Chancellery itself kept track of immigrants to ensure the repayment of monies advanced. Some colonists dropped out of the parties travelling to Saratov because of illness or other personal reasons: so the Frenchman Saunier, recruited by Beauregard, whose wife fell sick and who, on repayment of expenses incurred on his behalf, was released by Beauregard and the Chancellery 'for free residence in St Petersburg'.[88] Some were military men, like the Swedish army Ensign Klass Magnus von Werdenhof – 'dismissed from the Chancellery with a passport to find himself a post'[89] – or Cornet Georg von Helden, a more successful soldier, formerly in Prussian service, who made only a brief appearance in Petersburg before taking up a posting to the Smolensk Division, and who by 1781, when his file closed, had reached the rank of Major (*sekund-mayor*).[90]

One of the Chancellery's debtors in this category was a would-be recruiting agent, an associate of d'Harcourt, Jean Bois de Chêne. Like others of his occupation – Florentin, who settled in Saratov as a merchant, or Georges Henri Goguel, who entered State service after working for Le Roy[91] – Bois de Chêne stayed on in Russia even when all employment in the immigration programme, for him, had ceased. He did not remain long in Petersburg: in July 1765 the Chancellery recorded that he had been given a passport to go to Moscow 'to settle'; his debt amounted to 543 roubles 79 kopecks. Tikhmenev in Moscow had some difficulty in tracing him to the aristocratic home of Count Ivan Semyonovich Hendrikov, where he held a post for a time as tutor, and where his wife remained as governess (*pri detekh madamoyu*). Neither Bois de Chêne nor Hendrikov showed any eagerness to satisfy the Chancellery's demands for debt repayment, or even payment of interest: in fact Bois de Chêne's contention, that under the terms of the 1763 Manifesto he should pay no interest, had to be accepted. In 1769 Tikhmenev reported him in a new position, again as tutor, with the major's wife (*mayorsha*), Yelena Bibikova. She agreed to stop money from his wages, so that by 1773 only 12 roubles 62 kopecks of the debt remained, and the Chancellery pursued the matter no further.[92]

Other immigrants took employment with government bodies in Petersburg. Master mason Johann Jakob Tietzius from Potsdam was prepared to settle in any part of the Empire, but thought he could probably be more useful as a mason in the capital, since few colonists were likely to seek his services. He asked permission to settle in or near Petersburg, with a loan: 'and time will show whether the Crown receives profit from that or not'. He was also thinking of setting up a snuff factory. The Chancellery agreed with the reasoning, but not to the request for a loan, and found Tietzius a post as master mason with the Police Chancellery (*Glavnaya Politseymeysterskaya Kantselyariya*), at 250 roubles per annum.[93] A similar case was that of Jakob Christoph Ketscher, who had come from Berlin with von Werdenhof and who joined the Medical College as an instrument maker; he worked in this capacity for six years before leaving Russia in 1771.[94] In all these cases, the only interest retained by the Chancellery was in the debt owed to it.

Despite the low priority assigned to it by the Chancellery of Guardianship in the context of the special immigration programme, the policy of welcoming foreign (Western) artisans in general was adhered to, broadly speaking, throughout Catherine's reign and for long afterwards. In the first decade of the nineteenth century special artisan colonies were created in the Ukraine to answer specific local or governmental needs;[95] but in overall policy on the admittance of foreigners within the specific context of the 1763 rules – and particularly after 1804, when new and stringent criteria were introduced – the view of the Chancellery of Guardianship was adhered to, and artisans were neither actively sought, nor accepted, as 'colonists'. However, the favourable conditions open to those who came to settle at their own expense continued to attract such immigrants, and the authorities were pleased to receive them on this basis. An extract from one further official document on the question, a memorandum of 1809, at once summarizes official policy and gives a succinct – if also slightly self-contradictory – account of the position of foreign craftsmen in Russia at the turn of the eighteenth century.

It is well-known that only the capital cities can give these people permanent occupation and a reliable livelihood. In other towns they are in no wise able to live without poverty. Even the principal provincial towns (*gubernskiye goroda*) cannot give them continual work, and therefore the majority will have insufficient means to maintain themselves; and it cannot be supposed that, with all their diligence, they could bring any solid advantage to themselves or to the state in these circumstances.

The wealthy nobility in the provinces has no need of them, since it either orders all needful articles from the capitals, so as to obtain the best standards of work and the latest fashion, or, in accordance with accepted custom, sends its own people to the capitals to learn trades, and always has in its own home good workmen of almost every craft. The other inhabitants of the towns borrow these workmen from the nobles, or content themselves with their own local craftsmen, although these are not everywhere sufficiently expert; or else they obtain articles they need at the annual fairs, whither these things are brought from the capitals. At the same time, in the provinces, taste in interior furnishings, in carriages and so on, is not subject to such frequent fluctuations as in the capitals, where luxury ceaselessly devises new fashions and provides craftsmen and hand-workers with constant work.

If for these reasons it is difficult for a foreign craftsman to find the necessary livelihood for himself in the provincial towns, how much more is this the case in the district centres (*uyezdnyye goroda*), where for the most part there reside only officials living solely on their salaries, petty towns-folk (*meshchane*), and middling merchantry, who cannot possibly occupy such a craftsman. And if foreign craftsmen should be needed anywhere in greater numbers than at present, then of course sufficient will come in without any official aid or invitation; for the experience of many years has shown that daily more and more of them are coming to Russia of their own accord, and that it is difficult to find a provincial or a significant district town, in which there are not a few of them, and in some places, especially in the capitals, their numbers have increased to such an extent that they can scarcely all find work.

The by no means insignificant advantages given to them in Russia, and the freedom from many dues to which they are liable in their native land, will always be a reliable and trustworthy means to their increase here, without any other outlay on the part of the government.[96]

Petersburg and the north: entrepreneurs

As was the case with the artisan population, foreigners occupied a relatively large place among the entrepreneurs of the capital in the period under consideration. An official list drawn up in 1775 of enter-prises under the jurisdiction of the Office of Manufactures (covering, it will be recalled, Petersburg itself and some of the surrounding area), shows a total of 104, of which, however, at least 24 were not in opera-tion.[97] The number of foreign owners was 46; the majority were German, but other foreign nationals listed included British and French, several other Westerners, and at least 2 Armenians. These figures are not comprehensive, and in any case they only show licensed under-takings. Thus they include 7 hat manufacturers (5 foreign or with foreign names, at least 2 not in production); but only the previous year, 4 licensed hatters, none of whom appear on the list, had presented a petition complaining of unlicensed competition, and naming 13 alleged unofficial producers.[98] However, these unlisted and unlicensed manu-facturers were also mixed from the point of view of nationality,[99] so that even allowing for the inaccuracy of eighteenth-century records and statistics, the figures may be held to offer at least a fair indication of the position of foreigners in Petersburg light industry at the time.

The latter decades of the eighteenth century saw, of course, a rapid growth in the number of industrial units in Russia, so that our list reflects a situation slightly different from that in 1763. The ban on new industry in the capitals[100] tended to slow down development there, but did not stop it altogether; many new ventures were started, particularly small enterprises, and such as did not require much fuel or a large work-force. The list shows 43 enterprises established in the years 1763–75, of which at least 28 were in Petersburg itself, and at least 13 elsewhere.

During the 1760s, the Chancellery of Guardianship received a variety of applications to set up factories in or near the capitals. Some were unacceptable. The would-be ribbon manufacturer Major Johann von Gommel (Hommel?), it turned out, had been living for some time in Russia and so did not qualify under the terms of the Manifesto; 'and in any case his factory is not such that there are none in Russia'. He was therefore addressed to the Office of Manufactures. The Office gave him a licence, under which he set up in Ropsha in 1767.[101] A Captain von Schmettau, from Danzig, likewise sent on to the Office of Manufactures, in 1765, demanded large sums for a new chemical dyeing process he had discovered; but the Office found his claims exaggerated, and turned him down. However, 'so that he should have no grounds for complaint, and equally so that the Crown by dissemination by him of false rumours should not lose credit in the recruiting of foreigners both for manufactures and factories, and for other handicrafts', von Schmettau was given 'adequate compensation' for the expenses involved in his journey and stay in Petersburg.[102]

Other applicants were accepted, but failed to find their feet. The sealing-wax manufacturer Heinrich Arnold Trüper, also directed to the Office of Manufactures, was allowed to settle in Ropsha (on the grounds that new factories were forbidden in Petersburg itself). But 'as he could not gain his living there' he finally went on in 1765 to join the Saratov settlement, where he intended 'together with agriculture to set up a sealing-wax, tobacco and starch factory, and in addition to make malt in the German manner, brew beer and vinegar and distil Danzig vodka'. Such at any rate were his hopes. The Chancellery of Guardianship bought 200 pounds of sealing-wax from him to lighten his journey.[103]

The case of the Amsterdam *fabrikant* Joseph Ratke was referred simultaneously to the Office and the Chancellery in 1764. Ratke proposed to manufacture various sorts of velvet and other cloths. He offered to bring 3 or 4 skilled assistants with him, and asked for a loan of 4,000–5,000 roubles. The Chancellery seems to have left a decision to the Office, which replied that since these particular materials (except for velvets) were not being produced in Russia, Ratke would be a useful acquisition. He should bring all necessary equipment, or models of it, with him; and if he could get production started (outside the city) and prove his reliability, he would be given the ten-year loan that he requested.[104] The Office heard nothing further in the matter; but some time later Ratke came himself to Petersburg and started negotiations with the Chancellery. The Chancellery gave him an advance of 50 roubles, with which he tried to make a start; but the money was not enough, and the enterprise collapsed from lack of funds.[105]

Other applicants turned out to be little more than artisans. So the German Johann Gottlieb Otto from Copenhagen, originally engaged to work in a projected 'gold factory' (*Goldfabrik*) in Petersburg, who in 1764 took advantage of the Manifesto to switch to making order ribbon on his own account. On security offered by his brother, employed in the Imperial Petersburg tapestry manufacture, Otto received 200 roubles to allow him to recruit workers in Copenhagen and bring in the necessary implements. The Chancellery allowed him to site his venture in Petersburg itself, but left supervision to the Office of Manufactures. Otto found the workers he wanted, but then his money ran low, and he had to allow them temporarily to work for another manufacturer (*master*). In August 1765, Ivan Kuhlberg was sent by the Chancellery to inspect the premises and check the solvency of this debtor. He found one loom, a certain amount of ribbon and braid produced, but barely as much as – taken altogether with Otto's personal effects – would cover the 200 rouble outlay. The Chancellery reacted by demanding Otto's inscription in the tape- and braid-makers' guild as a craftsman. Although he claimed to have set up a factory, 'that cannot be considered accurate, or compared with factories established in Russia, because all foreigners call any handicraft a factory without distinction'.[106]

There were, however, some successes, at least initially. Six enterprises were set up in Petersburg on the basis of the 1763 Manifesto, one in Reval, one in Moscow, and one in Petrozavodsk; and several were established in Yamburg during Yelagin's reconstruction. The Petrozavodsk enterprise stood under the jurisdiction of the College of Mines;[107] those in Yamburg were controlled first by Yelagin, later by the local administration. At least in the beginning all the others were subject to the Chancellery itself, independent of the Office of Manufactures. In the unsuccessful cases quoted above, the Chancellery evidently felt that the enterprises proposed were not of sufficient value for it to back them without the approval or participation of the Office.

The six enterprises created in Petersburg catered almost without exception to the luxury needs of the upper classes; and this, together with the fact that they placed little pressure on local resources of fuel and labour, must explain why they were permitted inside the city. They included a silk and semi-silk factory (Johann Miller); lace and cotton production (Christian Schulz and Johann Michaelis respectively, each with a loan of 600 roubles); a snuff and tobacco factory (Johann Theophile Boucher or Bucher[108]); a group of Swiss watch- and clock-makers headed by Robert Jurrine; and a jewellery 'factory' (*galantereynaya fabrika*) (Jean-Pierre Ador). To these names should perhaps be added that of an Italian cheese-maker, Garibaldo, who settled in Petersburg in 1769, although his profession, and the loan he received (50 roubles), indicate the artisan rather than the large-scale producer. The others were a clock factory in Moscow (Marc Fazy and François Ferrier) and a joinery works in Reval (Pierre Galant).[109]

By far the largest of the Petersburg six were Ador, Jurrine and Boucher. Ador was one of a group who had come from Berlin after negotiations there with Dolgoruky; others in the company included the *vyzyvatel'* D'Haucourt, Bois de Chêne, and the sericulturist Bousserole.[110] Ador, a Swiss, described in one document as a *fabriquant bijoutier*, signed an agreement in 1764 to set up a factory for the production of

all sorts of jewellery (*galantereya*) with various colours and in enamel, with both flat and embossed designs, also stamped and various other articles, as for example gold chains for gentleman's and ladies's watches with keys, toothpick cases (*futlyary zubochistnyye*), enamel eggs (*yaichki*), sword hilts and all other similar articles, such as may be ordered by the court or desired by the quality; [and] he can show his artistry not only in the ordering of this work, but also in the making of various machines conducive to the establishment of that factory.[111]

Ador was to receive an eight-year loan of 12,000 roubles, plus 1,800 roubles for expenses in engaging foreign workers, and a large state-owned building in Petersburg. Necessary equipment could be imported duty-free to the value of 3,000 roubles. Exact standards were set for the quality of materials to be used, and Ador promised to meet most of the home demand for his products, at a cost below that of imports. He also agreed to take 14 Russian apprentices, maintained at state cost, and to train them fully within an eight-year period. The loan was to be repaid over three years, from the ninth year onwards, and any apprentices not then fully skilled would be kept on until they completed their training.[112]

Things went well in the first years for Ador. His returns for 1773 show production of 2,000 items worth 15,400 roubles.[113] In 1776 his contract was renewed, as from 1774, for a further four years, on approximately the previous basis. The apprentices, not yet fully trained, were now to be paid wages, ranging from 64 to 48 kopecks daily, for which they all had 'to work for twelve hours with diligence and loyalty'.[114] Ador's returns to the Office of Manufactures for 1774 did not mention the apprentices. He showed a work force of eight foreigners and three Russians. In addition to the grant of 13,800 roubles, the house in which his enterprise was situated had cost the Office 12,668 roubles $51\frac{1}{2}$ kopecks.[115]

However, the end of the additional four years found Ador in difficulties. He had insufficient ready money to meet the repayment due on the outstanding part of his loan, which under the new contract had been made payable to the Chancellery in one sum in 1778; he now owed 9,921 roubles $28\frac{1}{2}$ kopecks, plus the full sum expended on his building. Over the next three years he presented to the Chancellery of Guardianship as earnest of payment a number of overdue accounts and protested bills, totalling 19,942$\frac{1}{2}$ roubles, which give an interesting glimpse of his clientele. The largest sum outstanding (11,850 roubles) was owed by the Cabinet of Her Majesty. In the list of private clients, Princes Meshchersky and Dolgorukov stand next to Oberinspektor Nikita Shemyakin and Major-General Peter de Melissino, while a Kammerherr and two Councillors of State bring up the rear. As the only 'free' *galantereynyy fabrikant* in Petersburg, not attached to the jewellers' and goldsmiths' guild,[116] Ador had evidently established himself with the upper strata of society; and he suffered in the same way as many other suppliers from the extreme disinclination of such circles to pay their debts. The Chancellery, while refusing the bills as payment, had to help Ador to collect the sums owing on them, a long drawn-out process not completed until Meshchersky and Kammerherr Zinoviev had been sold up for bankruptcy.[117]

Of a similar nature were the two clock and watch enterprises established in Petersburg and Moscow. The contracts for these were signed at the same time as that of Ador, in March 1764, and all three were transferred together from the control of the Chancellery to that of the Office of Manufactures, three months later.[118] The clock-makers' conditions, identical in the two cases, were also much the same as those of Ador: a large building, 18,000 roubles for ten years, duty-free import of equipment and also spare parts; and 12 young Russian apprentices, from 12 to 15 years old, to be trained over twelve years, the first six years at state cost, thereafter on a salary.[119]

At the time of their transfer to the Office of Manufactures, all three contracting parties were already engaged in seeking their Western specialists, and in buying necessary instruments; in due course money was transferred for these purposes to Hamburg, Paris and Berlin. Meanwhile Fazy found a house in the German Suburb in Moscow, at a total cost of 9,150 roubles, and Jurrine another on Vasil'evskiy Ostrov for 7,500 roubles.[120] Both undertakings got successfully under way, Fazy's after some problems for Ferrier abroad. In his efforts to find the work-force he needed, Ferrier had extreme difficulty in obtaining the funds due to be paid over to him in the West, and then was arrested in France and spent nearly six months, together with his brother Jacques, in the Bastille.[121] Jurrine's enterprise began operations under his associates Sando and Basselier,[122] since Jurrine himself soon died. In 1774 the latter venture produced 46 clocks and watches of varying kinds,[123] and the following year it was employing 7 foreign and 13 Russian workers, besides its apprentices.[124]

The conditions negotiated with the three sets of entrepreneurs went beyond the provisions of the 1763 Manifesto, and in fact the Chancellery had to obtain special authorization for them.[125] At the same time, this type of undertaking had relatively little to contribute to the overall growth of Russian industry; and one can agree with Stolpyansky's conclusion in his otherwise rather garbled account of the Petersburg clock-makers: 'It would seem that the twelve-year privileges resulted finally in nothing more than that a few clocks with the inscription of this company are preserved in the Hermitage.'[126] However, these enterprises did represent a deliberate effort on the part of the government to cut into the much-expanded import trade in luxuries, which was an object of concern to political economists in the second half of the eighteenth century, and to provide a home source of supply which might replace it. Stolpyansky mentions a number of other Russian enterprises which appeared in Petersburg at about this time, and evidently served a similar function.[127]

Much the same things might be said of the snuff and tobacco manufacturer Theophile Boucher. But his products at least had a considerably wider appeal, and his arrival in Russia also coincided with a period of heightened interest in tobacco trade and manufacture, when efforts were being made to increase both imports and home production.[128] Boucher came from Lübeck in 1766 and the first result of his negotiations with the Chancellery was permission to sell tobacco of his own manufacture wholesale and retail throughout the Empire under the Imperial coat of arms, for one year.[129] Then, 'so that this craft should always remain in Russia', the Chancellery made a ten-year contract with him in April 1767.[130] The agreement denied Boucher any monopoly privileges, and stipulated the precise types of tobacco he could import – Virginia and Amersfort were banned, since they were shortly to be grown in Russia (though Boucher was allowed to buy them locally). Exact conditions of sale in Russia, and of export, were laid down, as well as for the purchase of other materials needed in the manufacturing process. Boucher was promised a suitable building, and received altogether 28,000 roubles in loans from the Chancellery.

Finally, he undertook to train 20 state apprentices. The Chancellery hoped to add merchants' children to this number so that ultimately more private factories would be set up. The apprentices' living conditions were minutely regulated, and Boucher undertook to teach them not only his trade, but French, German, arithmetic and geography as well. He was also to take an active part in the development of Russian tobacco plantations.

Boucher had only been waiting for a firm contract before summoning his family and German workers from Lübeck; and he was soon in business, with a shop of his own as well as his factory. In 1768 he processed some 4,000 puds of Ukrainian leaf tobacco, more than he was able at this stage to sell; so that in 1769, to help him over the initial period, the Chancellery advanced to him 12,000 roubles originally assigned for successive annual payments of the costs of his apprentices. In agreeing to this extraordinary grant, the Chancellery valued Boucher's building, equipment and stock at 60,000–70,000 roubles.[131]

In the following two or three years the factory flourished. Boucher made monthly returns to the Chancellery, which give considerable detail on operations at this time. Production for the year June 1769 to June 1770 was 3,600 puds of 13 different kinds of tobacco and snuff, valued at 22,370 roubles 80 kopecks. Sales reached 1,645 puds 31 lbs. bringing in 9,599 roubles 11¾ kopecks. Expenses were as follows: for other materials and incidentals – 3,450 roubles; wages – 8,008 roubles; 'for the hire of shops and attendants, for paper, sealing-wax and pictures (*kartinki*)' – 3,524 roubles; altogether 14,962 roubles.[132] In June 1771 Boucher was employing 38 workers, apparently all foreign, in addition to 19 state apprentices and 5 'hired children'.[133]

There were, however, grounds for reproof. In March 1772 the Chancellery found that Boucher was falling behind with his reports of tobacco purchases. Inspection visits in the following May and June showed that little progress was being made in the apprentices' language studies: 'The pupils have little success in German language, reading and writing, and do not study French at all, despite the fact that according to the contract they should be found foreign correspondents in good time, for which they must unavoidably know one of these languages.' Still, these were relatively minor blemishes. The same inspector reported that Boucher maintained his apprentices well, and that his books appeared to be entirely in order.[134] Boucher did not in fact pursue his business long enough to fulfil all the Chancellery's requirements. Before his obligations were met he made over both his factory and his debts to a Russian entrepreneur, and withdrew. The records quoted here end with the laconic note that 'as Boucher's factory has been given over to Shemyakin, who is paying the state debt for him, this file is to be sent to the archives'.[135]

Boucher is described at some length in the memoirs of Nikolai Grech, who portrays him as an attractive personality, and as a great 'projector'. Grech tells exotic stories of his life, beginning with his marriage in Martinique to a beautiful Creole girl who made him change his original German name of Fleischer (Butcher) to the French form Boucher, and ending with his death in 1800, which rumour had it was the work of his last wife, a mature lady whom he had married for her dowry when he was already seventy, and in search of funds for yet another new project.[136]

The Petrozavodsk enterprise, the so-called 'French factories' (*frantsuz-skiye fabriki*) set up on Lake Onega by two Frenchmen, Barral and Chanony, began in a way rather different from the other undertakings created under the immigration programme. In 1762 Pierre Barral, a merchant of Lyons, had tried to set up in his native town a tin works on the English pattern, in association with Denis Chanony, who had experience both in metallurgy and in the Lyons silk industry. The venture failed, however, and the two men decided to recoup their losses by answering the Russian proclamations to foreign entrepreneurs.[137] But neither appears to have treated with the Chancellery of Guardianship. They evidently had good connections in Petersburg, since in 1765 they were able to conclude an advantageous contract with the College of Mines, for 'the making of tin (*belogo zheleza*) and from it all sorts of cooking-ware; the galvanizing of sheet-iron, the manufacture of steel, cuirasses, scythes, sickles and thimbles'.[138]

The Empress confirmed the contract with the words: 'So be it, and the guarantors are known to me alone' – an unusual mark of distinction. Barral and Chanony received fuel and labour at cost, metal supplies from state stocks (at normal prices) and a 20,000 rouble loan, to be repaid within ten years.[139] The French Consul reported to Paris: 'With this help they will set up a tin works on Lake Onega, and they are positive that the Swedish and other producers will be unable to withstand the competition.'[140]

The associates were joined by another metallurgist, a French expert named Caron, who, however, died soon after, and by Barral's brother, David. David Barral ran a drapery and furrier's business for which he travelled to Russia, trading Lyons silk for furs. In 1765 the frequency of his visits, and the known plans of his brother Pierre, brought down on him the denunciations of the French diplomats in Petersburg, and the following year he was arrested in Lyons and imprisoned in the Bastille, on suspicion of recruiting workers for the Onega venture.[141] There were good grounds for this. His brother's associate, Chanony, was actively engaged in recruiting 'manufacturers' (*fabricants*) in 1765 and 1766, and is mentioned in a contemporary French report as a *directeur*, one of the principal organizers of the Russian recruitment. The report credits him personally with raising altogether about 100 families. This number, if correct, was probably in excess of the needs of the new enterprise, though of course small by comparison with the recruits of other *vyzyvateli*. Some of Chanony's people may have joined the general flow of immigrants; his agent, Goguel, was cousin to the agent of the same name working for Le Roy.[142]

The new Onega works began operations in January 1768,[143] and their owner's descriptions from the following years show them in a flourishing state. In 1773 Barral wished to return to Lyons on personal business, and to insure himself against possible reprisals in France, he turned for help to the French Ambassador in Petersburg. The memorandum describing his enterprise, which he drew up for the occasion, gives a fine – rather too fine – picture of energy and success. The initial factory had been joined by another processing steel, and by saw-mills, and production of kitchen-ware of all types and finishes was in full swing. Barral made the claim that the venture had cost him and Chanony over 500,000 livres, with a ten-year grant of 100,000; and that production capacity in tin (among other products) was about twice the total Russian consumption. The French Ambassador, in an accompanying note, described Barral as 'a very intelligent man, whose establishment in Russia seems to me useful to the commerce of France. . .'.[144]

In 1773 Barral and Chanony planned a new foundry on the river Megra, 25 versts from Lake Onega, to replace their annual state supply of Urals iron, which was to be withdrawn in 1775. Their Megra-

Mikhaylovsky plant began operations in 1776;[145] but two years later, with a new associate, also French, the Petersburg merchant Foullon, they were seeking postponement of their loan repayments;[146] and in the same year all their property was placed under sequester. The reasons advanced for the failure, at the time and later, are various: unfair competition from British merchants at Petersburg in the sale of their products; the extravagance of Barral, who was the company representative in the capital; ignorance of the poor quality of the ore on the river Megra.[147] The debt amounted to 193,977 roubles; the partners had no resources with which to meet it, and the enterprise never recovered.[148] When the outstanding sums were written off in 1793 Chanony was dead, and Barral living without means in Petersburg.[149]

The 'French factories' on Lake Onega formed one among several ephemeral enterprises set up in the area in the 1760s. Lyubomirov in his discussion of the region points out that several works shut down simultaneously in 1778, but he offers no satisfactory explanation for this sudden decline.[150] In the case of the 'French factories', Barral and Chanony had simply overstretched their resources, and were unable to make repayments of cash and materials which fell due in 1776 and 1777. The only partner who survived the crash was Foullon. He, fortunately for himself, had placed his property in the name of someone else.[151] In 1788, on the intervention of Charles Gascoigne, the director of the Olonets state metallurgical complex, already mentioned for his work in the south, Foullon was again given charge of the Megra-Mikhaylovsky plant; but he had insufficient funds to put it back into a profitable state.[152] Subsequently his son joined the state service under Gascoigne and made a notable career, in 1818 succeeding Adam Armstrong in Gascoigne's former position as director of the Olonets and Petersburg foundries.[153]

Like the 'French factories' of Barral and Chanony, the industrial development at Yamburg differed somewhat from the enterprises established under the aegis of the Chancellery of Guardianship. It formed part and parcel of Yelagin's reconstruction of the town; and it was therefore appropriate that it should include the only state industrial enterprise to emerge from the immigration scheme: a state textile mill in a state plan for urban renewal.

Before Catherine's reign, Yamburg had been a place of little note; earlier in the century it had formed part of Menshikov's vast estates in Ingermanland. The reasons and origins for Yelagin's work in the town are hard to discover, unless one assumes him really to have been inspired by J. G. Eisen.[154] Certainly he planned his new project on a large scale, so much so that Catherine had to restrain his enthusiasm after seeing Yamburg for herself during her Livonian tour of 1764.[155] Even so, the results were striking. As the geographer Polunin described it in his *New and Complete Geographical Dictionary* (1788–9),

> the broad straight road leading into the town, at the town entrance, is built up on both sides with stone houses. This street ends in an octagonal place, around which is situated the market hall (*gostinyy dvor*), with a gallery. In the middle of this square is placed an obelisk, farther on, on the so-called Ugorka, is erected a magnificent stone church.[156]

This was presumably the cathedral church of St Catherine the Great Martyr, built by the architect Mylnikov in 1782 under Yelagin's supervision.[157] The old Yamburg settlement, of wooden buildings, lay further towards the river Luga. 'In the newly-built street is established a post-house, in which travellers can get all they need, an apothecary's shop, and three factories, making cloth, stockings, and gloves; also the crystal and glass works which by decree of 7 March 1725 belonged to Prince Menshikov.'[158]

Yelagin's reconstruction of the town was elegant and ambitious; but by the end of the century, although Yamburg had now been raised to the status of a district centre, it was looking shabby. A traveller passing through in 1799 noted the architectural qualities of the place, but commented on the neglected state of the buildings, and predicted that they would soon fall into ruin for lack of repair.[159]

The industrial development survived Catherine in an equally diminished form. Altogether there were six enterprises, of which by far the largest and most significant was the state mill. The others consisted of a glove manufacture, another making baize, an undertaking producing mock velvet on three looms, a stocking factory (also three looms) run by a German, Walzer, and a cambric factory.[160] The latter may well have been the concern of the Frenchman Pierre Dumoutier, who appears in French diplomatic correspondence. In March 1767 the French Embassy reported in code to Paris that

> the Sr Dumoutier, a Frenchman of the Reformed faith, whose family is established at St Quentin where it has a quite considerable trade in batiste and cambric, the same who was for a long time in London and who is even well known there to the Comte de Guerchi [French Ambassador], has come to this country for the second time, and having pursued several different projects, has now decided on a scheme to establish a factory for fine fabrics and batiste at Yamburg near Narva where he has been granted the status of citizen with an Italian, Val, his associate.

The Sr Dumoutier has since left for London where he says he is going in order to receive an inheritance. I know that he plans to go also to Holland and to Hamburg, so as to be in a position in these two places to gather the various workmen whom he intends to recruit for his factory, in Holland and in the region of St Quentin.

The report continued: 'Another Frenchman named Dubousquet who had a factory at Nîmes has also obtained permission to set up a textile factory at Yamburg, and is working for his part to recruit workmen in Languedoc.'[161] Which of the Yamburg enterprises may have belonged to Dubousquet, is not clear.

None of these small private undertakings lasted more than a few years. The state mill, however, continued through at least till 1789, when it was destroyed by fire.[162] It had been established (according to Georgi[163]) in 1764, and was directed by another Frenchman, Pierre Levallier. An anonymous French informant at The Hague, an extract from whose letter to the authorities in Paris is preserved in the Bastille Archive, noted that Levallier and his son were natives of Carcassonne.[164] In October 1766 Levallier *père* had passed through The Hague on his way to France, in the same illegal search for skilled workmen which had taken Dumoutier and Dubousquet on like journeys. He evidently avoided the French police, to whose attention the letter-writer had recommended him; and his recruitment must have been successful, either in France or elsewhere. At least, most of his skilled work-force in the beginning was foreign; and in 1777 the French Consul in Petersburg had to arrange the pardon of three Frenchmen, 'deserters from the forces of the King and currently employed at the Imperial textile factory at Yamburg', who wished to take advantage of a French amnesty for military deserters but were tied for the moment by their contracts.[165] Levallier himself stayed on in Russia until his death in December 1781, shortly before he was due to take charge of 'the setting up of new mills in the interior' of Russia.[166] These presumably included the large mill established by Potemkin on his estate of Dubrovna in Mogilyov province in the 1780s, and which was transferred to Yekaterinoslav in 1794.[167] Potemkin also looked abroad at this time: in September 1784 the French Consul wrote that

The careful attention and the means which the Prince Potemkin is employing for the establishment which he has set in motion of several textile mills to produce woollen, silk, and other fabrics, in various places in this Empire, lend credibility to the reports that he had taken many workmen from us, and that he is expecting still more.[168]

The state mill itself at Yamburg produced very fine-quality fabrics.

It was a considerable enterprise, with 36 (Storch says 40) looms, and up to 600 workers, probably including some colonists.[169] A full discussion of it appears in H. Storch's *Historical-Statistical Depiction of the Russian Empire*,[170] which was published at the end of the century. According to Storch, its products were outstanding both in quantity and quality, equalling the best foreign fabrics in strength, fine weave, beauty and fastness of colour. They included both fine, light fabrics in the French fashion, and strong, thick materials of the British type. The factory had its own retail outlet, a shop in Petersburg, where the best grades sold from the outset at the modest price of 5 roubles per arshin, 'at a time when money was worth much more than it is now'. The wool used came at first almost entirely from Spain, although Ukrainian wool was used later for coarser ranges. Initially the majority of skilled workers came from abroad, but in time Russian workers learned the processes as well, and altogether the mill gave significant employment in an agriculturally infertile area.[171]

Thus Storch's description of the mill suggests great success. However, Storch did not approve of state-run concerns and he duly drew his own lessons from the Yamburg experience.[172] While valuable to the Empire, he pointed out, the mill could not be profitable to the Crown: state-run enterprises rarely prosper. But their failure – a recurrent phenomenon in many lands – does not deter wise princes from sponsoring such undertakings when their governments cannot otherwise overcome local prejudices, or when the costs and risks of some new branch of industry are beyond private means. These enterprises are then, however, to be made over to private ownership as soon as they are properly under way. This was what Peter I had done with his new cloth yard in Moscow; and this was Catherine II's intention with Yamburg. The mill was offered for sale. But it found no buyers, because the price asked took into account the very large initial outlay. So the factory remained in state ownership until it burned down in 1789.[173]

Storch's views on this case echoed ideas which, as he said, were common in Russian ruling circles in the eighteenth century: Catherine, for example, had used almost identical words when entrusting the reorganization of the Imperial tapestry manufacture to N. I. Panin in July 1763.[174] Storch's strictures notwithstanding, however, his own account indicates that the Yamburg mill was not a failure – on the contrary; it was simply very expensive to set up.[175] It did achieve its intention of producing fabrics not previously manufactured in the Empire. After its destruction only Potemkin's mill at Dubrovna, later at Yekaterinoslav, which derived from it, continued to produce fine cloths in any large quantity: and Storch himself noted the heavy import costs of fine grades of textiles at the end of the century.[176] Moreover, even in its destruction the school became a significant source of technical skills.[177] Some of the machinery was saved, and with part of the work-force was used to start textile production on a small scale in the new town of Sophia near Tsarskoye Selo. Catherine encouraged other workers to set up for themselves elsewhere in the Empire, and continued to pay their salaries for some time after the Yamburg closure; and in the 1780s and later other small textile enterprises appeared in Yamburg itself.[178] Levallier's mill would thus seem to be in fact an exception in the completely negative assessment which Storch gave to the Yamburg project as a whole.[179] Certainly the other enterprises were of no great importance or longevity; in this case therefore it is precisely in the private sector that the failure of the government's attempts to stimulate industry through the immigration policy is most clearly apparent.

Everything considered, it is evident that the welcome extended to entrepreneurs under the 1763 Manifesto brought little immediate advantage. It established no significant new industries or enterprises, with the exception of the Yamburg mill, and that apparently was un-acceptably expensive. Furthermore, again with the same exception, the new foreign enterprises failed in their second major purpose, the training of Russians in industrial processes and skills. This purpose can be traced in almost all the Chancellery's contracts, and it was in fact characteristic of most state-aided enterprises in Russia in the eighteenth century. The Chancellery was very solicitous of the apprentices whom it did place with immigrant entrepreneurs. But as far as the scanty evidence goes, the results were not impressive.[180] And, finally, foreign-owned factories continued to appear in the years 1763–6[181] and there-after quite independently of the Chancellery of Guardianship.

However, the 1763 Manifesto did leave some further trace in foreign entrepreneurial activity in Russia. Immediately upon its appear-ance, it became part of the body of legislation referred to when the authorities considered any new foreign application for an industrial enterprise; and although such references often had little significance, this represented one further factor, however small, in favour of the foreign entrepreneur. Thus the Manifesto was one of the decrees quoted on the application of the Englishman Gardner in 1765 to set up a porcelain factory (subsequently famous) near Moscow.[182] And nearly forty years later it stood to the advantage of Charles Baird, one of the outstanding entrepreneurs of his time.

Baird came to Russia in 1786, with Charles Gascoigne. Four years later he launched out on his own in Petersburg, becoming the partner of the English instrument-maker and iron-founder, Francis Morgan.[183] Baird claimed that the foundry relied upon § 131 of the Urban Statute of 1785, which in general terms permitted foreigners to establish industrial enterprises. In fact, however, it contravened the ban, still in force, on industrial development within the city. The authorities caught up with Baird only in 1802, when he sought permission to buy peasants for his labour force. The Senate at once demanded that the College of Mines examine whether or not Baird's works could be allowed to remain in Petersburg. The enquiry showed that annual production at the works had now reached some 138,600 roubles, much of it for state authorities, the Admiralty and the Department of Artillery; the work force totalled 133, including 67 assorted apprentices. Among other connections with the Admiralty, Baird had a contract to train 20 state employees over a seven-year period, with heavy penalty clauses for non-fulfilment.

The College of Mines referred in its summing up to the law of 1762 which had been infringed; to the 1763 Manifesto (VI, §§ 3, 9); to the Urban Statute; and to the law of 31 July 1802[184] limiting the purchase of peasants for industrial purposes. The College's judgement, finally pronounced in 1804, went in Baird's favour. The number of workers involved was too small to affect the price of food in Petersburg; wood and coal prices were also unaffected because Baird imported most of his fuel (coal) from England.[185] And not only would it be very costly to move the foundry elsewhere, but it was a positive advantage in its present position, ensuring a source of government supply should state enterprises fail. As far as the labour question was concerned, however, Baird was to meet his needs by hiring artisans, or peasants seeking work on the free market. This solution would have the additional advantage of spreading technical skills among Russian artisans, some of whom might later be able to set up on their own 'or, offering their skill to someone among the great owners of capital, establish works such as Baird's'.[186]

Subsequently, in 1805 or 1806, Baird approached the Ministry of Finance with the proposal that, in view of the short-fall in skilled labour being trained in state concerns in the Urals, he should take from 50 to 100 young workers from different enterprises for five-year apprenticeships (a useful source, in fact, of cheap labour). Detailed negotiations were begun with Imperial approval in 1806.[187] Baird, at least, discharged his obligations exactly. Not only was his works a leader –

together with the state-owned Olonets-Petersburg group, still directed at this time by Gascoigne[188] – in the development of metallurgy and machine-building in Russia;[189] but, in the words of the official *Survey of Different Branches of Manufacturing Industry in Russia for 1865*, his foundry 'educated the first generation of machine-building workers' in the country.[190]

Baird's son Francis carried on the business. He achieved ennoblement and became a serf-owner before freeing his 442 peasants in 1852.[191] But Charles's grandson finally sold out to French interests in 1881 and returned to England with his family. The Baird reputation remained. There is still today a phrase remembered in Leningrad, describing something well-organized and running smoothly: *kak u Berda na zavode* – 'like at Baird's works'.[192]

6

Immigration and colonies 1797–1804

General policy on immigration

Catherine II died in November 1796 and was succeeded by her son, Paul. The brief reign of the new Emperor (1796–1801) was distinguished, according to one nationalistic Russian writer, 'by a quite parental concern for the foreign colonists'.[1] This is a somewhat extreme view, though not without its element of truth. Under Paul, thorough surveys of the colonies were conducted, and generous efforts made to improve their condition. In fact, however, these activities formed part of a much wider process, a deliberate and comprehensive effort by the government to systematize and develop certain areas of the economy. For this purpose there was created in 1797 a new 'Board (*Ekspeditsiya*) of State Economy, Guardianship of Foreigners and Rural Husbandry', attached to the Senate, and under the overall charge of the Procurator-General. The new organ's sphere of competence was defined as, initially, 'all those things which under individual administrations already existing – as for instance commerce, manufactures, and matters pertaining to mining, salt and spirits – are relevant in general to a consideration of the state economy, to draw up further measures as We shall desire'. The Board was further to discover 'reliable and useful means to improve the condition of agriculture, arts, crafts and various manufacturing trades (*remesl, khudozhestv, raznykh rukodeliy*), of factories and works, and in general everything relating to the real advantage of the state in internal and external trade'. As far as foreigners were concerned, their interests were to be safeguarded, 'setting up according to need some offices for the most immediate assistance and protection required in guardianship of them'.[2]

In practice, the main activities of the Board lay in the sphere of agriculture, and it became the earliest forerunner of the Ministry of State Domains. It has been suggested that the idea of the new agency originated with Paul's spiritual adviser, A. A. Samborsky, noted for his Anglophilia and interest in agriculture, and that it had been prompted by the recent creation of the British Board of Agriculture.[3] The inclusion of foreign colonists under the Board's jurisdiction made for the first time an institutional link between immigrants and agricultural amelioration. The idea of an explicit and institutionalized didactic role for the foreigners seems to have been adumbrated first in a Board report of 1797,[4] and the general idea found final expression in the new Rules of 1804. The new office dealt too with questions affecting the state peasantry, and this was also new: one manifestation of a growing awareness that the Russian, as well as the foreign, rural population deserved special care and attention.[5]

But if the Board of State Economy represented to some extent a new departure in official attitudes towards foreign and native peasantry, other aspects of immigration policy remained unchanged. In the south, the process of development and settlement begun under Catherine's favourites was continuing; and one of the notable measures by which the authorities now sought to further it was the declaration of free-port status for the whole of the Crimean peninsula for a period of thirty years, a declaration including special provisions for foreigners who might wish to settle there. The Manifesto published on 13 February 1798[6] was designed only for the Crimean ports. It therefore did not include Odessa, which was still enjoying the ten-year privileges conferred by Catherine at its foundation. Proposals for free-port status for Odessa, instead of the Crimea, were in fact put forward at the time, but not accepted; local pressures for such status continued over the years, however, and finally achieved their object with the support of the then Governor, M. S. Vorontsov, in 1817.[7] In the intervening period, partial measures, such as the creation of special civic administration and the extension of Catherine's privileges, allowed Odessa to maintain its favoured status, and contributed in some degree to the rapid growth both of the town and of its foreign population.[8]

In respect of foreign settlement, the 1798 Manifesto was fully in keeping with its predecessor of 1784, except that Sebastopol, 'being a military harbour', was now excluded, and attention concentrated on Eupatoria and Theodosia. Settlement in the latter was offered especially to Greeks, 'as descendants of its ancient founders'; all other nationalities were directed to Eupatoria. Among a wide range of privileges and incentives offered, three stand out. Special Imperial 'benevolence' and a suitable reward were promised, firstly, to anyone bringing in and establishing foreigners at his own expense on land in the peninsula. The recruits of such *poseliteli* were to remain free in perpetuity, to settle and work on a contractual basis, to have the right to move on on expiry of contract, and even to acquire land of their own (§ 9).

Secondly, the right of land purchase was extended by the Manifesto to all foreign immigrants of any category, and tenure was to be hereditary, 'on the same basis as nobles' (*na prave dvoryanskom*), conditional only on sale should the owner wish to leave the country (§ 2). As with the right to buy serfs offered to foreign industrialists in 1763, the authorities were prepared to go outside existing laws in order to attract immigrants. Only two years before, Paul had forbidden all movement by the peasantry of New Russia (including many foreign immigrants already settled), thereby greatly increasing the dependence of peasants on landlords, and setting off a wave of flight to the Don.[9] And the opening of land purchase to non-nobles anticipated by three years Alexander I's restoration of that privilege to Russian nationals in 1801.[10] Thirdly, the final article (§ 12) promised that all foreign settlers (including therefore town-dwellers) should be under the special protection of the Board of State Economy: an extension of the 'guardianship' principle to areas where the former Chancellery of Guardianship had only limited powers.

The new Manifesto raised the hopes of many foreigners,[11] but, implementation took time, and seventeen months later, before it had been properly put into effect, the free-port system was suspended indefinitely, on the grounds that the disturbed situation created in Europe by the French revolutionary wars made such measures impracticable.[12] Interest and belief in the idea of foreign settlement as a means to develop the south remained strong, however, and throughout Paul's reign the Board of State Economy received, and duly considered, a variety of projects for recruitment abroad. Paul's fear of subversion, and the restrictions placed on travel in and out of Russia, were limiting factors; and the negotiations and proposals of which we learn were mainly concerned either with people who had suffered directly in the French Revolution and its aftermath, or those of whose 'sound principles' there could be no doubt.

The most important case was that of the French Royalist army under the Prince de Condé. Condé's corps stood in Russian service from 1797 to 1800; and even earlier, in 1792, plans had been made for its settlement in New Russia.[13] On Paul's accession, Condé reopened this question as part of his general negotiations with Russia. Representatives were even sent to examine on the spot lands allocated on the Sea of Azov. But then the difficulties involved, and particularly a change of policy on the part of Paul, finally caused the idea to be abandoned: 'a project, the announcement of which had resounded throughout Europe, and had stirred all [French] émigrés to movement and expectancy, finally dissolved in smoke'.[14]

The negotiations with Condé were conducted through a member of the Russian mission to the Imperial diet in Regensburg, M. Alopeus, who in 1797 received in this connection a considerable sum of money, and instructions to offer asylum and settlement to all needy French rank-and-file émigrés, including peasants.[15] A dispatch early in 1798 ordered him in addition to search for 'skilful manufacturers, broad-cloth makers and dyers, also people knowledgeable in viticulture and the making of wine. . .'.[16] For such immigrants the Board of State Economy planned to establish a state cloth mill in Oryol Province, and to settle other categories in the Crimea under the 1798 free-port rules.[17]

However, while welcoming such people in principle, the government was not prepared to undertake heavy expenditure, and this combined with the political situation to hinder recruitment. Alopeus wrote in April 1798 that

as regards farmers, it is scarcely possible to have any significant number, unless one seeks them out and advances them more than has been stipulated, for travel expenses. The good characters among them have engaged themselves with peasants in Germany, who employ them for labouring, and whence it would be necessary to draw them through accredited and reliable persons such as priests, etc.[18]

and a month later: 'on the conditions which I am authorized to accept, it is scarcely possible to engage any colonists at all, and a large part of those who intended to settle in Russia have gone to Hungary. I have had only one single individual. . .'[19] His April report had noted that, in any case,

it is very difficult to form with certainty any plan whose execution would fall a few months ahead, the situation in the south of Germany being the most precarious in the world, in view of the ferment of minds excited either by the huge vexations which result from the passage and support of troops, or by the infernal manoeuvres of the cruel and perfidious policy of France, seeking only destruction.[20]

The confused situation did not, however, prevent George Trappe, the organizer of the Danzig Mennonite migration of the 1780s and early 1790s, from offering his services once more to the Russian government, this time (1798) for the recruitment of Swiss colonists for the Crimea. Trappe claimed extensive connections in the Neufchâtel area;

and the Board considered his plan well founded. But it could not proceed immediately 'in view of the fact that the new administration of the Crimea has not yet been established'; in the meantime, Trappe was appointed to the Board's staff.[21] Hopes of further Prussian Mennonites were also raised at this time, and also deferred, despite the express wish of the Emperor for their settlement and the grant in 1800 of an Imperial Charter which gave final formulation to their rights.[22] The obstacle in this case was the attitude of the Prussian government, which delayed further Mennonite emigration until 1803.[23]

If then, altogether, one can point to little immigration in Paul's reign – the Holy Cross Armenians at the beginning, a handful of Swabian peasants at the end – this was clearly not for lack of inclination in official circles; the authorities were if anything enthusiastic. Outside New Russia, an order was given to prepare land in the Saratov colonies for up to 1,000 possible new settler families;[24] and the Board did show a truly parental concern for the ninety-one Swabians, originally established on Austrian territory, who crossed the border into Russian Volhynia in 1800 and expressed the wish to settle there. A special official from the Board travelled to Zhitomir, and under his care the newcomers were finally placed on very favourable terms in the existing New Russian colony of Josephstal.[25]

Official enthusiasm for group immigration did not extend to the individual émigrés who had been arriving in Russia since the French Revolution, and who had initially enjoyed much success. Catherine in her last years had been tiring of them, of their pretensions and squabbles; and the granting of land to them had proved singularly unproductive.[26] Paul followed a stricter line; Alopeus' instructions on the subject were to admit only those noble émigrés who could show written proof that they had Imperial permission to enter the country.[27] There were some among them, however, who had projects of their own to offer, and in a few cases Alopeus, seeking recruits in the approved categories, made the first approach himself. The Baron d'Oberkirch proposed Alsatian peasants; the Abbé le Cordelier, Canon of Troyes, hoped to use his metallurgical knowledge; the Baron de Neubeck wished to establish a colony producing cloth and glass.[28] Most of these were flatly rejected, usually on the grounds of cost; but a few were more favourably received, among them an Alsatian nobleman named Siegfried, who was allowed to come to Russia to visit the southern provinces and to negotiate further with the Board of State Economy.

Siegfried was a follower of Condé, and claimed to be experienced in viticulture. He wished to set up a colony of some 250 wine-growers, most of whom, 'before the revolution, enjoyed possession of property which their attachment to sound principles had caused them to lose'.[29] These later turned out to be Germans from the Rhine. Siegfried's conditions were heavy, but the Board felt justified in meeting his expenses for the journey. Accordingly, in 1798 Siegfried made a long trip to the Crimea, from which he returned to Petersburg with detailed proposals for a large establishment producing silk, wine, tobacco, glass and wool.

There were, of course, drawbacks and difficulties. The estimated costs were high, much of the land required already occupied. The political situation in Europe remained uncertain, and the passage of migrants was therefore problematical. And Siegfried himself could produce no personal guarantors. The matter went to the Senate, which on the basis of the Board's reports rejected the plan. One additional reason adduced in justification of the refusal was the nationality of Siegfried's colonists: as Germans they were outside the instructions given to Alopeus. But the Board agreed to meet Siegfried's living expenses for the period spent in Petersburg awaiting the Senate's decision, and the costs of his journey back to Germany.[30]

More successful than Siegfried was the Frenchman Rouvier, who came to Russia at about the same time, and who was to play some part in economic development in the Crimea during the years that followed. Rouvier early became a friend of P. S. Pallas, who had settled in the Crimea in 1795; and it was in Pallas' house near Akhmechet (Simferopol) that Condé's emissary de Castres met him in April 1798. Pallas, wrote de Castres, had not been alone in urging the advantages to Condé of a settlement in New Russia. He had been seconded by

an émigré merchant of Marseille, named Rouvier. Having transported his fortune and his commerce to Malaga,[31] [Rouvier] had associated himself with one of the most considerable houses of that town and had conceived the idea of forming an establishment in the Crimea, and of setting up there manufactures of soap, candles and silk, cotton dyeing in imitation of that of Smyrna, and even of treating the wines of the country after the manner of those of Malaga.

He had disembarked at Caffa[32] with a cargo which he valued at 170,000 roubles, mainly Malaga wine; and he declared himself possessor of a letter of credit on Constantinople for 40,000 piastres. It was with the presentation of such a guarantee that Rouvier was going to solicit certain privileges from the Russian government, when there appeared the Imperial decree which, declaring free the ports of the Crimea, gave him far more than he would have dared to ask.[33]

Rouvier's projects, and his representations, were supported (according to de Castres) by Pallas, by the Governor, Kakhovsky, and by the leading landowners of the Crimea. They also encouraged him to seek concession of what remained of the silk farm set up there abortively under Catherine. Rouvier planned to supply labour for it by settling Greeks from Smyrna, whom he could engage through the Greek captain of his ship. But beyond this, he dreamed of the creation in the Crimea of a large French colony, which would both give him support, and in its turn draw assistance from his contacts and resources. 'He made this idea the text of all our conversations at Pallas' house, where we met together.'[34] It was only some years later, from Rouvier's son-in-law, that de Castres heard of the difficulties which his friend had subsequently to face:

> He told me that as soon as the merchants of Moscow had learned of Rouvier's projects, they had employed all their credit and set in motion all sorts of intrigues to make them fail. They possessed the right of acquiring annually all the raw products of the Crimea, to use in their own mediocre manufacturing, and of paying for them only the year following, by taking back there an inconsiderable part of the manufactured goods; and they feared that the establishment in the country of the smallest factory would soon attract more, and would finally deprive them of this highly lucrative branch of commerce.
>
> Acting through Petersburg merchants, they worked so successfully on the government, that despite the recommendations of Count Kakhovsky and all the proprietors of the peninsula, all Rouvier's requests were refused. He was subjected to a thousand petty annoyances; and finally, disgusted with all the obstacles placed in his way, he was only too happy to devote himself to the only occupation which did not excite the jealousy of the Russians, that of the rearing of sheep.[35]

Conspiracy theories are always a useful explanation of failure, and, while Rouvier certainly had difficulties, credence should perhaps not be given to every word in this account. Some of his plans were unrealistically grandiose.[36] In any case he soon received recognition, with the award of the new title of Commercial Councellor,[37] and he was not wholly unsuccessful in other undertakings. He helped the Board of State Economy set up a school of viticulture under Pallas in 1804 and founded his own very successful school shortly afterwards.[38] But it was certainly as a sheep farmer that he made his reputation: Skal'kovsky called him with some justification the founder of merino sheep-breeding in New Russia.[39] However, these events belong to the following reign.

The accession of Alexander in 1801 brought a number of changes in matters affecting immigration and the southern provinces. The administrative divisions of the region, for example, altered in 1797, reverted to their previous form. So did the general laws governing entry into and exit from Russia, which had been tightened under Paul; and, more specifically, new regulations were shortly promulgated governing the reception of immigrants on the borders.[40]

But basic policy remained the same; and so, despite some administrative re-organization, did the role of the Board. The desirability of attracting foreigners, particularly to the south, was accepted without question throughout the government. In a private letter of 1802 the future Minister of the Interior, V. P. Kochubey, remarked that one outstanding qualification of a governor of the Taurian Province would be an ability to attract foreigners to the area.[41] N. Mordvinov, in a memorandum dealing with proposals for the private settlement of foreigners in the Western provinces, repeated almost exactly the ideas on the value of foreign skills which Musin-Pushkin had expressed forty years before;[42] and in an official paper written the following year (1803), Minister of Commerce N. P. Rumyantsev stressed the need for foreign merchants and their capital in Odessa, because 'as yet there is none of our own'.[43] Serious attempts were made finally to settle the outstanding problems of the Crimea – in particular a Land Commission was created to resolve the tangle of property relationships which had persisted ever since the annexation of the area in 1783[44] – and to define its administrative and economic organization. In 1801, apparently at the instance of Karl Hablitzl, a member of the Board and himself a former Taurian Vice-Governor, a special high-level committee was set up 'on the establishment of the New Russian province' (*komitet o ustroyenii novorossiyskoy gubernii*).[45]

The Committee considered it axiomatic that 'the Taurian Province, in view both of its present and its future population in greatest part with foreign peoples, requires a special statute concerning its administration'.[46] (The 'foreign peoples' of course included Tatars.) This was especially important since the Committee proposed the reintroduction of the 1798 free-port system, of which Hablitzl had been one of the original authors.[47] In the event this particular measure was not carried out; it was replaced by privileges announced at the same time as the territorial re-organization (also a Committee recommendation), for Kherson, Odessa, Taganrog and Theodosia. The most important of these was the appointment of town commandants (*gradonachal'niki*) to sponsor growth in general and trade in particular; it was in this capacity that Richelieu first came to Odessa in 1803.[48] Almost all other measures on the south taken by the government, in the years with which we are concerned, also emanated from or were discussed in the Committee. And it was likewise this body which considered private proposals concerning New Russia, including a paper submitted by Rouvier.[49]

Group immigration: the Rules of 1804

Paul's reign, as has been remarked, produced few new immigrants; but within six months of his death the floodgates opened, and the authorities were confronted with a flow of both applicants and migrants which increased steadily until 1805, and ran on in the years following.[50] First to come were Greeks and Bulgarians, fleeing from Turkish bandits under the rebel Pasvan-Oglu who were ravaging Rumelia (Southern Bulgaria). The earliest arrivals, 19 families led by their priest, had been picked up by a Greek skipper sheltering from bad weather under the Rumelian coast, and were landed unexpectedly in Odessa in September 1801. Others followed. They were entrusted by Imperial decree to the Board and its newly-created New Russia Guardianship Office,[51] to be settled on the basis of the 1763 regulations, with special provision for exemptions and privileges adjusted to their situation.[52]

This marked the beginning of the Bulgarian colonies properly speaking in Russia, which in the following decades grew to form large and prosperous communities (not purely composed of Bulgarians[53]) in the Crimea, near Odessa and in Bessarabia. The Russian authorities valued these settlers highly. Co-religionists oppressed by a hostile power, they were hardy, and used to conditions similar to those of New Russia. They also showed great skill and diligence, particularly in horticulture; and subsequent Bulgarian migrants were always welcomed. Their recruitment and reception, however, at least in peace-time, could be a somewhat hazardous operation, in view of their subjection to Turkey. In 1803 Richelieu described his *modus operandi* as follows:

Today a ship leaves here for the Rumelian coasts, on the pretext of purchasing wine and timber, but intended to bring in colonists; never was the moment more favourable, the whole country is on fire, and I am assured that several thousands of individuals are only awaiting a propitious occasion to come over to us, on the ship there is a very intelligent Greek who works as an interpreter in the quarantine station, and who has continual contacts with all the people there. The pretext we have taken is a little holiday to see his relatives at Constantinople, but as a precaution he will not go as far as that; I can assure Your Excellency that all this will not cause the slightest disturbance, and I hope that we shall have a few hundred good colonists for our steppes.[54]

While the Bulgarian immigration continued, various minor groups made their appearance in different places in 1802–3. A group of Montenegrins – or 'Slavyanoserbians' – settled in the village of Nikshich near Odessa.[55] In the Caucasus Scottish missionaries established the settlement of Karass not far from Pyatigorsk, hoping to buy children from the mountain peoples and educate them as Christians.[56] Land was granted in the Crimea to another religious group, the Catholic Frères de la Rédemption, who (like the Scots) took Sarepta as their precedent; but they failed to take up their allocation.[57] And from this time dates a project, realized only much later and in part, to settle sailors – in this instance Genoese ship-owners – on the Black Sea.[58]

More importantly, large-scale immigration started again from Central Europe. In 1803, after lengthy preparations conducted mainly through the Russian consul in Danzig, Trefurt, the first of the Prussian Mennonites whom Paul had hoped for entered Russia: 162 families settled on the Molochna river, north of the Sea of Azov. Between 1803 and 1809 the total number of Mennonite families rose to 484, most of whom went to the same area.[59] In 1804 Germans who had settled as colonists in Prussia re-emigrated to Russia; and in the same period Swiss and German emigrants recruited by the Swiss Major Hans Caspar von Escher and by the Lorrainer François Ziegler were arriving in the south.

Escher was a former Zürich merchant who after failure in business had entered Russian service; by 1803 he had spent eleven years in the army. He approached the Russian authorities early that year on behalf of fellow-countrymen wishing to emigrate to Russia. His petition was granted, but on a private basis; Escher then returned to Switzerland, where he published in the newspapers what he represented as a Russian government commission. This not only incensed Petersburg, it brought him additional applicants, some of whom arrived on his doorstep in Konstanz, expecting to travel on, in September 1803. Escher had planned to leave in spring 1804; now in an untenable position, he set off into the autumn without adequate funds, at the head of 229 colonists. After a difficult passage down the Danube and overland, while the Russian missions on his route refused financial help or tried to dissuade him from proceeding further, he was finally brought to a halt in the little Hungarian town of Rosenberg when smallpox broke out among the children of his party. The colonists spent the rest of the winter in Rosenberg – the smallpox fortunately was kept in check – and finally reached New Russia the following summer (July 1804). They were settled in the Crimea, forming the colony of Zürichstal.

Meanwhile one of Escher's sons, who had travelled with his father, had returned to Switzerland and started further recruitment, which resulted in the gathering in 1804 of some 1,000 emigrants in Konstanz. With new rules limiting admission to Russia the Russian government, fearing a repetition of the father's indiscretions, forbade the son to proceed; and Escher junior simply left the assembled would-be colonists to their own resources and the Swiss authorities.

Escher's story has been told, if in somewhat summary and not entirely accurate form, on the basis of his family archives.[60] Ziegler's activities seem to have gone so far unchronicled. Yet Ziegler, though himself of little significance, was for a moment to have an important influence on the development of immigration policy. The Russian government's views on the purpose and consequently the character of foreign settlement were undergoing gradual change at this time, a change reflected in the Rules of 1804. But the immediate stimulus to the 1804 legislation was the government's experience with Escher and particularly with Ziegler, in 1803. These two *vyzyvateli* caused the authorities to reconsider both their system of recruitment and the number and nature of the colonists being enrolled. It is therefore worth following Ziegler's doings in some detail.

Ziegler had first appeared on the scene late in 1802: on 10 January 1803 Count N. P. Rumyantsev sent him with a letter of recommendation to Kochubey, Minister of the Interior, as the man 'of whom I informed Your Excellency'. Ziegler presented to Kochubey a 'Project for the Establishment of a Colony in Russia', addressed to the Tsar, and in which he described himself as 'a retired officer of the service of the King of France, and who having been like so many others affected by the French Revolution, sees himself reduced, with a number of nearly eighty families of German nationality, to seeking a new Motherland'.[61] The project resembled others presented in this period, not least those of Escher and Siegfried:

There will be among the said colonists farmers, wine-growers and people of all sorts of occupations; François Ziegler, Joseph Schurtter, former Councillor of the Tribunal of the Superintendence of Waterways and Forests of the King of France, and Valentin Guérinot, formerly employed in the collection of taxes at St Davaux, who are at the head of this establishment, direct all their attention to erecting factories in which they could use the products of the country such as flax, hemp, wool, etc.

Ziegler requested permission to visit the site of the settlement, as well as a cash grant for the maintenance of himself and his partners, and for the establishment of colony and factories.

The caution and financial stringency exhibited in Siegfried's case seem now not to have applied. Was it that Ministers took a broader view than mere civil servants, however highly placed? Or did the new Emperor feel himself less circumscribed than his father? Whatever the reason, Kochubey shortly informed D. Gur'yev, director of the Imperial Cabinet, that Alexander had approved both the project and a 1,000 rouble grant from the Cabinet for its realization.[62]

Less than a month later, and evidently without visiting New Russia, Ziegler set off 'to Switzerland', with the intention of gathering settlers. The Foreign Minister, A. R. Vorontsov, sent instructions at the same time to the Russian Chargé d'Affaires at the Court of Württemberg in Stuttgart, L. A. Yakovlev, who became the Russian representative abroad most closely involved.[63] But since Ziegler based his subsequent operations on Ulm, and dispatched his colonists by boat down the Danube to Galati (Galatz), other diplomats stationed at points along the route were drawn in: the new Resident in Regensburg, P. Klüpffell, the Chargé d'Affaires Anstedt in Vienna (in the absence of Ambassador Razumovsky), and A. Gervais, the Russian Consul at Iasi (Jassy).

Before Ziegler's departure, a set of conditions for his operation had been agreed with him; in particular, § 2 stipulated that the Russian Government would advance no money, but would take charge of the colonists and pay accounts properly presented for their journey only on their arrival at the Russian frontier. This stipulation Kochubey had taken as a general rule for all recruiting operations under his Ministry.[64] However, on arrival at Stuttgart at the beginning of May with his associate, Ziegler immediately turned to Yakovlev with a request for funds, without which he claimed to be quite unable to proceed. Yakovlev with some hesitation complied. He simultaneously wrote to A. R. Vorontsov, his direct superior, and to Kochubey, asking instructions on finance and suggesting the appointment of an experienced and reliable director to oversee the whole operation.[65]

Subsequently letters from him stressed the need for prompt action. Ziegler was reporting a daily increase in the number of families awaiting departure in Ulm and there was danger that they might go elsewhere, to avoid the expense of a long wait, 'since the agents of the Prussian Government and those of Austria are continually seeking to profit from the inclinations of these emigrants, to persuade them to go to Poland or Galicia'. Yakovlev had written to the Russian representatives in Munich, the Bavarian capital, and in Regensburg, so that they could give assistance as necessary, and he promised to inform Vienna. These measures were essential for the smooth passage of the emigrants, who could play a crucial role by sending back good reports of their journey and settlement: 'nothing will be more apt than such news to encourage their compatriots and the inhabitants of the surrounding countries, whose disposition to emigrate seems to be growing'.[66]

At the same time Ziegler wrote to Kochubey, in letters of 14/26 May and 24 May/16 June, announcing that the number of colonists now promised to be much larger than anticipated. He was sending out agents, in order, he said, to collect families who had already agreed to leave, one Joseph Pascal to Switzerland, and a Swabian (with a French name), Jean Philippe Etimes, to the Palatinate. His brother-in-law Guérinot would stay in France, 'to make the necessary acquisitions there'. But money was essential, and lacking. Ziegler requested a monthly allowance of 500 Austrian florins, and the indication of a banking house with whom he could open credit to get his operation started. His second letter promised the first transport within four weeks.[67]

Ziegler's original offer to settle 80 fellow-sufferers and their families was now becoming – as Escher's was threatening to do at about the same time – a full-scale recruiting operation in the name of the Russian government. Kochubey's reply to Yakovlev stressed the conditions agreed with Ziegler, the rule of 'no money before the frontier', and told Yakovlev to restrict himself to non-financial assistance.[68] But at the same time, apparently accepting the course of events, Kochubey presented a report to the Emperor, which resulted in authorization in early July of a grant of two thousand Imperials (*chervonnykh*) to be placed at Yakovlev's disposal 'for the migration of colonists from Switzerland'.[69] Yakovlev himself was to exercise the supervision which he had recommended, and to give Ziegler and the colonists 'all possible help'.[70] Kochubey justified the change of attitude to Yakovlev on the grounds that advances could be made now that more was known of Ziegler and his ability to carry out his proposals. He also explained that the 2,000 Imperials was an interim sum, based on Ziegler's own estimate of monthly expenses.[71] Two weeks later, Imperial authorization was given for a further 4,000 Imperials for the same purpose.[72]

Meanwhile, a report from Ziegler dated 21 June/3 July announced the departure of the first transport from Ulm the previous day. Ziegler praised the ship-wrights, who had allowed dispatch of the party without receiving agreed advance payment, 'so as not to lose us the credit and confidence of the public': Ziegler was without the ready cash required.

Some of the colonists, too, had used up their resources while waiting, and Ziegler had therefore simply asked the Russian missions in Vienna and Regensburg to help them, these advances to be deducted from the money they would receive on arrival. He also enquired whether any assistance could be given to French would-be emigrants, who Guérinot reported were prevented from making the journey to Ulm by lack of funds, 'since they have been crushed (*écrasé*) by the French Revolution'.[73]

In reply, Kochubey told Ziegler that he had 'every reason to be well satisfied with the way in which you have directed this affair', and informed him that special funds had been placed at Yakovlev's disposal. Instructions had also been sent to Moldavia and New Russia for the reception of the colonists. As far as assistance to Guérinot's Frenchmen was concerned, although this lay quite outside the agreed terms, small advances could be made.[74] Yakovlev was also informed of this.[75] These letters crossed with another from Ziegler, of 1/13 July, notifying departure of the second transport. Ziegler ended with a further plea for money, both for the maintenance of himself and his companion, and to facilitate the dispatch of the colonists: 'we are in a position to supply His Majesty with as many persons as He may desire'.[76]

However, the first transport on its journey down the Danube had by now reached Vienna, and was causing trouble to the mission there. Anstedt wrote angrily to Ziegler that he had given 'all my care to your colonists, and I do not think that it was superfluous. Their spirit was depressed by the idea of the journey which remained for them to make, because all thought that at Vienna, they had covered three-quarters of the route.' Anstedt had to make advances of 1,000–1,100 florins to indigent emigrants, in clear breach, he said, of § 2 of Ziegler's agreement with Kochubey. Ziegler had appointed no leader in the party to maintain morale and discipline, and Anstedt found that even the most prosperous of the travellers were starting to demand maintenance payments, claiming that the Russian government was obliged to defray their costs en route.[77] Further upstream, at Regensburg, Klüpffell had likewise had to give financial help.

The voyage down the lower reaches of the Danube involved some risk, since the rebel Pasha Pasvan-Oglu was active in the area. To secure the colonists' passage as far as possible, Anstedt gave them passports in Russian, German, Turkish and Latin, and wrote in advance to all Russian diplomats who might be concerned, including the mission at Constantinople.[78] These precautions were approved by Yakovlev and the government; and in the event all the transports did arrive safely in New Russia, except one, the fourth, which was attacked and plundered to the tune of 19,000 florins.[79]

The arrival of the second transport in Vienna in mid-July placed Anstedt in the same position as with the first, since his reports on the latter to Petersburg had as yet brought no response. Anstedt's situation was especially difficult: in the absence of the Ambassador he had not been fully accredited, and could raise money only in his private capacity. He sought reassurance from Klüpffell, who pointed out that, to judge by their correspondence, Ziegler and Schurtter seemed 'personally to be very honest and capable', and that Yakovlev was supporting them positively, in daily expectation of affirmative instructions.[80] Anstedt accordingly came to the aid of the second transport as well. He wrote to Vorontsov: 'It was as denuded of funds as was the first. It was Mr de Klüpffel who gave it at Ratisbonne the means to reach here, and I for my part have arranged the advances and the contracts for its navigation as far as Galati.'[81]

Schurtter, in announcing to Kochubey the departure of the third transport from Ulm (16/28 July), tried to defend himself and Ziegler against Anstedt's recriminations over § 2: 'we could not send away these excellent fathers of families who were imploring the favours and protection of His Majesty, simply for lack of funds'.[82] But this carried little weight with the Minister, in the light of the Vienna and Regensburg reports. Repeating Anstedt's strictures on the organization of the transports, he again adopted the stern tone which he had previously abandoned. Ziegler and partners were to look for assistance only to Yakovlev; the Government had in fact no obligations beyond the points agreed with Ziegler, and any predicament arising from insufficient funds would be wholly the fault of the partners.[83]

The transports meanwhile continued. The fourth left Ulm on 31 July, the fifth eighteen days later.[84] On 2 August, Yakovlev wrote acknowledging Kochubey's letter of 4 July and the first 2,000 Imperials – which would in fact only cover expenses so far. The letter was very optimistic about emigration in general, and Ziegler in particular. Ziegler had been most grateful for news of the funds authorized. He had been intending to suspend operations for the year, since despite his difficult situation he had dispatched considerably more families in his four transports to date than the 80 contracted for. But Yakovlev had now engaged him to continue until the end of the season, and to prepare new transports for next year. Yakovlev went further:

I must...on this occasion give full justice to his zeal and his activity. If despite the lack of resources and the obstacles with which he has had to contend, he has been able to organize hitherto four transports, which can presently be followed by several others, it seems to me that he deserves preferably to be employed in these matters, and one cannot doubt that with more efficacious support he would completely fulfil the aims and intentions of our Government.

Yakovlev felt that, in any case, the tendency to emigration in southern Germany and particularly Switzerland was increasing, and offered great possibilities for the future. In the same letter he enclosed for the government's information a copy of newly-published Prussian regulations designed to control and limit the flow of immigration into Prussia.[85]

Even Yakovlev, however, the most well-disposed of the Russian diplomats towards Ziegler, always had reservations, particularly on the financial question. On receipt of the additional 4,000 Imperials, he did not tell Ziegler of them, allowing the latter to think that further advances came from his own funds, since Ziegler's demands had risen on his hearing of the first 2,000.[86] And shortly afterwards, towards the end of the month, Yakovlev sent to Ulm a member of his mission, Struve, who negotiated a new contract for the supply of boats at 700 instead of 1,100 florins each: an economy which led Yakovlev to reflect on the neglect of Russian financial interests by foreigners and the consequent advantages of entrusting the immediate direction of present affairs to official personnel.[87]

This less cheerful note harmonized with the changing attitude of Kochubey, on whom Anstedt's and Klüpffell's reports of the colonists had evidently made a bad impression. He wrote to Yakovlev on 8 September that

by the description of their beggarly, so to say, condition and the high cost of the transports, I do not anticipate any benefit from their settlement in our country; and therefore I do not wish that any new colonist transports should be undertaken, at least until spring. Success in colonies can only be expected when the migrants bring, besides their own persons, some fortune (*dostoyaniye*) as well; and then it is suitable for the Government to give grants and other assistance.

This, and ignorance of the characters of Ziegler and Escher (news of whom Yakovlev had also mentioned) were the reasons for the conditions originally imposed upon them. Kochubey therefore approved Yakovlev's caution over the 4,000 Imperials and was writing to Ziegler (and Escher) to cease further dispatches for the year.[88]

With letters taking nearly a month between Petersburg and southern Germany, however, Ziegler could not be stopped at once. His reports of the fifth and sixth transports came in after Kochubey's letters had been sent, and provoked a repetition of the order. The Minister added that in future the rule of 'no money before the frontier' would be strictly observed, and said, 'I consider the principles of the Prussian government, which apportions the aid it gives in accordance with the fortune brought by the colonists, to be extremely sound.'[89] Shortly afterwards came notification of the seventh transport (dated 2/14 September).[90] The instructions reached Yakovlev in time for him to order Ziegler to stop after the eighth,[91] but in fact ten transports went through altogether. Ziegler himself accompanied the last on a new land route across the Carpathians.[92]

The original route via Galati had been suggested in a letter from Kochubey in February. During the year, proposals for an overland alternative had been put to Yakovlev by one Charles von Otto, who had some association with Ziegler; and after protracted discussion, which even threw up the suggestion of a sea route via Trieste, it was proposed that one transport should travel experimentally from Budapest via Halitsch (near L'vov) to the Russian frontier at Radzivillov.[93] The final transport of the year made very good time on the journey to Radzivillov, where it wintered; and this was the route adopted for the immigrants of 1804. Ziegler, on arrival in Radzivillov in mid-October, declared his intention of going to Odessa, 'to make sure' of the transports he had dispatched, and from there to Petersburg.[94] This he did, obtaining 700 roubles from Richelieu in December for expenses on the way.[95] His season's work had brought in over 1,000 colonists: the nine transports (out of ten) for which figures are given in the records totalled at their departure 1,014 colonists of both sexes.[96]

The remaining correspondence between Petersburg and the missions abroad during September 1803 was largely concerned with financial matters, but hopes were expressed of more profitable immigration in the following year. Yakovlev declared that the 1803 operation should be seen as no more than a trial run, and that 'if Your Excellency is pleased to instruct me, I shall take advantage of the winter to take new measures'.[97] Kochubey returned repeatedly to the theme that only reasonably prosperous colonists could be beneficial to the state, and that missions should avoid any except diplomatic and consular help to migrants: 'all difficulties should be overcome once we return to the rule from which Ziegler ought never to have departed. . .'. But he was still prepared to have Ziegler come to Petersburg (at his own expense) 'for the composition of new measures should these be necessary'.[98]

In January 1804 Ziegler, undeterred by his difficulties, presented plans for the continuation of the previous year's operations.[99] However, the Ministry of the Interior had meanwhile found time to formulate its own intentions on further immigration, and these were now submitted for Imperial approval in a report signed by Kochubey, Hablitzl, and the head of the Board's First Section, Zhukovsky. The report summed up the position to date, discussed the aims and methods of immigration into Russia from the West, and laid down norms and procedures for the future.[100]

The new terms applied neither to immigration from the Balkans nor to the Mennonites, who as acknowledged experts in farming had special conditions of their own based on the Charter of 1800. The report's proposals were prompted immediately by the difficulties experienced with Ziegler and Escher, and by the evidence of a growing tide of emigration in Europe,[101] though they also reflected wider policy issues which will be mentioned later. It is tempting to speculate on the possible influence of the Prussian statute sent in by Yakovlev five months previously, but no firm evidence is available for this.

Catherine II, the report stated, had encouraged foreign immigration

from a desire to populate the empty steppes. But when overcrowding and the increase of population in the internal provinces may require the settling out of [Your Majesty's] own subjects, and lands in the southern region suitable for settlement are already no longer plentiful; then the aim should be less their population with foreigners, than the settlement on them of a limited number of such immigrants as might serve as examples in peasant occupations or in handicrafts.

State land was becoming scarce in the south; therefore to avoid long and expensive delays it was essential to determine and obtain beforehand plots suitable for colonists, 'by the choice of state [land] or by purchase from land-owners'. This latter solution had in fact frequently to be adopted: the land so generously and freely distributed to all comers only a few years before was now purchased back, often still completely empty, into the Treasury.[102]

The categories to be settled on the land thus chosen were carefully defined. Those most welcome were

good farmers and people sufficiently skilled and experienced in wine-growing, the raising of mulberries and other useful cultures, also those expert in stock-breeding, and especially in the maintenance and increase of the best breeds of sheep, and having in general all necessary knowledge of the best agriculture.

'Rural craftsmen' could also be included; other artisans 'who are of no use for rural life' would not be accepted under the colonist regulations, though if need arose, small numbers might be recruited specially for southern towns.

Any sort of enticement or persuasion, and special agents and commissions to encourage immigration, were (the report continued) undesirable. Foreigners wishing to settle in Russia as colonists should present themselves to Russian missions abroad, which would supply passports for the journey. Testimonials of good character from the authorities of the previous domicile were demanded, as well as proof of fulfilment of all obligations there, and of payment of debts. To facilitate the passage of the colonists, Klüpffell in Regensburg was empowered to make up transports of 20 to 30 families together and – contrary to the suppositions of the previous year – to dispatch them by boat or cart at government expense, under the orders and leadership of an Elder selected from their number. The report proposed Ziegler as Klüpffell's assistant, 'in view of his suitability to this, and his energy and resourcefulness (*rastoropnost'*)'.

The number of immigrants to be admitted each year was set at 200 families, as the maximum which could be conveniently settled in one season. Klüpffell himself was to select only 100 to 150 of these, since it was assumed that the remainder of the quota would be filled by others coming in by different routes. A means test was imposed. Would-be colonists had to prove possession of at least 500 talers (later 300 guilders) in cash or goods, 'for experience has taught that the establishment of poor immigrants both proceeds slowly and gives little success'. No maintenance grant would be given before the Russian border.

Furthermore, only families (*lyudi semyanistyye*) would be accepted. Childless couples were admissible, though undesirable; single people were quite excluded unless taken on as members of another family.

To the fecund, upright, skilful and prosperous peasant *paterfamilias* who thus remained eligible, the report extended all the by now traditional rights, exemptions and privileges. In some cases, the new rules improved upon the old. The normal land grant became 60 desyatinas (with special rules for the Crimea), maintenance payments were not to be refunded unless the immigrant left the country, and the establishment grant of 300 roubles could be increased for any special undertaking on the part of particularly wealthy colonists.

The report was approved in draft by the Emperor on 5 February 1804, and finally on 20 February. It was followed by other measures designed to systematize and facilitate settlement in the south. A decree of 23 February, 'on places for the settlement of foreigners', set specific priorities in the choice and distribution of land.[103] Another of 1 March allowed foreign settlers to buy land in New Russia:[104] an explicit extension of the general right of land purchase granted in 1801, and a privilege widely used, especially by the Mennonites, in subsequent years. In April, permission was renewed for colonists to settle on land-lords' estates, and the terms of such settlement were redefined.[105]

The provisions of the February report were given definitive form as a set of Rules, which were shortly printed for distribution.[106] Ziegler, now in government service, received the rank of College Secretary, and 300 Imperials for the journey to Regensburg. The new dispensation gave him a monthly salary of 600 florins, to cover both his own and administrative expenses, and the prospect of a cash reward for success-ful work. But he was in all things completely subject to Klüpffell.[107] Meanwhile, copies of the report were sent south, and Klüpffell was informed of his new task, his main responsibilities being the efficient and economical organization of transport, and above all 'the choice of the colonists, which must be sufficiently rigorous to give us only indi-viduals who are healthy, strong industrious and prosperous (*aisés*)'.[108] The Foreign Ministry was asked to prepare French and German trans-lations for dispatch to all relevant missions, so as to establish exact guidelines and 'to free us from the projects which are constantly being sent in in this field'. The Ministry was to emphasize separately to its diplomats abroad the government's intention 'not to attract large numbers of foreigners, but to open the way only for good farmers and other useful and well-provided (*bezbednykh*) people'.[109]

One problem raised by the new system was the time limit to be set for its introduction. Individual immigrants were continually appearing from various parts of southern Germany who could not have heard of the new requirements, and could not meet them, but who would be completely ruined if simply turned away. It was suggested that the deadline should be the entry into force of new frontier regulations already promulgated, which would become effective in May and which also covered colonists entering Russia.[110] However, an Imperial order of 20 March merely decreed that the new Rules should not be rigorously applied at once to poor immigrants: 'these foreigners should not be oppressed by any premature hindrances (*zatrudneniya*), lest on return-ing to their former homes they spread abroad a damaging impression'. Instructions to this effect went out with the new Rules to the Governors of the Western border provinces.[111]

In the midst of these precautions, there arrived a completely un-expected letter from Schurtter in Ulm. Left by himself while Ziegler was in Russia, and not knowing how to answer applicants who approached him during the winter, he had been enrolling them provisionally, warning against the sale of property until instructions were received. Then on 21 February he received a letter from Ziegler announcing 'the continuation of the Commission'. The news spread rapidly; now, said Schurtter, 'everybody is eager to be the first to leave'. The numbers were growing daily, nearly 1,500 families were enrolled, 'and are taking with them at least one million in property either now or to follow; an infinite number of the richest families await Mr Ziegler's return with impatience. . .'. But Schurtter did not know Ziegler's whereabouts, and appealed to Kochubey for help. Navigation opened in April. Money was running low, since a letter of credit promised by Ziegler had not arrived. Worse, the Bavarian Commissioner-General at Ulm had just officially forbidden any further enrolment or dispatch of colonists without his permission, an action Schurtter considered to be both in conflict with the expressed benevolence of the Bavarian Elector, and extremely detrimental to his undertaking – 'such a proceeding could destroy any project, and the public would lose all confidence'.[112]

Schurtter's letter was left unanswered for some time; then Kochubey administered a sharp rebuke. Ziegler had no right to speak of the commission continuing. He had never had authorization in the first place to set up a recruiting office; and sole authority for colonist affairs was now vested in Klüpffell, who would disavow anyone falsely claiming official Russian accreditation of any kind.[113]

By now Klüpffell had received notification of his new responsibilities, and had written at the end of March acknowledging them. After the experiences of the previous year, and personal acquaintance with Ziegler, he was on his guard, and had not a single good word now to say for his new assistant:

He has great faults, by which he can easily compromise both himself and those over him. He likes to boast, to cut a dash by his manner and by pretensions to rank, and to give himself great importance. In view of their possible consequences, I cannot but point out these facts to Your Excellency, to anticipate the equally possible case of his arrest during one of his various errands, and reference back to me, which would become most embarrassing. For this reason I shall not let him set foot on French territory.

I know that he has begun to give offence [in Ulm]; but it is there that he will need to go again, especially as his associate Schurtter has remained there and maintained his relations with the surrounding areas, and without this Schurtter he can do absolutely nothing, being himself illiterate and only able to sign his name. Such ignorance in a man who claims to have been, and has the papers of, an officer, has always seemed suspicious to me, and I must confess to Your Excellency that, all things considered, it will be difficult to expect a continuation of useful services.[114]

These forebodings were amply borne out in the months following. But meanwhile a new complicating factor arose: the reappearance of Charles von Otto, the person who had proposed the overland route the previous year. Otto had already once written to Petersburg, in November 1803, from Switzerland, claiming to be there under Ziegler's instructions and to have 200 families, 'artisans, farmers and manufacturers', ready to leave the following year. He was disturbed by the curtailment of official Russian support, and sought Kochubey's protection.[115] This letter went unanswered. In mid-April 1804 there arrived another, from Stuttgart, declaring that Otto, now independent of Ziegler, had some 700 families from Alsace and the Rhine wishing to settle in Russia, 400 of them prosperous, with property to the value of 80,000 florins. He asked only passports and protection for the journey, and said that he expected to arrive with his first party at his chosen collecting point of Lauingen, near Ulm, in three to four weeks' time.[116]

Official reaction to this was simply that the new Rules should apply in Otto's as in other cases; and this was the answer sent to Yakovlev when he wrote for instructions following an approach from Otto in Stuttgart.[117] Yakovlev thereupon contacted Klüpffell to suggest that, if convenient, the latter should handle Otto's colonists with the rest.

Klüpffell had already met Otto the previous year, and had in fact had difficulty in escaping his importunities. From Klüpffell's letters, and other papers of the case, a fairly clear picture of Otto emerges. As a former Austrian officer, he had first made proposals for the recruiting of settlers to the Austrian government. Rebuffed, he tried in 1803 to join Ziegler's venture. During the winter he was able to recruit on the basis of a loose association with Ziegler and Schurtter, claiming at the same time to be an official Russian agent. But in the spring of 1804 they fell out, and the latter two hastened to denounce Otto to Klüpffell, quite accurately, as an unprincipled adventurer. Otto went his own way, and in April assembled some 1,000 recruits in Lauingen. According to some of his victims, he distributed printed certificates signed by himself for the emigrants' admission into Russia; he furnished printed descriptions of the country, with details of colonists' privileges;[118] and he gave printed receipts for the 35 Rhenish guilders he demanded of each family, and which went in part to pay the passage down to Regensburg. Finding the Russian door closing, however, he hurriedly sent off two transports in order, as Klüpffell said, to relieve some at least of the pressures which his actions had built up upon him.[119] A German newspaper report received in Petersburg described how the first transport had set off 'in two craft down the Danube under the direction of the Russian Court's Commissioner Herr von Otto. Both vessels have a magnificent Russian flag, hung out to the sound of Turkish music (*vystavlennomu s Turetskoyu Muzykoyu*)'.[120]

The first of Otto's transports reached Regensburg at the end of April, shortly after Ziegler, who was belatedly on his way from Petersburg to organize his own dispatches. He reported that only four families qualified under the new regulations. Then he hastened off to Ulm, Klüpffell being already glad to be rid of him.[121] Otto's first transport was followed shortly by a second, all the families of which, like those of the first, were expecting to be accepted. Further close inspection of both groups showed that Ziegler had exaggerated and that about one third of the total 77 were eligible. Klüpffell even thought at first that they would almost all pass muster, 'since they had had the idea of helping each other by passing among themselves the money which each family had to prove it possessed. I could only avoid cheating in this respect by demanding the placing together of all their purses.'[122] It took Klüpffell eight days to sort out the situation and persuade the emigrants, who desperately wanted to stay together, that they would have to split up. He accepted 24 families for entry into Russia, and sent them on downstream in early May to Vienna, where the Ambassador, Razumovsky, arranged their onward journey by the overland route.[123]

Klüpffell found that Otto's recruits were mainly from Alsace and Baden, whereas Ziegler's came largely from Württemberg and Swabia. Klüpffell gave preference to Otto's Alsatian colonists, justifying the choice on the grounds that they were relatively well-to-do, that they were only a few weeks from home – and so had not exhausted their resources like some of Ziegler's people, who had been waiting since the previous year – and that in any case they had emigrated only to avoid unbearable taxation and conscription. Ziegler was accordingly told to send from Ulm only as many as would make up the quota.[124] Otto's third transport arrived in Regensburg from Lauingen on 14 May, and the families qualifying, 22 in number, set off again two days later.

The poorer colonist families of Otto's transports were simply left to their own devices. But 65 of them, in all 305 people, refused to accept their rejection by Klüpffell and sailed on at their own expense. They made their way without help to Budapest, then struggled further via Duklo and L'vov, receiving some help with transport for their sick from local Austrian authorities, and finally reached the Russian border at

Brody, where their resources failed. From Brody on 2 July they addressed a petition to the Tsar, begging protection and declaring their devotion to Russia which had led them in Vienna to reject various offers to settle in Austrian territory. The case of the stranded families was taken up by Richelieu, and Imperial approval soon granted for their admittance, on the basis of the decision to continue acceptance of poor immigrants for the time being. The 65 families were sent on down to Odessa on the same footing as the rest.[125]

On 15 May, Ziegler arrived in Regensburg from Ulm, bringing with him the full number of families which he was allowed, 72. Rather to Klüpffell's surprise, the majority of these were acceptable, despite the speed with which Ziegler had put his party together.[126] Ziegler's haste to return to Regensburg was occasioned in Klüpffell's view by the growing seriousness of the situation in Ulm. Bavarian disquiet was justified: Schurtter's excessive enrolment had brought German and some French families into the town and its environs 'to the number of 1,474, who only subsist on public charity and help given by the town authorities, without even knowing what fate awaits them'.[127] Otto in Lauingen also had recruits on his hands. On 19 May the Bavarian Minister Rechberg officially notified Klüpffell of the situation, presented complaints from emigrants against Ziegler and Schurtter, and promised shortly to start formal communications on the matter. The Bavarian position was especially delicate since the Elector of Württemberg had protested at the toleration of a foreign recruiting office so close to his borders, and Klüpffell was apprehensive that Bavaria might finally have recourse to forcible repatriation of the Württembergers among those now stranded and destitute, a proceeding likely to be resisted by Württemberg.[128]

This news, received in Petersburg in June, decided the Russian government to suspend all further transports for the year. Additional immigrants might be accepted only as a last resort to save families enrolled by the self-styled commissioners from total abandonment. Ziegler's salary was stopped, and he himself declared removed from any part in colonist affairs; the only crumb thrown to him was permission to go to Richelieu in Odessa if he chose.[129] Klüpffell's next letters, received at the beginning of July, reported the departure of further transports, the sixth and seventh, in the last week of May, and forwarded to the Foreign Ministry the Bavarian Note from Rechberg. Klüpffell had been able to give a satisfactory answer, using Kochubey's earlier correspondence with Schurtter.[130]

Russian measures to rectify the situation continued. Articles were placed in the newspapers of Frankfurt and Hamburg announcing cessation of admission to Russia, and stressing that Petersburg had no authorized commissioners anywhere in Germany.[131] Yakovlev secured Württemberg permission for those who had left the Electorate to return, and for those preparing to leave, to remain. And he had Otto arrested in Stuttgart for misrepresentation and fraud.[132]

At the same time, an official Note delivered by the Bavarian Ambassador in Petersburg indicated that the Electoral authorities had been guided in their initial permissive attitude to Ziegler and Schurtter by the representations of Russian diplomats at Munich and in Swabia. Hitherto Kochubey had tended to the view that some blame at least for the situation attached to the Bavarian government, which had made too little effort to check on the supposed commission. However, in view of the Bavarian Note, orders were sent to Klüpffell (29 July) to try to persuade emigrants to return home, but to ensure that any remaining without means who still wished to go to Russia were sent on, with payment of all expenses if necessary. This operation was to be kept secret, to avoid renewed applications.[133]

During July, Klüpffell had to deal with additional transports of 72 families, allowed by the Bavarian authorities to pass through to Regensburg at the express request of the Russian Ambassador in Munich, and to whom Klüpffell therefore could not refuse passports.[134] These, however, he considered the last, and at the end of the month sent in his accounts for the costs of eleven transports to the Russian frontier: 30,763 florins, 11 Kreutzer.[135] To fulfil the instructions on help for possible destitute colonists, Struve repeated his journey of the year before to Ulm, and visited Lauingen. In both places, all the emigrants had dispersed, and only one group of 49 Württemberg families, who had already once approached Klüpffell, were found to be stranded because of difficulties over their rights of citizenship. They were of good character and some means, and were allowed to set out at once, despite the – by now – late season.[136]

With that, the affair was more or less closed. In all, the lists for Klüpffell's official colonists (not including the 65 'poor' families and others who made their own way) show a total of 323 families dispatched in 1804, 2,213 people.[137] In succeeding years the Russian recruitment was influenced by various factors, both in Europe and at home, while immigration continued at a fairly high level. But the regulations laid down for the different colonist groups – the 1800 Charter to the Mennonites, the decree of 23 October 1801 to Greeks and Bulgarians, and finally the Rules of 1804 governing other European immigration – formed the basic framework for the colonization of Alexander's reign, as the 1763 Manifesto had provided the 'civic constitution' for settlers under Catherine.

Neither Escher nor Ziegler, who had so contributed to the appearance of the 1804 Rules, profited from their ventures in the end. Escher tried over several years to justify himself before the authorities, and suffered arrest and penury before achieving partial success in 1806, when he was granted a small pension and land in New Russia. This did not satisfy him, however, and he returned to the charge, until in 1808 he was told bluntly that his case was closed.[138] Ziegler was even less fortunate. The salary owing to him when his employment was cut short was insufficient to satisfy his creditors in Ulm and Regensburg, and special grants had to be made to deserving cases there, as well as in Odessa. Ziegler received passports to take his family to New Russia, and went as far as Brody, though Guérinot refused to accompany him. Our last glimpse of him is in 1805: living with his family in Brody, ever deeper in debt, he had renewed his pretensions to help from the Russian government – and received a definitive refusal.[139]

The New Russian Guardianship Office and the settlement of new colonies

The body to whom it fell to organize the settlement, not only of Escher's and Ziegler's recruits, but of the Mennonite and Balkan immigrants who continued to arrive, was the New Russian Guardianship Office. The renewed use of local supervisory organs for colonists was envisaged at the foundation of the Board of State Economy; and first the Saratov Office was resurrected (30 June 1797),[140] then, three years later, came the foundation in Yekaterinoslav of the 'Office of Guardianship of New Russian Foreign Settlers', usually shortened to the title above.[141]

The first Chief Judge, or Principal, of the New Russia Office was College (shortly State) Counsellor Samuel Contenius, appointed from the Geographic Department of the Board of State Economy on the founding of the Office in 1800. Born in Westphalia in 1748, son of a poor pastor, Contenius came to Russia as a private tutor, then entered state service in 1785.[142] He was one of those rare persons, rarer still in the Russian bureaucracy, who inspire sympathy and respect in all who know them. During his tenure of office, 1800–1818, he worked incessantly for the colonists, much to the detriment of his own health, and stayed on even after his final retirement, at the request of the Emperor himself, to help in a re-organization of the colonist administration then impending.

It is difficult to avoid superlatives in speaking of Contenius. Contemporary references and the archives of the Board contain scarcely a word of hostility to or criticism of him. When in 1807 his health became too bad for him to continue running the Office, Richelieu recommended that he should be given instead the narrower task of supervising the economic development of the colonies, retaining his previous rank and salary.[143] On this basis Contenius remained a valued member of the administration. In 1818 the Emperor personally decorated him with the ribbon and star of St Anne, first class, a distinction shared – according to A. M. Fadeyev, then an official in the Office – only by Karamzin, the distinguished writer and historian.[144] On his death in 1830, Contenius left a considerable sum towards the training of teachers and clergy for the colonies;[145] and his work was finally commemorated in the name of the colony Konteniusfeld.

However, Contenius' place as overall head of the Guardianship Office was not adequately filled after 1808, and this had serious consequences, especially as many of the Office's other members were men of less attractive qualities. One of the most prominent in the early stages was Ivan Brigonzi, of Italian parentage. He became Director of the New Russian Colonies in 1797, succeeding the first two holders of the office, Major J. von Essen and Baron Johann von Brackel,[146] and joined the Office on its formation as Deputy (*Tovarishch*) to Contenius. Although Brigonzi appears in the files of the Board as an honest and efficient administrator, de Castres, for whom he served as interpreter in 1798, gave him a very bad character.[147] Other members were often no better. Contenius' other Deputy, Dizdarev, and the accountant Gzel', were later found guilty of large-scale embezzlement. An official enquiry instituted in 1812 into the running of the Office revealed a state of chaos and negligence going back several years,[148] while officials in charge of particular areas – the Molochna and the Odessa German colonies – proved unable to justify their accounts. (It was characteristic that the official in charge of the investigation finally laid himself open likewise to suspicions of embezzlement.)

The Supervisor of the Odessa German colonies, Rosenkampf, was a special protégé of Richelieu, and the Duke took responsibility for him. From the time of his appointment in 1803 as Town Commandant of Odessa, Richelieu had taken a close interest in the colonies. In his official capacity he was in any case involved in the efforts of the Office to find temporary accommodation for Ziegler's recruits. But he went further and in October 1803 asked to be given special charge of their settlement. The Emperor immediately agreed; in fact, Alexander stated: 'I shall consider this a personal favour to Me'.[149] In February 1804, Richelieu was given general charge of the Guardianship Office and the whole settlement programme.

The next year this situation was regularized with his promotion to the Military Governorship of Kherson Province, based on Odessa and with responsibility for the other two provinces of New Russia.[150] Richelieu's jurisdiction now extended over all the areas where settlement was taking place, and he co-operated actively with Contenius in the Office's work, though still retaining a closer interest in the Odessa settlement. His excellent connections with Petersburg facilitated considerably the flow of funds and government attention to the southern colonies.[151]

Richelieu has been regarded as outstanding in his administration of New Russia, and he himself considered the colonies the most successful part of his work.[152] Even after his departure to France following the Bourbon restoration, he asked the Russian Minister of the Interior to keep him in touch with their development.[153] In respect of the embezzlement and maladministration uncovered by the 1812 enquiry, and which caused him unpleasantness with Petersburg, he could justifiably claim that the extent and complexity of his responsibilities made personal supervision impossible: 'How could I be responsible for a theft committed five hundred versts from my place of residence, obliged as I am in any case to be almost continuously on the move in order to attend to the different matters entrusted to me?'[154] Nevertheless, it was for Richelieu to ensure adequate supervision in the absence of a satisfactory replacement for Contenius; and for all his undoubted energy and concern, there may have been some truth in a later assertion that he spent time writing to Petersburg which should have been used for action on the spot.[155]

The first immigrants to require the assistance of the Guardianship Office were the Greek and Bulgarian arrivals of 1801. The Board of State Economy ordered Contenius from the Office in Yekaterinoslav to Odessa, to take charge of the newcomers and plan their settlement in detail. Meanwhile the New Russian Civil Governor,[156] Miklashevsky, started repairs to empty barracks in Odessa, to provide quarters for the winter.

It turned out that the first party were all Greeks. Contenius wrote with approval of their skills in wine-growing and sericulture, and of their cleanliness and tidiness, maintained despite their poverty.[157] In the spring of 1802, Brigonzi was sent down to direct the process of settlement, and he remained the official most closely involved. Arrivals of Bulgarians and Greeks continued through 1802 and in the following seasons, the largest numbers falling in 1804. Some of the foreigners were settled in the former Turkish colony of Ternovka near Nikolayev, others on land near Odessa, and in the Crimea.

By February 1803 Brigonzi was painting a fine picture of the first colonies. In Malyy Buyalik, on the Adzhelik stream by Odessa, the full complement to date of 54 stone houses had been built 'with the requisite exactness'. Each household had 'places for a yard, garden and orchard'; many had 'already managed to surround these with a ditch, and to make stone shelters for the cattle'; and some had started the spring ploughing and sowing. Lack of water was overcome 'by the increase of wells' and the construction of a dam. All the settlers had 'everything required for the full establishment of their economy', at a cost, including their houses, of 260 roubles 90 kopecks per family (below the regulation grant); it would be cheaper still, Brigonzi remarked, in Ternovka where houses were still standing and prices lower.[158] Brigonzi's zeal, and that of his two local assistants, was noted and earned him an official commendation.[159] By 1806 the total number of Greeks and Bulgarians of both sexes thus settled, in six villages, was 2,897.[160]

The first Bulgarian colonists were scarcely established when the new wave of Mennonite immigration began. This was well organized, and the newcomers were greatly helped by the presence in Russia of their Khortitsa co-religionists. Contacts between Khortitsa and the parent communities in Prussia had played in fact a considerable part in the migration, much to the pleasure of the Russian authorities. Most of the new Molochna colonists were prosperous, even wealthy, and their settlement was accomplished with a minimum of difficulty.[161]

Not so that of the Germans arriving at the time down the Danube. They came in larger numbers than anticipated, not a few sick or with resources exhausted on the journey. Less prosperous and organized than the Mennonites, less hardy and adaptable than the Bulgarians, they required in Richelieu's view considerably more care and guidance.[162] It is therefore not surprising to find a note of anxiety in correspondence between Petersburg and the south. When in October 1803 Kochubey sent to Richelieu the rescript approving the latter's supervision of the Odessa colonies, he added a personal letter, which he concluded:

The Emperor, in signing the rescript which you receive today, my Lord Duke, charged me to write to you particularly to direct your full attention to our colonists. He fears that they may experience all the disorders which the first colonists underwent in the reign of the Empress Catherine, and requests that you neglect nothing to ensure that these poor people have no cause to repent their departure from their native land.

Similar instructions went to Contenius at about the same time.[163]

The German immigration of 1803–4 certainly had features in common with the influx of the 1760s, though as numbers were fewer the problems were not so severe, while the Russian authorities showed greater determination in dealing with them. From the outset, the passage down the Danube in the conditions of summer was prone to cause illness, despite Anstedt's efforts from Vienna to prevent it. Where discipline and leadership were lacking, as in most of the early transports, precautions were neglected, while the river water, and ripe fruit along the banks, proved irresistible temptations. Many colonists of the first transports fell sick, and emergency medical care had to be provided at Galati and Dubossary, the entry into Russia. Nearly 100 immigrants died on the journey in 1803.[164]

Meanwhile in July 1803, in response to the first letters from Ulm, instructions had gone from Petersburg to all the relevant authorities in New Russia to ensure the best possible treatment of the new German immigrants. Richelieu was made responsible for their immediate needs, while the Guardianship Office was to receive special instructions from the Board concerning their settlement.[165] Directives to the Governor-General, Bekleshov, showed a particular interest in the wine-growers among the newcomers. His active assistance was desirable particularly because

according to the information received here these colonists are largely of good standing (*khoroshiye khozyayeva*), being specifically wine-growers, agriculturists and handicraftsmen, of whom each must receive a fair establishment according to his occupation. The wine-growers should be settled in the Crimea, the farmers in the Kherson and Yekaterinoslav Provinces on fertile land, and the hand-workers should be offered the opportunity of staying in the towns.

Furthermore, future immigration would inevitably depend upon the reports sent back by the present colonists.[166]

Information on the colonists from Anstedt reached Odessa even before the July instructions from Petersburg. Richelieu wrote at once to Kochubey promising barracks to house the impending arrivals and assuring the Minister that immediate requirements would be met. He had difficulties in fulfilling his promise, but when the colonists of Ziegler's first transport reached Odessa on 12 September 1803, accommodation was ready for them.[167] Under the joint direction of Contenius and Richelieu, successive transports were housed for the winter in Odessa, land allocations were sorted out in consultation with representatives of the colonists, and suitable families were selected for the Crimea.

In 1804 the process of settlement itself got under way. The distribution of Ziegler's recruits followed very much the pattern prescribed to Bekleshov, which was also that laid down in the decree of February 1804 on settlement priorities.[168] Under these rules, settlement was to begin as near as possible to seaports, which would give the best market for agricultural produce: for example Odessa and Theodosia. Subsequent immigrants could settle progressively further inland. The environs of Theodosia and the mountainous part of the Crimea in general were designated priority areas for viticulture and horticulture. And while artisans could settle in any town in the region, the first of the newcomers, those arriving at the time of the decree, were to stay in Odessa.

Accordingly, the largest contingent of new settlers, and of those following them in the next few years, established colonies on lands around Odessa. Some went to the older Yekaterinoslav colonies and to the Molochna region, which were approved because of the proximity of the Mennonites; while others, together with Escher's Swiss, formed six new villages in the Crimea. Artisan families settled in several towns: Grigoriopol, Odessa, Simferopol, Theodosia and Yekaterinoslav (which also received some Mennonites).[169]

The actual task of establishing the settlers presented familiar difficulties. Expenses for all immigrants were as always relatively high. In December 1803 Contenius estimated the total cost for the coming year of maintaining and settling even those already arrived (of all groups) at 361,000 roubles. The Germans received a larger establishment grant than the Bulgarians – calculated at 355 roubles per family, as against 277 – besides incurring higher transport costs; and their expenses consequently represented the largest part of the total.[170] House-building in the Odessa German colonies went slowly because of the failings of the contractors, who had labour problems. Of 500 houses needed, only 90 were finished in August 1804; and the colonists themselves had been set to break stones for building. This proved quite effective, but it took them away from essential work in the fields.[171]

Even with colonist labour and extensive use of dug-outs, by the end of 1804 many of that year's arrivals were still unhoused, so that recourse was made again to the (inadequate) barracks of Odessa and Ovidiopol.

Meanwhile many of the 1803 immigrants had again fallen sick in the summer weather: during August and September 1804 fever and dysentery struck some 500 of the Odessa contingent, causing those affected to miss the autumn sowing.[172] But still, Brigonzi was able to find some consolation. The immigrants of 1804, who had undergone Klüpffell's selection process, he thought much superior to their predecessors; and during the work in the Odessa German colonies he continued to supervise the Bulgarians, expressing admiration both for their diligence and their success.[173]

The events of 1804 foreshadowed the pattern of colonist affairs in New Russia for several years to come. Reports in 1805 already indicated a need for still more land and, with regard to the Germans, stressed the urgency of a strict application of the 1804 rules, both abroad and on the frontier. The Odessa German colonies in particular gave concern to Richelieu and the Guardianship Office; but in the decade following their settlement, and despite the rules of 1804, the Germans at large proved themselves less self-sufficient and adaptable than either the Mennonites or the Bulgarians. In October 1806, Richelieu summed up the situation:

> What shall I say to you of our colonists? They are the same as ever, that is, the Mennonites are astonishing, the Bulgarians incomparable, and the Germans intolerable. The harvest of the latter was worse than mediocre, and in large measure they are themselves the cause. They will have nothing to live on, at least those around Odessa, and however regrettable it may be, we shall not be able to avoid giving them assistance, since otherwise they will die of hunger. The Crimean colonists will manage without maintenance payments, as will those living on the Molochna Waters. The Bulgarians are rich, and had a good harvest.[174]

While this judgement may be coloured by Richelieu's nearness to the Odessa colonists, they certainly deserved their special mention. Finally, in 1812–14, the weakest among them had to be sifted out, an operation based explicitly on the 1775 selection in the Saratov colonies;[175] and again as in Saratov, it was only in the second generation that they really found their feet.

Yet in spite of this, the authorities still considered immigration of great importance for the development of the region. Not only did the good qualities of the Bulgarians and Mennonites to some extent balance the deficiencies of the Germans, in the years following 1804 the agricultural colonies were complemented by special artisan settlements in urban centres: Khar'kov, Odessa, Poltava, Taganrog.[176] Both Richelieu and the Petersburg government thus remained strongly in favour of continuing immigration from any source, provided it was sufficiently selected and controlled; and the policy was not difficult to execute. In the first nine years alone of the nineteenth century, 6,082 colonist families of various nationalities came to New Russia, 21,986 persons in all, at an average cost to the government per family of 480 paper and $17\frac{1}{2}$ silver roubles: altogether somewhat over 3,000,000 paper roubles.[177]

The re-organization of the colonies' administration

Parallel with the negotiations of Paul's reign and the renewed immigration under Alexander, the local administration of the foreign colonies underwent considerable re-organization; the creation of new Guardianship Offices was merely one step in this process. Shortly after its creation, the Board of State Economy instituted a comprehensive survey of the colonies, designed to systematize and improve their position: a process carried out in the six years after 1797 for all the original settlements. Each colony or group of colonies was 'revised' by an official of the Board, and on the basis of the latter's reports steps were taken to rectify the defects uncovered. In most cases, this entailed the allocation of additional land, and often the adjustment of the colonists' financial position.[178] The creation of Offices for the largest settlements was paralleled by the appointment of a supervisor (*smotritel'*) for the Petersburg group;[179] and all colonies were placed under the direct jurisdiction of the Board.[180]

Another measure was the standardization of colonist status. Despite the abortive free-port proposals of 1798, by 1800 the sphere of control of the Board had been defined and restricted to settled agricultural groups, and the foreign colonist artisans and others scattered in the towns of the south were therefore excluded from its jurisdiction.[181] Other anomalies were cleared up. The Swedish colonists had never had full status under the 1763 rules, since they had migrated within the Empire. It was now recognized that their change of environment had been so radical that nonetheless they deserved to be considered on the same basis as foreigners.[182] On the other hand, the Bulgarians who had settled by contract at the Monastery of the Brethren, near Kiev, were refused colonist status and assigned to the state peasantry, even though the monastery lands had reverted to the Treasury. The Senate decided that in such cases the 1763 Manifesto could apply only to those settled by the state.[183]

The new colonist offices received detailed Instructions on their duties, and on administrative procedure. Perhaps the single most significant clause in these documents was the ruling that all communication with the colonists should be conducted 'in their dialect': German and Bulgarian.[184] Efforts were made at the same time to encourage the spread of Russian: the New Russian Office was to send colonist orphans to state schools for this purpose, so that they could later act as secretaries and teach other children in the colonies.[185] But this was a mere palliative measure; there is little evidence on how it was carried out, but it seems to have had no significant practical effect. From this time onwards the colonists had little incentive to learn Russian, and the lack of it permanently hindered integration with their surroundings. Altogether, in fact, the changes now introduced, confirming the colonists' separate civic status, their special financial arrangements, different language and administrative system, all strengthened their separation from their Russian environment.

The new organization also gave added impetus to the colonies' economic development. The Instruction for the New Russia Office, for example, demanded particularly 'the development of artificial meadows, the planting of mulberries, vine-stocks, sesame and other useful cultures, the increase of sheep-farms of the best breeds, and the establishment of coarse and broad cloth, leather and other production'.[186] Of considerable advantage in this respect was a decree of 1798 which permitted the use of colonist debt repayments for the colonists' own benefit.[187] The repayments formed the basis of a so-called 'community fund' in each colony, which was put to good use during the nineteenth century, particularly in the New Russian settlements.

The same concern for agricultural and economic efficiency showed itself in a second set of Instructions, composed as the final step in the general review of the colonies, and regulating their 'internal order and administration'.[188] One article of the Saratov Instruction stressed the need, 'concerning garden plots and orchards, to encourage colonists to plant them with various necessary fruits and plant products; and especially, where it is convenient to increase potatoes ("earth apples") and the peasantry have become accustomed to their use, to ensure the sowing of fields with them'.[189]

This greater emphasis on progressive, rational farming and horticulture explains the directives to Bekleshov in 1803[190] and foreshadows the Rules of the following year. Both sets of Instructions looked back in some respects to their predecessors of the 1760s; but the immediate model was the recent Statute on Imperial (Appanage) Domains.[191] It provided the basis both for the new colonist legislation and for the 1797 re-organization of the state peasantry,[192] and it was here that concern with agricultural amelioration was first expressed in practical terms. The Saratov regulation on potatoes reproduced in fact almost verbatim a clause[193] of the Appanage Statute, which itself represented something of a new departure in the government's attitude to the peasantry.

In general, standards of agriculture subsequently rose higher in the foreign colonies than among the peasants of either the appanage or the state domains. A number of factors influenced this development – more advanced methods, colonist privileges, the amount of land held, the system of tenure. One element, however, was undoubtedly the screening and selection of settlers practised from the beginning of the new immigration and the deliberate use of the colonies by the Russian authorities as channels for amelioration.

The view of the colonies as pace-setters, as centres of innovation, became much more pronounced after 1804 and the application of the new Rules. The government's general plans for economic development in several fields envisaged a definite role for the colonists, as well as for such foreign entrepreneurs as Rouvier, or the Prussian sheep-farmer Müller.[194] In the south, sheep-breeding, sericulture and viticulture were to the fore; in Petersburg and Riebensdorf, the local popularization of potatoes. In Saratov, besides 'earth apples', tobacco already figured largely in the colonist economy, and for a time the authorities toyed with the idea of a tobacco factory there.[195] The view of the colonist as a model farmer found characteristic expression in the wish expressed by Arakcheyev in 1821 to settle expert farmers in Novgorod Province as examples to the military colonists of the region:

The best husbandmen of this sort are by common consent the foreign colonists. Arable farming and stock-breeding form the sole object of their activity. Considering their entire well-being to lie in the working of the land, they extract from it all those benefits which are the deserts only of unceasing labours and of patience. Besides, their very way of life, their sobriety, the cleanliness and order in their houses, can serve as useful examples.

Arakcheyev's proposal received Imperial approval, and the Inspector of the Petersburg colonies, after calling for volunteers, selected the 'two best' among the families willing to make the move.[196] In 1828 Saratov colonists were similarly appointed to direct agricultural settlements set up in that region for graduates of the Moscow Foundling House;[197] later, in the 1840s, Mennonite model farmers (*Musterwirte*) settled in the New Russian Jewish colonies.[198] (None of these 'models' proved very effective in influencing those around them.)

The new emphasis on quality rather than quantity among colonists reflected directly the growing concern with the welfare of native peasantry which had found expression in the appanage and state peasant legislation. One of the reasons given for the composition of the 1804 Rules, as we have seen, was the necessity, with land becoming scarcer and the native population growing, of putting available space to the best possible use. It followed that there remained less and less justification for the gross differences between privileges and assistance given to foreign, and those given to native migrants. Richelieu himself remarked on this, and the thought became increasingly common in official circles.[199] One early result of the changing official attitude was that in 1805 Russian state peasants from Smolensk Province, transferred to the south, were given advantageous conditions and placed under the jurisdiction of the New Russia Guardianship Office.[200] The Office was also required to supervise the Jewish agricultural colonies after their initial foundation in 1806; and a few years later it took charge of peasant migrants from the Bobyletskoye Starostvo in White Russia, displaced for the first of Alexander I's military colonies, the mishandling of whose transfer and settlement became, however, something of a *cause célèbre*.[201]

These new responsibilities of the colonist authorities coincided with the creation of new state agencies exclusively concerned with native migrants. The decree regulating the Smolensk peasants' migration gave rise in 1806 to an 'Office for the Establishment of Peasants Entering the Caucasus Province for Settlement'.[202] Already in 1802 orders had been given to investigate and improve the extremely bad conditions of migration to Siberia: the first move towards what finally became, for a time, a reasonably well-organized and well-controlled migration system.[203] Thus the new role of the colonist in the eyes of the state was only part of a much wider revision of policy towards the peasantry as a whole: in this field 'the Government was moving over from the former system of settlement to a new direction, in which the interests of the [native] colonizers themselves were given equal weight with the advantages of the region to be settled'.[204]

The role of colonists and foreigners in
specialized branches of agriculture after 1797

In the matter of improving the quality and techniques of agricultural
production, the Petersburg authorities and Richelieu in Odessa did not
limit their hopes of the colonists to any particular or exclusive fields.
Ideally they were looking – in the words of the decree of 20 February
1804 – for people 'having in general all necessary knowledge of the
best agriculture'. But some specific areas do stand out. The government
was concerned with them for their own sake, and the measures taken to
develop them extended beyond the colonies. Fields of especial interest
were sericulture, viticulture and fine-wool sheep-breeding; and these
were also singled out in the 1804 decree.[205]

All three fields had been objects of persistent, if spasmodic and un-
fruitful, government attention throughout the eighteenth century, frequently involving the employment of foreign skills.[206] The factors
determining official interest in them were similar to those already
observed with the colonist entrepreneurs of the 1760s: the desire to
reduce imports and increase self-sufficiency by improving home production, this time primarily of raw materials. All the three branches
were largely limited by geographical conditions to the south – which in
this context includes the lower Volga. As effective control was extended
progressively into hitherto undeveloped lands – as the expanses of the
southern Ukraine, the Caucasus, and later Bessarabia, came within
Russia's expanding borders – all three were much in the minds of those
administering the new territories.

In fact, they had long been established in these areas, but at a low
level or on a small scale. Raw silk produced in Russia was quite insufficient to satisfy home demand and it was often of poor quality or
spoilt by ignorance of spinning techniques. Like the mulberry, the vine
grew wild in many parts of the south. But local wines were un-
distinguished and could not stand comparison with those imported;
while the Muslim Tatars grew grapes for eating which were ill-suited to
wine-making. Similarly, Russian sheep-farmers produced very little
fine- or medium-grade wool, despite occasional government attempts
from Peter I onwards to introduce foreign fine-wool stock for breeding
purposes. The raw material for fine fabrics frequently had to be
imported, as were often the fabrics themselves.

The three branches, and particularly viticulture and sericulture, are
frequently mentioned together. Already in 1700 Peter I had ordered

the voyevoda of Astrakhan to 'develop a mulberry plantation and vine-[yard], in order to set up a silk-farm and vineyards in good places'.[207] And from the early stages of Catherine's colonization programme they were linked with the new settlements. The Plan of 1764 for New Russia offered special concessions to 'anyone setting up a silk-farm, vineyard, tobacco factory and other such of which there are very few or none at all in the state';[208] (while almost simultaneously the Little Russian College was considering foreign specialists for horticulture and Silesian stock to improve sheep-breeding further north in the Ukraine).[209] The 1764 regulations governing the settlement of the Volga colonists, who included immigrants from wine-growing regions of Germany, expressly mentioned vineyards, and several are recorded. One of the most successful was at Sarepta.[210] Besides encouraging individual silk-growing enterprises, notably those of Bousserole, Sarafov and Verdier, the Chancellery of Guardianship also tried in 1775 to involve the Volga colonies at large in sericulture: Ivan Reuss was assigned to this project as his principal field of responsibility. He also received instructions 'equally to encourage all, with diligence, concerning the increase of tobacco plantations'.[211] Tobacco, already grown extensively in Little Russia, prospered in the colonies; silk took hold only considerably later, and on a very small scale.

None of these colonist beginnings amounted to very much, however; and a similar lack of success on any significant scale attended the efforts of others, both private and public. Storch's comment on Russian eighteenth-century silk-growing can stand for all three branches: 'Even the progress which this culture has made since its first introduction, has been so insignificant, that it has in no way corresponded to the extremely favourable natural conditions.'[212] It was against this background that the Board of State Economy began its work in 1797. The first step in each field was an examination of the existing situation, and the composition of plans for future systematic expansion. In the light of such plans, the colonies seemed to offer one ideal channel for controlled development; but Petersburg and the New Russian authorities were also quick to welcome serious initiatives from individuals, both foreigners and native Russians.

Sericulture

The first measures of the new reign concerning sericulture involved not the Board of State Economy but the newly re-established College of Manufactures. The College had always been closely involved with silk

218 Human capital: the settlement of foreigners in Russia

production, and the two bodies now worked to some extent in parallel. The Board was drawn in when in April 1797 it received for consideration a script composed by Academician Lepekhin, entitled 'A Short Outline Concerning the Establishment of Silk Farms'.²¹³ (This subsequently became, apparently, the standard manual on the subject.)²¹⁴

Hablitzl, to whom the memorandum was referred, found it silent on two crucial questions: the reasons for the lack of success hitherto in Russian sericulture, and the means to remedy this; and he set about supplying the answers himself.²¹⁵ Firstly, he drew up a system of fines and rewards designed to encourage the planting of mulberries and the production of raw silk in suitable places throughout the south. Secondly, while laying primary responsibility upon provincial Governors, he proposed supervisors for closer control in each main silk-producing region: the Crimea, the lower Volga and Astrakhan, and the Caucasus Line. Thirdly, in order to improve the poor quality of the silk thread spun in these areas, one skilled silk-spinner was to be appointed to 'each of the places where at present a considerable quantity of silk is produced by the inhabitants, i.e. Simferopol, Astrakhan and Kizlyar. . .'.

Hablitzl succeeded in carrying his proposals through the Board. Supervision in the Crimea was entrusted to the overseer of the existing state farm at Novyye Vodolagi in the Ukraine. Responsibility for the Volga and Astrakhan devolved upon the supervisor of the long-established and unsuccessful Akhtuba state farm near Tsaritsyn, now being revived by the College of Manufactures.²¹⁶ For the Caucasus Line the Board engaged Baron Marschal von Bieberstein, a German of distinguished family and some reputation as a naturalist.²¹⁷ The annual reports of the Board over the next several years were most encouraging, and the Emperors – first Paul, then Alexander – expressed great satisfaction, often translated into promotions and rewards.²¹⁸ The measures of 1797 were however only a beginning. In 1799 a small special committee was appointed to gather information 'on the perfection of sericulture and of wools in Russia. . .as also in the field of manufactures generally', and to make recommendations.²¹⁹ Those on sericulture were published in a decree of 1800.²²⁰ Perhaps the most important proposal was for the distribution of land for mulberry plantations to all those wishing it, under clearly-formulated conditions. This practice was later extended to other crops of particular interest to the authorities, as well as to sheep-breeding. At the same time, the general rules established in 1797 concerning fines and rewards were retained; but the farms hitherto run by the state were to be made over to private enterprise. The Akhtuba and Novyye Vodolagi farms passed into the hands of their inhabitants as unprofitable to the state, while special measures were applied to two private plantations which had previously received state assistance. That of the Armenian entrepreneur Khastatov near Kizlyar, already long under state control following non-repayment of a loan, was finally sequestrated. Khastatov's 40 serfs became state peasants, while Armenians and Georgians who had settled there by contract with him retained possession of their land and use of the plantation, as well as all 'the rights and privileges granted [to their nationalities] by YIH'. The Saratov enterprise set up by Verdier, and then sold to a local merchant, was to be handed over to the Saratov Town Duma. The latter thereby became subject to the general regulations in force for sericulture in the province, including the penalties prescribed. The Saratov townsfolk at large had in any case the right to use their common land for horticultural purposes; and so the committee charged the Saratov Civil Governor to encourage them to plant mulberries as well.[221]

The spinners envisaged in 1797, and not yet appointed, were to be chosen 'from the Armenians and Georgians of Kizlyar or other suitable people'.[222] It was of course natural for the authorities to look to the Transcaucasian nationalities who were traditionally experienced in this field, and Armenians in particular figure repeatedly in government recommendations. In April 1799 the homes of Armenians in Kizlyar and the new settlement of Holy Cross were freed from quartering on condition that they took up silk production.[223] And the committee considered among other southern districts suitable for new silk production 'the remaining part of the New Russian Province, particularly among the Greeks and Armenians settled there, who engaged in this occupation in their former homeland [i.e. the Crimea]' – though the committee also added to this 'the southern lands of Saratov Province, where particularly certain foreign settlers who learned in Germany and other lands to raise mulberries and breed worms, give hopes of success'.[224]

Another measure proposed was the purchase of home-grown silk at the same price as the imported article; and the committee also called for the accelerated settlement of Astrakhan Province and the Crimea as the areas most suited to further development, the lack of population of the latter region being a constant complaint at this time. The supervisory system was elevated to an Inspectorate, with six staff under Bieberstein, who became Chief Inspector.[225]

The distribution of land proved difficult to implement for administrative reasons, and the rules governing it had more than once to be redefined.[226] One of these provisions stipulated that land could be

granted 'with or without populating it with people', 'people' meaning
not only serfs but 'also free people and foreigners, if any such should
agree to settle on the land for the purposes for which it is granted, on
conditions agreed with the owners'.[227]

The committee's recommendation appeared less than a year before
the first of the Board's 'Instructions' on the internal administration of
the colonies, which made so much of specialized economic development. Contenius took his Office's obligations in this sphere seriously;
and foreign settlers – both Asian and European – figure prominently
among those commended by Bieberstein for their efforts in sericulture.
His report for 1802, for example, singled out for especial praise
the Armenians of Holy Cross and Nakhichevan, and the 'German'
(Mennonite) colonists of Yekaterinoslav Province. In particular two
Mennonites 'who have worked with excellent zeal in this field' were
recommended for reward. And Bieberstein went out of his way to

render due justice, in the success of this culture, to the New Russian
Guardianship Office and the Nakhichevan Armenian Magistrature, which
without waiting for instructions or reminders from the Inspectors take all
necessary steps to that end, with a care superior to others. . .[228]

The duties of the southern colonists in the economic sphere were most
clearly set out in the Supplement to their Instruction published in 1803,
of which §§ 6 and 7 are devoted to viticulture and sericulture respectively. In each case precise regulations were laid down for the number
of trees or vine-slips to be planted, the care to be given and reports to
be made, all – predictably – on pain of punishment.[229] Under the
guidance of Contenius, sericulture gradually took hold, at least in the
Yekaterinoslav colonies.[230] In those of Odessa according to an official
reporting in 1815, there were many mulberries, especially in the
Bulgarian settlements. But silk production was negligible, as the
colonists concentrated on other branches of agriculture; and the
Germans had never tried it at all. Steps were however being taken to
begin production in Grossliebenthal, using mature trees already growing there.[231] Sericulture in the Crimean colonies followed much the
same pattern.

In general the Bulgarians showed more inclination to silk-growing
than did their German neighbours, especially around Odessa; and in
1808 the Bulgarian colony of Parkany, near Tiraspol, was set up
deliberately on the site of old plantations to house skilled horticulturists,
who succeeded with both silk- and wine-growing. Skal'kovsky recorded
in 1836: 'Now two settlements have been created there, in which both

branches are. . .in the most flourishing condition possible'.[232] From about 1810 onwards, individual Saratov colonists also began to receive awards and commendations for silk production.[233]

Thus in measures on sericulture after 1797, colonists featured prominently. And in the succeeding decades of the nineteenth century several foreign entrepreneurs, notably the Frenchmen Castella and Didelot in Georgia, also attempted to set up silk farms and factories. However, overall results in this sphere came to very little. Neither the colonists nor the entrepreneurs justified the broad hopes placed in them. The first serious success was achieved by a Russian land-owner, Rebrov, in the 1830s; but generally in the nineteenth century Russian raw silk production was quite insufficient to meet home demand.

Viticulture

At the end of the eighteenth century, there were three main wine-growing areas in the Russian Empire: the Crimea, the Don, and Astrakhan and the Terek. In these regions grapes and wine were traditional products, though generally of low quality. Only Astrakhan had been a centre of official efforts to produce high-quality grapes and wine, with the employment of a series of foreign experts. Yet even here success was slight.[234] In the view of the Board of State Economy in 1798, with the one possible exception of the Don,

in all countries of Russia where there are wine-growing establishments, everywhere there are the same deficiencies and errors; everywhere young vines are planted without distinction between different varieties and without careful choice of position, everywhere there is ignorance of the proper art of making wine and almost everywhere a lack of good barrels and cellars, and therefore the wines produced are bad, or only mediocre, and sell at a low price.[235]

From an initial consideration of the sad state of the Astrakhan vineyards, the Board proceeded to an examination of viticulture in the south at large. It was joined in its deliberations by Joseph Banq, recruited by Potemkin from France and already mentioned for his work in the Crimea. Before moving to the Black Sea, Banq had spent 1779–84 as *Inspecteur des Vignobles* in Astrakhan.[236] The Board's discussions led it to the conclusion that the most appropriate means of developing viticulture would be the creation of three state training schools. These should be situated respectively on the Caucasus Line near Kizlyar, on the Don and in the Crimea. One of a number of problems to be solved would be that of personnel: not that many would be needed, only one skilful wine-grower, a wine-cooper (*kupor*), a wet cooper (*bochar*) and 20 labourers. The first might perhaps be found among the Saratov colonists; otherwise it would be necessary to hire the skilled staff from abroad.[237]

The Board's plans met with approval, and in March 1798 it proceeded to the first practical steps. Requests went out to the Civil Governors of New Russia and Astrakhan, and to the Ataman of the Don Cossacks, to find suitable sites for the schools. The New Russian Civil Governor and the Chief Judge of the newly-reconstituted Saratov Guardianship Office were to discover whether the colonists of their respective regions could supply the requisite specialists.[238]

In May the New Russian Governor, I. Ya. Seletsky, reported that he had assigned land in the Sudak and Koz valleys of the Crimea, with a labour force conveniently available in nearby villages. The colonists and Mennonites of New Russia could not supply the specialists requested, but a suitable wine-grower and wet cooper had been found on the spot.[239] The Board for its part had wished to entrust the school to the new Crimean administration then under discussion, and the delay in the formation of this body appeared to prevent further action. Consideration of the Crimean school was therefore postponed – like George Trappe's proposals for the recruitment of Swiss wine-growers – until the inauguration of the new authority.[240]

The Astrakhan Governor, N. Arshenevsky, had entrusted selection of a suitable site on the Terek to Bieberstein, who was then about to make a tour of inspection. He reported back only in March 1799. There was no news from the Don; but the offer of posts in the new schools brought a response from four Saratov colonists, all experienced in viticulture. Two wished to go to the Don, and one each to the Terek and the Crimea.[241]

However, despite these developments, the Board felt unable to proceed. In August 1799 it reported to the Senate that an adequate number of qualified staff for the new schools could not be found in Russia, 'and for this reason the said intention could not be put into practice': none of the schools could be set up. Instead, as a trial venture (*dlya pervogo opyta*), a state vineyard should be established near the Stavropol fortress of the Caucasus Line. This could be staffed by two suitable horticulturists recruited from among the Slavs of Upper Hungary, 'who more than other people, both by their speech and their way of life, are similar to Russians, and can therefore advance this matter so much the better'. In addition a skilled wine-cooper could be hired from Württemberg, who should have one of the Saratov colonists as his assistant. The Senate in reply stressed the importance of wine-making for the economy of southern Russia, and wholeheartedly approved the new proposals.[242] The drafting of a final plan was entrusted to Bieberstein, who submitted a detailed scheme and cost estimates in the following March (1800).[243] But there the matter rested for eighteen months. In the veiled words of the Board's next report of January 1802 – already after the death of Paul – 'there were difficulties in recruiting abroad the skilled people required'. With the new reign, however, these obstacles vanished: 'since by the [new] Emperor's will free entry into Russia is permitted to everyone, it would be much better to obtain [the necessary personnel] from France and other European powers, where this branch has been brought to perfection'.[244] So the Board took up its previous plans once more, reverting to the proposals of 1798; and in a somewhat recast form these finally reached the Emperor for confirmation in December 1802.

Kochubey's report now postulated two schools, one on the Caucasus Line and one in the Crimea. Suitable staff to establish and run both institutions were to be hired from France;

and as it is known to me that Commercial Counsellor Rouvier, at present in Tauria, and due to set out for Spain in connection with his own private speculations, will be in Marseilles, I consider it most suitable to entrust [this] to him, as a person extremely knowledgeable, and always appearing to me in a most favourable light.[245]

A year previously, Rouvier had made detailed if rather over-ambitious proposals to the Committee on the Establishment of the New Russia Province, which had apparently played some considerable part in reviving both the Board's interest in viticulture and its plans for sheep-breeding.[246] (Hablitzl, it will be recalled, was a member of both the Committee and the Board.) Now Rouvier was requested to recruit six staff for each of the new schools; to buy several thousand slips each of the best French and Spanish vines; and to obtain models of the best wine-presses, 'of which there is a great lack in the southern Russian regions'. An additional commission concerned the purchase of seeds of the best strains of white mulberry, to be obtained from Southern France or Italy. Credit facilities of up to 5,000 roubles were made available for these purposes in Marseilles.[247]

The new provisions formed the basis for the two state schools of viticulture which were finally established in the south. Pallas received responsibility for the first, opened at Sudak in the Crimea in 1804, with vineyards in the Sudak and Koz valleys. (The Sudak valley was the most important wine-growing area in the Crimea.) The second school started only in 1807, near Kizlyar, under the direction of Bieberstein. The early history of both was recorded by Köppen, and the Crimean school has recently been described by a Soviet scholar, S. A. Sekirin-sky.[248] Both institutions had foreign personnel. Late in 1803 Rouvier sent two master wine-growers and a wine-cooper from Marseilles for Sudak, together with the vineslips and press models requested. The Kizlyar school was staffed by Germans from the Rhine, engaged some-what later through Bieberstein's brother, who occupied a high post in the state government of Nassau-Using.[249]

The schools existed for several decades, and went a long way towards fulfilling their intended function. Sekirinsky sums up on Sudak:

With all the faults and deficiencies characteristic of all institutions of feudal-absolutist Russia at that time, the Sudak school of viticulture already in the first decade of its existence became an important institu-tion for the preparation of cadres of experienced wine-growers and wine-makers, and a major centre of scientific (*kul'turnogo*) viticulture and wine-making in the south of Russia.[250]

But Pallas' school was not the only venture of its kind at that time in the Crimea. On his return from Spain in 1804, Rouvier brought with him Malaga vineslips and two Malaga wine-growers and their families, to whom he had promised official posts and salaries. Sudak proved too cool for the Malaga vines, and Rouvier therefore undertook to create his own nursery and school elsewhere on the southern shores of the peninsula. In return he received a loan of 12,000 roubles and other assistance.[251] Apparently his establishment prospered: in 1807 Richelieu praised it 'above all those in the Crimea, and even above the school of Herr Pallas'.[252]

Meanwhile, efforts to utilize the new immigration from Germany in restoring viticulture were also vigorously pursued. The first directive to Bekleshov dealing with the subject, of July 1803,[253] had laid on the Taurian Governor the responsibility for finding suitable land for settle-ment, with old vineyards; and the Acting Civil Governor of the province, A. I. Shostak, proved very co-operative. In Odessa, Contenius gathered volunteers to settle in the Crimea. By December 1803 he could report that the eight transports then arrived from Germany included 87 suitable families, and that he expected about 100 in all.

In fact, Contenius' hopes were not quite fulfilled in that year; but the total number of German families settled in the Crimea in 1804 and

1805 reached 142, while Escher's Swiss added a further 62. Besides the six new colonies established in the southern half of the peninsula, 17 Swiss and German families settled in Simferopol and Theodosia, and 7 wine-growers just outside the latter.[254]

One of the new Crimean colonies resulted directly from an inititative by Pallas in connection with his school. He suggested a special settlement in the Koz valley. Accordingly, in consultation with Pallas himself, the new Supervisor of the Crimean German colonies chose 18 of the best wine-growers among his charges, and arranged special conditions for them. This group finally settled in 1805 at Sudak, along the coast from Koz and very close to the school.[255]

The broader hopes of the Board of State Economy, expressed in the Instruction for the colonies and its Supplement, that *all* southern colonists should engage in viticulture, were not immediately realized. Some development took place in the second decade of the century; and according to one account, the Odessa colonists were solitary pioneers in their region until at least 1820.[256] But in the great expansion of viticulture which took place in the south in the 1820s and 1830s, colonists played a subordinate role.

Merino sheep-breeding

The first official proposals from the Board of State Economy for the proper establishment of fine-wool sheep-breeding in Russia were made in a memorandum of June 1797, which dealt primarily with the abolition of former Tatar levies on the grazing and transfer of stock in the Crimea. Exchequer losses from this measure, it was hoped, would be amply repaid by a resultant increase in stock-breeding, which should both supply home needs and leave a surplus for export. A small merino sheep farm, 'on the pattern of the stud planned for the region and approved by Your Highness', would give both an example to local breeders and a supply of pure-bred rams.[257]

These general proposals were followed two months later by a detailed scheme, worked out with the guidance of Hablitzl. It envisaged a flock of Spanish merinos tended by two Spanish shepherds and their own sheepdogs, under the direction of an official Supervisor. The Imperial note of confirmation added an instruction to create similar farms in other climatically suited areas.[258] However, political difficulties similar to those which hindered the recruitment of colonists and wine-growers under Paul interfered in this case as well. Danger from French privateers in the Mediterranean caused the purchase and dispatch of

Spanish animals to be postponed, and on Russia's declaration of war against Spain in 1799, the money was reallocated to the acquisition of stock in England.[259]

This new direction seems to have produced no serious results, although it may have led to the small model English farm established near Petersburg in 1802, whose situation suggests a connection with the ill-fated School of Agriculture organized by Samborsky.[260] The active interest of the Board of State Economy in the import of pure-bred sheep for southern Russia was only revived in 1801, apparently by Rouvier's memorandum on the Crimea.

Now, however, official measures were rivalled by private initiative. The first small merino flocks which appeared in S. Russia at this time belonged to private owners. The flock of Count N. P. Rumyantsev on his estate at Gomel in Mogilyov Province (1802) was followed by two others in Poltava Province in 1802 and 1803. Rumyantsev acquired Silesian merinos, together with an experienced shepherd from Saxony.[261] At the same time, in 1802, Kochubey agreed to the proposals of a sheep-farmer from Prussian Silesia, George Müller, to establish a large farm in the south on land to be given him for the purpose;[262] and Rouvier's offers to the same end, following on his memorandum to the Committee on the Establishment of New Russia, had been readily accepted. Rouvier and his son-in-law, Vassale, even obtained use of a transport ship from the Russian Black Sea fleet for their trip to Spain in quest of stock;[263] while Müller returned by himself to Saxony for the same purpose.

Both Rouvier and Müller were back in New Russia by 1804. Müller had not communicated with the Russian authorities during an absence of more than a year, and his sudden arrival in Odessa caused Richelieu some embarrassment, since he was accompanied by 1,200 sheep and 25 German shepherds, and the land near the town effectively promised to him in 1802 had been given to someone else.[264] Rouvier had made more careful arrangements, and had no such difficulties in establishing himself in the Crimea.

In the same year (1804) the government finally took active steps to implement its own plans. The Russian Ambassador in Vienna, Razumovsky, arranged the purchase of 200 pure-bred sheep from the farm of Prince Johann of Liechtenstein; the animals arrived in Odessa that summer. The Liechtenstein purchase attracted the attention of a prominent Austrian breeder, Prince Esterhazy, who made extensive and detailed proposals to the Russian government for the expansion of merino breeding in Russia. No proper farm had yet been created for the Liechtenstein sheep, and the Ministry of the Interior decided to accept Esterhazy's plan in principle, while reducing its scale. The Ministry experts (unnamed in Kochubey's report, but presumably the members of the former Board) assured the Minister that the two areas most suited to the scheme were the Crimea – similar in climate and topography to the sheep-breeding regions of Spain – and the environs of Odessa, where 'important ordinary sheep-farms, the confluence of many foreign colonists, the ease of trade, and other considerations' were all propitious. Kochubey wished to entrust the matter to a private individual who would have a personal stake in it, rather than repeat attempts at state intervention which, he said, had failed in the past. This view harmonized with the policy of placing silk production in private hands. Kochubey's first choice was Rouvier; but it soon became clear that a farm at Odessa offered a useful solution to Müller's awkward position, which was still not entirely settled. Contracts were therefore signed with both men early in 1805.[265]

Rouvier received 100,000 roubles over five years, repayable with interest in a further five, and land grants of 5,000 desyatinas in the mountainous, and 25,000 in the low-lying, parts of the Crimea. Since he could not offer sufficient sureties for the sum involved, payment of the money was entrusted to the Taurian Civil Governor, while a large part of it was earmarked for the purchase of stock from Esterhazy. Rouvier for his part undertook to increase his flock from 10,000 in 1805 to 100,000 in 1817; to acquire 50 additional pure-bred rams from Spain at his own expense; to sell improved stock to local farmers at reasonable prices; and to keep and teach up to 100 'apprentices', to be sent to him either by the government or by private farmers. The contract also included severe penalty clauses, extending Rouvier's liabilities to his heirs and placing all his personal possessions at risk. Müller's contract contained provisions similar to that of Rouvier, though on an altogether smaller scale. The Liechtenstein sheep and their shepherd were made over to him as part of his initial flock; and he also took an option on the establishment with government assistance of a mill to work his own wool.[266]

Both Müller and Rouvier were ultimately very successful, though the latter had some difficulties and took several years to reach a profitable position.[267] Müller soon fulfilled his obligations, and in 1808 the government approved a scheme for large-scale purchase of his animals for redistribution to local breeders.[268] Müller subsequently sold off his farm.[269] Rouvier continued his enterprise, very lucratively, and his son-in-law and heir, Vassale, remained one of the leading breeders in the south. These successes proved the viability of the new and potentially hazardous industry, and provided a readily accessible source of stock. Requests to the government from private individuals were met by publication in 1804 of a scheme for land grants on advantageous terms to would-be merino breeders in New Russia.[270]

All this encouraged an increasing number of imitators: in 1808 a government inspector recorded at least 11 *pomeschchik* merino breeders in Yekaterinoslav Province alone, with over 8,000 Silesian and Spanish animals between them – although he found only two minor breeders in the Crimea, besides Rouvier.[271] In the early stage, however, it was foreign breeders who set the pace. According to A. A. Skal'-kovsky,

From 1811, fine-wool sheep-breeding began to become so attractive, and its advantages so convincing, that at one and the same time the following obtained land in Kherson province and brought their flocks over: from Central Europe (Saxon Electoral stock) the rich Swiss sheep-farmer and agronomist Pictet de Rochement; from Moldavia and Wallachia, captain Revelio; and many others from other places. The latter [sic] was imitated by the Odessa merchant d'Epinais, to whom the government gave large areas of land gratis. The Dutchman Pau, the *pomeshchik* G. Shostak and many others also set up their own sheep farms. All the Mennonites settled after 1804...on the Molochna Waters began to pursue the same course. The last projects for land and financial grants from the exchequer we see in 1817, when the veterinary doctor Salos offered proposals not only for model merino farms, but also for schools for shepherds in southern Russia; while Messrs Argiot (*Arzhio*) and Durand, landowners from Provence, asked only land for sheep-farming, promising to transfer their valuable flocks to southern Russia [without financial assistance]. But the industry was now in any case firmly established: sheep farming was going ahead with giant strides, and in 1817 a strict prohibition was issued against any further grant of land, very little land now still remaining.[272]

Among the 'many other' foreigners mentioned above can be named Rouvier's other son-in-law, Potier, and the agents of the Dukes of Württemberg and Anhalt-Köthen, who founded respectively the sheep colonies of Carlsthal and Ascania Nova – the latter now famous as a wild-life reserve.[273]

Thus, in the words of the Soviet scholar S. V. Klimova, 'in pursuit of fat profits, foreigners came hastening to the south of Russia'.[274] Successful farmers could certainly hope to make a fortune. Yet as in other cases, such as that of Baird, the profit to the foreign entrepreneur was balanced by the expertise and above all the commercial initiative which he brought to his undertaking, and which the host country was unable in equal measure to supply. Klimova concludes that 'altogether, in the first quarter of the nineteenth-century, foreign sheep farmers in Russia played a positive role and furthered the spread here of fine-wool sheep-breeding'.[275]

The role of colonists in the early years was slight, although both on the Volga and in New Russia traditional breeds were well established, and the colonies loomed as large in official planning in this field as in the others. When in 1805 the already extended exemption period of the first Mennonite settlers in Khortitsa expired, they obtained a reduced rate of debt repayment on condition 'that they shall try to merit this favour by diligence in the improvement of sheep-breeding, the development of fruit-orchards and gardens, of woodland, and of mulberry plantations. . .'.[276]

Colonist involvement in merino-breeding began in 1803, when it was introduced into the Khortitsa Mennonite colonies. Sheep bought from Müller in 1808 – the year of Contenius' secondment to this work – were distributed throughout the colonies, and further purchases from Liechtenstein were put to the same use.[277] In the following period Richelieu authorized expenditure from the 'communal fund' of the Odessa colonies to build sheep-folds and buy stock.[278] But the colonists' flocks, slowly built up, suffered severely in the disastrous winter of 1812–13, which killed nearly 1,000,000 head of livestock in New Russia. Real success in merino-breeding among the colonies came in the 1820s.[279]

Conclusion

The new rules of 1804 on immigration did not remain long without modification. In 1810 the pressures of the Continental blockade and the Turkish war led to a cessation of all financial help to immigrants; in 1819 a 'temporary' ban marked the end of the large-scale immigration previously encouraged. The final cessation of government-sponsored immigration on the existing pattern in the 1830s was followed shortly by the subordination of the established colonies to the Ministry of State Domains. Further immigration later in the nineteenth century took place on different bases.

The rules of 1804 focussed firmly on the cultural and didactic role of foreign settlers. This role was consequently taken as a starting point by many nineteenth-century observers when commenting on immigration policies in the eighteenth. Philip Vigel, for example, wrote sneeringly of efforts under Catherine 'to establish European culture' in Russia through foreign settlement, and of the 'whole masses of light' which were to 'pour in upon us with thousands of German yokels (*muzhikov*)'.[1] But as we have seen, Catherine's purpose was not primarily to recruit Europeans, or to find foreign teachers for her subjects, although the opportunity to use settlers for the improvement of agricultural techniques and to encourage new industrial production was not overlooked. In accordance with the theories of state-craft of the time, with the common practice of other powers, and with the demographic needs of the Empire, her basic intention was to increase the population in general, and to use foreign settlers to accelerate the settlement and development of empty territories. The 1763 Manifesto and its accompanying legislation, which laid the basis for the immigration of the later eighteenth century, were to create an administrative system at national level which could organize both the recruitment and the settlement of immigrants from all sources, and supervise their use in whatever fields the government might find advantageous. The new Chancellery of Guardianship accordingly maintained direct control not only over the recruiters and over the major settlement on the Volga, but also over the entrepreneurs with whom it made special arrangements independent of the College of Manufactures. It played a direct role, too, in other fields outside its proper sphere of competence, as in the case of the Livonian Jews, or that of J. G. Eisen. But in these cases it was collaborating with or facilitating the work of other authorities; and where existing structures were already competent to supervise foreign settlers, or where direct control would have been too cumbersome or costly, the Chancellery relinquished authority to other government organs. This was the case with artisans who were placed under the Magistrature, and with the small settlements which were made under special contract in different parts of European Russia in the 1760s, and most of which stood under the jurisdiction of the local government authority. It was also the case in the far south; here the re-organization of the Serbian military colonies and the working out in 1764 of the Plan of Settlement of New Russia made intervention by the Chancellery unnecessary. The Plan, drawn up in close connection with the immigration decrees of 1763, formed the basis for the settlement of the southern border regions into the nineteenth century.

The Volga region itself was border territory in one sense, the frontier zone of settlement of its time. And it was primarily in the settlement of new border lands that foreign immigrants were used after the 1760s. From 1775, when the Volga settlement was completed, and the government had taken stock of the working and results of the new policy, immigration was pursued on a more flexible and less systematic basis during the progressive settlement and consolidation of the territory around the Black Sea which Russia acquired from Turkey under Catherine and Alexander I. Initially the emptiness of the land and the urgency of securing it against possible counter-attack led to radical measures on the part of Potemkin and his successors to acquire new inhabitants. But at the turn of the century, as the Turkish threat became somewhat more distant, and the hitherto abundant supplies of land showed signs of exhaustion, the view of the authorities began to change: the disadvantages of unrestricted foreign settlement loomed larger, and local considerations, together with a shift in overall government policy on the native peasantry, contributed to the establishment of the Rules of 1804 for general European immigration. The political factors which had led the government to encourage Transdanubian migrants, and the acknowledged agricultural skills of the Mennonites, ensured exemption for these groups from the new restrictions.

The foreigners who thus contributed to the development of Russia's southern borders, however, like their counterparts on the Volga, were only one small element among the native settlers who formed the bulk of the new population. And in general the foreign settlers of Catherine's reign and the first years of Alexander's all took longer to adapt to their new surroundings, and cost the Russian government far more both in cash and administrative terms, than did their native counterparts. Judged by itself, therefore, and in terms of its proclaimed intentions, the immigration policy and its results in the forty-year period under consideration were not particularly successful. Costs were much higher than anticipated, and higher than was really acceptable; the basic function of settling new land was fulfilled primarily by native elements. The hopes expressed by some for a cultural gain from the colonists were realized only marginally in the eighteenth century, although this aspect became much more important in the nineteenth; and in the industrial field the more modest plans of the Chancellery of Guardianship produced equally modest results. But the government's activities did nonetheless have their positive side. They did bring into the country tens of thousands of new inhabitants, whose descendants, if not they themselves, contributed notably to the areas in which they settled. And immigration should in any case not be approached in isolation, but as a constituent part of general policy. Considered as one strand in Russian policy on population and general economic development in the later eighteenth and early nineteenth centuries, the measures of Catherine and her successors on foreign immigration and settlement were constructive and, within limits, effective.

Looked at in the wider context of Russia's economic development at large in the period we are considering, the immigration and its results raise some more general questions. These concern both industrial and agricultural development, and the broader question of population growth and general economic advance. In Russia's industrial sector, the colonist entrepreneurs and artisans were merely one element among the foreigners to be found establishing and running enterprises in the eighteenth century; and a full discussion of the role of foreign economic enterprise in Catherine's Russia lies beyond the scope of the present study. Similarly, a proper evaluation of the economic significance of rural colonization will require further study of the rural colonies' development in the nineteenth century, when they reached maturity, and considerable prosperity. But we can attempt some tentative generalizations here.

The foreign entrepreneurs who contracted with the Chancellery of

Guardianship in the 1760s illustrate the problems facing industrialists generally, and foreign industrialists in particular, in eighteenth-century Russia. Industrial investment was rarely attractive to foreign capitalists unless backed by government grants, contracts, or guarantees. Foreign capital was engaged most obviously in foreign trade, which allowed operations to be based outside the country; another concentration was to be found among the bankers to the Court. In the latter case, the connection with government was again important; and entrepreneurial activity could be as risky for a banker with large resources as for someone less well placed, as was shown by the disaster of William Gomm in his Onega timber development.[2] A more successful attempt to combine merchant banking with other activities was that of the house of Stieglitz later in the century.

With very few exceptions, foreigners who did establish their own enterprises in eighteenth-century Russia operated on a small scale; the few with larger hopes and ambitions almost universally relied upon government help in some form or other. The most successful foreign entrepreneurs seem in fact to have been those actually in government service and who functioned as government employees: Levallier and Gascoigne are two examples. Foreigners with particular skills and know-how to offer could establish and maintain themselves successfully, as happened for instance in the case of the first cotton-printing concerns, all foreign – of Cozens and Chamberlain, Lieman, and Scheidemann;[3] but here again government backing was decisive. Lieman, furthermore, was at first in partnership with the Court broker (*makler*) Siritsius. Otherwise, foreigners were faced by all the difficulties of the Russian industrial environment of the eighteenth century: small, uncertain and unreliable markets; lack of a reliable financial and credit system other than government loans; lack of a suitable labour force and technological base; the dominance of a non-industrial landed class which also made its weight felt in industrial enterprise; and economic ideas in official circles which did not favour large-scale industrialization, except for state requirements and in so far as it did not conflict with agriculture.

The colonist entrepreneurial legislation and the approach to the question of the Chancellery of Guardianship suggest both the authorities' awareness of the situation, and their tendency to develop industry along existing lines. The entrepreneurs recruited in the 1760s were almost all producers of luxury goods; their purpose in the eyes of the government was to supply a home demand which had expanded rapidly in the eighteenth century and which was felt to impose an unacceptable burden on the country's balance of payments. The relatively short life of some of the these undertakings was characteristic of numerous native enterprises at a time when a supporting industrial and commercial environment was only emerging.

Among the several individual industrial fortunes built in eighteenth-century Russia, there were few belonging to independent foreign entrepreneurs. Charles Baird is one of the earliest examples in the Imperial period of a foreigner who established himself as a major Russian industrialist. Like his non-noble Russian predecessors, however – the most obvious case is the Demidov dynasty – he too made his money largely through government contracts; and like them he and his heirs succeeded in achieving recognition in the highest circles, ennoblement, and absorption into the non-industrial landed elite. Baird also enjoyed monopoly rights and a cheap labour supply. Unlike the colonist entrepreneurs of Catherine's reign, however, the Bairds created a major enterprise of lasting significance; and their success evidently reflects the greater possibilities offered by the more developed economy of the early nineteenth century.

Baird stood of course in the older, non-colonist tradition of the individual foreign entrepreneur in Russia. His counterpart in the agricultural field in our study is Rouvier, who did for sheep-farming something of what Baird did in metallurgy and engineering, and who succeeded for similar reasons. Sheep-farming was eminently suited to the conditions of the southern Ukraine, provided that the necessary technical skills were also available. At the same time, physical security and a basic infrastructure were also essential. Hence the authorities' concern above all to populate the new area, as a preliminary step to development of the various sides of its economy. It is notable that of the specialized branches of agricultural industry discussed in the last section, wine-growing and sheep-breeding reached maturity in the 1820s–1840s, by which time the southern Ukraine had passed beyond its pioneering stage: and the colonist and the foreign entrepreneur in these fields soon became merely part of a relatively well-developed Russian industry, largely independent of direct government support.

Eighteenth-century official attempts to develop these branches failed because they were unsystematic and not sustained, despite the use of considerable resources and foreign skills; in part they failed also because, even with these skills, technological levels were insufficient. But finally such attempts failed because they hung largely in the air, lacking essential acceptance and support from the economic and social environment of their time. Similar causes – the complexion of an economy still in the eighteenth century partly natural, deficient in means of communication and transfer of technology and technical skills, and based in attitudes engendered by the serf system – seem to have minimised the possible effectiveness of foreign settlements in the model role posited, for some of them at the outset, for most after 1804. It was once again only in the nineteenth century, and primarily among the educated classes, that the pre-eminence of colonist farming became a commonly-received idea.

Parallel with the economic development of the later eighteenth and early nineteenth centuries went not only the populating of border areas, but a continual growth in overall population which brought with it, already before 1800, the first signs of regional land shortage. The lack of population which underlay and suggested Catherine's initiative of the 1760s, was of long standing, and had had important effects upon Russia's social and economic development. E. P. Domar has recently examined the connection between serfdom and underpopulation, and his study suggests that emancipation, whether of slave or serf, may be related to the exhaustion of free land resources.[4] The population growth of European Russia in the eighteenth and early nineteenth centuries finally in large measure reversed the long-standing imbalance between land and population; and while in 1800 the authorities lamented the emptiness of the Taurian Province, in older areas of settlement peasant farmers were falling below the land norms which the government itself prescribed as necessary for subsistence. The change in official attitudes at the beginning of the nineteenth century, towards both native and foreign settlement, reflected the changing demographic position of the country at large. In the long view, large-scale foreign settlement was begun, in the 1760s, at a time when native population growth was already likely to make it superfluous; its limitation in 1804 and its later complete cessation correspond to the growing pressure of native population on the land supply. Thus the patterns of mass immigration follow closely the overall dynamic of settlement and of population growth in European Russia; and it was a natural outcome when in 1871, ten years after the emancipation of the landlords' peasants, the re-organization of both serf and state peasantry was extended to the foreign colonists, and their special status was abolished.

Outside of European Russia, foreign settlement had little impact. Siberia and Central Asia, the great colonial regions of the nineteenth century, seem to have been too remote and too difficult of access to attract any direct immigration from abroad. Some colonists from existing foreign settlements joined the movement east and south-eastwards; and in the 1860s the urgent need to populate new territory on the Amur led to some ineffectual efforts to attract foreign settlers to that area. But otherwise official policies, as well as the alternative attractions to nineteenth-century European emigrants of settlement overseas, in the Americas, gave little incentive to renewed foreign settlement in underpopulated areas of the Russian Empire in the later part of the century. Apart from isolated episodes of immigration, the two significant areas of new foreign settlement after 1804 were Bessarabia (now in Moldavia), taken from the Turks in 1812, and attracting population for the same reasons as the rest of New Russia, and Volhynia (now part of the Ukraine), on the western edge of European Russia, where at different times in the century opportunities for private land purchase, and the labour needs of the region's landowners, attracted numbers of foreigners from Polish territory and from Central Europe on a private basis, with little official intervention or support.

These later events, and the subsequent history of Imperial Russia's foreign settlements, are not our present concern.[5] The later life of the colonies, the place of groups and individuals in Russian society and the Russian economy, deserve attention, as do the changing attitudes of Russian authority to the 'foreigners' in its charge and to the question of further immigration. These developments remain subjects for further study, within the wider frame of Russian and Soviet history. The earlier stages have been charted here.

Appendix I

The official English-language version of the Manifesto of 1763 TsGADA f. 248, kn. 3398, ll. 263–50b.

of *Moscovia, Kiovia, Uladimiria, Novogardia, Czarina of Casan, Czarina of Astracan, Czarina of Siberia, Lady of Pscovia, and Great Duchess of Smolensko, Duchess of Estonia, Livonia, Corelia, Tueria, Ingoria, Permia, Viatka, Bolgaria and others Lady, and Great Duchess of Lower Novogardia, Tzernigovia, Resania, Rostovia, Iaroslavia, Belooseria, Udoria, Obdoria, Condinia and of all the Northern Coasts Dominatrice, and Lady of the Land of Iberia, the Czars of Cartalinia and Gruzinia, as likewise of Cabardinia, the Dukes of Czircassia and of the Mountains, and many others, Heir, Successor, Lady and Ruler.*

Whereas we knowing the vast Extent of Lands in our Empire, find amongst the rest a great many very advantageous and convenient Places for the settlement and Habitation of Mankind, which remaine yet uncultivated, and amongst which many have unexhaustable Treasures of divers metals hidden in the Bosom of the Earth; and they having Woods, Rivers, Lakes, and Seas belonging to Commerce, enough, are very convenient for the increase and augmentation of many Manufactures, Fabricks, and other Works. This induced us for the benefit of all our faithfull subjects to issue out a Manifest the 4. day of December 1762. past. but having declared therein Our will and Pleasure tending to those Foreigners, who are desirous to settle themselves in Our Empire, in Short; We, in addition thereto, order to be made known to all of the fallowing ordinance, which we do most solemnly constitute and command to be observed.

I.

We allow and give Leave for all Foreigners to come into Our Empire and settle themselves wheresoever they shall desire in all Our Governments.

II.

Such Foreigners may come and appear not only in Our Residence to the appointed for that purpose Guardian-Office for Foreigners, but even in other bordering City's of Our Empire, where any one may find it more convenient, to the Governours, and where are none, to the Chief Commanders of those City's.

III.

As amongst the said Foreigners, that are desirous to settle themselves in Russia, may happen to be such, who have not substance enough for to undertake the voyage, those may appear to Our Ministers or Residents, residing at Foreign Courts, who will not only dispatch them forthwith to Russia upon Our own Cost and Expenses, but even supply them with money for their Iourney.

IIII.

As soon as the said Foreigners come into Our Residence, and appear to the Guardian-Office, or in any of Our Bordering City's or Towns, they are to declare their final Intention, whether they desire to list themselves for Trade, or Handy-Crafts, and be Citizens, and in which City they wish to be, or whether they desire to settle themselves in Colonys or by Places upon the free and convenient Grounds for Tillage and many other advantages? which will be immediately resolved upon, and be alowed them according to their desire. As what tend's particularly to those Places in Our Empire, where the said free Grounds fit for Plantations do ly, they are to be seen in the fallowing List, nevertheless there are a great many more vast spaces of Grounds, which do far exceed the above mentioned Number, supplyed with all other necessary's for the sustenance of human Life, which we give Leave likewise to be inhabited by all, whosoever shall chuse for their Profit to settle themselves thereon.

V.

As soon as any Foreigner arrives into Our Empire for settlement, and appear's to Our Guardian-Office, which is appointed for them, or in any other of our bordering City's or Towns, he is to declare at first, as is prescribed in the 4. precedent Article, his Intention, and then conformably to his Religion and its Rite to take the usual Oath of subjection and Fidelity to Us.

VI.

And to the end, that all Foreigners, as are desirous to settle themselves in Our Empire, may see, how far our good will extend's to their Profit and Advantage, We do grant, that. (1) All such Comers into our Empire for settlement may enjoy the free Exercise of their Religion conformable to their Rites and Ceremonies, without any hindrance or molestation; and that those, which are desirous to settle themselves not in the City's or

Towns, but separately in the open Fields, in Colonys or by Places, may build themselves up Churches with steeples for Bells, and keep as many Parsons and Clergy-men as will be needfull, excluding only building up Monastery's: admonishing however hereby, that none of the divers Christians dwelling in Russia presume under what Pretence soever it be, to persuade or turn any one to his Religion or Community, under Penalty of suffering the Rigour and severity of Our Laws, except the Mahometans of different Nations dwelling near to the Borders of Our Empire, whom we do allow in a decent manner to be persuaded to embrass the Christian Religions, but even to be made band-men to any one. (2) Such Foreigners, as come for settlement to Russia, shall be exempt of all Tributs payable into Our Treasury and of all ordinary and extraordinary services or Duties, as likewise of giving Quarters to Soldiers, and in short, they shall be free from all Taxes and Burdens as fallow's, viz. Those which come over by many Familys and by whole Colony's and settle themselves on the open Fields or uncultivated Grounds are to enjoy the above said immunitys for thirty Years; but those, which desire to abide in the City's, as also to list themselves for Handy-Crafts or Trade in Our Residence in St Petersburg or in the adiacent places, in the Citys of Livonia and Estonia, Ingermanlandia, Corelia and Finland, or in Our Capital City of Moscow, for five Years; and in the other Citys of Our Governments and Provinces, for ten Years; moreover to every one of them, who come into Russia not for a short time, but for to settle themselves, will be given free Lodgings for half a Year. (3) All those Foreigners, which come for settlement to Russia, shall according to their Inclinations, either to Husbandry, or any Handy-Craft, or the setting up of Manufactures, Fabricks or Works, receive all aide and Assistance therein, as also shall be given them for that purpose sufficient Lands, and all needfull help and assistance proportionable to every ones Condition, observing in the meantime the necessity and advantage of erecting new Fabricks and Works, especially such as have not been hitherto established in Russia. (4) For the Building of Houses, and providing themselves with all Kind of Cattle needfull in Husbandry, as likewise all necessary utensils for Tillage and Handy-Crafts, Provisions and Materials, shall be given them out of our Treasury a sufficient sum of money without Interest or per cent, upon Condition of paying back only the said sum, after the Expiration of ten Years, in three Years time by equal Parts. (5) Such, as have settled themselves in separate Colonys and Places, we leave their inner Iurisdiction to their own good disposition, so that Our Commanders shall no ways concern themselves with the Management of their Affairs; but in the rest they must submit themselves to Our Civil Law; and in case they should desire of Us, from themselves to have a proper Person appointed to them with a Safe-Gard of well disciplined Troops, for their security and safety, till they become well acquainted with the neighbouring inhabitants, it shall be granted to them. (6) Every one of those Foreigners, who are desirous to come and settle themselves in Russia, we do allow the Importation of their goods and Effects consisting in any thing what so ever, without Toll or Custom, provided they be for their own use and not for sale: But in Case any one would import more Merchandizes, than he has need of, for sale, we give him Liberty to do it, allowing every Family the Import of such goods without paying any Toll or Custom, to the Value of, and not exceeding three hundred Rubles, on Condition, that they remain in Russia no less than ten Years; otherwise they will be obliged at their Leaving Russia to pay down for the above said Merchandizes the usual Tolls and Customs of Importation and Exportation. (7) Such Foreigners, that have settled themselves in Russia, as long as they remain in the empire, shall not be appointed to any Military or Civil-Duty against their will, except Land-Dutys, and even that after the prescribed Years of Respit be expired; but in case any one should desire of his own accord to enter into Our Military service, and List himself for a soldier, such a one at his appointment into the Regiment shall receive a Reward of thirty Rubles above the usual salary. (8) As soon as the said Foreigners appear to the appointed Guardian-Office for that purpose, or in any other of Our Bordering Citys, and declare their desire to go and settle themselves into the inner Parts of Russia, they shall have Diet-money given them, as also free Horses to carry them to the intended Places. (9) If any of those Foreigners that have settled themselves in Russia. shall erect Fabricks or Works, and manufacture there such Merchandizes, as have not been made yet in Russia; We do allow and give Leave to sell and export the said Merchandizes out of our Empire for ten Years, without paying any inland Tolls, Port – Duties or Customs on the Borders. (10) If any Foreign Capitalist will erect Fabricks, Manufactures or Works in Russia, We allow him to purchase for the said Fabricks, Manufactures and Works a requisite Numbre of Bond – People and Peasants. (11) To those Foreigners which have settled themselves in Our Empire by Colonies or Places, we do allow and give Leave to appoint such Markets and Fairs, as they themselves shall think most proper, without paying any Toll or Custom into Our Treasury.

VII.

All the above said Avantages and Ordinance are to be enjoyed not only by those, who have settled themselves in Our Empire, but even by their Children after them and their Posterity, though they might be born in Russia, reckoning the said Years from the Day of their Ancestors coming into Russia.

VIII.

After the Expiration of the above said Years of Respit, all those Foreigners, who have established themselves in Russia, must pay the accustomed Taxes, which are very tolerable, and perform the Land-Duties, as Our other Subjects do.

IX.

At last, if any of the said Foreigners, which have settled themselves in Our Empire, and are come under Our Subjection, should desire to go out of Our

Empire, we give them Leave and free Liberty always to do the same, on such Conditions however, that they deliver, of all their wellgotten Wealth into Our Treasury, as fallows, viz: those that have lived in Our Empire from one to five Years the fifth part; from five to ten Years and further, the tent Part; and then they may set out to any Parts, whither they have a mind, without any hindrance or Molestation.

x.

But in Case any of the Foreigners, which are desirous to settle themselves in Russia, shall for some particular Reasons demand besides the prescribed Conditions, other Privilages more: Such may address themselves either in writing or Personally to Our appointed Guardian-Office for Foreigners, which will circumstantially represent it to us, and then according to the Conjunctures We shall give a more favourable Resolution there upon, which they may expect from Our Equity. Given at Peterhoff the 22. day of July 1763. and of Our Reign the Second.

The Original Her Imperial   (L.S.)   Printed in St Petersburg at the
Majesty Signed with Her   Senate the 25. day of July 1763.
own Hand thus:
      CATHERINE.

A List Of the Lands in Russia, which are free and convenient for Plantations

1. In the Government of Tobolsk in the Land of Barabin, are Some hundred thousand Desiatins* of Grounds, which are very fertile and convenient for Plantations, having woods, Rivers and Fischeries enough.
2. In the Said Government under the Iurisdiction of the Fortress of Ust-Kumenegorsk all along the Rivers Uba, Uloe, Beresowka, Gluboca, and other Rivulets, which fall as well into the Said Rivers, as into the River Irtisch, are likewise very advantageous Grounds for Plantations.
3. In the Government of Astracan from Saratoff up to the River Volga, in the Territory of Rasdory, where the River Karaman in its Current divideth itself into two parts near the River Telausica, are besides Sufficient Corn-Lands 5,478 Desiatins of meadow – Ground, and 4,467 of Woods for Fewel and fit for building of Houses.

    Adjoining to the Territory of Zaurnorsko Rwoik, are 810 Desiatins of meadow – Ground and 1,131 of Woods.

    Near the Rivulet Tishan, are 469 Desiatins of meadow – Ground and 496 of Woods.

    Near the Rivulet Wertubany are 2,979 Desiatins of meadow – Ground and 3,607 of Woods fit for Building.

* A Desiatin is a Piece of Ground of 36 Perches, 2 Yards in Length, and of 13 Perches 3 Yards and a half in breadth.

Near the Rivulet Irgise, are 5,418 Desiatins of meadow – Ground, and 2,575 of Woods.

Near the Rivulet Sanzaley, are 1,789 Desiatins of meadow – Ground and 1,711 of Woods.

Near the Rivulet [B]eresowka, are 1,325 Desiatins of meadow – Ground and 1,606 of Woods.

Near the Rivulet call'd the litte Irgise, are 731 Desiatins of meadow – Ground and 712 of Woods.

From Saratoff down the River Volga below the Rivulet Muhar Tarlick, are besides sufficient Corn – Grounds, 6,366 Desiatins of Meadow – Ground, and 943 of Woods for Fewel and fit for building of Houses. By the Rivulet Besimianna, are 962 Desiatins of Meadow – Ground, and 609 of Woods.

Along the Rivulet called the little Tarlick are 3,509 Desiatins of Meadow – Ground and 840 of Woods.

Along the Rivulet called the litle Tarlick are 3,509 Desiatins of Meadow – Ground and 2,118 of Woods.

Between the Rivulets call'd the great Tarlick and Kamischew Bujarack, are 3,433 Desiatins of Meadow – Ground and 1,828 of Woods.

Near the Rivulet Kamischew Bujarack, are 1,751 Desiatins of Meadow – Ground and 2,254 of Woods.

Along the Rivulet Eruslan, are 1,744 Desiatins of Grass-Ground, and 523 of Woods.

At the Mouth of the Rivulet called the Lower Eruslan, are 1,770 Desiatins of Meadow – Ground and 1,104 of Woods.

Near the Rivulet Jablonnoy Bujarack are 4,003 Desiatins of Meadow – Ground and Woods.

And in all there are 70,000 Desiatins of Such Grounds, which are convenient and fit for Plantations.

4. In the Government of Orenburg along the River Sacmara, forty Werst distant from Orenburg and below the River Samara within three hundred Werst of the said City to the River Canel, as also below the Town Samara along the River Volga as far as the mouth of the Rivulet Irgise and up the said Rivulet, are so much very fertile and convenient Grounds for plantations, as will be enough for some thousands of Familys to Settle themselves upon.

5. In the Government of Belogorod in the District of Waluy along the Rivulets Jurawka, Derkul, Bitka and Oskul, are free Grounds and meadows enough for the Plantation of some hundreds of Houses, which consequently may be of great advantage to the new Colony's

Appendix II

One important form of publicity used by recruiting agents in Europe was the broadsheet, a printed or manuscript handbill. Among the papers of the Chancellery of Guardianship relating to the cancellation of Beauregard's contract is a Russian translation of such a broadsheet, used by Beauregard and his agents, and dated 1765.
TsGADA f. 248, kn. 3762, ll. 491–40b. (Author's translation from Russian.)

An Announcement Concerning the Benefits and Advantages
of the Colony Katharinenlehn, which is being established
on the patterns of the Swiss cantons

This colony is situated between 50 and 52 degrees of latitude from the Equator, opposite Saratov on the river Volga. The climate, as far as concerns the mildness of the air, is similar to that of Lyons in France, for the cold continues for scarcely three months. The soil, which is blackish in quality, is extraordinarily fertile, and without manuring, in return for little labour, gives fifteen and sixteen times the amount sown; and there are incontestable proofs that new settlers who arrived there in the spring of last year received peas one hundred fold over their sowing, although that sowing was done hastily and later than usual.

There are the most magnificent meadows there, also a great quantity of stock. The cows are similar to the Dutch breed both in quality and size, and the horses are so swift that they can travel from twelve to fifteen German miles in a day, and they cost no more than five or six roubles. The price of a milch cow is not above three to four roubles; the very best and fattest meat, such as beef, veal, mutton and pork can be bought for a kopeck per pound. All sorts of victuals, such as rice, beans, rye, barley, oats, peas, millet, flax, hemp and so on grow there in great abundance. In some places the ground is very suitable to the growing of the vine, which has already had astonishing success in surrounding places. The grapes gathered there and the wine made from them have a splendid flavour; and the wild mulberries which are found on the islands of the said river Volga promise equally magnificent benefits from the nurture of silk worms.

It was possible to obtain almonds; cherries and all sorts of fruit grow in great plenty, while garden vegetables [491ob] are accounted almost as nothing, because in the depth of winter one can obtain them amply at an extremely cheap price. Melons are extremely good there, and very abundant, and wild asparagus grows there in the meadows and valleys, as do hyacinths, tulips and other flowers.

Already on the 18th of April last, the grass there had grown up half as tall as a man, as is attested by a certain foreign clerical person and by many trustworthy people among the foreigners settled there. And all sorts of game and animals so abound, and are sold so cheaply, that three people can get a good luncheon and dinner for themselves for five or six kopecks. Doves, of which great numbers breed there, geese, canaries, hazel and black grouse, snipe, and also fish of all kinds with which the rivers teem, are sold at the lowest of prices. Deer, hares and other animals live in those parts in no less profusion than other game.

There are also places extremely suitable to the culture of tobacco and all kinds of herbs for dyeing; and the position of the town, and of the various large and small villages and other communities being set up in that settlement, on the banks of small rivers falling into the Volga, will contribute to the easy transport of foodstuffs and provisions even as far as the borders of Persia; and from there rich objects and goods can be brought back again.

By the same river Volga it is possible through Kazan' to reach Moscow and St Petersburg, and even as far as the Baltic Sea; and during the winter, which lasts only three months there, carriage of goods costs the slightest sum. Furthermore, trade can be conducted [492] along the river Don, or Tanais, to Lake Tavan, and also to the Archipelago and Mediterranean Sea. Wax and honey are found in those parts in plenty; all kinds of animal skins, also furs and Russian tanned hides, for which there will always be found many buyers abroad, make a very considerable trade.

It would be superfluous here to show in detail the benefits open to craftsmen of all kinds, manufacturers and entrepreneurs, and particularly to industrious farmers (*khlebopashtsy*) in respect of rural husbandry, from settlement there; or to describe how prosperous their condition will be with all the assistance and advances which HER IMPERIAL HIGHNESS THE AUTOCRAT OF ALL THE RUSSIAS, with the greatest bounty, graciously pleases to give them, as well as with the efforts which the Director of this colony and his assistants will make to ensure that each new settler according to his particular condition shall be able to enjoy a peaceful and plentiful life. Likewise care shall be taken for all that can further the education of the young, the elevation of the sciences and of useful crafts, and the provision of honourable support for widows and orphans according to the circumstances in which they find themselves.

1. HER IMPERIAL HIGHNESS, by a law established in perpetuity allowing to each one free practice of his religion according to the rites of his own Church, permits new settlers to build churches and belfries, to

which shall be appointed the requisite number of clergy of the Catholic, Reformed and Lutheran confessions. [4920b]

2. All and every foreign settler in this colony, also their children even though born in Russia, shall be free for 30 years from all taxes and state services of any kind, and on expiry of that period shall be obliged to pay only the usual moderate land taxes at the same rate as native and long-established inhabitants of the Russian Empire.

3. Everyone will be permitted to leave the Empire permanently, whenever he wishes, provided only that he shall have returned the money spent on him by the Treasury; he may also take with him possessions acquired in Russia, paying only one fifth part to the Treasury if he has stayed not more than five years, and only one tenth if longer than the five-year limit. Treasury monies shall be repaid [by other settlers] only after passage of the first ten years, in three equal parts over three years and without payment of interest.

4. It is permitted to everyone to bring into the country all his own property, also everything else needful for his own expenditure; and to each family, goods to the value of 300 roubles, for sale, without payment of any duty unless any family wishes to leave the country before the passage of the first ten years when it will have to pay duty on the 300 roubles' worth of goods imported.

5. The Director of the settlement intends to give every facility to those unable to acquire for themselves the merchandise which HER IMPERIAL HIGHNESS [493] allows each family to import into Russia on the basis of the Manifesto and the conditions set forth in it, so that regardless of the great profit likely to accrue from this, the Director leaves to the settlers themselves or their families the disposal and sale of the goods, deducting only not more than three per cent commission for the merchants from whom these goods shall come.

6. It is also permitted to the new settlers to establish their own fairs and trading points, without any payment of dues to the Treasury, and in addition after ten years they may export overseas all articles and wares produced in the colony, also without payment of taxes to the Treasury.

7. Money for transport and maintenance on the journey to the capital will be given them from the Treasury of HER IMPERIAL HIGHNESS, and from there they will be transported free of charge to the place of settlement itself; where besides all necessary help and an advance in money they will receive daily maintenance payments for a whole year counting from the time when houses are ready for them. [They will also receive] all materials necessary for house-building, and sheds and stables in due relation to the condition of the members of each family and the quantity of land allocated to it.

8. Seed will be given for the first sowing, both winter and spring.

9. They will also be given one horse for each worker, and over and above that one horse as a reserve for each family. [4930b]

10. All horse harness, carts, ploughs, sledges, household equipment, also

farming and household implements, and in addition one of each sort of tool per family.

11. Cows, sheep and pigs in due proportion and according to the number of people of each age[?], also money for the purchase of livestock, garden seeds and other petty items.

12. Handicraftsmen settling in the villages according to the lands allocated to them will receive as much raw material as they and their family can work in two months, and those settlers in the town as much as they can work in six months as well as land as much as they can plough or have need of, besides the other monetary advance and necessary help on the same basis as promised to farmers.

13. HER IMPERIAL HIGHNESS permits the Director of this settlement, as a special grace, to engage for it people of different status with retention of the ranks and characters acquired by them in foreign countries. He also has the right to establish this settlement on the same basis as the Swiss cantons, under its own internal jurisdiction and police, appointing to it colonels, lt. colonels, majors, captains, ensigns, high bailiffs (*Oberamtmänner*), higher and lower judges, village mayors (*Schulzen*), beadles (*Vögte*) and overseers (*Forstjäger*), who shall receive a specified salary from the produce of the colony and also in advance, while they are occupied with the gathering and dispatch of colonists, in addition to the land which will be given to them in hereditary possession [491] according to the number of families consisting of (?) their own labourers, viz. a captain or a judge will receive 150 desyatinas for each five families.

An overseer knowledgeable in rural economy and able to read and write, having also wife and children or two servant girls, will have supervision over his own area of jurisdiction (*forshtyegerstvo*) in which his village (*derevnya*) will be first and which will comprise 21 persons, viz. seven married farmers including the overseer himself, then (*sledovatel'no*) seven women, two labourers and five children, counting them more or less. For seven married families the overseer will receive in hereditary possession for himself and his family 75 desyatinas. The second farmer of the *forshtyegerstvo* will receive 25 desyatinas, the third – 24, the fourth – 18, the fifth – 15, the sixth – 12, and a shepherd in the number of those seven married men will also receive 12 desyatinas. The two labourers shall receive 10 desyatinas each.

If any wish to have part in the benefits of this colony stated above, they may correspond with Mr Caneau de Beauregard in the Castle of Brockhausen, in Utrecht province, or address themselves to the Russian IMPERIAL Commissioner Schmidt in Lübeck and to the Russian IMPERIAL Consul Aldekot in Amsterdam; also in Koswig on the Elbe to Capt. Kindermann, in Roslau to Capt. Kotzer, in Köln on the Rhine to Capt. Weimar [494ob] in Hamburg, Taunitz St., to Major Monjou, and finally in Frankfurt on the Main, to Lt. Col. Monjou, as being assistants to the Director who have from him letters of accreditation to that effect and have been appointed Commissioners.

Beneath this proclamation, on the printed sheet which the Chancellary obtained by chance, is written and signed in Beauregard's hand:

We Alexander Vorontsov, Count of the Holy Roman Empire, Gentleman of the Chamber of HIH THE EMPRESS OF ALL THE RUSSIAS, and Minister Plenipotentiary to Their Excellencies the Estates General of the United Netherlands, hereby certify that the benefits hereinabove described conform in all points to the truth, in proof whereof we have personally signed this certification and set our seal to it. Done at The Hague, the 23rd day of August, 1765.

Appendix III

Lloyds Evening Post and British Chronicle, vol. xiv no. 1040, 9–12 March N.S. 1764, p. 243: 'Account of the Weekly Papers'.

To the North Briton, March 10th

Sir,

In No. 75 of your Paper, you mentioned that 248 Persons, of various occupations, had engaged with the Russian Ambassador to form a settlement in his Mistress's dominions, having previously met with a denial in their application for encouragement to do so in Florida. In the public Papers of this week I find the States of Holland have issued an arret, strictly forbidding, under the severest penalties, any of their subjects to accept the invitations given by the Ambassadors of that Power, at the several Courts where they reside, to foreigners to settle on some waste Lands of Russia, at the sole expence of the Empress. The Dutch, Sir, are a wise nation, and know the value of people too well to part with them. We have not only lost the service of these 248 persons, but that of their posterity. In a generation or two, thousands who *might* have been English subjects, will *all* be Russians. Every subject, on an average, consumes, I have been told, to the value of five pounds per annum in food and apparel; for the supply of which divers persons are employed. When an individual, therefore, removes to a foreign State, it causes a proportionable loss of trade, and the Government is also deprived of that advantage which it must have reaped from his stay, in respect to the taxes raised, by customs and excise, on those commodities he would naturally have used. Besides this, the strength of the nation, by such measures, becomes enervated; one fourth of the inhabitants being usually reckoned capable of bearing arms.

But to my purpose: This migration of the 248 persons, I am informed, is not the whole. Others are daily making the same agreement. I was last night in company with a *reduced* Lieutenant, who assured me, that he was soon to go to Russia as Superintendant of another cargo of Manufacturers and private Soldiers; that he was to have the rank of Captain in the Czarina's troops, and command of a fine settlement in one of the

Southern and Asiatic provinces of that extensive empire. I enquired of him, where he had served during the late war? His answer was, in Germany, and had, therefore, no right, according to the late Proclamation, to any establishment in America. 'Besides, Sir', says he, 'if I had, what should I do with my land? I have no slaves, no labouring utensils, no money. My arrears, too, are in an inaccessible fund; but in the Russian service I enter into present pay, and am provided, by that Government, with a capital to carry on any reasonable scheme.'

On hearing this, I could not help reflecting on the surprizing mutability of things. Russia, so late the most ignorant nation in Europe, is now become one of the wisest. England, once so much her Superior in the Art of Government, now gives place to Russia. In the name of Prudence, Mr North Briton, have our Worthy Great Men no intelligence? Or are there no laws in England that prohibit Manufacturers from going abroad, and forbid our private men to enlist in foreign service? I have somewhere read, that it is highly penal to decoy a Manufacturer over sea. If there are such laws, why are they not put into execution? Policy should make us keep our people at home; and Religion, as well as Policy, commands us to provide for them.

(No signature)

Appendix IV

Observations Sur La Levée des Colonies Russes & L'Emigration des Familles Françoises

ll. 222–220b.

Le Sr Chanoni de Lyon, agé de 40 ans, taille de 5 pieds 5 pouces, assés joli de figure, un peu chauve au front, dirigeant les manufactures de fer blanc et emploié dans celle d'étoffes de soie.

Passa à Hambourg dans le mois de Novembre 1765, allant en Saxe avec un nommé Florentin pour y débaucher des manufacturiers; il en est revenu peu après mais sans succès, a pris la route d'Hollande ou il s'est arreté fort peu, en est parti pour se rendre à Bâle pour être proche de Montbeillard et du rendés-vous avec un nommé Goguel, ci-devant Lieut^t au Reg^{mt} D'Alsace, taille de 6 pieds, agé de 22 ans, assés bel homme.

Ce même Goguel est de Montbeillard et y aiant tout sa famille qu'on y dit tres estimée, il étoit...sous le pretexte de l'...est... [document dirty, 2 lines illegible at this point].

Il est à remarquer que la régence du Duc de Wirtemburg commençoit a sentir l'effet de cette émigration et avoit Consequemment donné les ordres les plus rigoureux pour en prevenir les Suittes. Il fallut donce se tenir caché, ce que fit le Sr Chanoni qui en partie [l. 220ob.] s'est tenu à Bâle ou autres endroits de la Suisse ou à Montbeillard chés le d^t Goguel.

Leurs opérations ont été fortes lentes au commencement, de façon que quand le Sr Chanoni est parti de là pour se rendre a St. Petersbourg, il n'y avoit que 30 familles de fabricans de levées, mais au moi de mai le Sr Goguel en avoit près de Cent tant du Pais que françoises. Je ne les ai point vû, car elles n'ont pas passés par Hambourg.

ll. 223–224

Le Roy de Flagis, de Paris, taille de 5 pieds 1 pouce, chevalure brune, agé de 34 ans, a été Jesuite Suivant les uns ou Oratorien suivt d'autres.

Directeur d'une colonie aiant fait son contract pour 3000 familles & eu sous lui pour le travail des Levées des Colons.

Florentin, d'Aix-la Chappelle, taille de 5 pieds 5 pouces, gras, blond, homme intelligent.

Goguel, de Montbeillard, ci-devant Cap^{ne} Lieut: au Reg^{mt} d'Alsace, cousin de celui qui est avec Chanoni, grand de 5^{pds} 10^{pces}, bel homme.

Dreischok, homme de rien, du Pais de Maience, brun, petit, maigre, laid de figure.

Le Doulx de Ste Croix, de Bourdeaux, ancien^{mt} au Regt. de Poitou, agé de 31 ans, taille de 5^{pds} 2^{pces}, marié, aiant avec lui son beaufrere nommé Deschamps, taille de 5^{pds} 4^{pces}, blond et fort maigre, agé de 36 ans.

Rubertus, Camelotier de Saxe, agé de 30 ans, taille de 5^{pds} 6^{pces}.

Planchenaud, de Paris, ci-devant Perruquier, marié à une Comedienne franç^{se} a St. Petersbourg.

Cordier, François, Comédien a la Haie, c'est lui qui a Composé Zarucma.

Departemens des susd^{ts} commissaires.

à Ratisbonne, *Florentin* fit en 1765 environ 550 familles toutes allemandes, partie Bavaroises, Palatines ou Wurtembergeoises, environs 15 familles d'Alsace qu'il a engagées à Wurms dans un voïage qu'il y fit.

En 1766, il y a fait prés de 300 familles Palatines, Bavaroises ou Bohemiennes.

à Nuremberg: id^m en 1766, aux Environs de 150 familles en partie Wirtembergeoises [l. 2230b].

Rubertus à Ulm, en 1765 il y a levé pas loin de 110 familles toutes allemandes a 2 ou 3 familles Franç^{ses} refugiées prés.

Goguel à Ulm, en 1766 y a engagé pres de 100 familles presque toutes Wirtembergeoises & si les ordres de la Cour de Russie de cesser les opérations n'étoient pas venues, 400 fam^{les} Wirtembergeoises étoient pretes à Suivre.

Dreischock à Franckfort, en 1766 y a levé presque 1000 fam^{les} du Païs de Maience, Treves, La Hesse, Palatin, 25 familles franç^{ses} tant de la Loraine, en partie Vignerons, que refugiées protestantes de Sarbruck, Nassau, Darmstadt, Giessen & [sic].

Il est a observer que cette partie de L'Allemagne ou est Franckfort, a fourni cette année plus de 3500 familles et qu'elles etoient d'autant plus agréeablement reçues, que presque tous les Chefs de Famille savoient ecrire, connoissoient mieux le Labourage et étoient plus industrieux que les Bavarois.

Uchtritz à Zerbst, en 1766. Il y a levé jusqu'à 230 fam^{les}, parmi lesquelles se sont trouvées 5 fam^{les} françoises perdues pour la france depuis la paix.

Chevalier, Fabri^{et} de Velour de Coton avec sa femme et un enfant.

Louvelle, aussi de Rouen, Fabric^t d'Etoffe de soye, sa femme et deux enfans.

Gerard, Vigneron de la Lorraine, sa femme et huit enfans.

L. Bourgneuf de Toulouse, sa femme et un enfant.

Aux environs de 50 Familles de Brandebourg, des Colons que le Roi de Prusse avoit fait venir de tout coté pour cultiver la marche Brandebourgeoise, parmi les quelles il s'est [l. 224] trouvé aussi 5 à 6 familles de la Lorraine.

Hambourg, Lubeck, Kiel en 1766, pas plus de 100 familles et une famille françoise nommée Deuza, de Valencienne, Fabricant de Cambrai.

Le Doulx en 1766, prés de 200 familles pour la plupart composées de Colons que le Roi de Dan[k] avoit fait venir pour defricher les Bruïere de la Jutlande.

Cordier en *Hollande* en 1765. 5 familles françoises, fabricants de Cambrai.

ll. 224ob.–225

Meunier de Precourt de Paris, taille du 5[pds] 2[pces], blond, la voix roque; ci devant emploié dans Les vivres. *Directeur*, aïant sous lui le chevalier Pignalvert que je ne connois pas.

Rolwagen Officier au Service de Bronswick, de la taille de 5[pds] 5[pces], blond, assés bel homme.

Meunier de Beljean de Metz fils d'un regisseur d'Abbaïe prés de cette Ville.

En Hollande Meunier D[r] en 1765 a levé environ 200 familles, parmi lesquelles il y avoit près de 30 familles Françoises, plusieurs Fabricants, 3 officiers franc[s] & 2 bas officiers.

On pouroit savoir plusieurs particularités d'un nommé Dèschamps, ci devant attaché à la Police de Paris demeurant ruë de la Pelterie, ou par le susd[t] Meunier de Beljean qui est retourné à Metz chés son Père. Ce jeune homme s'étoit engagé par misere comme Colon et est parvenu à être Secretaire de Mr Meunier.

a Hambourg Lubeck en 1765. Par la soit disante femme de Meunier Le D[r] et le nommé Chev[r] de Pignalvert, prés de 370 famil: toutes allemandes a quelques deserteurs françois pres.

a Wurms, Rollwagen en 1766. Mr Meunier compta faire un dernier effort en envoïant ledit Rollwagen. Dès le mois de fevrier il en recut une liste de 2800 Tetes, mais le mauvais traitement qu'on leur fit essuïer en route, les reduit a 1300 parmi [l. 225] les quels il s'en trouva peut-etre une 3one De françoises, Déserteurs, fabricans de bas, forgerons reformées pour la plus part. Le Sr Meunier a recu 16000 roubles et n'a levé que 970 familles.

l. 225ob.

Mr *de Beauregard*, aiant sous ses ordres:

Mrs le Lieut Colonel & Major de Monjou, Les Cap[ne] Kotzer, Beckstein et autres, Les Lieut. Oldenbourg, Kesseler, Lagarde & autres.

Il avait quatre Rendes-vous Roslau en Zerbst, Furth prés de Nuremburg, Franckfort, Amsterdam. Je ne compte ni Hambourg, ni Lubeck, ces deux Villes faisant le rendes-vous general.

a Roslau, Le Cap^ne *Kotzer.* Cette petite Ville a produit plus de 700 familles, tous fabricans du pais d'Anhalt, Cöthen, Zerbst, Dessau, Bernbourg, de la Saxe, du Brandenbourg, ces derniers en passant Magdebourg se disoient saxons.

a Furth. A 20 familles franc^ses prés composées de Cloutiers, Tisserans, Bucherons tirées des Ardennes ils n'y ont eu que 200 fam^les.

a Franckfort. Pres de 450 familles je ne les ai point vues.

a Hamburg. Le Cap^ne Beckstein, secondé du Lieutenant Oldenbourg y a fait cent quelques fam^les.

a Lubeck. Le Lieutenant LaGarde y a levé plus de 200 familles. Je n'y ai remarqué que peu de françois.

l. 226

Lembke, Facius, Florentin. Tous trois Commis^fr Imperiaux.

Lembke, proposé pour embarquer les Colons n'a presque point enrollé de familles, mais son predecesseur en avoit engagé plus de 1400. pend^t l'espace de deux. ans, parmi les quelles se sont trouvées quelques françoises malheureuses depuis Longtemps dans le Pais.

Facius a Franckfort il a fait pour Compte de la Couronne plus de 1400 familles en un an de tems, j'y ai trouvé peut-être 80 familles franc^ses, soit Loraines, soit Alsaciennes, composées de deserteurs mariés an Allemagnes, quelques Vignerons Laboureurs et peu de fabricans.

Dans la route de *Ratisbonne* a *Lubeck* Le nommé *Florentin* a fait 630 a 50 familles; il y avoit plusieurs familles franc^ses d'origine, mais perdues depuis Longtems pour le Roiaume et etablis a Bareith, Erlang et réformées pour La plupart.

Un nommé Gerard Colon s'etoit engagé d'aller à ses depens chercher des filleuses a Valenciennes Mons et Païs circonvoisin, Il avoit sur lui 1200 Frederics d'or qu'il avoit volé de la Caisse du Domaine De Berlin, mais à la réquisition du Roi il fut rendu, on assure qu'il l'a fait pendre.

l. 227

Recapitulation Générale des Observations

Directeur	Emploies	Villes	Ans	Familles Allemandes	Familles Françoises	Total des Familles
Chanoni	Goguel	Montbeillard	1766	60	40	100
Le Roy	Florentin	Ratisbonne	65	535	15	550
			66	300		300
	Rubertus	Ulm	65	107	3	110
	Goguel	idem	66	100		100
	Dreischock	Franckfort	66	990	20	1010
	Uchtritz	Roslau	66	225	5	230
		Hambourg ⎫		⎫		
		Lubeck ⎬	65 ⎱ 66 ⎰	299	2	301
		Kiel ⎭				
	Cordier	Hollande	65		5	5
Meunier	Lui-même	Hollande	65	175	25	200
	sa soidisante	Hambourg ⎫		⎫		
	femme	Lubeck ⎬	65 ⎱ 66 ⎰	400		400
		Eutin ⎭				
	Rollwagen	Wurms	66	330	20	350
Beauregard	Cap. Kotzer	Roslau	66	700		700
	Monjou	Furth	66	390	10	400
		Amsterdam	66	180	20	200
		Frankfort	66	450		450
	Beckstein	Hambourg	66	100		100
	Lagarde	Lubeck	66	200		200
Lembcke		Lubeck		1400		1400
Facius		Francfort	66	1330	70	1400
Florentin		dans la route de Ratisbonne à Lubeck	66	630		630
		Nuremburg	66	150		150
				9051	235	9286

D'aprés ce tableau, quoique pas tout a fait exact, le nombre des Familles qu'on nomme françoises n'est pas si considerable que nous l'avions craint, et si on épluchoit bien exactement cet Etat il ne s'en trouveroit peut etre pas [l. 227ob.] 150 de veritablement françoises, Car il n'y a personne qui ne Convienne que l'absence de differentes familles pendant 30 40 ou 50 ans et plus nous les rend etrangeres.

l. 228

Etat
de Dépense pour la Chancellerie de protection de St. Petersbourg
à la levée de 9000 familles.

Pour 40 Roubles par famille rendue à Lubeck	...	360000
Leur Entretient à Lubeck a 8 roubles	...	72000
Frais de passage a 12 roubles	...	108000
Paye pendant un mois a Oranienbaum a 12 Roubl	...	108000
Pour la somme de 300 Roubles promis par S. M^{te} Imp. a chaque famille, portée a la moitié	...	1350000
Fraix de transport d'oranienbaum a Saratoff à 8 Roub	...	72000
Gratification accordée a chaque Directeur a 10 Roub:	...	90000
Pour faux frais	...	15000
Pour L'etablissement des maisons a 30 Roub:	...	270000
Pour L'etablissement general de chaque 100ne de fam^{le} a 3000 familles	...	270000
	Roubles	2 715 000

Voici un Etat de depense tres considerable pour la Cour de Russie, si elle avoit été obligé d'en sortir les deniers de ses Coffres, mais on observera que la Noblesse du Pais en a fait les Frais de moitié et la Cour n'a fait les avances que d'une partie.

A l'arrivée des Colons a Oranienbaum la Noblesse choisit ceux dont Les métiers leur conviennent. Le Colon pour eviter un plus grand éloignement contracte avec ce Noble pour 20 ans et plus, fait reimbourser la Chancellerie par ce seigneur les frais qu'il a occasionné, dès cet instant il est libre vis a vis de la Couronne, mais rengagé sous le seigneur. Par la les sommes passées dans L'étranger par la levée ont été en parti remplacées dans le trésor par la Noblesse du Pais. Qu'on observe de plus, que l'allemagne n'a eu que 445000 roubles pour 9000 familles environ qu'elle a perdu.

Quant a l'article 5 quoique la dépense n'en soit portée qu'a moitié elle peut etre reduite au tier etant assuré que nombre de familles n'ont recu que 70 Roubles et d'autres n'en ont pris que 60 pour être plûtot dans le Cas de rembourser. D'ailleurs les familles cedées a la Noblesse n'ont rien Reçu.

Si les directeurs etoient paies, l'article 7 seroit une depense réele.

Les articles 9 et 10 peuvent souffrir un tier de Diminution.

N.B.:

(1) All orthography as far as possible is that of the original (identification of capitals is sometimes difficult). Italics indicate larger script.

(2) The document is held in the Mss. Dept. of the Saltykov-Shchedrin State Public Library, Leningrad (ORGPB): Bastille Archive, *Avtograf* 121, no. 107. It is reproduced as an appendix to the Library's internal typescript

catalogue of this archive: *ORGPB, Dokumenty iz Bastil'skogo Arkhiva, Annotirovannyy Katalog*, sost. A. D. Lyublinskaya (Leningrad 1960). On the Bastille Archive and the Leningrad holdings, see A. D. Lyublinskaya, 'Bastiliya i yeyo arkhiv', *Frantsuskiy Yezhegodnik za 1958 g.* (M. 1959), pp. 104–26. The document was not published in the collections of material from the archive printed by Ravaisson, La Ferrière and Hovyn de Tranchère; but it was known in a very bad copy to P. d'Estrée, 'Une Colonie franco-russe au XVIIIe siècle', *Revue des Revues*, 1896 no. 19 (1 octobre), 15–16.

(3) Lyublinskaya (catalogue p. 40) suggests very plausibly that the document was prepared at official request by a French consul located in Hamburg or Lübeck, in an attempt to estimate the number of French families lost to the Russian recruiting agents in general, and in particular to the agent Rollwagen, who was imprisoned in the Bastille and to whose case the document belonged (Archives de la Bastille, Bibl. de l'Arsénal, Paris, no. 12299). A request to the French Ambassador in Petersburg for similar information is given in *SIRIO*, cxli, 158. The document appears to have been composed in late 1766 or early 1767. Rollwagen was subsequently found innocent of charges of suborning French subjects, and was released. Further details on him, and on others including David Barral, can be found in vol. 19 of Ravaisson's collection: L. Ravaisson-Mollien, *Archives de la Bastille: Documents inédits...t.19: Règne de Louis XV (1765–69)* (Paris 1904), pp. 170–235.

(4) While in many respects the information contained in the document is unique, it is not entirely accurate. Totals for recruitment appear to be much too high (but see p. 283 n. 66); some details of the 'directors' contracts are incorrect; and insufficient distinction is made between different categories of agent.

Appendix V

Der zu Strelina mit denen Collonisten, so nach der Ukraine sich zu Etabeliren willig gemacht geschlossener Contract

TsGADA f. 283, op. 1 d. 16 (contracts with the Chancellery of Guardianship), contracts nos. 48 and 49, ll. 128–32 and 133–70b.

Two contracts between the colonists settling in Belovezh, and Premier-Major Jacob Freyhold on behalf of the President of the Little Russian College. Signed in Strelna, outside Petersburg; undated. (The Belovezh colonies were set up in 1766.)

The colony was to include an agricultural and an urban or artisan settlement; the first contract (no. 48) was made with the farmers, the second with the artisans. The texts are in large part very similar. Italics in the text indicates words written in Latin script and slightly larger than the Gothic script of the remainder. All orthography as in the original, except for the German ß.

The first contract has 115 colonist signatures or marks, the second 51.

no. 48 no. 49

Wir endes Unterschriebene die zu der *Etabelirung nach der Ukraine* bestimmte *Colonisten*, bescheinigen und bekräftigen hiemit dass auf hohen Befehl d.H. *Major Freyhold* uns nachfolgende *Conditiones* bestehend in „7„ Punkte bekannt gemacht hat gegen welche wir auf nichts einzuwenden haben, sondern vielmehr mit selbigen völlig zu frieden sind und demnach verlangen nach der *Ukraine* etabeliret zu werden.

Wir verbünden uns sowohl als die Persohnen von unsern Familien dass

Wir endes Unterschriebene die zu der *Etabelirung nach der Ukraine* bestimmte *Colonisten*, bescheinigen und bekräftigen hiemit dass auf hohen Befehl d. H. *Major Freyhold* uns nachfolgende *Conditiones* bestehend in „7„ Punkte bekannt gemacht hat gegen welche wir auf nichts einzuwenden haben, sondern vielmehr mit selbigen völlig zu frieden sind und demnach verlangen nach der *Ukraine* etabeliret zu werden.

Versprechen wir Endes unter-schriebene und verbünden uns sowohl

wir den uns von S^r hochgräfflichen
Excellence hochbestalten *General
en Cheff, General Gouverneur* von
Klein Russland *President* des dasigen
Collegii, Cheff des *Ukrainschen*
und Klein Russischen *Corps,* des *St.
Andreas* und *St. Alexander Newsky*
und des holsteinischen *St. Annen*
Ordens Ritter Graffen von *Rumantzoff*
in den neuen *Collonie* Aus-Länder
gennant Catharinen Polsche Kreis in
Klein Reussen gelegen, angewiesenen
Theil und District Ländereyen so viel
wir mit unsern Familien in Vermögen
sind zu bearbeiten, getraulich bewohnen und zu unsern *Establissement* in
der *Collonie* gehörig bearbeiten und
cultivieren wollen.

als die Persohnen von unsern Familien
dass wir den uns von S^r hochgräfflichen
Excellence hochbestallten *General en
Cheff, General Gouverneur* von
Klein Russland *President* des dasigen
Collegii, Cheff des *Ukrainschen* und
Klein Russischen *Corps,* des *St.
Andreas, St. Alexander Newsky* und
des holsteinischen *St. Annen* Ordens
Ritter Graffen von Rumanzoff in den
neuen *Collonie* Aus Länder, gennant,
Catharinen Pohl in Klein Reussen
gelegene Stadt bewohnen wollen.

2.

Dass weder wir noch die Unsrigen
von bennanten Ländereyen ohne
Erlaubniss unserer obenerwehnten
Oberhaupts des *General Gouvernements* verlassen wollen uns anderswohin, es sey wo es wolle zu begeben
und zu *Etabeliren,* vielmehr wollen
wir uns daselbst, so wie es ehrlichen
Männern geziemt verhalten, und
aufführen und uns nicht nur denen
hiesigen und künftigen Gesetzen des
Reichs, sondern auch denen für die
Collonie besondern festgestellten
Reglements und innerlichen Verfassungen unterwerfen, dahingegegen
wird uns auch das angewiesene Land
eingetheilet, nach eines in den
Vermögen und Stärke der *Familie*
[*sic*] und so wie es Sr Erlauchten
d. H. Graff vor gut befinden wird: so
dass wir es zu bearbeiten in Stande
seyn können, wogegen auch die
qualitet des Ackers, Bau und übrige
Land Wirtschaft Wesen *taxiret* wird,
zu dem wird auch einer jeden *Familie*
bestanden in Natura zu geben, als
nehmlich ein Wohnhauss, nebst
Scheune und gehörige Stallungen,
so wie es Sr Erlauchten für gut und

2.

Dass weder wir noch die Unsrigen
aus der bennanten Stadt ohne Erlaubniss unsere obenerwehnten Oberhaupts
oder des *General Gouvernements*
verlassen wollen uns anderswohin, es
sey wo es wolle zu begeben und zu
Etabeliren, vielmehr wollen wir uns
daselbst, so wie es ehrlichen Bürgern
geziemet verhalten, und aufführen
und uns nicht nur denen jetzigen
und künftigen Gesetzen des Reichs,
sondern auch denen für die *Collonie*
besondern festgestellte *Reglements* und
innerlichen Verfassungen unterwerfen.

bequem halten wird, an aus saat
Rocken 3 Schetwert, Weitzen 4
Schetwerik, Haber 5 Schetwert und
zum Unterhalt das erste Jahr an
Rocken 10 Schetwert, so wohl auch
über dem zur Haushaltung 2 Pferde,
2 Kühe, 3 Schafe, 3 Schweine, 4
Gänse, 4 Hüner und zur Bearbeitung
des Landes ein Wagen nebst Pflug 2
Eggen eine Axt, ein Gestühl mit einer
Sense zum Hexelschneiden, eine Sense,
ein Beyl ein Bohrer und ein Meisel.

3.

Dass wir für Betrag des zu unsren
Etablissement verwanten Vorschuss-
geldes ausser die zwey ersten Jahre,
die folgenden aber zu sechs *procent*
jährlich zu entrichten verbunden, bis
wir im Stande seyn werden selbiges
Capital gänzlich abzutragen wie auch
vor die uns zu ernannten Ländereyen,
als Acker und Wiesenland, jährlich
ausser das erste Jahr die folgenden
nach Berechnung ihres Werths zu fünf
procent oder von ihrem Gewinnst zu
fünf und zwanzig *procent* jährlich zu
entrichten verplichtet seyn.

4.

Dass uns auch verstatten und
behältlich sey, wenn einige dienlich
fanden, sowohl selbsten als auch mit
unserer *Familie* Russland wieder zu
verlassen, unsere *Effecten* und die
bey der *Collonie* erübrigten Vortheile
ungehindert mit zu nehmen, jedoch

3.

Im gleichen verbünden wir uns vor
unsere Erben und unsere Nachkommen
dass die auf uns von der hohen Crone
nebst dem Vorschuss angewandte
Gelder laut allerhöchst Ihro *Majestet*
Emanirten Manifest nach Verflüssung
zehn frey Jahren in dreyen Jahren zu
bezahlen, und nach Verfluss der in
solchen *Manifest* festgestellten frey
Jahren sind wir schuldig und gezwungen alle die *Honora publica* gleich
den andern Bürgern zu entrichten, die
Art und Weise aber dieser Entrichtung
soll in Zukunft festgesetzt werden
dahingegen wird uns von Seiten
der hohen Crone versprochen, den
gehörigen Vorschuss, und alles zu
unserer Hanthierung Nöthige ohne
Mangel, so wohl in Natura als am
Gelde, wie es sich am füglichsten und
vortrefflichsten thun läst, zu reichen,
da es aber unterschiedene *Profession-*
alisten giebt, und man jetzt nicht
determiniren kann was ein jeder
bekommen soll: so bleibt selbiges bis
in Zukunft ausgesetzt.

4.

Dass uns auch verstatten und
behältlich sey, wenn einige nach
Bezahlung der Crone Schulden
dienlich fänden, sowohl selbsten als
auch mit unserer *Familie* Russland
wieder zu verlassen, unsere *Effecten*
und die bey der *Collonie* erübrigten

nur in so weit als es nach dem Inhalt
des Kayserlichen *Manifests* zu gestanden und erlaubt worden ist in gleichen
dass wir unsere Versprechungen und
Verpflichtungen unsers *Contracts*
erfüllet haben müssen, wobey wir uns
gleich wohl aus bedingen dass wir das
einige nicht mit *restituiren* dürfen, was
zu unsere Transport und Unterhalt
von *St. Petersbourg* bis in *loco* des
Etablissements erforderlich gewesen,
angesehen *Ihro Majestet* diese Gelder
ohne Wiederersetzung allergnädigst
eingewilliget haben.

Vortheile ungehindert mit zu nehmen,
jedoch nur in so weit als es nach dem
Inhalt des Kayserlichen *Manifests* zu
gestanden und erlaubt worden ist in
gleichen dass wir unsere Versprechungen und die Verpflichtungen unsers
Contracts erfüllet haben müssen,
wobey wir uns gleich wohl aus
bedingen dass wir das einige nicht mit
restituiren dürfen, was zu unsern
Transport und Unterhaltung von *St.
Petersbourg* bis in *loco* des *Etablissements* erforderlich gewesen, angesehen
Ihro Majestet diese Gelder ohne
Wiederersetzung allergnädigst eingewilliget haben.

5.

5.

Der ganzen *Collonie* wird bestanden
an oben erwehnten Ort, der *Protestant-
ischen Religion* nach eine Kirche
nebst dazu gehörigen Priester mit
freyen Unterhalt auf zwei Jahre von
der hohen Crone, vom dritten aber
an wird er von uns *saloriret*, beträffend
aber der Kirche so wird selbige uns mit
allen zugehörigen Nothwendigkeiten,
ohne unsere Bezahlung aber, von der
hohen Crone versehen und erbauet
nach Verflüssung der zwey Jahre aber,
verbünden wir uns, den Geistlichen
derselbiger uns schon von der hohen
Crone gegeben worden mit einem
jährlichen Unterhald von 180 Rubl.
selbsten zu versorgen; zu dem wird uns
auch bestanden bey selbiger Kirche
einen Kister der zugleich auch unsere
Kinder im Lesen Schreiben und
Christenthum unterweisen möchte,
mit Unterhalt ebenfalls wie den
Geistlichen, in zwey Jahren von der
hohen Crone, vom dritten aber von
uns *saloriret*, dergestalt dass eine
jedwede *Familie* ihm geben wird jährl:
so viel dass er sein Unterhalt haben
kann. Die Häuser aber so wohl für
den Geistlichen als auch für schon
erwehnten Küster zum Pastor-Rath
werden von der Hohen Crone ohne
unsere Bezahlung erbauet, die künftige

Der ganzen *Collonie* wird bestanden
an oben erwehnten Ort der *Protestant-
ischen Religion* nach eine Kirche
nebst dazu gehörigen Priester mit
freyen Unterhalt auf zwey Jahren von
der hohen Crone, vom dritten aber
an wird er von uns *saloriret*, betreffend
aber wegen der Kirche so wird
selbige uns mit allen dazu gehörigen
Nothwendigkeiten, ohne aber unsere
Bezahlung, von der hohen Crone
versehen und erbauet nach Verflüssung
der zwey Jahren aber, verbünden wir
uns, den Geistlichen derselbiger uns
schon ein mahl von der hohen Crone
gegeben worden mit einem jährlichen
Unterhalt von 180 Rubl. gut zu thun,
zu dem wird uns auch bestanden bey
selbiger Kirche einen Küster der
zugleich auch unsere Kinder im Lesen
Schreiben und Christenthum unterweisen möchte, mit Unterhalt ebenfalls
wie den Geistlichen, in zwey Jahren
von der hohen Crone, vom dritten aber
von uns *saloriret* dergestalt dass eine
jedwede *Familie* ihm jährlich so viel
geben wird dass er sein Unterhalt
haben kann. Die Häuser aber so wohl
für den Geistlichen also auch für schon
erwehnten Küster zum Pastor-Rath
werden von der hohen Crone erbauet
ohne unsere Bezahlung, die künftige

Reparatur so wohl an der Kirche als
an den andren dazu gehörigen
Gebäudern verbünden wir uns nach
Verflüssung der zwey Jahre auf unserm
eigenen Unkosten alle Wohl zu thun.

Reparatur so wohl der Kirche als
anderer dazu gehöriger Gebäude
verbünden wir uns nach Verflüssung
der zwey Jahren auf unsern eigenen
Unkosten alle Wohl zu thun.

6.

6.

Da hingegen verbünden wir uns in
Einrichtung der fernern, wie zur
Unterhaltung derer Strassen in einer
ordentlichen Zustand, zu denen
Einquartirungen, zur Wahrnehmung
derer Wälder, also auch überhaupt in
Ansehung der Policey, und unsern
innerlichen Gerichts Ordnungen, als
auch in Streitigkeiten, so sich zwischen
uns, und den dasigen Einwohnern
ereigen könnten, erbitten wir der
hohen Crone, eine Land Gerechtigkeit,
von der besonderen Vorsorge S^r
Erlauchten d. H. *General en cheff* und
Ritter Graffen von *Rumanzoff* zu
welchen wir unser besonder Zutrauen
gefast haben, und demnach von uns
Collonisten, auch schon vorhero mit
Einwilligung geschehen ist, und nur
dazumahl *per appellation* uns an die
Tutel Cantzeley zu wenden, wenn
solche Fälle sich ereignen sollten, als
im obenerwehnten *Confirmierten
Doclad* vorgeschrieben steht, als nehmlich alle Aus-Länder der [= oder? RPB]
Fremdlinge, welche sich bequemen
gutwillig, sich so wohl bey *particulair*
Persohnen, auf deren eigentumlichen,
als auch auf Crons für sie *expres*
abgemessnen Ländereyen zu setzen,
verbleyben in der zeit freye Leute auf
gleichem Fusse mit denen Crons
Collonisten, und unter der Vormundschaft der zu solchen Endzwecke
errichteten *Cantzeley*, deren Gewald
und Oberaufsicht sich in diesem
Falle nicht weiter, als nur in so fern
erstrecken mag, dass die von beyden
Theilen geschlossenen *Contracte*, wie
mit *particulair* Persohnen, so auch mit
der Hofs *Cantzeley* oder mit andern
Gerichts Stühlen, wenn im Nothfall

Da hingegen verbünden wir uns in
Einrichtung der fernern, wie zur
Unterhaltung derer Strassen in einer
ordentlichen Zustand, zu denen
Einquartirungen, zur Wahrnehmung
derer Wälder, also auch überhaupt in
Ansehung der Policey, und unsern
innerlichen Gerichts Ordnungen, als
auch in Streitigkeiten, so sich zwischen
uns, und den dasigen Einwohnern
ereigen könnten erbitten wir der
hohen Crone eine Land Gerechtigkeit,
von der besonderen Vorsorge S^r
Erlauchten d. H. *General en cheff* und
Ritter Graffen von *Rumanzoff* zu
welchen wir unser besonder Zutrauen
gefast haben, und demnach von uns
Collonisten, auch schon vorhero mit
Einwilligung geschehen ist, und nur
dazumahl *per appellation* uns an die
Tutel Cantzeley zu wenden wenn
solche Fälle sich ereignen sollten, als
im oben erwehnten *Confirmierten
Doclad* vorgeschrieben steht, als nehmlich alle Aus-Länder der [= oder? RPB]
Fremdlinge, welche sich bequemen
gutwillig, sich so wohl bey *particulair*
Persohnen, auf deren eigentumlichen,
als auf Crons für sie *expres* abgemessnen Ländereyen zu setzen, verbleyben
in der zeit freye Leute, auf gleichem
Fusse mit denen Crons *Collonisten*
und unter der Vormundschaft der
zu solchen Endzwecke errichteten
Cantzeley, deren Gewalt und Ober
Aufsicht sich in diesem Falle nicht
weiter, als nur in so fern erstrecken
mag dass die von beyden Theilen
geschlossenen Contracte wie mit
particulair Persohnen, so auch mit
der Hofs *Cantzeley* oder mit andern
Gerichts Stühlen, wenn im Nothfall

solches jemahls erheischen würde,
unerbrüchlich beobachtet, ja nichts
dem *Interesse* des Reichs nachtheiliges,
und dem wegen der Fremdlinge
*publicierten Manifeste prejudicir*liches
in selbige eingerücket werden möchte.
Wannenhero solche *Contracte* zur
Approbation bey der *Tutel Cantzley*
derer Fremdlinge einzubringen sind,
allwo auf selbige verwahrlich aufge-
hoben, und denen *Contrahenten* unter
deren Glieder ihrer Unterschrift denen
Particulair Collonisten, aber unter
Beydrückung des Insiegels sothaner
Cantseley gleich lautende *Copeien*
davon gegeben werden soll. Folglich
mögen alle solche Fremdlinge die
sich vermittelst derer *Contracte* mit
particulair Persohnen in der *Ukraine*
und mit Gerichten in andern Kreisen
sich zu setzen einlassen, ihre Klagen
bey der *Tutel Cantzeley* als dem
eigentlichen zu ihrer Schützung
errichteten *Foro* an bringen, welches
zu unserer Nachricht auch dem
Contracte von Worte zu Worte ein
verleibet worden ist.

solches iemahls erfordern würde,
unerbrüchlich beobachtet, ja nichts
dem Interesse des Reichs nachtheiliges,
und dem wegen der Fremdlinge *publicierten Manifeste prejudicir*liches in
selbige eingerücket werden möchte.
Wannenhero solche Contracte zur
Aprobation bey der *Tutel Cantzley*
derer Fremdlinge einzubringen sind,
allwo auf selbige verwahrlich aufge-
hoben, und denen Contrahenten unter
derer Glieder ihrer Unterschrift denen
Particulair Collonisten, aber unter
Beydrückung des Insiegels sothaner
Cantzeley gleich lautende *Copeien*
davon gegeben werden soll. Folglich
mögen alle solche Fremdlinge die
sich vermittelst derer *Contracte* mit
particulair Persohnen in der *Ukraine*
und mit Gerichten in andern Kreisen
sich zu setzen einlassen, ihre Klagen
bey der *Tutel Cantzeley* als dem
eigentlichen zu ihrer Schützung
errichteten *Foro* an bringen, welches zu
unserer Nachricht auch dem *Contracte*
von Worte zu Worte ein verleibet
worden ist.

7·

Uber diese angeführte Puncten
versprechen und verbünden wir uns
und unsere Erben, dass so lange wir der
hohen Crone alle an uns angewandte
Unkostungs Gelder nicht erlegt haben
sind wir schuldig und gezwungen
unsere Wohnungen und Wirtschaft auf
keinerley Art und Weise zu verlassen,
und in allen gehalten zu seyn nach
unsren geschlossenen *Contract* ohne
fernere Beziehung auf *Emanirten
Manifest*, und wenn bey iedem vor-
kommenden Fall, da nothwendig
irgend eine neue Verfügung zu treffen
oder eine bereits getroffene abzuendern
wäre, dergleichen Abänderungen
ohne Vorweisse und *Aprobation* der
Tutel Cantzeley derer Aus Länder
durchaus nicht verstattet werden:
sondern dass ein *Consens* wohlerfolgen

7·

Uber diese angeführte Puncten
versprechen und verbünden wir uns
und unsere Erben, dass so lange wir der
hohen Crone alle an uns angewandte
Unkostungs Gelder nicht erlegt haben,
sind wir schulig [sic] und gezwungen
unsere Wohnungen und Wirtschaft auf
keinerley Art und Weise zu verlassen,
und in allen gehalten zu seyn nach
diesen unsren geschlossenen *Contract*
ohne fernere Beziehung auf *Emanirten
Manifest*, und wenn bey jeden vor-
kommenden Fall da nothwendig irgend
eine neue Verfügung zu treffen oder
eine bereits getroffene abzuendern
wäre, dergleichen Abänderungen ohne
Vorweise und *Aprobation* der *Tutel
Cantzeley* derer Aus Länder durchaus
nicht verstattet werden, sondern dass
ein *Consens* wohlerfolgen und ein

und ein blosser Entwurff zu machen
sey, und so dan zur Bestätigung
alle Zeit an der *Tutel Cantzeley*
eingesendet werden soll.

In Kraft dieses habe ich gegenwärtigen *Contract* unterzeichnet, um
dadurch zu bezeugen dass alle oben
angeführte Vortheile von Seiten der
hohen Crone durch Sr Erlauchten den
Herrn Graff von *Rumanzoff* würcklich
an die unterschriebene *Collonisten*
versprochen sind. Alle oben angeführte
Verheissungen von Seite der hohen
Crone so wohl, als unsere Verbün-
dungen dagegen bekräftigen wir
hiedurch.

[Signature of Prem. Maj. Jacob
Freyhold and the signature or mark
of 115 colonists.]

blosser Entwurff zu machen sey, und
so dan zur Bestätigung alle Zeit an
der *Tutel Cantzeley* eingesendet
werden soll.

In Kraft dieses habe ich gegenwärtigen *Contract* unterzeichnet, um
dadurch zu bezeigen dass alle oben
angeführte Vortheile von Seiten der
hohen Crone durch Sr Erlauchten den
Herrn Graff von *Rumanzoff* würcklich
an die unterschriebene *Collonisten*
versprochen sind. Alle oben angeführte
Verheissungen von Seite der hohen
Crone so wohl als unsere Verbün-
dungen dagegen bekräftigen wir
hiedurch.

[Signature of Prem. Maj. Jacob
Freyhold and the signature or mark
of 51 colonists.]

Appendix VI

Rules concerning the reception in future of colonists

The official printed Rules based upon the Imperial decree of 20 February 1804. (Author's translation from Russian.) TsGIAL f. 383, op. 29, d. 220, ll. 66–90b.

Rules selected from the Statute, confirmed by His Imperial Highness, concerning the reception in future of Colonists wishing to emigrate to Russia for settlement

I

Foreign Colonists are to settle in the New Russian region.*

II

This settlement is to be composed only of such people as may be most useful for that region, for example: good farmers, people accustomed to viticulture, the growing of mulberries and other useful plants, also such as are skilful in stock-breeding, and especially in the maintenance and increase of the best breeds of sheep, and such as have in general all necessary knowledge of the best agriculture. Rural artisans, for example: carpenters, blacksmiths, potters, millers, weavers, stone-masons and other craftsmen necessary in the rural way of life, may be accepted; but all other handicraftsmen and artisans who cannot find a living in the villages may not be numbered among the Colonists; for although there is need of urban artisans in the southern region, since it is not possible to limit the number of such immigrants, and the present small population of the region's towns does not yet allow of large numbers of such artisans, especially of one and the same trade, therefore they cannot find good advantage for themselves there.

---

* The Provinces of Kherson, Tauria and Yekaterinoslav compose the New Russian region. It stretches from the Dnieper to the Black and Azov Seas.

III

It is stipulated that no means whatsoever of enticement should be used, and that neither special Commissions, nor private individuals should be appointed for the recruitment of colonists. Persons wishing to emigrate to Russia for settlement may present themselves to HIS IMPERIAL MAJESTY'S Ministers, Residents, chargés d'affaires or Consuls, who, having taken information on such persons' circumstances and, as far as possible, their good behaviour, may furnish them with passports for their journey to the Russian border, where such Foreigners will be admitted according to these passports.

IV

All such foreigners presenting themselves to a minister or other plenipotentiary of HIS MAJESTY are absolutely obliged to show a testimonial from the local administration or social authority of their place of residence, that they are good householders and with regard to their present landlord have fulfilled everything which the law requires of them. Without this no one may be accepted.

V

Several families who have reached agreement to migrate together may choose one, two or more persons and send them in advance on behalf of the rest to inspect the lands assigned to them and to discover their qualities.

VI

Ministers, Residents, chargés d'affaires or Consuls of HIS IMPERIAL MAJESTY may give financial advances to no one.

VII

They must further observe that those presenting themselves to them furnish testimonials, or sure guarantees, that they possess and will bring with them possessions, either as cash capital or in goods, to a value of not less than 300 guilders. Those not furnishing such testimonials shall not be accepted, since experience has shown that the establishment of poor persons both proceeds slowly and gives small success.

VIII

They are to observe that those emigrating for settlement have a family. Individuals may in no case be accepted, except where someone wishes to take them into his family.

IX

As a family consisting only of husband and wife has great difficulty in maintaining its household and achieving a prosperous condition, if they have not and cannot maintain labourers, a situation of which there are sufficient examples in the Colonies already established in Russia: it is desirable that such people of small family, and in general poor people, should not emigrate [to Russia].

x

Foreigners wishing to emigrate to Russia on the above bases enjoy all those rights and privileges accorded at large to the Colonists now settling in the New Russian region, viz.:

1. Freedom of belief.

2. Freedom from payment of taxes and from all local service obligations (*povinnosti*) for ten years.

3. On expiry of these ten years, they shall pay the Treasury a land tax, in the first ten years of 15–20 kopecks per desyatina per annum; on expiry of this [second] period, this tax will be adjusted to the level of taxation common to other peasants (*poselyane*) settled on state lands in that place. Land service obligations shall be performed equally with the Russian subjects among whom the colonists shall be settled, immediately on expiry of the [first] exemption period, with the exception of military quartering, from which they are freed, except for those occasions when military detachments pass through their settlements.

4. Freedom from Military and Civil service; but all are free to register for this of their own accord, which nonetheless shall not give exemption from payment of debts to the Treasury.

5. The payment of monies advanced by the Treasury, on expiry of the years of exemption, is spread over the following ten.

6. All Colonists shall receive, free, 60 desyatinas of land for each family, excluding the mountainous part of the Crimea, where because of the scarcity of land special rules exist for its distribution.

7. From the day of arrival on the frontier begins payment of a maintenance allowance per head of 10 kopecks for adults and 6 for children per day, right until arrival at the place of settlement. These monies shall not be required back from the colonists, unless anyone wishes to leave Russia. In that case they must be repaid to the Treasury.

8. On arrival at the place of settlement, until their own first harvest, each person shall receive from 5–10 kopecks, depending on the price of essential victuals. This sum shall be repaid to the Treasury, together with the general loan, as explained below.

9. The loan made for the building of houses, purchase of cattle, and in general for all aspects of domestic establishment, totals 300 roubles. For persons arriving with considerable property, this sum may be increased if they request it to finance any useful enterprise.

10. On settlement, they are permitted to import their property, of whatever form, free of customs duties. In addition each family – by which is meant a husband and wife and small children, or 2 adult workers, or 4 women – may import once only goods belonging to themselves, for sale, at a price up to 300 roubles.

11. If any person, at any time whatsoever, wishes to leave the State, he is free to do so, on condition however of payment to the Treasury

of a sum equivalent to three times the annual tax payment by persons of his condition, over and above payment of all debts outstanding.

12. It is permitted to set up factories, and to follow any trade; to enter merchant and craft guilds, and to sell one's products throughout the Empire.

13. Foreigners are permitted to buy land in the New Russian region from landowners, and to hold it as private property with no other tax than that paid for the same land by the previous owner, according to the rules in force in the region. But any Foreigner buying land as private property must, if he wishes to leave Russia once more, sell the land or transfer it (*ustupit'*) to someone else remaining within the State.

14. In addition to this, should any Foreign settlers, after prior offer or agreement, wish to settle on the lands of private Owners, in any Province whatsoever, then Owners are permitted to receive such people on voluntary terms. These migrants shall also enjoy freedom of belief and shall be exempted from Military and Civil Service and from all taxes to the Treasury, except for that which the Landowners must pay for them, and which shall be adjusted to accord with the tax received by the Treasury from the landowners' native peasants.

XI

For the securing of greater conveniences and protection to Foreigners settling on state lands, they are to be entrusted to a special authority under the name of Office of Guardianship of Foreigners, which is to have charge of their settlement.

XII

If any among those arriving for settlement prove unheeding and disobedient to the constituted authority, or indulge in dissipation, such persons after confiscation from them of the amount of their debts to the Treasury, shall without fail be sent out of the country.

Notes

Introduction

1. V. O. Klyuchevsky, *Sochineniya*, I (Moscow 1956), 30–1.
2. D. K. Fieldhouse, *The Colonial Empires* (London–New York 1966), 334.
3. Cp. for example, P. Dukes, *The Emergence of the Superpowers. A Short Comparative History of the U.S.A. and the U.S.S.R.* (London 1970), passim. Attempts have also been made to apply F. J. Turner's frontier thesis to Russia, most recently by J. K. Wieczynski, *The Russian Frontier: The Impact of Borderlands upon the Course of Early Russian History* (Charlottesville 1976). For a critical Soviet comment on the 'frontier tradition' of historical writing, including Klyuchevsky, see A. V. Fadeyev, *Rossia i Kavkaz pervoy treti XIX v.* (Moscow 1960), 33–4. A full comparison of land settlement systems such as the American Ordinances of 1785 and 1787 or the provisions of the Wakefield theory as applied in Australia and New Zealand, with Russian provisions for foreign and native settlement, would be of great interest.
4. Native historians of some of the different national groups involved have stressed the extent to which they maintained and have maintained their ethnic identity, under the Tsarist and the Soviet regimes. Recent Soviet writers in the field, on the other hand, have tended to treat the foreign settlers more as part of the Empire's population as a whole, and have also highlighted their involvement in class struggle and revolutionary activity. Cp. in the first category K. Stumpp, *Die Russlanddeutschen. Zweihundert Jahre unterwegs* (Freilassing 1966); A. Giesinger, *From Catherine to Khrushchev. The Story of Russia's Germans* (Battleford Saskatchewan, 1974); F. C. Koch, *The Volga Germans in Russia and the Americas, from 1763 to the Present* (University Park, Pennsylvania and London 1977). In the second, particularly the monographs of Ye. I. Druzhinina on the southern Ukraine, and her articles 'Klassovaya bor'ba krest'yan Yuzhnoy Ukrainy v pervoy polovine XIX v.', *Yezhegodnik po agrarnoy istorii vostochnoy Yevropy, 1964 g.* (Kishinyov 1966), 572–83; 'Volneniya kolonistov Novorossii i Yuzhnoy Bessarabii', *Problemy istorii obshchestvennogo dvizheniya i istoriografii. K 70-letiyu M. V. Nechkinoy* (Moscow 1971), 102–9. Also V. V. Mavrodin, 'Ob uchastii kolonistov Povolzh'ya v vosstanii Pugachova', *Krest'yanstvo i klassovaya bor'ba v feodal'noy Rossii. Sb. statey pamyati I. I. Smirnova,* = *Tr. In-ta Ist. A. N. S.S.S.R., Leningradsk. otd., vyp. 9* (Leningrad 1967), 400–414; I. I. Meshcheryuk, *Pereseleniye Bolgar v Yuzhnuyu Bessarabiyu 1828–1834 gg.* (Kishinyov 1965), esp. 206–7.

1. Antecedents

1. B. Nolde, *La Formation de l'Empire Russe*, I (Paris 1952), 219. *Orenburgskaya Ekspeditsiya*: name given to the new administration of the region set up in the 1730s.
2. *PSZ*, IX, 312, no. 6571, 1 May 1734.
3. The latest study is A. S. Donnelly, *The Russian Conquest of Bashkiria 1552–1740* (New Haven–London 1968); cp. also Nolde, *La Formation*, I, 192–231.
4. V. P. Semyonov-Tyan-Shansky, ed., *Rossia, Polnoye Opisaniye Nashego Otechestva*, V (SPb 1914), 140.
5. *PSZ*, IX, 323–30, no. 6576, 18 May 1734; 740–1, no. 6889, 11 Feb. 1736 (Barayev, § 5); P. E. Matviyevsky, 'O roli Orenburga v russko-indiyskoy torgovle v XVIII v.', *Istoriya SSSR*, 1969, no. 3, 106.
6. *PSZ*, XIII, 655–6, no. 9995, 2 Sept. 1752.
7. P. Rychkov, *Topografiya Orenburgskaya, to yest' obstoyatel'noye opisaniye Orenburgskoy gubernii*, II (SPb 1762) 28–30; cp. *PSZ*, XII, 39–41, no. 8893, 8 March 1744.
8. Matviyevsky, 'O roli Orenburga', 107–8.
9. Semyonov-Tyan-Shansky, *Rossia*, V, 138; Nolde, *La Formation*, I, 204–5.
10. Nolde, *La Formation*, I, 192.
11. Ibid., I, 204–5; Semyonov-Tyan-Shansky, *Rossia*, V, 140; V. N. Vitevsky, *I. I. Nepluyev i Orenburgskiy Kray v prezhnem yego sostave do 1758 g.*, 5 parts (Kazan 1889–97), II, 276.
12. Donnelly, *The Russian Conquest*, 22; Nolde, *La Formation*, I, 191–5, 204–7.
13. Vitevsky, *I. I. Nepluyev*, III, 463–4; V. I. Semevsky, *Krest'yane v tsarstvovaniye Imp. Yekateriny II*, 2nd ed., I (SPb 1903), 188–9.
14. S. M. Solov'yov, *Istoriya Rossii s drevnyeyshikh vremyon*, ed. L. Cherepnin 29 vols in XV (Moscow 1959–66), XII, 220.
15. Vitevsky, *I. I. Nepluyev*, II, 339; cp. on such fugitives Got'ye, Yu., 'Iz istorii peredvizheniya naseleniya v XVIII v.' *Chteniya*, 1908 no. 1, *Smes'*, 1–26.
16. *PSZ*, XII, 183–6, no. 9006, quoted in Vitevsky, *I. I. Nepluyev*, III, 488.
17. Ibid., III, 489. *Odnodvortsy*, 'one-court-holders', were former petty servicemen who in the eighteenth century were assimilated to the state peasantry. Cp. below, p. 73, n. 97.
18. Cp. Nolde, *La Formation*, I, 177–8.
19. *PSZ*, XII, 51, 8901, 15 March 1744; Vitevsky, *I. I. Nepluyev*, II, 219–20.
20. *PSZ*, IX, 1013–4, no. 7136, 27 Dec. 1736.
21. Vitevsky, *I. I. Nepluyev*, III, 482.
22. *PSZ*, no. 7136; cp. no. 6889, § 14.
23. *PSZ*, X, 207–9, no. 7315, 6 July 1737; Vitevsky, *I. I. Nepluyev*, III, 483.
24. Ibid.; Solov'yov, *Istoriya Rossii*, XIII, 237–8.
25. *PSZ*, V, 485–7, no. 3062, 14 Jan. 1717.
26. Vitevsky, *I. I. Nepluyev*, III, 516.
27. *PSZ*, XII, 308–28, no. 9110, 15 Feb. 1745.
28. N. Popov, *V. N. Tatishchev i yego vremya*...(Moscow 1861), 263–4. A full account of the Stavropol colony in Vitevsky, *I. I. Nepluyev*, III, 502–616. The account of the Soviet writer, T. I. Belikov, *Uchastiye Kalmykov v krest'yanskoy voyne pod rukovodstvom E. I. Pugachova (1773–75)* (Elista 1971), 21–35, stresses the difficult and oppressive conditions there for the colonists.
29. TsGADA f. 248, kn. 3398, ll. 121–2. Senate aide-memoire for the Empress,

3 June 1763. On the Dzhungars see I. Ya. Zlatkin, *Istoriya Dzhungarskogo Khanstva (1635–1758)* (Moscow 1964).

30. TsGADA f. 248, kn. 3398, l. 119. Children were to be placed in Baltic regimental schools.

31. Ibid., ll. 120, 123. In January 1761 the Senate also accepted a College proposal that escapers of noble birth should have the right to live where they wished in Russia. But this was to be kept secret, in order not to encourage flight.

32. Rychkov, *Topografiya*, II, 94; Solov'yev, *Istoriya Rossii*, XII, 45–6; Vitevsky, *I. I. Nepluyev*, III, 466–70.

33. Ibid.

34. Ibid., 487. Italics in the original.

35. A. A. Kaufman, *Pereseleniye i kolonizatsiya* (SPb 1905), 12–14.

36. Cp. Semevsky, *Krest'yane*, I, 178ff.

37. *PSZ*, IV, 192–4, no. 1910, 16 April 1702; B. Ischchanian, *Die ausländischen Elemente in der russischen Volkswirtschaft* (Berlin 1913), 16–18; E. Amburger, *Die Anwerbung ausländerischer Fachkräfte für die Wirtschaft Russlands vom 15ten bis ins 19te Jhdt.* (Wiesbaden 1968), 75–6.

38. *PSZ*, VII, 167–74, no. 4378.

39. *PSZ*, no. 1910; XXVI, 593–5, no. 19801, 22 March 1801 and note.

40. Numerous examples in Amburger, *Die Anwerbung*, *passim*.

41. V. Veuclin, *Les Lyonnais et la Russie au siècle dernier* (Lyon 1896), 14.

42. *PSZ*, XIII, 875–6, no. 10129, 12 Aug. 1753.

43. *PSZ*, XV, 863–5, no. 11379, 15 Dec. 1761.

44. S. M. Troitsky, 'Novyy istochnik po istorii ekonomicheskoy mysli v Rossii v seredine XVIII v. ("Rassuzhdeniye o rossiyskoy kommertsii" sekretarya senata F. I. Sukina)', *Arkheograficheskiy Yezhegodnik za 1966 g.* (Moscow 1968), 246; TsGADA, f. 248, kn. 3396 (Senate minutes for College of Manufactures for 1762), d. 7, Po donesheniyu vyyekhavshego iz kenigsberga v sanktpeterburg sherstyanikh i parchits mastera Yakova Ratke o proizvozhdenii yemu na propitaniye iz manufaktur kantory po 25 k. na den' i o prochem, 25 April 1762, l. 107, Senate 'extract'.

45. TsGADA f. 248, kn. 3396, d. 7, *passim*.

46. *PSZ*, VII, 157–8, no. 4357, 10 Nov. 1723; XII, 77–8, no. 8919, 13 April 1744; XII, 581–3, no. 9311, 5 Sept. 1746.

47. V. A. Khachaturyan, 'Naseleniye armyanskoy kolonii v Astrakhani vo 2-oy ½-e XVIII v.', *Izvestiya A. N. Armyanskoy SSR (obshchestvennyye nauki)*, 1965 no. 7, 18.

48. *PSZ*, XVI, 31–8, no. 11630, § 16. This addition is not reproduced in *PSZ*: 'and drawing up a draft text (*formulyar*) of the said charter, taking everything necessary for it from that given to Orenburg, also from the descriptions of lands belonging to the border areas in order to make them as widely-known as possible, present it to the Senate for approval'. TsGADA, f. 248, kn. 3398, l. 52, Senate 'extract' of 1762 on legislation relevant to Baratayev request: see below, p. 37.

49. *PSZ*, XVI, 77, no. 11680, 10 Oct. 1762; XVI, 290–3, no. 11857, 11 June 1763.

50. Khachaturyan, 'Naseleniye armyanskoy kolonii', 79; *PSZ*, XII, no. 8919, 13 April 1744, § 1. Kizlyar was founded in 1731 on the Terek, near the Caspian coast.

51. On Nezhin cp. G. L. Arsh, *Eteristskoye dvizheniye v Rossii* (Moscow 1970), *passim*, but esp. 129–30, and the works cited there; Ye I. Druzhinina, *Kyuchuk-Kaynardzhiyskiy Mir 1774 goda* (Moscow 1955), 58–9.

52. Decrees confirming the Nezhin Greeks' privileges are printed in *PSZ* for March 1710, Feb. 1736, Dec. 1742, Dec. 1769, Sept. 1785, Aug. 1797, Dec. 1801. Armenian colonies in the Ukraine: Ya. R. Dashkevich, *Armyanskiye kolonii na Ukraine v istochnikakh i literature XV–XIX v.* (Yerevan 1962); *Istorich. svyazi i druzhba ukrainskogo i armyanskogo narodov. Sbornik materialov nauchnov sessii*, 1 (Yerevan 1961), 2 (Kiev 1965), 3 (Yerevan 1970).

53. G. I. Pylayev, *Ocherki po istorii yuzhnoslavyanskoy i moldavanovoloshskoy kolonizatsii v Rossii v 50–60kh gg. XVIII v.*, Moskovskiy Gos. Ped. Institut im. Lenina, kandidatskaya dissertatsiya, Moscow 1950, 66–7, 81–5; N. D. Polons'ka-Vasylenko, 'The Settlement of the Southern Ukraine 1750–75', *Annals of the Ukrainian Academy of Arts and Sciences in the U.S.A.* (N. York (Summer/Fall) 1955), 40–1; A. A. Skal'kovsky, *Khronologicheskoye Obozreniye Istorii Novorossiyskogo Kraya*, 1 (Odessa 1850), 15–16.

54. Polons'ka-Vasylenko, 'The Settlement', 108. A very full account in ibid., 40–180, Pylayev, *Ocherki*, 88–278. See also V. F. Shishmaryov, 'Romanskiye poseleniya na yuge Rossii', *Akademiya Nauk SSSR, Trudy Arkhiva*, vypusk 26 (Leningrad 1975), 32–41. I have been unable to locate M. Gjuric, *Ueber die Auswanderung der Serben aus Ungarn nach Russland in den 50-er Jahren des 18ten Jahrhunderts*, unpub. Inaug. Dissertation (Vienna 1941). A. P. Bazhova, 'Iz yugoslavyanskikh zemel' – v Rossiyu', *Voprosy Istorii* 1977 no. 2, 124–37, and the work of V. I. Sinitsa quoted there, ignore earlier works and add nothing new. For an instructive comparison of Russian and Austrian border systems, see A. Ferguson, 'Russian Land-militia and Austrian Militärgrenze', *Südostdeutsche Forschungen* 13 (1954), 137–58.

55. The Russian Minister Obreskov reported from Constantinople on 22 June 1752: 'One cannot depict the joyous exclamation with which the news of New Serbia has been received among all the Orthodox Christian nationalities'. Pylayev, *Ocherki*, 100.

56. Ibid., 210–19, 229–45; Polons'ka-Vasylenko, 'The Settlement', 106–7, 171, seems inaccurate here. On the Montenegrins, also the future role of Ezdemirovich, see further Solov'yov, *Istoriya Rossii* XII, 214–15, 488–90; XIV, 304, 312.

57. *AKV*, IV, 59–61, Foreign Ministry report to Senate, Nov. 1752; Polons'ka-Vasylenko, 'The Settlement', 47.

58. Vitevsky, *I. I. Nepluyev*, III, 473–7.

59. Pylayev, *Ocherki*, 219–21; Rychkov, *Topografiya Orenburgskaya*, II, 105; Vitevsky, *I. I. Nepluyev*, III, 478–81.
    SA, XII, 235–7; *SIRIO*, XLVIII, 565, no. 594; Polons'ka-Vasylenko, 'The Settlement' 105.

61. G. G. Pisarevsky, *Iz istorii inostrannoy kolonizatsii v Rossii v XVIII v.* (Moscow 1909), 42–3. On Weissbach, see Polons'ka-Vasylenko, 'The Settlement', *passim*.

62. Pisarevsky, *Iz istorii*, 29–32.

63. On the Karelians, see A. S. Zherbin, *Pereseleniye Karel v Rossiyu v XVII v.* (Petrozavodsk 1956). In 1689 the Russian government had issued a proclamation to French Huguenots on the same grounds as those now proposed by Lafont: religious persecution. The decree granted a request from the Elector of Brandenburg, following the revocation of the Edict of Nantes, that Huguenots be permitted to settle in Russia and enter Russian service

(*PSZ*, III, 3–9, no. 1331, 21 Jan. 1689). Reports of a large response appear exaggerated (E. Haumant, *La Culture Française en Russie 1700–1900* (Paris 1910), 16–17), but some immigration took place. However, this in no way represented a programme. Further on Huguenots, Calvinists and their descendants in Russia see E. Amburger, 'Hugenottenfamilien in Russland', *Herold*, Bd. 5 (1963–5), 125–35; F. Tastevin, 'Les calvinistes français en Russie (xvii–xix s.)', *Feuilles d'Histoire du XVII au XX s.*, t. 54 (1910), 197–206, 295–304.

64. Pisarevsky, *Iz istorii*, 20–3, 32–7. The terms offered included: settlement on the Dnieper 'near the Polish border' or on the Volga 'near Moscow' (to mention distant points might discourage immigration); freedom of religion and of re-emigration; 20-year tax exemption; diplomatic and financial assistance for the journey to Russia; material and financial help in settlement, interest-free loans and land-grants for entrepreneurs and a year's maintenance for artisans; Russian peasant labour for the agricultural needs of entrepreneurs; and special commissioners, Russian and French, to manage the colonies' affairs, under direction of the College of Foreign Affairs. Additional requests from immigrants would be received and considered.
Pisarevsky gives the Danish Manifesto in full.

65. Pisarevsky, *Iz istorii*, 37–40.

66. Ibid. The report is published in *AKV*, xxv, 206–11.

67. Pisarevsky, *Iz istorii*, 40–2. Pisarevsky's ascription of the Senate's attitude to preoccupation with the war (41) seems questionable. It found time for both the Montenegrins and the Sukin mission.

68. G. von Frantzius, *Die Okkupation Ostpreussens durch die Russen im 7-jährigen Kriege*...(Berlin 1916), 22, 37; *Beyträge zur Kunde Preussens*, I (Königsberg 1817), 532, note ***, 534. The idea of thus exploiting the Russian occupation of Prussia also occurred, if only in retrospect, to Diderot: cp. D. Diderot, *Oeuvres Politiques*, ed. Vernière (Paris 1963), 385–6. Any such actual exploitation is vehemently denied by the Soviet historian N. Korobkov, *Semiletnyaya Voyna* (Moscow 1940), 4, note 1. See also E. Amburger, *Die Anwerbung*, 136.

69. Pisarevsky, *Iz istorii*, 43–5. Government plans to recruit artisans abroad were allegedly also held up for financial reasons: *PSZ*, xv, 575–6, no. 11158, 7 Dec. 1760.

70. W. Conze, *Hirschenhof, die Geschichte einer deutschen Sprachinsel in Livland* (Berlin 1934), 27.

71. Autobiographical notes by Eisen pub'd in *Provinzialblatt für Kur-, Liv- und Esthland*, 1828, no. 1, 2; also quoted by Conze, *Hirschenhof*. The German (Holstein) regiments were indeed decreed into existence (*PSZ*, xv, 893, no. 11416; Solov'yov, *Istoriya Rossii*, xIII, 26), but they did not survive their creator.

72. M. Stepermanis, 'J. G. Eisen et ses luttes pour l'abolition du servage en Livonie et en Courlande', *Pirmā Baltijas vēsturnieku konference Riga 1937* (Riga 1938), 504–5.

73. *Provinzialblatt*, 1828, no. 4, 14.

74. 'Economie et population. Les doctrines françaises avant 1800', Institut National d'Etudes Démographiques, *Travaux et Documents*, Cahier 21 (Paris 1954), 129–35.

75. *Lloyds Evening Post and British Chronicle*, xIII, no. 968, 23–26 Sept. 1763, NS, (London), 298.

76. See below, p. 27, and J. Letiche, ed. *A History of Russian Economic Thought, 9th through 18th Centuries* (Berkeley and Los Angeles 1964), 394.

77. J. von Sonnenfels, *Grundsätze der Polizey, Handlung und Finanzwissenschaft, Erster Theil* (Wien 1768; the preface is dated 1765 – I have used here the 3rd edition, of 1770), 36–8, §§ 24–8. This is a classical statement of Sonnenfels' views, in summary form:

> The *enlargement of society* thus subsumes within itself all the subordinate separate means which, collectively, further the *general welfare*. As soon, therefore, as it is proven of an institution or a law, that it is advantageous for the enlargement of society or at least is not opposed to it: then this proof at the same time contains the higher proof within it, that the given institution or law is likewise conducive to, or at least not restrictive of, the general welfare, from the point of view of security or the convenience of life. Accordingly we take the increase of civil society through encouragement of population [growth], as the chief and general principle of statecraft and of the sciences contained within statecraft; and the test of every measure adopted to further the general welfare is: is it conducive to population [growth]; is it disadvantageous to population [growth]? (§ 24).

This work appeared in Russian as *Nachal'nyye osnovaniya politsii ili blagochiniya* (Moscow 1787). For a general discussion of Sonnenfels' views see F. Spitzer, *Joseph von Sonnenfels als Nationalökonom*, Inaugural Dissertation (Bern 1906); K. H. Osterloh, *Joseph von Sonnenfels und die österreichische Reformbewegung im Zeitalter des aufgeklärten Absolutismus* (Lübeck–Hamburg 1970).

78. *Politische Korrespondenz Friedrich's des Grossen. Ergänzungsband: Die Politischen Testamente Friedrich's des Grossen*, red. G. B. Volz (Berlin 1920), 126–7.

79. 'Economie et Population', Cahier 21, 129–35; V. Riqueti, Marquis de Mirabeau, *L'Ami des Hommes, ou Traité de la Population* (nouvelle édition corrigée, Avignon 1757), III, 239.

80. K. Schünemann, *Die Bevölkerungspolitik Oesterreichs unter Maria Theresa* (Berlin 1936), 9–12; M. M. Shpilevsky, 'Politika narodonaseleniya v tsarstvovaniye Yekateriny II', *Zapiski Imp. Novorossiyskogo Universiteta*, VI (Odessa 1871), 4; M. Beheim-Schwarzbach, *Hohenzollernsche Colonisationen* (Leipzig 1874), 264–5.

81. 'Economie et Population', Cahier 28 (1954), 84; Pisarevsky, *Iz istorii*, 3–6.

82. *Provinzialblatt*, 1828, no. 4, 14; Shpilevsky, 'Politika narodonaseleniya', 82–3.

83. Schünemann, *Die Bevölkerungspolitik*, 7–10.

84. 'Economie et Population', Cahier 21, *passim*.

85. Solov'yov, *Istoriya Rossii*, IX, 455.

86. *SIRIO*, VII, 99–100, Notes of the Grand Duchess Catherine, no. 36 (ca. 1761). Cp. the discussion of 'The Black Sea Problem in the 1760s', on her own premises, by Ye. I. Druzhinina, *Kyuchuk-Kaynardzhiyskiy*, 47–68.

87. *SIRIO*, VII, 85, no. 9.

88. Pisarevsky, *Iz istorii*, 28; Zh. Ananyan, 'K. voprusu o zaselenii yuga Rossii Armyanami vo 2-oy ½-e XVIII v.', *Izvestiya A. N. Armyanskoy S.S.R.*, (*obshchestvennyye nauki*), 1963 no. 5, 44–6.

89. V. K. Yatsunsky, 'Rol' migratsiy i vysokogo yestestvennogo prirosta nase-

leniya v zaselenii kolonizovavshikhsya rayonov Rossii', *Voprosy Geografii*, Sb. 83 (1970), 34–44.

90. Ibid., 41.

91. A. L. Schlözer, *Von der Unschädlichkeit der Pocken in Russland und von Russlands Bevölkerung überhaupt* (Göttingen–Gotha 1768), 29. See also the comments in A. A. Geraklitov, *Istoriya Saratovskogo Kraya v XVI–XVIII vv.* (Saratov–Moscow 1923), 370–1. On the other hand, the opinion can already be found in contemporary Western writing on Russia that serfdom as an institution, generally, was an obstacle to population growth: cp. e.g. G. Wiegand, 'Russland im Urteil des Aufklärers Christoph Schmidt genannt Phiseldek', E. Lesky, u.a., hrsg., *Die Aufklärung in Ost- und Südosteuropa* (Köln–Wien 1972), 67–8. Schlözer also makes this point, but in carefully veiled terms: *Von der Unschädlichkeit*, 38.

92. *PSZ*, IV, 779, no. 2467, § 18. Cp. Shpilevsky, 'Politika', 62–3.

93. P. A. Alefirenko, *Krest'yanskoye dvizheniye i krest'yanskiy vopros v Rossii v 30–50 gg. XVIII v.* (Moscow 1958), 336.

94. Solov'yov, *Istoriya Rossii*, XII, 207. Peter Shuvalov's project *O raznykh gosudarstvennoy pol'zy sposobakh*, alternatively entitled *O sokhranenii naroda*, was published with a commentary by S. O. Shmidt in *Istoricheskiy Arkhiv*, 1962, no. 6, 100–18. Shmidt notes similarities with Volynsky's projects and with legislation of Peter I.

95. 'Slovo pokhval'noye Petru Velikomu...' M. V. Lomonosov, *Polnoye Sobraniye Sochineniy*, ed. S. I. Vavilov (Moscow–Leningrad 1950–9), VIII, 589; 'O sokhranenii i razmnozhenii rossiyskogo naroda', ibid., VI, 382–403. The latter work is also discussed in Alefirenko, *Krest'yanskoye*, 368–9, and Letiche, *A History*, 387–95.

96. Beheim-Schwarzbach, *Hohenzollernsche*, 277.

97. G. Schmoller, 'Die preussischen Kolonisationen des 17. u. 18. Jhdts.', *Schriften des Vereins für Sozialpolitik*, XXXII (1866), 9.

98. Beheim-Schwarzbach, *Hohenzollernsche*, 48–53.

99. Ibid., 272.

100. Ibid., 633, Table LXIV.

101. Schmoller, 'Die preussischen', 10.

102. Schünemann, *Die Bevölkerungspolitik*, 16.

103. Ibid., 378.

104. Ibid., 300ff; M. L. Hansen. *The Atlantic Migration 1607–1860* (Harvard U.P. 1940), *passim*; D. Häberle, *Auswanderungen und Koloniegründungen der Pfälzer im 18ten Jhdt.* (Kaiserslautern 1909), 51–60, 117–20; R. Hayes, 'The German Colony in County Limerick', *North Munster Antiquarian Journal*, vol. I, no. 2 (Oct. 1937), 45–53.

105. M. Defourneau, *Pablo de Olavide ou l'Afrancesado (1725–1803)* (Paris 1959), 180. Cp. R. Leonhard, *Agrarpolitik und Agrarreform in Spanien unter Carl III* (München–Berlin 1909), 284–323; Häberle, *Auswanderungen*, 153–61; P. J. Hauben, 'The First Decade of an Agrarian Experiment in Bourbon Spain: The "New Towns" of Sierra Morena and Andalusia, 1766–75', *Agricultural History*, 39 no. 1 (January 1965), 34–40.

106. Häberle, *Auswanderungen*, 139–44; Pisarevsky, *Iz istorii*, 20–27.

2. Catherine II and the Manifestos of 1762 and 1763

1. W. Tooke, *View of the Russian Empire during the Reign of Catherine the Second and to the Close of the Present Chapter*, 3 vols (London 1799), II, 241. Tooke's work largely reproduces H. Storch, *Historisch-statistiches Gemaehlde des Russischen Reichs*, 6 parts (Riga–Leipzig 1797–1802). Storch and Tooke both have extensive sections on measures to conserve and increase population.

2. *SIRIO*, VII, 85–6.

3. *Nakaz Imp. Yekateriny II, dannyy Kommissii o Sochinenii Proyekta Novogo Ulozheniya*, pod red. N. D. Chechulina (SPb 1907), CXXIX, 77–85.

4. M. M. Shpilevsky, 'Politika narodonaseleniya v tsarstvovaniye Yekateriny II', *Zapiski Imp. Novorossiyskogo Universiteta*, VI (Odessa 1871), *passim*.

5. Ibid., 4.

6. A. L. Schlözer, *Von der Unschädlichkeit der Pocken in Russland und von Russlands Bevölkerung überhaupt* (Göttingen–Gotha 1768), 120.

7. Appendix I.

8. K. Lodyzhensky, *Istoriya Russkogo Tamozhennogo Tarifa* (SPb 1886), 99–100.

9. E.g. von Klingshtet, *TVEO*, chast' I (1765), 161–2; M. M. Shcherbatov, *Neizdannyye Sochineniya* (Moscow 1935), 64–5, 144.

10. 'Economie et Population', Cahier 21, 88, 129, 334.

11. J. Letiche, ed., *A History of Russian Economic Thought, Ninth through Eighteenth Centuries* (Berkeley and Los Angeles 1964), 394; *Nakaz Imp., Yekateriny II...*, CXXXVI–CXXXVIII; Shpilevsky, 'Politika narodonaseleniya', 7–8.

12. E.g. H. Storch, 'Ueber die Bevölkerung. Ein staatswirtschaftlicher Versuch', *Journal von Russland*, hrsg. J. H. Busse, 2ter Jg., 2ter Bd., 12tes Stük (Junius 1795), 337.

13. P. G. Lyubomirow (Lyubomirov), *Die wirtschaftliche Lage der deutschen Kolonien des Saratower und Wolsker Bezirks im Jahre 1791* (Pokrowsk 1926), 3–5.

14. *PSZ*, XVI, 343–4, no. 11908, 1 Sept. 1763.

15. P. M. Maykov, *I. I. Betskoy, Opyt yego biografii* (SPb 1904), 143, n. 1; 149, n. 1. A similar case in G. G. Pisarevsky, *Iz istorii inostrannoy kolonizatsii v Rossii v XVIII v.* (Moscow 1909), X, 285.

16. H. Hafa, *Die Brüdergemeinde Sarepta, ein Beitrag zur Geschichte des Wolga-deutschtums* (Breslau 1936), 1–25. On the Herrnhut movement in Livonia, in the 1730s, see J. Eckhardt, *Livland im 18ten Jhdt.*, I (Leipzig 1876), *passim*.

17. A. Klaus, *Nashi kolonii. Opyty i materialy po istorii i statistike inostrannoy kolonizatsii v Rossii*, vypusk I (SPb 1869, reprinted Cambridge 1972), 32.

18. Quoted in Pisarevsky, *Iz istorii*, 46.

19. Cp. below, p. 83.

20. *SA*, XI, 273; Solov'yov, *Istoriya Rossii s drevnyeyshikh vremyon*, ed. L. Cherepnin, 29 vols in XV (Moscow 1959–66), XII, 48, XIII, 140; Pisarevsky, *Iz istorii*, 48.

21. *SIRIO*, CXL, 461, no. 263, Praslin to de Bausset, 3 Feb. 1765. On Pictet see below; Pisarevsky, *Iz istorii*, 93–5; and N. Hans, 'François Pierre Pictet, Secretary to Catherine II', *SEER*, 36 (1957–8), 481–91. Hans says nothing of Pictet's colonizing activities.

22. TsGADA f. 248, kn. 3398, ll. 3–30b., Senate minutes of 15 Oct. 1762.
23. Ibid., ll. 4–5.
24. *PSZ*, xv, 722, no. 11261, 1 June 1761.
25. *SA*, xii, 201.
26. *PSZ*, xv, 894–5, no. 11420, 29 Jan. 1762. According to G. Derzhavin, quoted by N. S. Sokolov, *Rasskol v Saratovskom Kraye*, t. 1 (Saratov 1888), 30, this decree was originally prompted by receipt of a project for the settlement of empty Volga lands by the Old Believers.
27. *SA*, xii, 201–2.
28. TsGADA f. 248, kn. 3398, ll. 530b.–56, n.d. The papers of the six cases occupy ll. 7–65.
29. TsGADA f. 248, kn. 3398, l. 55.
30. Schlözer wrote that with Catherine's accession 'there began a golden age for the composers of projects'. *A. L. Schlözers öffentliches und Privatleben, von ihm selbst beschrieben* (Göttingen 1802), 146.
31. Solov'yov, *Istoriya Rossii*, xiii, 140.
32. *SIRIO*, vii, 315 (italics in original).
33. TsGADA f. 248, kn. 3398, l. 540b.
34. Cp. above, p. 18.
35. TsGADA f. 248, kn. 3398, ll. 49–50. Baratayev appears in 1762 as Saratov Voyevoda, in N. S. Sokolov's account of Old Believer settlement on the Volga, *Rasskol*, 27–8, 33.
36. TsGADA f. 248, kn. 3398, ll. 56–65.
37. The extract of laws made for the Senate showed that a decree of 1740 had confirmed the right given in 1728 to Jews to enter Little Russia for commercial purposes. This was revoked in 1742. Following representations from Riga, the Senate suggested that permission be renewed to prevent serious loss of trade; the reply was the resolution quoted. TsGADA f. 248, kn. 3398, ll. 58–64.
38. Solov'yov, *Istoriya Rossii*, xiii, 111–12. Cp. Yu. Gessen, *Istoriya yevreyskogo naroda v Rossii* (Leningrad 1925–7), i, 56–7.
39. TsGADA f. 248, kn. 3398, l. 65.
40. See below, pp. 86–8.
41. *PSZ*, xvi, 126–7, no. 11720.
42. *SA*, xi, 304; Pisarevsky, *Iz istorii*, 48.
43. TsGADA f. 248, kn. 3398, l. 71, Senate minutes.
44. *SA*, xii, 201–6, 211–16; *PSZ*, xvi, 129–32, no. 11725, 14 Dec. 1762, amplified by xvi, 140–1, no. 11738, 20 Jan. 1763. Some of the lands listed in the appendix were already under consideration for other settlement: cp. *PSZ*, xv, 533–8, no. 11124, 17 Oct. 1760. Orenburg lands named were those originally assigned to the Montenegrins. On the Old Believers and their settlement, see Sokolov, *Rasskol*.
45. TsGADA f. 248, kn. 3398, ll. 92–103, list of addressees and numbers of copies, Senate minutes of 30 Dec. 1762.
46. Ibid., l. 92.
47. Ibid., ll. 103–8; *SIRIO*, xlviii, 251, no. 289. The College reported dispatch of copies to Constantinople, Copenhagen, Danzig, The Hague, Hamburg, Leipzig, London, Madrid, Mitau, Paris, Regensburg, Stockholm, Vienna, Warsaw. The usual number of copies was 5: Vienna and Warsaw received 10, Paris and Madrid 1. Berlin is a curious omission from this list.

48. G. I. Pylayev, *Ocherki po istorii yuzhnoslavyanskoy i moldavano-voloshskoy kolonizatsii v Rossii v 50–60kh gg. xviii v.*, kandidatskaya dissertatsiya, Moskovskiy Gos. Pedagogicheskiy Inst. im Lenina (Moscow 1950), 85–6 notes that Russian policy was particularly timorous in this respect. The Senate usually refused entry to immigrants without passports coming direct from Turkish territory, frequently directing such people through Austrian and Polish territory to avoid responsibility. But Turkey, while never issuing passports, never sought the return of fugitive subjects; Austria accepted all such immigrants, encouraged more, and never returned any. Russian policy continued until the war of 1768–74 and blocked the way into Russia for 'thousands of Turkish Christians'. Cp. ibid., 120; N.D. Polons′ka-Vasylenko, 'The Settlement of the Southern Ukraine 1750–75', *Annals of the Ukrainian Academy of Arts and Sciences in the U.S.A.* (Summer–Fall 1955, New York 1955), 103–4.

49. *SIRIO*, XLVIII, 329, no. 377, 19 Feb. 1763.

50. *SA*, XII, 222–3, 25 Feb. and 14 March.

51. *PSZ*, XVI, 247–8, no. 11815, Manifesto of 13 May 1763.

52. Pisarevsky, *Iz istorii*, 49.

53. Ibid., 50. No reference was made at any time to the initially very successful Danish colonization programme of 1759.

54. *SA*, XII, 223, 25 Feb.–15 March 1763.

55. *SIRIO*, XLVIII, 448–9, nos. 490–2.

56. *SA*, XII, 231, 22 May 1763.

57. Ibid., 218, 232; B. Nolde, *La Formation de l'Empire Russe. Etudes, Notes, Documents* (Paris 1952–3), II, 342–3.

58. *SA*, XII, 232. There is no indication of any action on this decision.

59. That discussed above, p. 17.

60. *SA*, XII, 232.

61. *SIRIO*, XLVIII, 524, no. 555.

62. TsGADA f. 248, kn. 3398, l. 180, report to Senate of 7 June 1763.

63. Ibid., ll. 195–6, College to Senate, 15 June 1763. The memo is marked 'Taken to the Senate 23 June'; another note says: 'Resolved by the decree of 22 July 1763...'

64. Ibid., ll. 188, 209–ob., College Office report and Senate resolution of 25 June 1763.

65. Solov′yov, *Istoriya Rossii*, XIII, 229: 1763, undated.

66. This term does not go easily into English. The Russian translations of the time used 'Guardian Office' (1763 Manifesto) and 'Office of Protection', *Public Advertiser* (London 29 Sept. 1763, NS); cp. Pisarevsky, *Iz istorii*, 47 footnote. Almost every writer on the subject has his own version.

67. *SIRIO*, VII, 301; TsGADA f. 248, kn. 3398, ll. 197–8, minutes of 30 June, 4 July 1763.

68. Ibid., ll. 196a, 30 June 1763.

69. Ibid., ll. 199–200.

70. *SA*, XIII, 148; the same, and details of its implementation: TsGADA f. 248, kn. 3398, ll. 210, 213–15, Senate minutes 9–11 July 1763. The London *Public Advertiser*, reporting this under the dateline Petersburg, July 27, noted that 'Orders are also given to the Custom House Officers, to acquaint all the Strangers, that arrive, therewith', no. 8995, Wed. 31 August 1763, NS, 2. The same day (9 July), the College of Foreign Affairs reported the arrival of 15 more immigrants from Rehbinder. They were accorded the

278 *Notes to pages 44–52*

same treatment as the others, benefiting also from the new accommodation arrangements. TsGADA f. 248, kn. 3398, ll. 210–ob.

71. On this colony see V. A. Bayburtyan, *Armyanskaya Koloniya Novoy Dzhulfy v XVII veke* (Yerevan 1969).
72. TsGADA f. 248, kn. 3398, ll. 201–4, n.d.
73. Cp. *PSZ*, xxviii, 512–14, no. 21458, 20 Sept. 1804.
74. TsGADA f. 248, kn. 3398, ll. 205–5a.
75. *SIRIO*, vii, 302, footnote 2. Pekarsky notes: 'Written in an unknown hand'. A third copy, marked 'from HIH Cabinet', but apparently not the one used by Pekarsky: TsGADA f. 16, d. 349, l. 1–20b. With the latter is preserved another project evidently submitted to Catherine: 'Notte pour servir d'indice de la base à donner aux Etablissement des Colons Etrangers Sur les Terres de quelque Seigneur Russe et des Conditions à leur accorder pour l'intérêt et le bien reciproque'. TsGADA f. 16, d. 349, ll. 5–7, without date or signature. The system of land-grants proposed is similar to that advertised by Beauregard: cp. Appendix ii.
76. Cp. *AKV*, vii, 615, correspondence of Catherine with M. L. Vorontsov, who proposed consultation of the Danish Manifesto; xxviii, 26.
77. *SIRIO*, vii, 303. I follow here the attribution of this document made by the editors of *SIRIO*. It could however with equal sense refer to the foundation of the Moscow Foundling House (which, unlike the Chancellery, did have 'Guardians' (*opekuny*)). Cp. below, p. 54.
78. *PSZ*, xvi, 312–13, no. 11879.
79. Ibid., 316–18, no. 11881; details of staff and salaries, xvi, 328, no. 11890, 7 Aug. 1763.
80. This figure was not in fact altered until much later: cp. *SIRIO*, v, 228–30.
81. Appendix i; *PSZ*, xvi, 313–16, no. 11880.
82. W. Tooke, *View of the Russian Empire*, ii, 243. There follows an excellent summary of the Manifesto.
83. TsGADA f. 248, kn. 3398, ll. 310–11, 31 July 1763.
84. Cp. above, p. 39. About 100 replies (but not that for Saratov) are filed in TsGADA f. 248, kn. 3398, ll. 111, 547a–686ob.
85. TsGADA f. 248, kn. 3398, l. 5600b.
86. Ibid., l. 581.
87. Ibid., ll. 616–ob., 670.
88. Ibid., ll. 548, 550–4.
89. Ibid., ll. 29–36, 43–6.
90. According to Ya. Zutis, *Ostzeyskiy vopros v XVIII v.* (Riga 1946), 304–5, the 1763 Manifesto stimulated the immigration of foreign merchants into the Baltic provinces. Cp. below, p. 86.
91. Full German text in M. Beheim-Schwarzbach, *Hohenzollernsche Colonisationen* (Leipzig 1874), 48–53; Russian translation, Pisarevsky, *Iz istorii*, 11–16.
92. Cp. above, p. 46, n. 76, and Pisarevsky, 23, 35. It was also in line with Prussian practice.
93. Hafa, *Die Brüdergemeinde*, 24–5.
94. *PSZ*, xv, 313–15, no. 10914, 12 Jan. 1759; xvi, 88, no. 11689, 23 Oct. 1762.
95. Pisarevsky, *Iz istorii*, 47; G. Bonwetsch, *Geschichte der deutschen Kolonien an der Wolga* (Stuttgart 1919), 11.
96. A. A. Kizewetter, 'Otzyv o sochinenii G. G. Pisarevskogo, "Iz istorii..."', offprint from *Otchot o 52-om prisuzhdenii nagrad gr. Uvarova* (SPb 1912),

29–30; P. A. Shafranov, 'Otzyv o knige G. G. Pisarevskogo, "Iz istorii...." ', *Chteniya* (1909), no. 4, *Smes'*, 30–5.

97. *Nakaz Imp. Yekateriny II*, 78. In an article praising the Russian immigration scheme, the London *Public Advertiser* of 29 Sept. 1763 (N.S.) (no. 9019) proclaimed: 'Population and Culture [i.e. agriculture] are of such infinite Importance that every Prince and Minister of true Political Ideas ought to have the most serious Attentions thereto, at any Expense'. The article was Russian-inspired (Pisarevsky, *Iz istorii*, 47).

98. Cp. Chapter 5.

99. *PSZ*, xvii, 7–9, no. 12307, 13 Jan. 1765.

100. As Kizewetter and Shafranov emphasized, see above, note 96.

101. See Chapter 3.

102. See for example the views of Sonnenfels on agriculture, and Spitzer's comments: F. Spitzer, *Joseph von Sonnenfels als Nationalökonom*, Inaugural Dissertation (Bern 1906), 68–9.

103. TsGADA f. 248, kn. 3398, ll. 321–4, minutes of 31 July 1763.

104. *PSZ*, xiv, 363–4, no. 10410, 23 May 1755 (a 'guardian' for widows' and orphans' interests to be appointed to the Survey Offices); xv, 360, no. 10972, 2 July 1759 (free medicines for poor mothers and new-born infants).

105. The draft project of this received Imperial assent on 10 June 1763; the final report of an official study group, making few changes, was approved on 23 August. Maykov, *I. I. Betskoy*, 120–21.

106. TsGADA f. 248, kn. 3398, l. 324.

107. Maykov, *I. I. Betskoy*, 207.

108. *SIRIO*, xlviii, 555, no. 579, 21 July 1763.

109. TsGADA f. 248, kn. 3398, l. 117, decree to the Senate. Cp. above, pp. 11–12 and B. v. Bilbassof, *Geschichte Katharina II*, i, ii (Berlin 1893), 135, no. 35.

110. TsGADA f. 248, kn. 3398, l. 117 (3 June 1763), ll. 124, 126 (10 June); *SA*, xiv, 93, no. 87; *PSZ*, xvi, 289, no. 11854, 10 June 1763 and 320–1, no. 11886, 28 July 1763.

111. *SA*, xiv, 93–5; TsGADA f. 248, kn. 3398, l. 168.

112. Ibid., l. 174, 14 March 1765.

113. TsGADA f. 248, kn. 3622, ll. 86–92, a test case heard in the Senate 15 March–5 May 1764; cp. chapter 4 below.

114. A. Klaus, *Nashi kolonii*, 11.

115. Schlözer, *Leben*, 147.

3. *The response: settlement 1763–1775*

1. *SIRIO*, cxxxiv, 159, Nakaz ot meshchan armyan i katolicheskogo verois-povedaniya zhiteley g. Astrakhani, para. 1. Could 1762 here be a mistake for 1763?

2. An extended and detailed but rather uneven account of the recruitment, based on the archives of the College of Foreign Affairs, is given in G. G. Pisarevsky, *Iz istorii inostrannoy kolonizatsii v Rossii v XVIII v.* (Moscow 1909), part III; supplemented by P. A. Shafranov, 'Otzyv o knige G. G. Pisarevskogo "Iz istorii inostrannoy kolonizatsii v Rossii v XVIII v."', *Chteniya* (1909), no. 4, Smes', 28–46.

3. *SIRIO*, LI, 164, no. 803; Pisarevsky, *Iz istorii*, 68. This was not inconsistent with the view taken by Austria of immigration into Russia in the 1750s: cp. *SIRIO*, LI, 483, no. 1004.

4. *SIRIO*, LI, 115, no. 762.

5. K. Schünemann, *Die Bevölkerungspolitik Oesterreichs unter Maria Theresa* (Berlin 1936), 304–5.

6. P. D'Estrée, 'Une Colonie franco-russe au XVIII s.', *Revue des Revues*, 1896, no. 9, 1–16. See further Appendix IV. While using the files of the recruiting agent Rollwagen from the Bastille Archive, D'Estrée makes no mention of the case of David Barral (discussed below, p. 172), whose papers are mixed with those of Rollwagen: Archives de la Bastille, Bibliothèque de l'Arsénal, Paris, no. 12299. Cp. also F. Funck-Brentano, *Catalogue des Manuscrits de la Bibliothèque de l'Arsénal*, t. 9: *Archives de la Bastille* (Paris 1892), 210–14; F. Ravaisson-Mollien, *Archives de la Bastille. Documents Inédits...*, XIX (Paris 1904), 170–223; *SIRIO*, CXL, passim.

7. E. Amburger, *Russland und Schweden 1762–1772. Katharina II, die schwedische Verfassung und die Ruhe des Nordens* (Berlin 1934), 106–8; Pisarevsky, *Iz istorii*, 66–7.

8. Ibid., 67–74.

9. M. Beheim-Schwarzbach, *Hohenzollernsche Colonisationen* (Leipzig 1874), 275–6; W. Kirchner, 'Emigration to Russia', *American Historical Review*, LV, no. 3 (April 1950), 192–209, reprinted in *Commercial Relations between Russia and Europe 1400–1800. Collected Essays* (Bloomington 1966), has useful material from Swiss archives.

10. E.g. *SIRIO*, LI, 126–7, no. 768.

11. Beheim-Schwarzbach, *Hohenzollernsche Colonisationen*.

12. Cp. French comment on the position of Saxony, *SIRIO*, CXLI, 103, no. 50.

13. Schünemann, *Die Bevölkerungspolitik*, 234–5.

14. Such claims are to be found especially among German writers sympathetic to the settlers: cp. most recently A. Giesinger, *From Catherine to Khrushchev*, 5; F. C. Koch, *The Volga Germans in Russia and the Americas, from 1763 to the Present* (University Park, Pennsylvania and London 1977), 6. Writers hostile to the German colonists or to Germany have sometimes suggested in contrast that German immigrants were or became a Prussian fifth column, part of the *Drang nach Osten*: cp. E. Lewin, *The German Road to the East* (London 1916), 298–301; *Istoricheskiy Vestnik*, XXXIX no. 3 (1890), 716–17; A. Velitsyn, 'Inostrannaya kolonizatsiya v Rossii,' *Russkiy Vestnik*, no. 6 (1889), 130. This view reappeared in Soviet historiography in the post-World War II period: F. A. Red'ko, *Kolonizatsionnaya politika russkogo tsarizma i nemetskiye kolonisty na*

Ukraine (*s kontsa XVIII do nachala XX st.*), aftoreferat kand. diss., Kievskiy Gos. Univ. (Kiev 1952).

15. Pisarevsky, *Iz istorii*, 74; D. G. Rempel, *The Mennonite Colonies in New Russia, A Study of their Settlement and Economic Development from 1789 to 1914*, unpublished PhD dissertation (Stanford, Calif. 1933), 119–20; id., 'The Mennonite Commonwealth in Russia: A Sketch of Its Founding and Endurance, 1789–1919', *Mennonite Quarterly Review*, XLVII (Oct. 1973), XLVIII (Jan. 1974), and separate off-print, 14.

16. Pisarevsky, *Iz istorii*, 69–70.

17. *SIRIO*, LI, 214, no. 844. Caucasian immigrants had already established the town of Mozdok, cp. above, p. 41.

18. Pisarevsky, *Iz istorii*, 58, records the disfavour with which the Württemberger Heinrich Gross, Russian Minister at The Hague, viewed French applicants.

19. Besides Pisarevsky's account, cp. documents in *SIRIO*, LI, nos. 721, 728, 762, 768, 803, 859.

20. *SIRIO*, LI, 69–70, no. 739; 126–7, no. 768.

21. Ibid., no. 739.

22. Ibid., 117, no. 762.

23. TsGADA f. 248, kn. 3622, l. 171, report from G. Orlov to HIH, approved 20 Aug. 1764. Later groups of the same type were incorporated in the Saratov settlement: so the German weavers from Stockholm, sent by Ostermann in 1764, whom Shafranov wrongly calls Swedes. TsGADA f. 283, d. 35, Delo ob otpravlennykh iz shvetsii inostrantsakh...18 June 1764.

24. TsGADA f. 248, kn. 3398, l. 492, Chancellery of Guardianship report to the Senate, 21 Oct. 1763; cp. *SIRIO*, LI, 44, no. 721.

25. Pisarevsky, *Iz istorii*, 60–2; *Buckingham Correspondence*, II, 122–3.

26. Pisarevsky, *Iz istorii*, 63–4.

27. Ibid.; appointed February 1764.

28. One early Russian contact, Colonel David Solomon Rapin, who ended up in the Bastille on suspicion of poaching French subjects, told his French interrogators that he had made a contract with Vorontsov in London only after a rebuff from the French Ambassador there and the failure of negotiations with the Spanish Ambassador. Ravaisson-Mollien, *Archives*, XIX, 182 (report of 25 Nov. 1765); further on Rapin see Pisarevsky, *Iz istorii* 83–4.

29. TsGADA f. 248, kn. 3398, l. 1, Register of contents.

30. TsGADA f. 16, 348, ll. 1–17. See further my article 'Culture and Enlightenment: Julius von Canitz and the Kazan' *gimnazii* in the Eighteenth Century', forthcoming in *Canadian–American Slavic Studies*, 1980.

31. 'Projet d'Une Compagnie pour la Découverte d'un Passage aux Indes par la Russie, présenté à S.M. l'Impératrice Catherine II', appendix to 'Voyage en Russie', *Oeuvres Posthumes de J.-H.-B. de Saint-Pierre*...ed. L. Aimé-Martin, I (Paris 1833), 32–40. Saint-Pierre tried to interest G. Orlov personally in his project, who however declared the ideas it contained 'contrary to the laws of the Empire and to the interests of the magnates'. Ibid., xxiv.

32. TsGADA f. 248, kn. 3398, ll. 535–40, d. 23, Po donosheniyu otstavnogo praporshchika Shirvanovicha, ob otkaze emu v vyvode syuda v Rossiyu na poseleniye inostrannykh lyudey, 17 Nov. 1763.

33. Pisarevsky, *Iz istorii*, 82–4.

34. TsGADA f. 248, kn. 3398, ll. 541–2, Senate minutes of 17 Nov. 1763, approved report to HIH by G. Orlov.
35. *SIRIO*, LI, 189, no. 830.
36. On different types of recruiting agent in Europe at this time, cp. Schünemann, *Die Bevölkerungspolitik*, 296ff.
37. See below, p. 97.
38. TsGADA f. 283, op. 1, d. 16, Contracts of the Chancellery of Guardianship, ll. 47–76, ob., 230–10b; Shafranov, 'Otzyv o knige G. G. Pisarevskogo', 39–40. After initial misunderstandings an official form of contract was drawn up: *PSZ*, XVI, 965–8, no. 12283.
39. TsGADA f. 283, op. 1, d. 16, ll. 71–2, contract of 20 April 1765; Pisarevsky, *Iz istorii*, 86.
40. N. D. Polons'ka-Vasylenko, 'The Settlement of the Southern Ukraine 1750–75', *Annals of the Ukrainian Academy of Arts and Sciences in the U.S.A.*, Summer–Fall 1955, (New York 1955), 250.
41. TsGADA f. 248, kn. 3622, ll. 232–43, d. 20, Po donesheniyu gen.-poruchika Mel'gunova, ob otsylke k nemu trebuyemykh im o inostrantsakh... ekzemplyarov, 7 March 1765.
42. Cp. below, pp. 86–8.
43. Yu. Gessen, *Istoriya yevreyskogo naroda v Rossii*, I (Leningrad 1925), 60.
44. Polons'ka-Vasylenko, 'The Settlement', p. 250.
45. Amburger, *Russland und Schweden*, 106–7. A fourth name, Norberg, was added later.
46. J. Etterlin-Adliswil, *Die ehemaligen Schweizerkolonien in Russland, die Ukraine, die Krim, das Donezgebiet, der Kaukasus, die Wolga und ihr Gebiet* (Zürich–Bern, duplicated typescript, 1945), 62–5; W. Kirchner, *Commercial Relations Between Russia and Europe 1400–1800. Collected Essays*, Indiana Russian and East European Series, vol. 33 (Bloomington 1966), 195–7.
47. Cp. Appendix IV.
48. A. A. Kizewetter, 'Otzyv o sochinenii G. G. Pisarevskogo "Iz istorii inostrannoy kolonizatsii v Rossii v XVIII v." ', *Otchot o 52-om prisuzhdenii nagrad grafa Uvarova* (SPb 1912), 33–4, corrects Pisarevsky's account of this group (*Iz istorii*, 89). These agents evidently knew each other and worked together when necessary. D'Haucourt first approached the Chancellery with two associates (*PSZ*, XVI, 632–3, no. 12109); later he came back with six, including two brothers Vandini (*PSZ*, XVI, 924–5, no. 12255). Finally he told the Chancellery that he had placed his recruiting operation in the charge of *k tomu sposobnogo direktora Deprekurta* (TsGADA f. 283, d. 29, l. 140b.).
49. Pisarevsky, *Iz istorii*, 94; TsGADA f. 283, op. 1, d. 16, l. 520b.
50. On Meusnier's police activities, see P. D'Estrée, 'Fermiers généraux et femmes galantes: un policier homme de lettres, l'inspecteur Meusnier (1748–1757)', *Revue Retrospective, Nouvelle Série*, XVII, July–Dec. 1892 (Paris 1893), 217–76. Both Meusnier and Beauregard later offered their services to Austria: some of their subsequent adventures are related by Schünemann, *Die Bevölkerungspolitik*, 299–303. See also Appendix IV.
51. *AKV*, XXXI, 424, and correspondence of M. L. and A. R. Vorontsov, *passim*.
52. K. von Stählin, *Aus den Papieren Jacob v. Stählins, Ein biographischer*

Beitrag zur deutsch–russischen Kulturgeschichte des 18ten Jahrhunderts (Königsberg–Berlin 1926), 333–5.

53. G. Vinsky, *Moyo Vremya* (SPb 1914), 68–9.
54. No results of any recruitment by him are recorded. Catherine thought at one time that she could identify Vandini with the somewhat mysterious Montenegrin pretender Stepan Malyy. In 1769 she wrote to Aleksey Orlov: 'Major-Gen. Podgorichani suspects, not without reason, that Stepan Malyy is that same Italian Vandini, who had dealings with the Chancellery of Guardianship here and, after tricking people here, having wheedled diamonds out of a Greek merchant and used them as security, took the money and rode off...', *SIRIO*, 1, 16.
55. Shafranov, 'Otzyv o knige G. G. Pisarevskogo', 38–9; TsGADA f. 248, kn. 3762, ll. 231–3, d. 10, ...o vydache inostrantsu Florentinu za nabranniye 492 familii kolonistov v nagrazhdeniye 2,400 roubles i o bytii yemu v Saratove na poselenii kuptsom (17 June 1768).
56. Pisarevsky implies (*Iz istorii*, 102–3) that the term *vyzyvatel'* was applied only to this group, as opposed to other recruiters who received merely a cash reward. In fact it seems that this distinction was made only with regard to the colonists recruited by these people, to distinguish them from the rest (*koronnyye*) who were to settle separately. But all foreigners who signed recruiting contracts with the Chancellery might be called *vyzyvateli.* The term 'director' appears to have originated with the principal *vyzyvateli* themselves, and to have been used usually only of those who actually controlled a colony (or group of colonies) and its establishment.
57. Pisarevsky, *Iz istorii*, Appendix, 15.
58. Ibid., 103; ORGPB, Bastille Archive, Avt. 121, no. 106, ll. 218, 2190b., 2200b.; Appendix IV.
59. Pisarevsky, *Iz istorii*, 98–101, Appendix, 11–14.
60. Cp. Appendix II.
61. *MIRF*, XI (SPb 1886), 256, 267, Admiralty College Board Minutes of 30 April and 7 Aug. 1766; *SIRIO*, x, 92.
62. Quoted in Pisarevsky, *Iz istorii*, 166.
63. TsGADA f. 283, d. 4, ll. 186–8, letter from Chancellery of Guardianship to A. Gross, Russian Minister in Saxony, concerning Lembke's service record, 2 Sept. 1779.
64. Beheim-Schwarzbach, *Hohenzollernsche*, 276; Pisarevsky, *Iz istorii*, 178.
65. *PSZ*, XVII, 1068, no. 12793; *SIRIO*, LVII, 546–8, nos. 1355, 1356.
66. According to an archival source cited by G. G. Pisarevsky, *Khozyaystvo i forma zemlevladeniya v koloniyakh Povolzh'ya v XVIII i 1-oy chetverti XIX v.* (Rostov 1916), 23, note. Whether this includes colonists engaged by *poseliteli* (p. 82) is unclear. The nature of the records, and fluctuations caused by flight, deaths, births and changes of status, make colonist statistics problematic. Shcherbatov, who had access to official sources, gave the overall total settled in 1772 as 28,893; 'Statistika v rassuzhdenii Rossii', *Chteniya* 1859 no. III, 54–5. See also Shafranov, 'Otzyv o knige G. G. Pisarevskogo', 43–5.
67. Christian Gabriel Lembke, a 'jurist', finally took over from Schmidt in mid-1766. He requested an increase on Schmidt's salary as he would have to employ five office staff 'who will be quite indispensable to him for paper work and other requirements in the matter of the colonists': TsGADA f. 283, d. 4, l. 23, copy of report from Vikhlyayev (here *S*ikhlyayev),

Hamburg 16/27 May 1766. Lembke remained accredited in Lübeck, receiving an official salary, until November 1774, although after 1767 he had 'almost no work at all' to do. Ibid., l. 188.

68. TsGADA f. 248, kn. 3398, ll. 216–36, d. 8, 'Po donosheniyu Kollegii Inostrannykh Del ob otsylke v Magistratskuyu Kontoru prislannykh iz Gdanska. . .inostranntsov remeslennykh lyudey 15 chlvk. . .'

69. Ibid., l. 225.

70. TsGADA f. 248, kn. 3622, ll. 171–2, report from Orlov to HIH, approved 20 Aug. 1764. Cp. the similar case of the foreign *master* Jackman (*Zhakman*): *SA*, xiv, 2–4. Vandier later tried to renew negotiations with the Chancellery: TsGADA f. 283, op. 1, d. 71, 'po prozhektu inostrantsov Dezartsa [Des-Essarts] i Vande. . .', 8 Feb. 1766.

71. TsGADA f. 248, kn. 3398, l. 492.

72. Quoted by G. Beratz, *Die deutschen Kolonien a. d. unteren Wolga in ihrer Entstehung und ersten Entwicklung*, 2nd ed. (Berlin 1923), 43.

73. Ibid.; *PSZ*, xvi, 731–2, no. 12146, 30 April 1764.

74. G. Bonwetsch, *Geschichte der deutschen Kolonien an der Wolga* (Stuttgart 1919), 29.

75. *PSZ*, xvi, 699–700, no. 12651, 19 May 1766.

76. Ibid., no. 12146.

77. *PSZ*, xliv, ii, 98, no. 12630, 28 April 1766; Beratz, *Die deutschen Kolonien*, 44.

78. Ibid., footnote, quoting Kuhlberg's reports to the Chancellery of June 1766; cp. A. A. Klaus, *Nashi Kolonii, Opyty i materialy po istorii i statistike inostrannoy kolonizatsii v Rossii*, (SPb 1869, reprinted Cambridge 1972), Appendix 1, 8. The book-binder is mentioned in *PSZ*, xvi, 915–16, no. 12248. – Kuhlberg was in fact proposing that non-farmers should set themselves up as rural craftsmen.

79. TsGADA f. 283, op. 1, d. 8, l. 1; 'osoblovo zhe nechinya nimaleyshikh obid, privyazok i volokit, pod opaseniyem neupustitel'nogo po ukazam shtrafa i nakazaniya'.

80. Ibid.

81. Ibid., l. 2.

82. Some moved to the Saratov colonies when they were established.

83. TsGADA f. 248, kn. 3398, l. 492, Chancellery report to Senate of 21 Oct. 1763; *SA*, xiii, 375–6.

84. TsGADA f. 283, op. 1, d. 15, l. 23, report from Reuss to Chancellery, 23 April 1764.

85. TsGADA f. 248, kn. 3622, ll. 199–200, Senate minutes of 10 Jan. 1765.

86. TsGADA f. 283, op. 1, d. 15, l. 25, register of reports from Reuss; cp. F. Ya. Polyansky, *Gorodskoye remeslo i manufaktura v Rossii v XVIII v.* (Moscow 1960), 145.

87. TsGADA f. 248, kn. 3622, ll. 99–102, 25 May 1764; cp. *SIRIO*, cxxxiv, 270, 281 § B.

88. *Trudy Saratovskoy Uchonoy Arkhivnoy Komissii*, 1887, g., ii, i (Saratov 1889), 176–85: figures for 1769; reproduced in Pisarevsky, *Iz istorii*, Appendix, 82.

89. TsGADA f. 248, kn. 3622, ll. 1–57, d. 1, Po donosheniyu. . .Orlova o podnesenii Ye. I. Velichestvu pri doklade ko oprobatsii priznannykh senatom dostatochnymi i poleznymi uchinyonnykh im gr. Orlovym o zdelanii dlya poselenii vykhodyashchikh inostrannykh lyudey porozzhim

zemlyam mezhevianiya i protchego uchrezhdeniy. 16 Feb. 1764; *PSZ*, XVI, 648–55, no. 12095, 19 March 1764.

90. Bonwetsch, *Geschichte*, 15–16.
91. Pisarevsky, *Iz istorii*, 84.
92. The line ran down the Volga from Chardym (? – 'Gordym island') above Saratov, to Tsaritsyn; followed the forts of the Tsaritsyn Line to the Don, and the Don itself westwards to its tributary the Vityug near Voronezh; ran up the Vityug, and from its headwaters to Novokhopyorsk on the Khopyor, up the latter to the village of Znamenskoye (apparently at the mouth of the tributary Argada), and then eastward along the Penza provincial boundary to Saratov *uyezd*, and back to the Volga.
93. According to a letter of G. G. Orlov, the norm of 30 desyatinas was fixed by the Chancellery in consultation with representatives of the colonists. G. G. Pisarevsky, *Vnutrenniy rasporyadok v koloniyakh Povolzh'ya pri Yekaterine II* (Warsaw 1914), 3. The Survey Instruction of 1766 (*PSZ*, XVII, no. 12659) doubled *odnovorets* holdings to sixty desyatinas; the colonist norm remained the same.
94. Only one twelfth of the total was to be left for craftsmen in the smaller villages where there was less need of them. The new families envisaged were those which would form by marriage.
95. The administration of the colonies is discussed at length by M. Langhans-Ratzeburg, *Die Wolgadeutschen. Ihr Staats- und Verwaltungsrecht in Vergangenheit und Gegenwart* (Berlin 1929).
96. Ultimogeniture was sometimes found in Russian customary law. See Brokgaus i Efron, *Entsiklopedicheskiy Slovar'*, XXXVII, 385–6, article 'Minorat'.
97. V. I. Semevsky, *Krest'yane v tsarstvovaniye Imp. Yekateriny II* (SPb 1901–3), II, 735–6; *SIRIO*, VII, 308. Further on the *odnodvortsy*, cp. T. Esper, 'The Odnodvortsy and the Russian Nobility', *SEER*, LXV, no. 104 (Jan. 1967), 124–34. The later status of the colonists is summed up in *Svod Zakonov*, XII, ii, Ustav o koloniyakh inostrantsev v Imperii, razdel vtoroy. These remarks apply of course only to those first called colonists, i.e. who settled in colonies.
98. TsGADA f. 248, kn. 3622, ll. 27–35, 143–65.
99. Including the father of the memoirist Philip Vigel': cp. *Zapiski F.F. Vigelya* (Moscow 1891), 22ff. The other two were Captains Popov and Liebhardt, who were promoted for the occasion.
100. G. G. Pisarevsky, 'Nizhneye Povolzh'ye v tretey chetverti XVIII v.', *Izvestiya Pedagogicheskogo Fakul'teta Azerbaydzhanskogo Gos. Univ., obshchestvennyye nauki*, XIV (Baku 1929), 224. The general survey ordered for all of European Russia in 1766 did not reach Saratov until the turn of the century (1798). The significance, special features, and results of Reuss's *opekunskoye mezhevaniye* are discussed by L. N. Yurovsky, *Saratovskiye Votchiny. Statist. -ekon. ocherki i materialy iz istorii krupnogo zemlevladeniya i krepostnogo khozyaystva v kontse XVIII i v nachale XIX stoletiya* (Saratov 1923), 29–37.
101. Pisarevsky, *Nizhneye Povolzh'ye*, 228.
102. TsGADA f. 248, kn. 3622, ll. 107–13. Correspondence between the Chancellery, the Senate and the Heraldry Office, 21 June–29 Nov. 1764.
103. Ibid., kn. 3398, ll. 543–5, d. 25. Po donosheniyu Kantselyarii O. I. o vybore dlya prismotru za otpravlyayushchimisya inostrantsami na poseleniye...

kantselyarii opekunstva sposobnogo chlena; *PSZ*, XLIV, ii, 98, 100, no. 12630, 28 April 1766.

104. Ibid., 99.

105. Ibid., 98–101; Pisarevsky, *Khozyaystvo i forma zemlevladeniya*, 6, footnote 1.

106. D. Schmidt, *Studien über die Geschichte der Wolgadeutschen*, 1 Teil (Moscow–Pokrovsk–Kharkov 1930), 49–51; Beratz, *Die deutschen Kolonien*, 51 and Appendix. The figure 104 includes Sarepta.

107. TsGADA f. 16, d. 351, l. 41, CGF General Account to 1770, item 9. The curious total is unexplained. Cp. *PSZ*, XVI, 913–14, no. 12246, 21 Sept. 1764.

108. *PSZ*, XVII, 373, no. 12503, 1 Nov. 1765; XVIII, 927, no. 13325, 23 July 1769.

109. *PSZ*, no. 13325; P. Koeppen, *Ueber die Deutschen im St. Petersburgischen Gouvernement* (SPb 1850), 10–11 (Russian version, P. Keppen, 'Ob inorodcheskom, preimushchestvenno nemetskom naselenii Sanktpeterburgskoy gubernii', *ZhMVD*, 1850, no. 11). The original name of the first colony was Malo-Saratovskaya: E. Koch, *Die deutschen Kolonien Nordrusslands. Eine siedlungs-wirtschaftsgeographische und kulturhistorische Untersuchung.* Inaugural Dissertation (Würzburg 1932), 9.

110. J. Georgi, *Versuch einer Beschreibung der russischen kayserlichen Residenzstadt Sanktpeterburg* (SPb 1790–Riga 1793), 561.

111. H. Reimers, *Sanktpeterburg am Ende seines ersten Jahrhunderts*, 1 (SPb 1805), 275–6; in the mid-19th century F. Matthäi described them as agriculturally outstanding: *Die deutschen Ansiedlungen in Russland. Ihre Geschichte und ihre volkswirtschaftliche Bedeutung für die Vergangenheit und Zukunft* (Leipzig 1866), 222–3. Klaus adduces no evidence in support of his statement (*Nashi Kolonii*, 128) that the Petersburg colonies had a model function.

112. The industrial development is described below, pp. 173–7. I am indebted to Professor E. Amburger who allowed me to consult the relevant pages of his forthcoming book on Ingermanland. Cp. also Koeppen, *Ueber die Deutschen*, 11–12; I. Pushkaryov, *Opisaniye Sanktpeterburga i uyezdnykh gorodov Sanktpeterburgskoy gubernii* (Spb 1839–42), IV, 82–7.

113. W. Conze, *Hirschenhof, die Geschichte einer deutschen Sprachinsel in Livland* (Berlin 1934).

114. TsGADA f. 248, kn. 3762, ll. 537, 541, CGF aide-memoire and Senate resolution, 12 May 1769: the colonists settled 'on his Shcherbinin's demand in consideration of the need there of people skilled in agriculture, and of craftsmen'.

115. On the Tevyashov family see V. P. Zagorovsky, *Istoricheskaya Toponimika Voronezhskogo Kraya* (Voronezh 1973), *passim*.

116. M. Bylov, Nemtsy v Voronezhskoy gubernii, *Pamyatnaya Knizhka Voronezhskoy Gubernii na 1894 g.* (Voronezh 1894), 119–20.

117. A. V. Veynberg, ed., *Materialy dlya istorii Voronezhskoy i sosednikh guberniy*, XVI (Voronezh 1890), 1945.

118. Sch., 'Geschichte der einsamen deutschen Bauernkolonie Riebensdorf in Zentralrussland', reprinted with additions in *HBR* (1958), 35–45. Another small colony of twenty families, Kalatsch, set up in 1766, was short-lived. Cp. also *Die evangelisch-lutherischen Gemeinden in Russland. Eine historisch-statistische Darstellung, hrsg. v. Zentral-Komite der Unterstützungs-Kasse für ev.-luth. Gemeinden in Russland* (SPb 1909–11), I, i, 37–8.

119. Veynberg, *Materialy*, xvi, 1944–5.
120. Ibid. S. G. Gmelin, in his *Reise durch Russland zur Untersuchung der drey Naturreiche*, 1 (SPb 1770), 97, noted that the colonists were mainly from Württemberg and the Palatinate, and included both Protestant and Catholic; he listed several artisans, including the pipe-maker, a Swede.
121. *PSZ*, xvii, 701–2, no. 12655, 22 May 1766.
122. Appendix v.
123. A. Shafonsky, *Chernigovskogo Namestnichestva Topograficheskoye Opisaniye s kratkim geograficheskim i istoricheskim opisaniyem Maliya Rossii... 1786 g.* (Kiev 1851), 395–403. The other colonies were named Belovezhskaya Koloniya; Gross Werder; Klein Werder; Rundewiese. Further on this group see J. A. Güldenstädt, *Reisen durch Russland und im Caucasischen Gebirge* (SPb 1787–91), ii, 370–72; anon., 'Belovezhskaya nemetskaya koloniya', *Pamyatnaya Knizhka Chernigovskoy Gubernii* (Chernigov 1862), 129–62.
124. *PSZ*, xviii, 391–2, no. 13015, 17 Nov. 1767.
125. Ibid., 38, no. 12836, 28 Feb. 1767. See below, pp. 81–5, on the private contracts.
126. *PSZ*, xviii, 391–2, no. 13015.
127. *PSZ*, xvii, 196–8, no. 12443, 30 July 1765; xviii, 35, no. 12836, 28 Feb. 1767; 137–8, no. 12905, 2 June 1767.
128. *PSZ*, xviii, 36–7, no. 12836. In settling them, Rumyantsev was to bear in mind the provisions of the 1763 Manifesto, and local Ukrainian conditions.
129. Pylayev, *Ocherki po istorii yuzhnoslavyanskoy i moldavano-voloshskoy kolonizatsii*, 281–2; Güldenstadt, *Reisen durch Russland*, ii, 379; 'Arkhiv voenno-pokhodnoy kantselyarii gr. P. A. Rumyantseva-Zadunayskogo, chast' 1: 1767–69', *Chteniya* 1865, no. 1, ii, 253–70.
130. *PSZ*, xviii, 39–49, no. 12836.
131. 'Arkhiv voenno-pokhodnoy kantselyarii gr. P. A. Rumyantseva-Zadunayskogo, chast' 1: 1767–69', *Chteniya*, 1865 no. 1, ii, 253–70.
132. V. Ruban, *Lyubopytnyy mesyatseslov na 1775 g.* (SPb 1775), 62; E. Zagorovsky, 'Inostrannaya kolonizatsiya Novorossii v XVIII v. (Po povodu issledovaniya G. G. Pisarevskogo, "Iz istorii...")', *Izv. Odesskogo Bibliograficheskogo Ob-va pri Novorossiyskom Univ.*, ii, vyp. 8 (March 1913), 113.
133. *Lyubopytnyy mesyatseslov*, 62.
134. Sometimes also called *Sarpinskaya Koloniya*, the Sarpa or Sarpinka colony, after the river Sarpa on which it stood.
135. *PSZ*, xvii, 151–60, no. 12411, 7 June 1765; Hafa, *Die Brudergemeinde Sarepta*, 25–44.
136. *PSZ*, xliv, ii, 99, no. 12630, 28 April 1766.
137. Hafa, *Die Brudergemeinde Sarepta*, 44.
138. Ibid., 34.
139. *PSZ*, xvii, 374–7, no. 12503.
140. V. Yakushkin, *Ocherki po istorii russkoy pozemel'noy politiki v XVIII i XIX vv. Vypusk I: XVIII v.* (Moscow 1890), 58–60.
141. *PSZ*, xviii, 130–1, no. 12897, 19 May 1767.
142. TsGADA f. 248, kn. 3762, ll. 196-ob., report by Orlov confirmed by HIH, heard in the Senate 16 April 1767.
143. Ibid.
144. *SIRIO*, xxxvi, 25, 17 Sept. 1768.
145. TsGADA f. 283, op. 1, d. 16, ll. 139–227, contracts of the Chancellery.

146. *PSZ*, XIX, 523, no. 13819, 13 June 1772.
147. *PSZ*, XXVII, 731–4, no. 20843, 11 July 1803.
148. *PSZ*, XXVI, 259–60, no. 19512, 11 Aug. 1800. The Senate decision in this case was clearly wrong.
149. *PSZ*, XXVI, 123, no. 19372, § 8, 6 April 1800.
150. Klaus, *Nashi Kolonii*, 24–55; E. J. Waltner, *Banished for Faith* (Freeman, South Dakota 1968), gives a translation of the Hutterites' own chronicle: on the Russian period, see 61–128. In 1802, after trouble with Rumyantsev's heirs, the Hutterites moved to Crown land at Radichev, 15 versts from Vishenki.
151. TsGIAL f. 398, op. 81, d. 95, ll. 13–16, report of Board of State Economy to HIH, 7 April 1798. The case was somewhat unusual – at least in Trappe's account, ll. 1–20b., letter to Prince A. B. Kurakin of 8 March 1798 – because of the involvement of highly-placed backers: Trappe's patron was Potemkin, to whom he had been recommended by Princess Marie Fyodorovna; behind the new applicant, Major-General Herrmann, stood (according to Trappe) Prince Zubov. The Board treated the case as a simple breach of contract.
152. Ibid., ll. 1–20b.
153. Cp. below, p. 197.
154. Zutis, *Ostzeyskiy vopros v XVIII v.*, 302–5.
155. Ibid., 321.
156. Ibid., 316 (*ostzeyskiy* as opposed to *baltiyskiy vopros*: cp. ibid., 5).
157. Ibid., 284.
158. Ibid., 305. In referring to the Manifesto, Zutis writes June for July, and gives a wrong *PSZ* number.
159. Gessen, *Istoriya yevreyskogo naroda*, I, 58.
160. Ibid.; A. Buchholtz, *Geschichte der Juden in Riga* (Riga 1899), 55–7.
161. Gessen, *Istoriya yevreyskogo naroda*, I, 58–9; Buchholtz, *Geschichte der Juden*, 57–8.
162. Gessen, *Istoriya yevreyskogo naroda*, I, 58–63.
163. *PSZ*, XVIII, 1018, no. 13383, 16 Nov. 1769; Gessen, *Istoriya yevreyskogo naroda*, I, 63; Buchholz, *Geschichte der Juden*, 57.
164. P. A. Ivanov, 'Delo o vykhodyashchikh iz-za granitsy v Novorossiyskuyu guberniyu zhidakh', *ZOO*, XVII (1894), 163–88; 120 families settled in 1775–7, and 32 more were admitted for temporary residence.
165. Gessen, *Istoriya yevreyskogo naroda*, I, 63.
166. *PSZ*, XVIII, 336–41, no. 12967, 22 Aug. 1767.
167. Ibid.
168. Zutis, *Ostzeyskiy vopros v XVIII v.*, 254–5.
169. Ibid. See also O.-H. Elias, 'Zur Lage der undeutschen Bevölkerung im Riga des 18ten Jahrhunderts', *JbfGO*, NF, 14 (1966), Heft 4, 481–4.
170. Zutis, *Ostzeyskiy vopros v XVIII v.*, 254–5.
171. Ibid., 256.
172. *PSZ*, no. 12967.
173. Zutis, *Ostzeyskiy vopros v XVIII v.*, 254.
174. Kh. P. Strod, 'Vliyaniye torgovoy politiki Rossiyskoy Imperii na razvitiye sel'skogo khozyaystva Latvii v XVIII v.', A. K. Biron, red., *Ekonomic-heskiye svyazi Pribaltiki s Rossiyey. Sbornik statey* (Riga 1968), 157.
175. Ibid.
176. Zutis, *Ostzeyskiy vopros v XVIII v.*, 275. Garlieb Merkel portrays in his

memoirs the personal life of Linke – or Godofredus von Link, as the latter (Merkel says) always signed himself – in his middle and later years; Linke and Merkel were related. Merkel ascribes the calm regularity of Linke's family routine, and the stoic impassivity with which he met repeated misfortunes, to a life-long absorption in the mysteries of alchemy. G. H. Merkel, *Darstellungen und Charakteristiken aus meinem Leben* (Leipzig–Riga und Mitau 1839–40), I, 70–84.

177. Strod, 'Vliyaniye', 57.
178. Ibid.; M. Stepermanis, 'Aizkraukles K. F. Šulcs un vina sabiedriskā darbība', *Latvijas Universitātes Raksti (fil. fak. ser.)* III, 5 (1935), 135–6.
179. Stepermanis, 'Aizkraukles K. F. Šulcs', 136–7.
180. M. Stepermanis, 'Pirmās ciņas par dzimtbūšanas atcelšanu Vidzemē 1750–64' (part ii), *Izglītības Ministrijas Mēnešrakts* (1931) no. 11, 447–8.
181. Ibid.
182. Stepermanis, 'Aizkraukles K. F. Šulcs' gives the fullest account of Schoultz's dealings with Eisen at this time.
183. Zutis, *Ostzeyskiy vopros v XVIII v.*, 336; V. I. Semevsky, *Krest'yanskiy vopros v Rossii v XVIII i 1-oy ½-e XIX v.*, I (SPb 1888), 14–15.
184. Zutis, *Ostzeyskiy vopros v XVIII v.*, 336; Stepermanis, *J. G. Eisen et ses luttes*, 505. The essay 'Eines Lieffländischen Patrioten Beschreibung der Leibeigenschaft, wie solche in Liefland ueber die Bauren eingeführet ist', appeared anonymously in F. G. Müller, ed., *Sammlung Russicher Geschichte*, IX (SPb 1764), 491–527.
185. *Provinzialblatt für Kur-, Liv- und Esthland* (1828), no. 2, 1.
186. Solov'yov, *Istoriya Rossii*, XIII, 316, 322.
187. *Provinzialblatt*, no. 2, 1: 'um durch mich die Leibeigenschaft abschaffen und Kolonien pflanzen zu lassen'. The association of colonization with liberty and civic virtues was by no means unique to Eisen. In 1774, for example, Diderot wrote to Catherine: 'If I had to create a nation at liberty, what would I do? I would plant in its midst a colony of men who are free, very free, such for example as the Swiss; I would ensure most strictly that that they retained their privileges, and I would leave the rest to time and to example.' *Mémoires pour Catherine II*, ed. P. Vernière (Paris 1966), 199. The idea recurs in Diderot's 'Observations sur le Nakaz', *Oeuvres Politiques* (Paris 1963), 350–1.
188. Zutis, *Ostzeyskiy vopros v XVII v.*, 336.
189. Ibid., 336–7; *Provinzialblatt*, no. 2, 1.
190. Zutis, *Ostzeyskiy vopros v XVIII v.*, 337–8.
191. See M. Belyavsky, *Krest'yanskiy vopros v Rossii nakanune vosstaniya Pugachova* (Moscow 1965); P. Dukes, 'Catherine II's Enlightened Absolutism and the Problem of Serfdom', *Russian Law: Historical and Political Perspectives*, ed. W. E. Butler (Leyden 1977), 93–115; R. Jones, *The Emancipation of the Russian Nobility 1762–1785* (Princeton 1973); I. de Madariaga, 'Catherine II and the Serfs: A Reconsideration of some Problems', *SEER*, LII, no. 126 (Jan. 1974), 34–62; V. Nedosekin, 'O diskussii po krest'yanskomu voprosu v Rossii nakanune vosstaniya Pugachova', *Izv. Voronezhskogo Gos. Ped. In-ta* 63 (1967), 326–46; H. Neuschäffer, *Katharina II und die baltischen Provinzen* (Hannover–Döhren 1975).
192. Cp. Neuschäffer, *Katharina II*, 398–426.
193. See works cited in n. 191 above.

194. *SIRIO*, xxxvi, 24.
195. Neuschäffer's assertion, 401, n. 117, that the 1765 law (*PSZ* 12503) is Eisen's Ropsha plan, seems to contradict the evidence.
196. *Provinzialblatt* (1828), no. 3, 11.
197. Conze, *Hirschenhof*, 27.
198. See below, pp. 173–7.
199. Quoted in Stepermanis, *J. G. Eisen et ses luttes*, 506.
200. Schlözer, *Leben*, 89–91.
201. Further on Eisen see H. Neuschäffer, 'Der livländische Pastor und Kameralist Johann Georg Eisen von Schwarzenberg. Ein deutscher Vertreter der Aufklärung in Russland zu Beginn der zweiten Hälfte des 18ten Jahrhunderts', *Kieler Historische Studien*, 22 (1974), 120–43. The monograph of E. Donnert, *Johann Georg Eisen (1717–1779). Ein Vorkämpfer der Bauernbefreiung in Russland* (Leipzig 1978) appeared too late to be used here.
202. Yurovsky, *Saratovskiye Votchiny*, 24–5.
203. *Chteniya* (1863), no. 2, 27–8, letters of Catherine to N. I. Panin, 3 and 4 June 1767.
204. Ibid., 28, letter of 4 June.
205. 'Biograficheskiy ocherk gr. V. G. Orlova, Sostavlen vnukom yego gr. V. P. Orlovym-Davydovym', *Russkiy Arkhiv* (1908), no. vii, 348–9. I. M. Katayev, *Na Beregakh Volgi: Istoriya Usol'skoy Votchiny Grafov Orlovykh* (Chelyabinsk 1948) is rather thin on the early period.
206. Orlov-Davydov, 'Biograficheskiy ocherk gr. V. G. Orlova', 349.
207. A number of studies have been made of the general settlement of the lower Volga at this time, which cannot be explored fully here. Besides Yurovsky, cp. the works already cited of Geraklitov, *Istoriya Saratovskogo Kraya*, Kizewetter, *Otzyv*, 13–24, and Pisarevsky, *Nizhneye Povolzh'ye*; also P. Lyubomirov, 'Zaseleniye Astrakhanskogo kraya v XVIII v.', *Nash Kray* (Astrakhan 1926), no. 4, 54–77; N. M. Vas'kin, 'Pomeshchich'e zemlevladeniye v Astrakhanskom kraye vo vtoroy polovine XVIII v.', *Problemy Istorii SSSR*, v (1976), 181–93.
208. Lyubomirov, 'Zaseleniye Astrakhanskogo kraya', 63.
209. Ibid.; *PSZ*, xvi, 827–32, no. 12198, 5 July 1764.
210. *PSZ*, xviii, 1,024–6, no. 13389, 30 Nov. 1769.
211. *PSZ*, xvii, 91–8, no. 12360, 22 March 1765; xvii, 451–8, no. 12519, 8 Dec. 1765; TsGADA f. 248, kn. 3622, ll. 244–325, d. 21, Po donosheniyu... Orlova ob otmerivanii vsem vladel'tsam koim krest'yan imet' dozvoleno zemli vo opredelyonnykh dlya poseleniya inostrantsov okruzhnosti po 30 desyatinam na kazhduyu dushu...8 March 1765.
212. *PSZ*, xvii, 590, no. 12581, 23 Feb. 1766.
213. Ibid.
214. TsGADA f. 248, kn. 3622, ll. 698–711, dd. 50 (6 Oct.), 51 (11 Oct. 1766): appointment of Durnovo; l. 787, d. 55 (14 Nov. 1766): appointment of Guards Lieutenant Pushin as his assistant in towns of Ustyuzhnya, Zhelezopol'sk, Poshekhon'e. In connection with these appointments *PSZ*, xvii, 590–92, no. 12581, 23 Feb. 1766; 1,022, no. 12763, 17 Oct. 1766.
215. TsGADA f. 248, kn. 3622, l. 676, decree to Kamer-Kollegiya following Senate report to HIH, 7 Sept.; f. 16, d. 351, l. 16, Orlov report to HIH, 26 April 1767; ll. 27–32, report to Chancellery from Durnovo, 27 April 1767; Pisarevsky, *Iz istorii*, Appendix, 82–3.

216. Defects in the financial administration further hampered the transport of colonists. At one point Catherine personally ordered advances to be made against sums due, but unavailable, to the Chancellery of Guardianship, which had been unable to dispatch Herrnhuters and others for lack of funds: *SIRIO*, VII, 335.
217. Pisarevsky, *Khozyaystvo i forma zemlevladeniya*, 23.
218. C. G. Züge, *Der russische Colonist oder Christian Gottlob Züges Leben in Russland. Nebst einer Schilderung der Sitten und Gebräuche der Russen, vornehmlich in den asiatischen Provinzen* (Zeitz und Naumburg 1802–3), I, 143. Züge's memoirs were written (in their published version) in old age, and details of chronology and numbers sometimes appear shaky. But his account seems otherwise generally accurate, and it provides a lively and coherent personal view.
219. *PSZ*, XVI, 436–7, no. 11980, Nov. 1763. It is not clear whether the medical personnel was ever provided.
220. *SIRIO*, XIII, 77; CXII, 442; *Un diplomate français à la Cour de Catherine II. 1775–80. Journal intime du Chevalier de Corberon*, I (Paris 1901), 298; Pisarevsky, *Iz istorii*, Appendix, 23–5, 47–67. Pictet tried unsuccessfully to enlist Voltaire's support in his defence: *Voltaire's Correspondence*, ed. T. Bestermann, LXVIII (Geneva 1962), 152–3, no. 16041, Voltaire to Catherine II, 12 March, NS, 1771.
221. Beauregard's widely publicized intention to model his colonies on the Swiss cantons came to nothing: 'The intention, however, to place the establishment of the new inhabitants to some extent upon a Swiss footing, was declared suspicious out of envy and for political reasons, and became impracticable because of other obstacles', *Eine Reise durch Deutschland und Russland seinen Freunden beschrieben von Johann Baptista Cataneo aus Bunden, gegenwärtigen Pfarrer einer reformierten deutschen Colonie zu Norka in der Saratofischen Statthalterschaft an der Wolga, in der russischen Tartarei in Asien* (Chur 1787), 117. Many of these colonies received Swiss names, however.
222. TsGADA f. 248, kn. 4076, ll. 149a–169, d. 11, ...o rassmotrenii v obshchikh zdeshnikh Senata departamentov sobranii doklada podnosimogo ot Kommissii uchrezhdyonnoy dlya rassmotreniya vyzyvatel'skikh del...11 Oct. 1777 (quotation l. 158). Cp. Pisarevsky, *Iz istorii*, 182–204, Appendix no. 32, 47–67.
223. Cp. G. G. Pisarevsky, *Vnutrenniy rasporyadok v koloniyakh Povolzh'ya pri Yekaterine II* (Warsaw 1914), 3. (This view was shared by contemporaries: cp. *Buckingham Correspondence* II, 65.) Beratz, *Die deutschen Kolonien*, 85–6; Koch, *Volga Germans*, 102, and the remarks of Shishmaryov, 'Nauchnoye naslediye', 105–6.
224. Klaus, *Nashi Kolonii*, Appendix I.
225. Züge, *Der russiche Colonist* I, 169–71. On the other hand, the Count von Dönhoff, an ancestor of the Volga German memoirist Bauer, was made of sterner stuff. According to Bauer, von Dönhoff joined the colonists at Oranienbaum, and was for some time their only Russian speaker. Although Bauer says nothing about his skills as a farmer, he supervised the establishment of the colony of Gololobovka or Dönhoff to which he gave his name, and in Bauer's account appears as a figure of considerable weight in his community. Bauer states that von Dönhoff always retained the German noble style of dress and hair with which he had come to the Volga, and that

he became a particular target for Pugachev's men during the insurgents' sweep through the colonies in 1774. G. Bauer, *Geschichte der deutschen Ansiedler an der Wolga seit ihrer Einwanderung nach Russland bis zur Einführung der allgemeinen Wehrpflicht* (*1766–1874*) (Saratov 1908), 16–18, 20–1, 32–5.

226. Pisarevsky, *Khozyaystvo i forma zemlevladeniya*, 24. M. Babintsev, 'Uchastiye nemtsev Povolzh'ya v vosstanii Pugachova', *Za Kommunisticheskoye Prosveshcheniye*, no. 1 (20) (Engels 1941), 62, gives rather improbable figures of 47.3, 44, 8.7 for the same year; no source given. Cp. further *Zapiski Puteshestviya Akad*. Fal'ka, *Polnoye Sobraniye Uchonykh Puteshestviy po Rossii*..., vi (SPb 1824), 114; Lyubomirow, *Die wirtschaftliche Lage*, 10–24; D. Schmidt, *Studien*, 38–46; P. Sinner, 'Kurzgefasste Geschichte der deutschen Wolgakolonien', *Beiträge zur Heimatkunde des deutschen Wolgagebiets* (Pokrovski [Kosakenstadt] 1923), 9: partial statistics from official immigration lists show 60% farmers.

227. Pisarevsky, *Iz istorii*, Appendix, 82; id., *Vnutrenniy rasporyadok*, 4.

228. *PSZ*, xx, 757–9, no. 14814, 27 Oct. 1778.

229. N. N. Selifontov, 'I. K. Boshnyak, komendant gor. Saratova, 1774', *Russkaya Starina*, xxvi, 199–216.

230. *Pugachovshchina* (*Materialy po istorii revolyutsionnogo dvizheniya v Rossii XVII i XVIII vv.*), pod obshchey redaktsiyey M. N. Pokrovskogo (Moscow–Lenigrad 1929), ii, 70–3, iii, 201–6.

231. Pisarevsky, *Khozyaystvo i forma zemlevladeniya*, 26. Cp. Babintsev, 'Uchastiye nemtsev Povolzh'ya'; V. V. Mavrodin, 'Die Teilnahme deutscher Ansiedler des Volgagebiets am Pugačevaufstand', *Jahrbuch für Geschichte der UdSSR* 7 (1963), 189–99; id., 'Ob uchastii kolonistov Povolzh'ya v vosstanii Pugachova', *Krest'yanstvo i klassovaya bor'ba v feodal'noy Rossii. Sb. statey pamyati I. I. Smirnova = Trudy In-ta Ist. AN SSSR, Leningradsk. Otd.*, vyp. 9 (Leningrad 1967), 400–14; A. G. Tatarincev, 'Zum Widerhall des Pugačev-Aufstandes im Saratower Gebiet. Aus der Geschichte der deutschen Kolonisation in der zweiten Hälfte des 18. Jhdts', *Zeitschrift für Slawistik*, xiii (1968), 196–206. For a forceful presentation of the 'German loyalist' view, Beratz, *Die deutschen Kolonien*, 170–7, who is followed by Koch, *Volga Germans*, 99–102.

232. Hafa, *Die Brudergemeinde Sarepta*, 75; TsGADA f. 248, kn. 4076, l. 112–140b., report to HIH by A. Vyazemsky, 6 June 1775.

233. *Zapiski G. R. Derzhavina*, ed. Bartenev (Moscow 1860), 92–3; Beratz, *Die deutschen Kolonien*, 189 has a slightly different version. Cp. Pisarevsky, *Khozyaystvo i forma zemlevladeniya*, 26.

234. Ibid., 27–8.

235. Pisarevsky, *Vnutrenniy rasporyadok*, 2–5.

236. Züge, *Der russische Colonist*, ii, 51–3.

237. Pisarevsky, *Vnutrenniy rasporyadok*, 8.

238. *PSZ*, xvii, 131, no. 12394, 5 May 1765.

239. On Forster and for the following see G. Steiner, 'J. R. Forsters und Georg Forsters Beziehungen zu Russland', *Studien zur Geschichte der russischen Literatur des 18ten Jahrhunderts*, hrsg. H. Grasshof u. U. Lehmann, ii (Berlin 1968), 245–311; R. P. Bartlett, 'J. R. Forster's Stay in Russia 1765–66: Diplomatic and Official Accounts', *JbfGO* 23 (1975) no. 4, 489–95; M. E. Hoare, *The Tactless Philosopher: Johann Reinhold Forster 1729–1798* (Melbourne 1976), 24–36.

240. The work he undertook on the journey was formally reported in the Academy of Sciences in 1765–6, and appeared in print in London in the Royal Society's *Philosophical Transactions*, in 1767 and 1768. See especially Forster's map of the colonies, based on Reuss's survey and his own observations, published with '*A Letter from Mr.* J. R. Forster, *F.A.S., to* M. Maty, *M.D., Sec. R.S. containing some Account of a new Map of the River* Volga', *Philos. Trans.* 58 (1768), 214–16.

241. Pisarevsky, *Vnutrenniy rasporyadok,* 5–6.

242. *PSZ,* XLIV, ii, 98, no. 12630.

243. Cp. *SIRIO,* CXLI, 78–9, no. 39.

244. Letters and notes to N. I. Panin, *Chteniya,* 1863 no. 2, 26, no. 53; 30, no. 59.

245. 'Biograficheskiy ocherk gr. V. G. Orlova', *Russkiy Arkhiv* (1908), no. 7, 314–45.

246. Züge, *Der russische Colonist,* II, 48–9.

247. Beratz, *Die deutschen Kolonien,* 126.

248. Pisarevsky, *Iz istorii,* Appendix, 64.

249. Ibid., 48.

250. Hafa, *Die Brudergemeinde Sarepta,* 43, n. 120. Herrnhut apparently did not meet this request.

251. Bartlett, 'J. R. Forster's Stay in Russia', 495.

252. Pisarevsky, *Vnutrenniy rasporyadok,* 11. The Instruction is printed here in full as an appendix. See also Beratz, *Die deutschen Kolonien,* 111–25.

253. Quoted in Pisarevsky, *Khozyaystvo i forma zemlevladeniya,* 31.

254. Ibid., 32, footnote; TsGADA f. 248, kn. 4076, l. 86, Senate minutes of 9 March 1775.

255. *PSZ,* XX, 125–6, no. 14302, 18 April 1775; Pisarevsky, *Khozyaystvo i forma zemlevladeniya,* 32–52. The poll tax was however instituted in the Volga colonies before the end of the century, in accordance with the 1763 manifesto.

256. Ibid. This change of attitude also coincided with Diderot's presentation to Catherine of a memorandum on the Saratov colonies: *Mémoires pour Catherine II,* LX, 260 and note, 317. There is no evidence for or against a connection between the two.

257. Cataneo, *Eine Reise durch Deutschland,* 131–3; Pisarevsky, *Khozyaystvo i forma zemlevladeniya*; Tatarincev, 'Zum Widerhall'. On attempts at greater government supervision of the Russian peasantry in the later eighteenth century cp. N. M. Druzhinin, *Gosudarstvennyye Krest'yane i Reforma P. D. Kiselyova,* I (Moscow 1946), 60–9.

258. P. S. Pallas, *Travels through the Southern Provinces of the Russian Empire in the years 1793 and 1794* (London 1802–3), I, 57–8.

259. *PSZ,* XXI, 491–2, no. 15383, 20 April 1782. This period of the Saratov colonies' development, sometimes wrongly portrayed as disastrous, is well discussed by Lyubomirow, *Die wirtschaftliche Lage*; cp. also Pisarevsky, *Vnutrenniy rasporyadok.* It was at this time that repartition of land-holdings was introduced into the Saratov colonies, as a purely administrative measure, parallel to its spread among the Russian peasantry at the time. Cp. Pisarevsky, *Khozyaystvo i forma zemlevladeniya,* 63–7, and further on the general spread of repartition, S. G. Pushkarev, *Krest'yanskaia pozemel'no-peredel'naia obshchina v Rossii* (Newtonville, Mass. 1976), ii: XVIII vek.

260. Cp. below, p. 205.

261. W. Kuhn, *Versuch einer Naturgeschichte der deutschen Sprachinsel*, quoted in Conze, *Hirschenhof*, 42.
262. Cp. above, p. 29, also the difficulties of Joseph of Austria described in W. Kuhn, *Die jungen deutschen Sprachinseln in Galizien (Ein Beitrag zur Methode der Sprachinselforschung)* (Münster 1930), 51–9.
263. Sch., 'Geschichte der einsamen deutschen'; Güldenstädt, *Reisen durch Russland*, ıı, 370, 379.
264. Conze, *Hirschenhof*, 47–9; TsGADA f. 248, kn. 4076, ll. 312a–83, d. 22, Po reportam...gr. Brouna otnositel'no do poselyonnykh v Liflyandii... kolonistov ot chego imenno preterpevayut oni nuzhdu...11 and 25 May 1781.
265. Hafa, *Die Brudergemeinde Sarepta*, 59–65; P. G. Lyubomirov, *Ocherki po istorii russkoy promyshlennosti* (Moscow–Leningrad 1947), 130, 602, 620.
266. Hafa, *Die Brudergemeinde Sarepta*, 77–87.
267. Ibid., 97–8. In 1772 Sarepta sought official support for plans to set up 'a settlement on the river Terek, after first sending its representatives to examine those countries and the springs of health-giving waters found there'. Although Catherine ordered Astrakhan Governor Beketov to give every assistance from the outset, evidently nothing came of it. TsGADA f. 248, kn. 3762, l. 698, copy of Catherine's personal decree to Beketov, 31 July 1772. Only in 1802 did Scottish missionaries establish the station of Karass in the Caucasus: see below, p. 189.
268. M. Woltner, *Das wolga-deutsche Bildungswesen und die russische Schulpolitik* (Leipzig 1937), 51; cp. Klaus, *Nashi Kolonii*, 81.
269. Klaus, *Nashi Kolonii*, 80.
270. TsGADA f. 248, kn. 3622, l. 273, also quoted by Kizewetter, 'Otzyv o sochinenii G. G. Pisarevskogo', 16: a report of 1765 gives a total of 8,443 male souls.
271. Falk, 'Zapiski Puteshestviya akad. Falka', 110, 114; cp. P. S. Pallas, *Reise durch verschiedene Provinzen des Russ. Reichs* (SPb 1771–6), ııı, 618.
272. E. Kusheva, 'Saratov v tretey chetverti XVIII v.', *Trudy Nizhne-Volzhskogo Oblastnogo Nauchnogo Obshchestva Krayevedeniya*, vypusk 35, chast' 2 (Saratov 1928), 36; Pallas, *Reise*, ııı, 619.
273. TsGADA f. 248, kn. 3622, l. 344, report to Senate of 4 June.
274. Falk, 'Zapiski Puteshestviya akad. Falka', 114. Rossoshi was the only colony with a predominantly French population. Departures continued. German settlers from other colonies moved into the empty places, and Pallas on his second visit in 1793 found only four French families remaining (*Travels*, ı, 64). The name Rossoshi was found in singular and plural forms in the seventeenth and eighteenth centuries, both in its original meaning of the confluence of small rivers, and as a place name. Zagorovsky, *Istoricheskaya Toponimika*, 41–2, 53, 111. Further on Rossoshi, cp. Shishmaryov, 'Nauchnoye naslediye', 111–12.
275. Vinsky, *Moyo Vremya*, 107.
276. Bonwetsch, *Geschichte der deutschen Kolonien*, 38; Pisarevsky, *Khozyaystvo i forma zemlevladeniya*, 23, 26–7.
277. *Memoirs of the Baron de Tott*, 2nd ed. (London 1768), ı, ii, 71–2.
278. Züge, *Der russische Colonist*. Other stories of attempted flight in Bauer, *Geschichte der deutschen Ansiedler*, 25–7.
279. Pisarevsky, *Iz istorii*, 311–14.
280. Ibid., 139; Shishmaryov, 'Nauchnoye naslediye', 120.

281. *SIRIO*, cxli, 99, no. 48.
282. *Voltaire's Correspondence*, lxii, 178, no. 14792, probably 14 July 1769. Voltaire proved an excellent public relations agent for Catherine. The present quotation leads straight on to Catherine's notorious assertion 'that our taxes are in any case so moderate, that there is no peasant in Russia who does not eat a chicken whenever he pleases, and that for some time now there have been provinces where they prefer turkey to chicken'. Catherine continues with the beneficial effects on agriculture of the newly-permitted grain exports, and concludes 'that the population has similarly increased by a tenth in many provinces over the past seven years'. The passage on peasants eating chicken alludes to a famous statement attributed to Henry IV of France – whom Catherine had very much admired – and so is not to be taken purely at face value. Henry's remark is also cited approvingly in a work of almost the same date on the emigration movement in Europe, and which attacked high taxation, princely luxury, and bad government as its causes: *Briefe über die Auswanderung der Unterthanen, besonders nach Russland* (Gotha 1770), 34–5. On Henry IV's remark, see e.g. Q. Hurst, *Henry of Navarre* (London 1937), 232; on Catherine's admiration, B. von Bilbassoff, *Geschichte Katharina II*, i, i, 318.
283. Pisarevsky, *Khozyaystvo i forma zemlevladeniya*, 36; Pallas, *Travels*, i, 58.
284. T. F. J. Basiner, 'Naturwissenschaftliche Reise durch die Kirgisensteppe nach Chiva', *Beiträge zur Kenntnis des Russischen Reiches und der angrenzenden Länder Asiens*, hrsg. Baer und Helmerson, xv (SPb 1848), 14–15. Cp. Vinsky, *Moyo Vremya*, 111.
285. *PSZ*, xxi, 569–70, no. 15411, 30 May 1782. Those who left the Livonian colonies on the same basis tended to move to Riga. Conze, *Hirschenhof*, 48.
286. TsGADA f. 16, d. 351, CGE General Account to 1770, ll. 44, 49. In fact, a proportion of debts had later to be written off.
287. The source quoted by Shafranov, 'Otzyv o knige G. G. Pisarevskogo', 44, gives a total of 5,682,306 roubles (3,655,852 roubles 86 kopecks returnable) for immigrants from southern and western Europe, including *fabrikanty*, during the whole of Catherine's reign. This is certainly too low: the Saratov colonies alone cost some 5,200,000 roubles, the Petersburg, Belovezh and Livonian settlements together nearly 288,500 roubles, and the Mennonite settlements of the 1780s and 1790s in the south over 358,000 roubles. Cp. 'Istoricheskoye obozreniye vodvoreniya inostrannykh poselentsev v Rossii', *ZhMGI*, lii, Sept. 1854, 35–78, *passim*; J. F. Erdmann, *Beiträge zur Kenntnis des Innern von Russland*, ii (Leipzig 1826), i, 282–3.

4. Southern Russia 1764–1796

1. *PSZ*, xvi, 961–2, no. 12277, 10 Nov. 1764; xvii, 133–6, no. 12397, 20 May 1765. H. Auerbach, *Die Besiedlung der Südukraine in den Jahren 1774–87* (Wiesbaden 1965), 19–20; N. D. Polons'ka-Vasylenko, 'The Settlement of the Southern Ukraine 1750–75', *Annals of the Ukrainian Academy of Arts and Sciences in the U.S.A.* (Summer–Fall 1955, New York 1955), 181–3.
2. The name New Russia came to be applied to all the lands north of the Black Sea which were successively absorbed by Russia in the last third of the eighteenth century, including the original Province of New Russia. Its use in this and following chapters designates the territory under Russian control and the boundaries in force at the particular time

referred to. A geographical account of New Russia and its formation is available in English in C. B. Peterson III., *Geographical Aspects of Foreign Colonization in Pre-Revolutionary New Russia*, PhD dissertation (U. Washington 1969), chapters i–iii.

3. *PSZ*, xvi, 297–9, no. 11861, 11 June 1763; 657–67, no. 12099, 22 March 1764; 795–9, no. 12180, 11 June 1764; Auerbach, *Die Besiedelung der Südukraine*, 28–31; Polons'ka-Vasylenko, 'The Settlement of the Southern Ukraine', 183–90.

4. A Cossack settlement adjoining New Serbia, established in 1753–4; cp. Polons'ka-Vasylenko, 'The Settlement of the Southern Ukraine', 64–5.

5. *PSZ*, xvi, 293, no. 11861, § 4 and 5, 11 June 1763.

6. *PSZ*, no. 12099.

7. *PSZ*, no. 12180; it differed little from that for New Serbia.

8. Auerbach, *Die Besiedelung*, 32–7; Ye. I. Druzhinina, *Severnoye Prichernomor'ye 1775–1800 gg.* (Moscow 1959), 58–66 (Druzhinina wrongly cites here *PSZ* no. 12095 which applied specifically to the Saratov colonies (66–7)); Polons'ka-Vasylenko, 'The Settlement of the Southern Ukraine', 200–18. J. A. Duran, 'Catherine II, Potemkin and Colonization Policy in South Russia', *Russian Review*, January 1969, 23–36, adds little to the earlier studies. The significance of the Plan was fully apparent to contemporaries: cp. the full summary by J. A. Güldenstädt, *Reisen durch Russland und im Caucasischen Gebirge* (SPb 1787–91), i, 120ff.

9. Polons'ka-Vasylenko, 'The Settlement of the Southern Ukraine', 202–3.

10. Ibid., 50.

11. Auerbach, *Die Besiedelung*, 32.

12. In view of the detailed descriptions available, only points of particular interest are dealt with here. Polons'ka-Vasylenko's account unfortunately has a number of errors and mis-translations, as compared with the Russian text in *PSZ*. The most important are as follows. i, § vi offered 12 roubles, not 6 (P–V, 204) to foreign and native settlers. ii, § 1 reserved sixteen districts for immigrants *wishing*, not unwilling (P–V, 204), to settle in separate settlements. And the 'biscuit factories' (vi § 1, P–V, 210) are in fact cloth mills.

13. Cp. similar arrangements for the Slavyanoserbian lands: *PSZ*, no. 12180.

14. If the heirs of a dead serviceman were too young or too infirm either to serve or to be peasants (civilian settlers), they were to be sent to the Orphanage and the plot given to someone able to serve. The movable property was to be sold up, and the money invested until the heirs should reach majority. This exactly repeated the procedure prescribed for minors in similar cases in the Volga colonies.

15. Except commercial or industrial grants.

16. Cp. below, p. 116.

17. *PSZ*, xxii, 974–93, no. 16603, n.d., 1787; cp. *SIRIO*, xx, 447–98.

18. Cp. V. I. Semevsky, *Krest'yane v tsarstvovaniye Imp. Yekateriny II*, (SPb 1901–3), i, 401.

19. Discussion and detailed measures relating to the Plan continued into the following year: cp. the detailed decisions, some of them secret, approved in the Senate on 21 Feb. 1765. *SA*, xiii, 50–5.

20. V. N. Kabuzan, 'Krest'yanskaya kolonizatsiya Severnogo Prichernomor'ya (Novorossii) v XVIII-i-oy ½e XIX vv. (1719–1857 gg.)', *Yezhegodnik po agrarnoy istorii Vostochnoy Yevropy za 1964 g.* (Kishinyov 1966), 319–20,

elaborated in idem, *Zaseleniye Novorossii v XVIII–1½ XIXvv. (1719–1858 gg.)* (Moscow 1976), 102–12. Female population in 1764 was 27,625, in 1772 – 45,429.

21. Kabuzan, 'Krest'yanskaya kolonizatsiya', 320.
22. This change, however, reflected also the increase in the reserves of land available after 1774.
23. Druzhinina, *Severnoye Prichernomor'ye*, 63–7, 121; Polons'ka-Vasylenko, 'The Settlement of the Southern Ukraine', 212–16. Cp. below, p. 134.
24. Cp. Auerbach, *Die Besiedelung*, 40, 47, 55; T. Adamczyk, *Fürst G. A. Potemkin. Untersuchungen zu seiner Lebensgeschichte* (Emsdetten 1936), 17.
25. Some scholars have denied the Project any serious content at all: E. Hösch, 'Das sog. "griechische Projekt" Katharinas II', *JbfGO*, NF, 12 (1964), 168–206; O. Markova, 'O proiskhozhdenii tak naz. grecheskogo proyekta (80-yye gg. XVIII v.)', *Istoriya SSSR* (1958), no. 4, 52–78. For an excellent discussion see D. M. Griffiths, *Russian Court Politics and the Question of an Expansionist Foreign Policy under Catherine II, 1762–1783*, PhD dissertation (Cornell University 1967), 144–75.
26. N. F. Dubrovin, 'Brat'ya Potemkiny na Kavkaze', *Russiky Vestnik*, cxxxviii (Nov. 1878), 30–9; A. R. Ioannisyan, *Rossia i armyanskoye osvoboditel'noye dvizheniye v 80–kh gg. XVIII st.* (Yerevan 1947), 189–94.
27. *PSZ*, xx, 476, no. 14552, 24 Dec. 1776.
28. *PSZ*, xx, 520–1, no. 14607, 24 April 177; also quoted in B. Nolde, *La Formation de l'Empire Russe. Etudes, Notes, Documents* (Paris 1952–3), II, 347; A. N. Fadeyev, *Rossia i Kavkaz pervoy treti XIX v.* (Moscow 1960), p. 37.
29. Quoted in G. G. Pisarevsky, *Khozyaystvo i forma zemlevladeniya v koloniyakh Povolzh'ya v XVIII i 1-oy ½-e XIX v.* (Rostov na Donu 1916), 54–5. The comment on Armenians and Greeks refers according to Pisarevsky to the Crimean Christians: cp. below, p. 130. On Catherine's and Potemkin's use of Jewish settlers in the south, see above, p. 86.
30. *PSZ*, xx, 757–9, no. 14814, 27 Oct. 1778. This decree also proposed the Russian peasantry as models for the unsuccessful colonists. Cp. also Pisarevsky, *Khozyaystvo i forma zemlevladeniya*, 54–5.
31. Nolde, *La Formation*, II, 348–9.
32. *PSZ*, xx, 374–5, no. 14464, 5 May 1776; Fadeyev, *Rossia i Kavkaz*, 37–8. For the Volga Cossacks, the move was a punishment for their part in the Pugachev rising. In general, the ripples of the revolt which spread south and westwards were a factor in the adoption of consolidating measures in New Russia, which will be mentioned in the next section.
33. Fadeyev, *Rossia i Kavkaz*, 38; id., *Ocherki ekonomicheskogo razvitiya stepnogo Predkavkaz'ya v doreformennyy period* (Moscow 1957), 31.
34. *PSZ*, xxi, 784, no. 15619, 22 Dec. 1782.
35. *PSZ*, xxii, 270–1, nos. 16113, 16114, 17 and 18 Dec. 1785; xxiii, 807–9, no. 17398, 11 Oct. 1795; xl, Appendix, 41, no. 21779a, 3 June 1805; S. Maksimov, 'Ocherk russkikh pereseleniy', *Morskoy Sbornik*, liv, no. 8 (1861), 217–20. This was in fact an extension of a decree of 1781 which allowed 'economic' peasants to settle in New Russia.
36. *PSZ*, nos. 16614, 17398.
37. Dubrovin, 'Brat'ya Potemkiny na Kavkaze', *Russkiy Vestnik*, cxxxix (April 1879), 862–6; *PSZ*, xxii, 388–92, nos. 16193, 16194, 5 and 9 May 1785.
38. Ibid., 358–84, no. 16187, 21 April 1785.

39. Ibid., 428–9, no. 16226.
40. G. G. Pisarevsky, *Iz istorii inostrannoy kolonizatsii v Rossii v XVIII v.* (Moscow 1909), 264.
41. Ibid., 264ff; cp. below, p. 127.
42. Cp. P. S. Pallas, *Travels through the Southern Provinces of the Russian Empire in the years 1793 and 1794* (London 1802–3), I, 320, 325, 332–3; Plate XI; and II, Appendix, Map II.
43. *PSZ*, XXIII, 536–9, no. 17230, 1 July 1794. The exact numbers given here are *remeslennikov i khlebopashtsev* 74 families, 184 male and 164 female souls. Most men were apparently labourers in the Saratov colonies. Cp. also Pisarevsky, *Khozyaystvo i forma zemlevladeniya*, 59–60.
44. *PSZ*, XXI, 1,013–17, no. 15835, 1783.
45. Dubrovin, 'Brat'ya Potemkiny na Kavkaze', *passim*; Ioannisyan, *Rossia i armyanskoye*, 189–94.
46. Cp. below, p. 140.
47. *PSZ*, XXIV, 761, no. 19189, 7 Oct. 1797. The number of those wishing to emigrate is given as 11,000 families; the actual figure was probably some 500 families. Cp. Fadeyev, *Ocherki ekon. razvitiya*, 44, further *PSZ*, XXV, 619–20, no. 18935, 15 April 1799. Some of the emigrants received permission to settle in Astrakhan and Kizlyar: *PSZ*, XXIV, 601, no. 17947, 1 May 1797.
  The new town was founded close to the site of the former German colony. The settlement of the Kuma region, and particularly the environs of the ancient ruins of Madzhary, had had many advocates. Tatishchev suggested it in 1744; in 1763 some Nekrasovtsy (Old Believer Cossacks living in Polish and Turkish territory) sought permission to settle there, but were directed to choose instead from lands listed in the immigration register (*SA*, XII, 239–41, report and Senate resolution of 28 Oct. 1763). Several of the Academicians writing under Catherine recommended settlement (S. G. Gmelin, *Reise durch Russland zur Untersuchung der drey Naturreiche* (SPb 1770–4), IV, 22–4 and note). The silk-inspector and naturalist von Bieberstein also saw opportunities there, and was late enough (1799) to comment on the Armenian settlement, for which he predicted the same role on the Kuma as that played by Kizlyar on the Terek (TsGIAL f. 398, op. 81, d. 1291, l. 86, part of report of Feb. 1799, Primechaniya o sostoyanii domovodstva na Kavkazskoy Linii voobshche, a osoblivo o tamoshnikh vinogradnykh sadakh). In fact Holy Cross itself never acquired great size or importance, although Armenians and Georgians in the Kuma and Terek area at large made a notable contribution to economic development. Fadeyev, *Ocherki ekon. razvitiya*, 44.
48. Fadeyev, *Rossia i Kavkaz*, 38–9.
49. A. Bennigsen, 'Un mouvement populaire au Caucase au XVIII siècle. La "Guerre Sainte" du *sheikh* Mansur (1785–91), page mal connu et controverseé des relations russo-turques', *Cahiers du Monde Russe et Soviétique*, V (1964), no. 2, 159–205.
50. Fadeyev, *Ocherki ekonomicheskogo razvitiya*, 34.
51. Cp. above, p. 118, n. 27.
52. Auerbach, *Die Besiedelung*, 62–70.
53. *PSZ*, XX, 53–5, no. 14251, 14 Feb. 1775; 190–3, no. 14354, 5 Aug. 1775; Auerbach, *Die Besiedelung*, 55–62.
54. Druzhinina, *Severnoye Prichernomor'ye*, 67–8.
55. *PSZ*, XX, 101–4 (first sequence), no. 14284, 28 March 1775; S. Safonov,

'Ostatki grecheskikh legionov v Rossii, ili nyneshneye naseleniye Balaklavy', *ZOO*, 1 (1844), 205–17; cp. below, p. 130.

56. A. A. Sergeyev, 'Nogaytsy na Molochnykh Vodakh (1790–1832)', *Izvestiya Tavricheskoy Uchonoy Arkhivnoy Komissii* 48 (Simferopol 1912), 11–14. One source shows 12,000 at this time, and probably many more followed. Lepekhin assessed their numbers in 1774 at not less than 30,000 (ibid.). Further on the Nogay see below, p. 139.

57. *Sbornik voyenno-istoricheskikh materialov*, izd. N. Dubrovin, vypusk VI (SPb 1893), Bumagi Potemkina, 119–20.

58. *SIRIO*, XXVII, 275; *PSZ*, XXII, 438–40, no. 16239, 13 Aug. 1785; Druzhinina, *Severnoye Prichernomor'ye*, 145–6.

59. A. A. Skal'kovsky, *Khronologicheskoye Obozreniye Istorii Novorossiyskogo Kraya, 1730–1823*, 1 (Odessa 1836), 142–3.

60. *PSZ*, XXII, 280, no. 16130, 14 Jan. 1785; cp. XXII, 324, no. 16167, 18 March 1785.

61. Details of these and other elements in Druzhinina, *Severnoye Prichernomor'ye*, 121–9.

62. Cp. above, p. 116.

63. Fedosy Makar'yevskiy, *Materialy dlya statisticheskogo opisaniya Yekaterinoslavskoy yeparkhii. Tserkvi i prikhody XVIII st.*, vypusk 2 (Yekat-slav 1880), 336; TsGADA f. 248, op. 58, d. 4338, ll. 437–99; TsGADA, Gosarkhiv, razryad XVI, op. 1, d. 796, chast' vii, ll. 58–9.

64. *ZOO*, XV (1889), 607–8; Skal'kovsky, *Khronologicheskoye Obozreniye*, I, 174–9.

65. Druzhinina, *Severnoye Prichernomor'ye*, 122–3.

66. *ZOO*, XII, ii (1881), 249–329, Potemkin to Kakhovsky, no. 264, 17 Aug. 1784.

67. TsGADA, Gosarkhiv, razryad XVI, d. 962, chast' ii, ll. 183–92.

68. D. Gray to Sir Robert Ainslie, British Ambassador in Constantinople, 24 June 1784, V. N. Aleksandrenko, *Russkiye diplomaticheskiye agenty v Londone v XVIII v.*, 2 vols (Warsaw 1897), II, 224–6. Other rejected applicants are mentioned by Pisarevsky, *Iz istorii*, 231–6.

69. Besides Klaus and Pisarevsky, Mennonite scholars have researched and written extensively on the Russian Mennonite settlements. Outstanding among recent writings are those of Dr D. G. Rempel: apart from works already quoted, see his 'From Danzig to Russia: The First Mennonite Migration', *Mennonite Life* 24 (1) (1969), 8–28. A new extensive non-Mennonite account is J. Urry, *The Closed and the Open: Social and Religious Change Amongst the Mennonites in Russia (1789–1889)*, unpublished D.Phil. dissertation (Oxford 1978).

70. On all these colonists cp. Druzhinina, *Severnoye Prichernomor'ye*, 68, 159–60, 164–6, 193; Pisarevsky, *Iz istorii*, 221–340. I have not used the documentary publications on the Swedish colony by A. Loit and N. Tiberg, *Gammalsvenskby-Dokument (Skrifter utgivna av kungl. Gustav Adolfs Akademien*, 31). (Uppsala–Copenhagen 1958) or the general account by J. Utas, *Svenskbyborna. Historia och öde fran trettonhundra till nu* (Stockholm 1959).

71. *AKV*, XI, 177–8, letter of 6/18 May 1801; cp. *AKV*, XIII, 101, and *Russkiy Arkhiv*, 1879, no. 1, 97–100, 'Iz pisem gr. S. R. Vorontsova k gr. A. A. Bezborodko', nos. 10 and 12; Auerbach, *Die Besiedelung*, 27–8. The traditional British system of transportation to America broke down in 1775 as a result of the revolution, and was finally stopped in 1788. Proper penal

colonies were established very soon after in Australia. A. E. Smith, *Colonists in Bondage. White Servitude and Convict Labour in America 1607–1776* (Chapel Hill 1947), 115, 123–4.

72. *AKV*, XI, 178.

73. *PSZ*, XXII, 50–1, no. 15935, 22 Feb. 1784. A petition (in French) from a Genoan merchant, Barthélemy Gallera, who responded and settled in Theodosia: *Arkhiv Grafov Mordvinovykh*, II (SPb 1901), 539.

74. D. Bagaley, 'Kolonizatsiya Novorossiyskogo Kraya i pervyye shagi yego po puti kul'tury', *Kievskaya Starina* XXV–XXVI (May–June 1889), 457.

75. *SIRIO*, XXVII, 257–8; Druzhinina, *Severnoye Prichernomor'ye*, 84.

76. Ibid., 165; Pisarevsky, *Iz istorii*, 289.

77. Amburger, *Die Anwerbung*, 132.

78. *SIRIO*, XXVII, 111; *PSZ*, XX, 404–5, no. 14494, 22 Aug. 1776. It is worth mentioning that this sum was paid from the revenues of the Chancellery of Guardianship of Foreigners. This was one of the rare occasions on which the Chancellery was involved in the financing of foreign settlement in the south, and reflects the fluid state of administration there at the time. A. G. Orlov, originally in charge of the establishment of the Greeks, was replaced before its completion by Potemkin. Subsequent immigration into New Russia was financed from the funds at the latter's disposal. The stated reason for using CGF funds now was that since, allegedly, the CGF had no further objects of expenditure following the cessation of recruitment abroad, the 'Albanians' were a worthy alternative. The allocation was paid regularly, switching to another source after 1782 (TsGIAL f. 383, op. 29, d. 176, l. 390b.).

79. TsGADA, Gosarkhiv, razryad XVI, d. 689, chast' 1, l. 181, Vedomost' o trebuyushcheysya na Albanskiye seleniya...summe. Ye. A. Zagorovsky, *Voyennaya kolonizatsiya Novorossii pri Potyomkine* (Odessa 1913), 31, gives an approximate total figure for 1776 of 1,300 males.

80. Zagorovsky, *Voyennaya kolonizatsiya Novorossii*, 33; Safonov, 'Ostatki Grecheskikh legionov', 220–1. The subsequent history of the Balaklava regiment was by no means as fine and heroic as Safonov suggests.

81. Pallas, *Travels*, I, 485. Pallas however was unimpressed by the qualities of these merchants.

82. Safonov, 'Ostatki Grecheskikh legionov', 209–14; TsGADA, Gosarkhiv, razryad XVI, op. 1, d. 689 (Potemkin papers), chast' 1, ll. 13–14. (Taganrog Greeks' petition to Potemkin, 1 Nov. 1783), l. 430b., 'Vedomost'...skol'ko grecheskoye kupecheskoye bratstvo v Taganroge kakikh stroyeniy iz sobstvennogo koshtu uchinilo i kapitalu denezhnogo imeyut', 7 June 1784; chast' 2, ll. 170–5, 'Spisok imyannoy sochinyonnoy v Taganrogskom Grecheskom Pravlenii o poselivshchikhsya grecheskikh kuptsakh...', 29 July 1783.

83. *PSZ*, XXIII, 724, no. 17348, 30 June 1795. On these and on all the Greek settlements in Southern Russia at this time, see also the Master's thesis of B. A. Karidis, *The Greek Communities in South Russia: Aspects of their Formation and Commercial Enterprise 1774–1829* (University of Birmingham 1976).

84. V. B. Barkhudaryan, *Istoriya novo-nakhichevanskoy armyanskoy kolonii (1779–1861 gg.)* (Yerevan 1967: in Armenian with Russian résumé).

85. F. Macler, 'Rapport sur une mission scientifique en Galicie et Boukhovine

(juillet–août 1925)', *Revue des Etudes Arméniennes*, VII, 1 (1927), 36–7. In 1784 404 Uniats lived together with 230 Greeks and 276 Armenians (named by religion): TsGADA, Gosarkhiv, razryad XVI, op. 1, d. 689, chast' 2, l. 116, 'Perechen' o chisle obitayemykh (sic) v Yekaterinoslave Khristiyan khozyayev s ikh semeystvami...', 10 May 1784.

86. M. Raeff, 'Der Stil der russischen Reichspolitik und Fürst G. A. Potemkin', *JbfGO*, N.F. 16 (1968), Heft 2, 169–70.

87. Skal'kovsky, *Khronologicheskoye Obozreniye*, I, 138.

88. Auerbach, *Die Besiedelung*, 82. This episode has been frequently described. The large document collection of N. Dubrovin, *Prisoyedineniye Kryma k Rossii* (SPb 1885) was not available to me. Apart from works already cited, see most recently M. Nersisyan, *Iz istorii russko-armyanskikh otnosheniy*, I (Yerevan 1956), 13–43; and the rather unsatisfactory analysis by A. Fisher, *The Russian Annexation of the Crimea, 1772–1783* (Cambridge 1970), 100–5. Lack of proper preparation by the Russian authorities, either for the journey or on the new site of settlement, inflicted extreme hardship and a high death toll on the migrants.

89. Bagaley, 'Kolonizatsiya Novorossiyskogo Kraya', 448.

90. Ibid., 448–9.

91. E. Bodemann, *Der Briefwechsel zwischen Kaiserin Katharina II von Russland und J. G. Zimmermann* (Hannover–Leipzig 1906), 20. D. C. Rempel, *The Mennonite Commonwealth in Russia*, 19–20, notes a suggestion that the Mennonites were intended particularly to develop dairy-farming.

92. Druzhinina, *Severnoye Prichernomor'ye*, 135–6.

93. Bodemann, *Der Briefwechsel*, 18–20; Amburger, *Die Anwerbung*, 130 and generally, 130–3.

94. *PSZ*, XXI, 993, no. 15814, 14 Aug. 1783; *SIRIO*, XXVII, 275; Druzhinina, *Severnoye Prichernomor'ye*. 137. Potemkin provided equally for his own personal estates in the south: cp. e.g. I. R. Christie, 'Samuel Bentham at Krichev', *SEER*, April 1970, 232–47.

95. *PSZ*, XXIII, 432–6, no. 17129, 30 May 1793; Druzhinina, *Severnoye Prichernomor'ye*, 231–9. On the Yamburg mill, cp. below, p. 175.

96. Ibid.

97. Ibid., 241–4.

98. Bodemann, *Der Briefwechsel*, 18–36.

99. TsGADA Gosarkhiv, razryad XVI, op. 1, d. 689, chast' 1, ll. 49, 55–6; excerpts in Russian translation from the original letter. Cp. also Bodeman, *Der Briefwechsel*.

100. Bagaley, 'Kolonizatsiya Novorossiyskogo Kraya', 452–6.

101. A. M. Fadeyev, *Vospominaniya 1790–1867 gg.*, I (Odessa 1897), 42.

102. *PSZ*, XXIII, 301, no. 17017. Kakhovsky's report is given in A. Skal'kovsky, 'Sravnitel'nyy vzglyad na Ochakovskuyu oblast' v 1790 i 1840 gg.', *ZOO*, I, iv (1844), 262–3.

103. *PSZ*, XXIII, 301–2, no. 17018, 26 Jan. 1792, esp. § 2.

104. *ZOO*, IX (1875), 319–31; TsGVIA f. VUA, d. 18336, ch. 1, ll. 9–196. The survey on which the 1792 figures are based covered most, but not all, of the region.

105. *PSZ*, XXIII, 356, no. 17068, 27 July 1792.

106. Ibid., 514, no. 17208, May 1794; Druzhinina, *Severnoye Prichernomor'ye*, 201.

107. *PSZ*, XXIII, 686–8, no. 17320.

108. Much material relating to the Greeks during and after the war is contained in *Arkhiv Grafov Mordinovykh*, 1 and 11.
109. De Ribas, of Spanish descent, and the effective founder of Odessa, was one of many foreigners who made a successful career in the administration of New Russia. In general, cp. *RBS*, vol. Reutern-Rolzberg (SPb 1913), 168–73. As Frenchmen were attracted to New Russia by the presence of Richelieu, whom we shall meet later, so De Ribas, who began his career in Italy, presided over an influx of Italians in the 1790s. V. F. Shishmaryov, 'Nauchnoye naslediye. Romanskiye poseleniya na yuge Rossii', *Trudy Arkhiva Akademii Nauk S.S.S.R.*, vypusk 26 (1975), 161.
110. *PSZ*, XXIII, 813–15, no. 17406, 14 Nov. 1795.
111. TsGIAL f. 383, op. 29, d. 176, O vosstanovlenii Grecheskogo Diviziona i ob otvode onomu zemli, 1801–10. Many decrees in *PSZ*.
112. *PSZ*, no. 17406.
113. Ibid.
114. *Istoricheskiy ocherk Odessy, k stoletnemu yubileyu so dnya zavoyevaniya* (Odessa 1889), 12–13. In 1797 this office was remodelled on the basis of those at Reval and Riga. A. Skal'kovsky, *Pervoye tridtsatiletiye Odessy 1793–1823* (Odessa 1837), 46–7, gives the *burgomistry* as Ivan Timoshenko and Fyodor Flogaiti.
115. Skal'kovsky, *Pervoye tridtsatiletiye*, 66. This coincided with the abolition of the Greek Division. Skal'kovsky takes further the colourful story of Kes-Oglu and the Magistrature for Foreigners.
116. *PSZ*, XXIII, 798–9, no. 17392, 2 Oct. 1795. A decree of 11 Oct. once again legalized state peasant migration to the south. It had originally been permitted in 1781 (cp. above, p. 120, n. 35); decrees of 1781, 1782 and 1787 allowed state peasants of all provinces except Orenburg, Irkutsk, Tobolsk, to go at their own wish to the Caucasus, Saratov and Yekaterinoslav Viceroyalties (in their then form), and to the Crimea. This was stopped in 1788 after the outbreak of war, and migration permitted only to Saratov, 'as being an interior Province'. *PSZ*, XXIII, 807–9, no. 17398, 11 Oct. 1795.
117. *PSZ*, no. 17392, 801–3.
118. *PSZ*, XXIII, 301–2, no. 17018, 26 Jan. 1792, § 4.
119. Pisarevsky, *Iz istorii*, 338–9; M. Popruzhenko, 'Iz materialov po istorii slavyanskoy kolonizatsii v Rossii', *ZOO*, XXVIII (1910), ii, materialy, 1–2.
120. *PSZ*, XXIII, 324, no. 17039, 27 April 1792; TsGIAL f. 383, op. 29, d. 159, 1797 report from New Russian Kazyonnaya Palata on colonists in general, ll. 23, 25–6, data on the Turks.
121. Mrs M. Guthrie, *A Tour, performed in the years 1795–6, through the Taurida, or Crimea...* (London 1802), 10.
122. *PSZ*, XXV, 920, no. 19929, 24 Dec. 1799.
123. Cp. above, p. 124.
124. Sergeyev, 'Nogaytsy', 14–16.
125. Ibid., 16.
126. Ibid., 16–20.
127. Ibid.
128. Zh. A. Ananyan, *Armyanskaya Koloniya Grigoriopol'* (Yerevan 1969) gives a detailed history. Cp. Druzhinina, *Severnoye Prichernomor'ye*, 199–201. In the last five years of Catherine's reign individual Armenian groups and families came in continuously to New Russia, and were placed in Nakhichevan as well as Grigoriopol. Similar Greeks were settled

in Mariupol. Skal'kovsky, *Khronologicheskoye Obozreniye Istorii Novo-rossiyskogo Kraya*, 1 (Odessa 1850), 226; Zagorovsky, 'Inostrannaya kolonizatsiya', 117.

129. D. G. Rempel, 'The Mennonite Commonwealth in Russia. A Sketch of its Founding and Endurance 1789–1919', *Mennonite Quarterly Review*, XLVII (October 1973), and XLVIII (January 1974), offprint, 40.
130. *PSZ*, XXIII, 454, no. 17147, 17 Aug. 1793.
131. Cp. below, p. 184.
132. *PSZ*, XXIII, 500–4, no. 17191, 25 March 1794.
133. Zagorovsky, 'Inostrannaya kolonizatsiya', 116.
134. TsGADA, Gosarkhiv, razryad XVI, op. 1, d. 689, chast' 2, l. 277; Zh. Ananyan, 'K voprosu o zaselenii yuga Rossii Armyanami vo 2-oy ½-e XVIII v.', *Izvestiya A. N. Armyanskoy S.S.R. (obshchestvennyye nauki)* (1963), no. 5, 46, note 7.
135. V. Yastrebov, 'Greki v Yelizavetgrade 1754–77', *Kievskaya Starina*, VIII (April 1884), 674–80.
136. *PSZ*, XXIV, 614, no. 17967, 20 May 1797.
137. *PSZ*, XXIII, 500–4, no. 17191, 25 March 1794; XXV, 619–20, no. 18935, 15 April 1799.
138. Cp. above, pp. 42, 97 and below, pp. 165, 192.
139. Druzhinina, *Severnoye Prichernomor'ye*, 160; Kabuzan, *Zaseleniye Novorossii*, 5, 14. V. Zagoruyko, *Po stranitsam istorii Odessy i Odesshchiny*, 1 (Odessa 1957), 60–1.

5. Urban and entrepreneurial settlement under the 1763 Manifesto

1. *PSZ*, VII, 167–74, no. 4378, 3 Dec. 1723.
2. *PSZ*, XX, 84, no. 14275, § 11, 13 March 1775.
3. D. Baburin, *Ocherki po istorii Manufaktur-Kollegii* (Moscow 1939), 147–69.
4. P. G. Lyubomirov, *Ocherki po istorii russkoy promyshlennosti* (Moscow–Leningrad 1947), 22, note 1. This division continued beyond the years discussed by Lyubomirov.
5. Cf. the case of the Saxon tapestry-maker Lehmann, set out at length in *PSZ*, XV, 247–50, no. 10868, 30 July 1758.
6. For a brief overview see E. Amburger, 'Der fremde Unternehmer in Russland bis zur Oktoberrevolution im J. 1917', *Tradition: Zeitschrift für Firmengeschichte und Unternehmerbiographie*, 4 (1957), 337–56.
7. N. N. Dmitriyev, 'Pervyye russkiye sitsenabivnyye manufaktury XVIII v.', *Izvestiya Gos. Akademii Istorii Material'noy Kul'tury*, no. 116 (1935), *passim*.
8. Cp. below, p. 178.
9. *PSZ*, XV, 215, no. 10845, 5 June 1758; XVI, 25–6, no. 11622, 19 July 1762; ORGPB, f. 741 (Stolpyansky), op. 1, no. 20, 'Peterburg Petra – Vasil'yevskiy Ostrov', chapter 11 (typescript), ll. 7–12.
10. *SIRIO*, XLVIII, 509, no. 545.
11. Cp. above, p. 67.
12. TsGADA f. 248, kn. 3622, l. 171, report from Orlov to HIH, approved 20 Aug. 1764.
13. *SIRIO*, LI, 459, no. 993.
14. Cp. *Nakaz Imp. Yekateriny II*, 89, § 314; K. Lodyzhensky, *Istoriya russkogo tamozhennogo tarifa* (SPb 1886), 107 and note.

304   *Notes to pages 146–151*

15. TsGADA f. 277, op. 10, d. 598, ll. 57–63, draft memorandum from College of Manufactures to College of Foreign Affairs, 1764.
16. TsGADA f. 277, op. 10, d. 3, ll. 21–7, College of Manufactures memorandum, 12 Sept. 1763. There is no record of any further developments. Cp. Catherine's negative comments on a proposal for a new playing-card factory put forward by Teplov 'who is demanding exclusive rights, which the Senate advises should be given, on the pretext of establishing a new branch [of industry]...*Chteniya* (1863), no. 2, 143–4, Catherine to Panin, n.d.
17. Cp. above, pp. 77, 93, and pp. 175–7.
18. Under Alexander I the practice of granting separate corporate organization was extended to German artisans who formed colonies in Odessa, Poltava, and Taganrog and elsewhere. Cp. below, p. 212.
19. Principal sources for the following: A. I. Gaysinovich, 'Tsekhi v Rossii v XVIII v.', *Izvestiya AN SSSR, otd. obshchestv. nauk* (1931) no. 5, 523–68; K. Pazhitnov, *Problema remeslennykh tsekhov v zakonodatel'stve russkogo absolyutizma* (Moscow 1952), 39–103; F. Polyansky, *Gorodskoye remeslo i manufaktura v Rossii v XVIII v.* (Moscow 1960), chapter 3.
20. *PSZ*, xv, 767, no. 11308, 10 Aug. 1761; Pazhitnov, *Problema*, 61.
21. Gaysinovich, 'Tsekhi', 531–2.
22. *SIRIO*, xvii, 219; J. Georgi, *Versuch einer Beschreibung der russischen kayserlichen Residenzstadt Sanktpeterburg...*(SPb 1790–Riga 1793), 189–90; Pazhitnov, *Problema*, 59–75.
23. *PSZ*, xv, 574–5, no. 11158, 7 Dec. 1760.
24. Cp. *SIRIO*, xliii, 250–2 (*Glavnyy Magistrat*); cvii, 219, § 21 (inhabitants of Petersburg).
25. V. A. Khachaturyan, 'Naseleniye armyanskoy kolonii v Astrakhani vo 2-oy ½-e XVIII v.', *Izvestiya A. N. Armyanskoy S.S.R. (obshchestvennyye nauki)* (1965), no. 7, 78–81.
26. Cp. V. A. Khachaturyan, 'Administrativno-pravovoye polozheniye astrakhanskikh armyan vo 2-oy ½-e XVIII v.', *Izvestiya A. N. Armyanskoy SSR (obshchestvennyye nauki)* (1963), no. 12, 57–68; A. I. Yukht, 'Pravovoye polozheniye astrakhanskikh armyan v 1-oy ½-e XVIII v.', *Izvestiya A. N. Armyanskoy SSR (obshchestvennyye nauki)* (1960), no. 12, 47–60. For a concise over-view of the colony's history, see V. A. Khachaturyan, 'Poseleniye v Astrakhani', *Literaturnaya Armeniya* (1972), no. 4, 92–7.
27. Yukht, 'Pravovoye polozheniye', 51–3.
28. *Opisaniye Koly i Astrakhani. Iz sochineniy akademika N. Ozeretskovskogo* (SPb 1804), 127–9; cp. further A. I. Yukht, 'Indiyskaya koloniya Astrakhani', *Voprosy Istorii* (1957), no. 3, 135–43.
29. Khachaturyan, 'Naseleniye armyanskoy kolonii Astrakhani', 78–9.
30. In 1758 and 1760 new companies were formed for the Caspian and Persian trade: *PSZ*, xv, 216–27, no. 10848, 15 June 1758; xv, 455–63, no. 11046, 30 March 1760. The former, the Persian Trade Company, contributed to the growth of Astrakhan Armenian commerce in Petersburg: ORGPB, f. 741 (Stolpyansky), op. 1, no. 20, ll. 14–17. Cp. also *PSZ*, xvi, 31–8, no. 11630, 31 July 1762; 291–3, no. 11857, 10 June 1763.
31. *PSZ*, xv, 389–90, no. 11009, 10 Nov. 1759; xvi, 287–9, no. 11853, 9 June 1763; xl, Appendix, p. 4, no. 13139a, 30 June 1768.
32. *PSZ*, no. 11853.
33. *PSZ*, xvii, 7–9, no. 12307, 13 Jan. 1765.

34. Khachaturyan, 'Naseleniye armyanskoy kolonii Astrakhani', 79; cp. above, p. 18.
35. Khachaturyan, 'Naseleniye armyanskoy kolonii Astrakhani', 83–4; Lyubomirov, *Ocherki*, 620.
36. Gaysinovich, 'Tsekhi', 545–6; further on Astrakhan textiles, cp. Lyubomirov, *Ocherki*, 633–59; A. Yukht, 'Armyanskiye remeslenniki v Astrakhani v 1-oy ½-e XVIII v.', *Izvestiya A. N. Armyanskoy SSR (obshchestvennyye nauki)* (1958), no. 1, 37–54.
37. Khachaturyan, 'Naseleniye armyanskoy kolonii Astrakhani', 86.
38. Khachaturyan, 'Naseleniye armyanskoy kolonii Astrakhani', 86–7. Cp. above, p. 117.
39. A. R. Ioannisyan, 'Armyanskoye natsional'no-osvoboditel'noye dvizheniye v 60-kh gg. XVIII v.', *Izvestiya A. N. SSSR (Istoriya i filosofiya)*, III (1946), no. 2, 141–2.
40. Ibid., 143–4. A first-hand account is to be found in D. M. Lang, 'Count Todtleben's expedition to Georgia 1769–71, according to a French eyewitness', *Bulletin of the School of Oriental and African Studies*, London, 13 (1949–50), 878–907.
41. *PSZ*, XVI, 387, no. 11937, 25 Sept. 1763.
42. TsGADA f. 248, kn. 3398, ll. 481a–491, d. 19, O vydache...Sarafovu... deneg 15,000 rubley.
43. TsGADA f. 16, d. 351, l. 199, memorandum from G. G. Orlov, 14 Oct. 1769.
44. *Russkiy Arkhiv* (1908), no. 7, 340.
45. *PSZ*, XVIII, 1,019, no. 13384, 17 Nov. 1769.
46. TsGADA f. 248, kn. 3762, ll. 562a–649, d. 17, Po donosheniyu kants. opekunstva inostrannykh o udovol'stvovanii...Astrakhanskogo sholkovogo zavoda soderzhatelya Moiseya Sarafova...23 Sept. 1769. Details of what appears to have been the crisis in Orlov-Davydov, see note 44.
47. *PSZ*, no. 13384.
48. Cp. *PSZ*, XVI, 786–90, no. 12174, 5 June 1764.
49. Cp. further Khachaturyan, 'Administrativno-pravovoye polozheniye', 59–60, and above, p. 71.
50. *MIRF*, XI, 749, Admiralty College Minutes, 26 Oct. 1771.
51. P. A. Shafranov, 'Otzyv o knige G. G. Pisarevskogo "Iz istorii inostrannoy kolonizatsii v Rossii v XVIII v." ', *Chteniya* (1909), no. 4, Smes', 33.
52. *Russkiy Arkhiv* (1908), no. 7, 340.
53. E. Kusheva, 'Saratov v tretey chetverti XVIII v.', *Trudy Nizhne-Volzhskogo Oblastnogo Nauchnogo Obshchestva Krayevedeniya*, vypusk 35, chast' 2 (Saratov 1928), 32.
54. *PSZ*, XVI, 968–9, no. 12284, 17 Nov. 1764.
55. 'Zapiski Puteshestviya akad. Fal'ka', *Polnoye Sobraniye Uchonykh Puteshestviy po Rossii*, 115.
56. Ibid., 115; A. Chernov, 'Iz istorii shelkovodstva v Rossii', *Krasnyy Arkhiv*, CVI (1941), 89; A. Leopol'dov, *Statisticheskoye Opisaniye Saratovskoy Gubernii*, I (SPb 1839), 146–8.
57. According to V. G. Orlov, *Russkiy Arkhiv* (1908), no. 7, 329.
58. Shafranov, 'Otzyv', 30–1; Kusheva, 'Saratov', 32.
59. Shafranov, 'Otzyv', 33. This is a more reliable figure than Züge's, below.
60. Kusheva, 'Saratov', 32.
61. Züge, *Der russische Colonist oder Christian Gottlob Züges Leben in Russ-*

306 *Notes to pages 157–160*

land. *Nebst einer Schilderung der Sitten und Gebräuche der Russen, vornehmlich in den asiatischen Provinzen* (Zeitz und Naumburg 1802–3), I, 173–6.

62. Kusheva, 'Saratov', 33; TsGADA f. 248, kn. 4076, ll. 4020b–4030b.: Senate hearing on old debts due to the Chancellery, 1781. The latter was still trying to extract the 500 roubles from the heirs of the Russian partners, deceased.

63. *PSZ*, XVI, 492, no. 12010, 13 Jan. 1764.

64. *PSZ*, XVII, 16–17, no. 12321, 29 Jan. 1765; XXIV, 794, no. 18240, 8 Nov. 1797; M. Chulkov, *Istoricheskoye Opisaniye Rossiyskoy Kommertsii...* (Moscow 1781–88), VI, iii, 659; A. Chernov, 'Iz istorii shelkovodstva v Rossii', *Krasnyy Arkhiv*, CVI (1941), 89.

65. *Voltaire's Correspondence*, LXXVII, 186–7, no. 15829, Voltaire to Catherine, 22 Dec. N.S. 1770 (Bestermann's note 4, suggesting that this is the first reference to the factory, seems to conflict with Catherine's mention of it in no. 15798, 155); LXXVIII, 51, no. 15954, same to same, 22 Jan. NS, 1771; 166, no. 16049, Catherine to Voltaire, 3 March 1771.

66. Züge, *Der russische Colonist*, II, 49–51, describes Orlov's superficial examination of Vorsprecher's factory, where the bad state of affairs had been covered up.

67. *Russkiy Arkhiv* (1908), no. 7, 330.

68. Shafranov, 'Otzyv', 33.

69. A footnote states that the figure 14 is taken from Georgi's account (1793); Greek and Turkish were not yet in use in Schlözer's time.

70. Schlözer, *Leben*, 172–5.

71. Diderot, *Mémoires pour Catherine II*, 180.

72. *PSZ*, XVI, 708–9, no. 12128, 13 April 1764.

73. Cp. K. von Stählin, *Aus den Papieren Jacob v. Stählins. Ein biographischer Beitrag zur deutsch–russischen Kulturgeschichte des 18ten Jahrhunderts* (Könisberg–Berlin 1926), 43–4.

74. *Istoricheskoye, geograficheskoye i topograficheskoye opisaniye Sanktpeterburga...sochinyonnoye g. Bogdanovym...a nyne dopolnennoye i izdannoye...Vasil'yem Rubanom. Izdaniye pervoye* (SPb 1779), 150, 164–5; P. Stolpyansky, *Peterburg, kak voznik, osnovalsya i ros Sankt-Piterburkh* (Petrograd 1918), 145.

75. J. G. Georgi, *Versuch einer Beschreibung der russisch-kayserlichen Residenzstadt Sanktpeterburg und der Merkwürdigkeiten der Gegend* (SPb 1790, Riga 1793), 191; cp. comments of H. Storch, *The Picture of St. Petersburg* (London 1801), 277–9.

76. G. Vinsky, *Moyo Vremya* (SPb 1914), 66–7.

77. *Grobovshchik*, the third of the Tales of Belkin. Among other literary portraits (apart from numerous Western tutors), cp. Gogol's *Revizor* – the German doctor – various artisans in the same author's Petersburg tales, and Leskov's *Ostrovityane* – a Petersburg artisan family.

78. C. Müller, *St. Petersburg, ein Beitrag zur Geschichte unsrer Zeit in Briefen aus den Jahren 1810, 1811 und 1812* (Mainz 1813), 100–1. Müller also speaks, however, of Russian 'hatred' of foreigners, 70–1.

79. Ibid., 266.

80. *PSZ*, XXXI, 53–60, no. 24116, § x (6), 2 Feb. 1810; *Zhurnal Komiteta Ministrov, 1801–20*, II (SPb 1891), 77, minutes of 4 August 1810. The tax was lightened in 1818.

81. F. Polyansky, *Gorodskoye remeslo*, 142.
82. TsGADA f. 248, kn. 3622, ll. 127–8, Chancellery memorandum to the Senate, 27 July 1764.
83. Ibid., ll. 130, 138–9, Senate minutes of 28 July, 1 Nov. 1764.
84. *PSZ*, xvi, 999–1,000, no. 12290.
85. *PSZ*, xviii, 336–41, no. 12967, 22 Aug. 1767; xvi, 907–10, no. 12242, 15 Sept. 1764.
86. TsGADA f. 248, kn. 3398, ll. 188, Senate resolution of 25 June 1763, 233–4, list of immigrants and costs.
87. Ibid., and f. 283, d. 14, l. 25, excerpt from Chancellery minutes of 17 Nov. 1770.
88. TsGADA f. 283, d. 79, O dache inostrantsu Andreyu Klode Zon'ye dlya svobodnogo v Sanktpeterburge zhit'ya pashporta, 10 Oct. 1766.
89. TsGADA f. 283, d. 29, l. 16, Chancellery minutes 27 July 1765.
90. Ibid., l. 15, passport; ll. 117–18; otherwise called Georg Gonsorovsky; promoted *sekund-mayor* 1773. Information from Professor E. Amburger.
91. Cp. above, p. 64, note 55; *RBS*, vol. Gerbersky-Gohenlohe (Moscow 1916), 43–6. G. G. Pisarevsky, *Iz istorii inostrannoy kolonizatsii v Rossii v XVIII v.* (Moscow 1909), Appendix, 47ff.
92. TsGADA f. 283, d. 29, passim: Chancellery papers and correspondence.
93. Ibid., d. 29, ll. 1–11, Tietzius' application to the Chancellery and ensuing correspondence, May 1764.
94. Ibid., ll. 76–7. Like Werdenhof, Ketscher was described as 'shvedskoy sluzhby'. A Christoff Ketscher, evidently his son, b. Stockholm 1757, d. Moscow 1829, also an instrument maker, worked in Moscow in the 1820s. He had numerous descendants in Russia. (Information from Professor E. Amburger.)
95. Cp. above, note 18 and below, p. 212.
96. TsGIAL f. 383, op. 29, d. 220, ll. 1210b.–124, memorandum 'O gorodskikh inostrannykh remeslennikakh', marked (l. 119) 'vysochayshe aprobovano – Genvarya 23 dnya 1809'.
97. TsGADA f. 1261, op. 1, d. 891, ll. 93–107, 'Vedomost' o sostoyashchikh v vedomstve Manufaktur Kontory fabrikakh...' (Jan. 1775). This document has recently been published by Ye. I. Indova, 'O rossiyskikh manufakturakh vtoroy poloviny XVIII v.', *Istoricheskaya Geografiya Rossii XII – nachalo XX v. Sb. statey k 70-letiyu prof. L. G. Beskrovnogo*, ed. A. L. Narochnitsky et al. (Moscow 1975), 326–45. Capital invested, shown in 74 cases, ranged from 195,875 roubles, 80,000 roubles, 75,430 roubles, down to 100 roubles. Of the 21 largest enterprises (over 10,000 roubles), 9 were foreign-owned; of the smallest 14 (less than 500 roubles), 4; 74 enterprises were situated in Petersburg itself.
98. Baburin, *Ocherki*, 149–50 and note.
99. Judging by their names, seven were French or German.
100. Cp. above, p. 51, note 94.
101. TsGADA f. 283, op. 1, d. 68, O byvshem v golshtinskoy sluzhbe artilerii maiore Iogane fongommele...; Indova, 'O rossiyskih manufakturah', 343. It will be recalled that the Crown estate of Ropsha had been given to the Orlov family. Von Gommel produced in 1767 1658 arshins of ribbon, of various grades, valued at 604 roubles 50 kopecks. But production stopped in 1768. Chulkov, *Istoricheskoye Opisaniye*, vi, iii, 665.

102. *SA*, xv, 210–13; TsGADA f. 248, kn. 3622, ll. 320–1, 'Proposal' by Orlov, confirmed by HIH, 19 Dec. 1765.
103. TsGADA f. 283, op. 1, d. 58, ll. 5, 9–90b, Chancellery summaries and decisions on the case, 16 May and 10 June 1765. Permission to distil vodka and brew beer for sale was refused.
104. TsGADA f. 277, op. 10, d. 349, ll. 2, 6–60b., copy of dispatch from Musin-Pushkin, Russian Minister in Hamburg, 2/13 March 1764, Office decision, 3 May 1764.
105. Shafranov, 'Otzyv', 32.
106. TsGADA f. 283, op. 1, d. 14, Po prosheniyu priyekhavshego syuda... inostrantsa Yagana Gottliba Otta..., ll. 2–23, Feb. 1764–Aug. 1765.
107. *PSZ*, xvii, 63–6, no. 12335, 24 Feb. 1765.
108. This man signed himself Bucher or Buchez; on the derivation of his name, however, see below, p. 171.
109. Shafranov, 'Otzyv', 31–3; *PSZ*, xvi, 494–5, no. 12013, 13 Jan. 1764.
110. Cp. above, p. 63, note 48; TsGADA f. 283, op. 1, d. 29, ll. 14, 85, Chancellery aide-memoires of 1764(?) and 1773 on Bois de Chêne. Ador came from Vuiteboeuf, Vaud. He died in St Petersburg in 1784. Information from Professor E. Amburger.
111. A rather careless transcription in Shafranov, 'Otzyv', 31–2; copies of the original in TsGADA f. 283, op. 1, d. 16, ll. 3–4; f. 277, op. 10, d. 476, ll. 25–260b.
112. Further on Ador's apprentices, TsGADA f. 283, op. 1, d. 31, O trebovanii ot voennoy kollegii dlya galantereynoy fabriki iz garnizonnoy shkoly shkol'nikov.
113. Chulkov, *Istoricheskoye Opisaniye*, vi, iii, 679.
114. TsGADA f. 283, op. 1, d. 16, l. 410b.
115. TsGADA f. 1261, op. 1, d. 891, Office of Manufactures *Vedomost'* (Jan. 1775), l. 1050b.
116. Information from Professor E. Amburger. No other *galantereynaya fabrika* appears in the Office of Manufactures list.
117. TsGADA f. 248, kn. 4076, ll. 280–93, Chancellery report to Senate, March 1781, and subsequent Senate minutes.
118. *PSZ*, xvi, 793–4, no. 12177, 8 June 1764. This explains why they, but none of the other entrepreneurs discussed, appear in the Office's statistical returns.
119. *PSZ*, no. 12013; TsGADA f. 283, op. 1, d. 16, l. 1–2; f. 277, op. 10, d. 476, ll. 19–200b., contracts with Fazy and Jurrine.
120. TsGADA f. 277, op. 10, d. 476, ll. 8, 33, 94: correspondence of the parties with the College of Manufactures; Indova, 'O rossiyskikh manufakturakh', 342.
121. Their entry and exit are recorded in Archives de la Bastille, Bibl. de la Ville de Paris, 12480 (entry of prisoners), f. 103–4, 7 Aug. NS, 1765, 12582 (releases), f. 104–5, 21 Dec. NS, 1765. Protocol of their interrogation: MAE CPR 78 (1765), ff. 253–5a. A list of those in Ferrier's party at his arrest, largely natives of Geneva like himself, is given (with incorrect dates) in V.-E. Veuclin, *L'Amitié Franco-Russe, Ses Origines: Le Génie Français et la Russie sous Catherine II* (Lisieux 1896), 6.
122. In another version Sandome and Basemir Brudel. Sando may have been of the Swiss family of Sandoz. Fazy is named Facius in some Chancellery documents, Ferrier as Franede Fermier. V. L. Chenakal, *Watchmakers and*

Clockmakers in Russia 1400 to 1850, Antiquarian Horological Monographs no. 6 (n.p. 1972), gives only Sando and Bazilier (*sic*) for the years 1774–7, Jean Fazy (Marc's brother: d. 476, l. 680b.) and a younger Ferrier, Jacob. One of M. Fazy's sons became secretary to John Paul Jones during the latter's Russian service; another reached the rank of general. Information from Professor E. Amburger.

123. According to inconsistent figures in Chulkov, *Istoricheskoye Opisaniye*, VI, iii, 678.
124. TsGADA f. 1261, op. 1, d. 891, l. 1050b.
125. *PSZ*, no. 12013.
126. Stolpyansky, *Peterburg*, 351–2.
127. Ibid.
128. *PSZ*, XVI, 176–94, no. 11777, 14 March 1763; W. Kirchner, *Commercial Relations Between Russia and Europe 1400–1800. Collected Essays*, Indiana Russian and East European Series, vol. 33 (Bloomington 1966), 186.
129. *PSZ*, XVII, 920, no. 12715, 4 Aug. 1766.
130. *PSZ*, XVIII, 92–104, no. 12878, 22 April 1767.
131. TsGADA f. 248, kn. 3622, ll. 694–5, report to HIH by G. Orlov, confirmed 18 March 1769.
132. TsGADA f. 283, op. 1, d. 137, ll. 52–6, general balance for year to 1 June 1770.
133. Ibid., d. 148, ll. 3, 9, 10, 29, reports from Boucher 1771–2.
134. Ibid., d. 148, ll. 26–ob., 40, 50, reports of Chancellery inspector F. Roggenbukke, May and June 1772.
135. Ibid., d. 137, l. 56. Evidently the customs-farmer N. Shemyakin. Cp. d. 148, l. 610b.
136. N. I. Grech, *Zapiski o moyey zhizni* (SPb 1886), 129–31.
137. V. E. Veuclin, *Les Lyonnais et la Russie au siècle dernier. Mémoire présenté au Congrès des Sociétés savantes à la Sorbonne en 1896* (Lyon 1896), 18.
138. *PSZ*, XVII, 63–6, no. 12335, 24 Feb. 1765; N. I. Pavlenko, *Istoriya Metallurgii v Rossii XVIII v.* (Moscow 1962), 210–11.
139. *PSZ*, no. 12335.
140. Veuclin, *Les Lyonnais et la Russie*, 19.
141. Ibid., 20; Archives de la Bastille, Bibl. de l'Arsénal, 12299, *passim*, esp. ff. 28–33, protocol of interrogation, 8 Aug. NS, 1766.
142. Appendix IV, p. 251. Cp. above, p. 162.
143. N. I. Pavlenko, *Istoriya metallurgii*, pp. 210–16.
144. Veuclin, *Les Lyonnais et la Russie*, 20–1. No source given; original in MAE CPR 91 (1773), ff. 30–1; 98–102a, Durand to d'Aiguillon, 29 Jan. 1773. The partners had also had negotiations with the Russian government over cannon production, and had even obtained French permission to hire a master cannon-founder in France, before the idea was dropped. See my article 'Scottish Cannon-Founders and the Russian Navy 1768–1785', *Oxford Slavonic Papers*, NS, X (1977), 55.
145. Pavlenko, *Istoriya metallurgii*, 211.
146. *PSZ*, XX, 738, no. 14782, 13 Aug. 1778.
147. Pavlenko, *Istoriya metallurgii*, 212–13.
148. Ibid.
149. Ya. Balagurov, *Olonetskiye gornyye zavody v doreformennyy period*

310   *Notes to pages 173–176*

(Petrozavodsk 1958), 93 note 2. Pavlenko, following Yartsov's contemporary account, says the debt was finally abandoned only in 1802.

150. Lyubomirov, *Ocherki*, 490–2.
151. Balagurov, *Olonetskiye gornyye zavody*, gives the 'someone else' as de Lozhegvil, 'probably de Longsevil'. Cp. K. Paustovsky, 'Sud'ba Shar'lza Longsevilya', *Sobr. Soch. v 8 tt.*, vi (Moscow 1969), 7–52. However, Longseville, a Bonapartist prisoner of war, only arrived in Petrozavodsk in 1810.
152. Balagurov, *Olonetskiye gornyye zavody*, 93; Pavlenko.
153. Pavlenko, *Istoriya metallurgii*, 212–13; *RBS*, vol. Faber-Tsyavlovsky (SPb 1901), 249, Aleksandr Andreyevich Fullon (1764–1844).
154. Cp. above, p. 93.
155. H. Storch, *Historisch-statistisches Gemaehlde des russischen Reichs* (Riga–Leipzig 1804–8), iii, 40–1.
156. *Novyy i polnyy geograficheskiy slovar' Rossiyskogo Gosudarstva* (Moscow 1788–9), vi, 269–70.
157. I. Pushkaryov, *Opisaniye Sanktpeterburga i uyezdnykh gorodov Sanktpeterburgskoy gubernii* (SPb 1839–41), iv, 84.
158. *Novyy i polnyy geog. slovar'*, 269–70.
159. l'Abbé Georgel, *Voyage à St.-Petersbourg en 1799–1800, fait avec l'Ambassade des Chevaliers de l'Ordre de Jean de Jerusalem...*(Paris 1818), 174–5.
160. Details from Professor E. Amburger.
161. AN, AE, B¹ 987, Corr. Cons. St Pétersbourg 1756–72, Rossignol to Praslin 10 March 1767. The official list of Petersburg enterprises cited by Chulkov from the 1770s shows production there of gold, silver and silk fringing by 'Pierre Joseph de Moutier' on 8 looms: Chulkov, *Istoricheskoye Opisaniye*, vi, iii, 700.
162. According to Storch, *Historisch-statistisches Gemaehlde*, iii, 256.
163. J. G. Georgi, *Geographisch-physikalische und naturhistorische Beschreibung des Russischen Reichs zur Uebersicht bisheriger Kenntnisse vom demselben*, ii (Königsberg 1797), i, 87.
164. Archives de la Bastille, Bibl. de l'Arsénal, 12299, ff. 133–133a, letter of 5 May 1767.
165. AN, AE, B¹ 988, Lesseps to Sartine, 4 Feb. and 15 April 1777.
166. AN, AE, B¹ 989, ff. 16–17, Lesseps to de Castries, 4 Jan. 1782.
167. Cp. above, p. 132; *PSZ*, xxi, 993, no. 15814, 14 Aug. 1783.
168. AN, AE, B¹ 989, ff. 148a–149, Lesseps to de Castries, 30 Sept. 1784.
169. B. J. F. Herrmann, *Statistische Schilderung von Russland in Rücksicht auf die Bevölkerung, Landesbeschaffenheit, Naturprodukte, Landwirtschaft, Bergbau, Manufakturen und Handel* (SPb–Leipzig 1790), 379, note, gives 'formerly 36 looms and over 600 workers'. Storch, *Historisch-statistisches Gemaehlde*, iii, 254, gives 40 looms and over 300 workers. There is some confusion from these sources and from Georgi's *Beschreibung des russ. Reichs* (above, note 163), since Georgi and Herrmann both refer to the mill as functioning, although their works appeared after 1789. The most probable explanation is that their data were collected before that date.
170. *Historisch-statistisches Gemaehlde*, iii, 39–42, 252–7.
171. Ibid., 253–4.
172. On Storch and his views see R. E. McGrew, 'Dilemmas of Development: Baron H. F. Storch (1766–1835) on the Growth of Imperial Russia', *JbfGO*, NF, 24 (1976), Hft. 1, 31–71.

173. *Historisch-statistisches Gemaehlde*, III, 254–6.
174. Chulkov, *Istoricheskoye*, VI, iii, 574. On the tapestry manufacture, its history, work-force native and foreign, and its products, see T. T. Korshunova, comp. and intro., *Russkiye Shpalery. Petersburgskaya Shpalernaya Manufaktura* (Leningrad 1975).
175. In 1788 Levallier's widow petitioned the Empress for payment of 43,386 roubles which she claimed were still unpaid from 47,445 roubles due to her husband in connection with the mill. A. Bychkov, ed., *Pis'ma i bumagi Imperatritsy Yekateriny II, khranyashchiyesya v Imperatorskoy Publichnoy Biblioteke* (SPb 1873), 57.
176. Storch, *Historisch-statistisches Gemaehlde*, III, 250–2, 257. Storch lists some other smaller producers of fine-quality fabrics.
177. Ibid., 255–6: 'eine nicht unwichtige Pflanzschule'.
178. Ibid., 256–7; further detail in Professor Amburger's forthcoming book on Ingermanland.
179. Storch, *Historisch-statistisches Gemaehlde*, III, 39.
180. The Chancellery carefully assured the financial position of these apprentices. The accounts to 1770 show 4,836 roubles 76 kopecks spent on food, clothing, and footwear for them: TsGADA f. 16, d. 351, l. 41. The slow progress of Ador's and Boucher's pupils has been mentioned. Baburin, *Ocherki*, 322–3, refers to the examination of Sando and Basselier's pupils by the Office of Manufactures. Further cp. Dmitriyev, 'Pervyye russkiye', 35–6, 98–100, 134.
181. The list of the Office of Manufactures already quoted gives three such new ventures in Petersburg for this period. These do not include Liemann's factory, for which permission was given in February 1763.
182. TsGADA f. 277, op. 10, d. 761, ll. 6–16, College of Manufactures summary of previous legislation. Further on Gardner, see Yu. Arbat, *Farforovyy Gorodok* (Moscow 1957).
183. *RBS*, vol. Aleksinsky-Bestuzhev (SPb 1900), 728. Cp. further E. Robinson, 'The Transference of British Technology to Russia: A Preliminary Survey', *Great Britain and Her World 1750–1914: Essays in Honour of W. O. Henderson* (Manchester 1975), 12–14.
184. *PSZ*, XXVII, 209–10, no. 20352.
185. Following the practice initiated by Gascoigne.
186. TsGADA f. 271, kn. 2648, ll. 445–76, d. 13, Po ukazu Prav. Senata, kakoe sostoyashchii sdes' inostrantsa Berda chugunyy liteynyy zavod imeyet ustroystvo...(Sept. 1802–Feb. 1806) (quotation l. 4750b.).
187. Ibid., ll. 4820b.–85; Cp. S. Strumilin, *Ocherki ekonomicheskoy istorii Rossii* (Moscow 1960), 433.
188. Gascoigne died in July 1806. Cp. *RBS*, vol. Gaag-Gerbel' (Moscow 1914), 258–9.
189. V. K. Yatsunsky, 'Rol' Peterburga v promyshlennom razvitii dorevolyutsionnoy Rossii', *Voprosy Istorii* (1954), no. 9, 99–101.
190. Quoted by Yatsunsky, ibid.
191. *RBS*, vol. Aleksinsky-Bestuzhev, 728; T. Tower, *A Memoir of the late Charles Baird, Esq., and of his Son Francis of St. Petersburg and 4 Queen's Gate, London* (London 1867), *passim*.
192. I am indebted for this information to S. G. Sakharova of the Leningrad State Historical Archive, and to Miss X. Howard-Johnston.

6. *Immigration and colonies, 1797–1804*

1. A. A. Velitsyn, 'Inostrannaya kolonizatsiya v Rossii', *Russkiy Vestnik* (1889), no. 3, 120.

2. *PSZ*, XXIV, 508–9, nos. 17865, 17866, 4 March 1797. The full Russian title was *Ekspeditsiya Gosudarstvennogo Khozyaystva, Opekunstva Inostrannykh i Sel'skogo Domovodstva.*

3. V. I. Veshnyakov, 'Ekspeditsiya Gosudarstvennogo Khozyaystva, 1797–1803', *Russkaya Starina*, CVIII (1901), 198.

4. *PSZ*, XXIV, 668–9, no. 18006, 20 June 1797, § 3, concerning Petersburg colonists.

5. Measures of the Board and other bodies at this time, e.g. *PSZ*, XXIV, 807–8, no. 18256, 27 Nov. 1797; XXV, 389–93, no. 18676, 24 Sept. 1798; 808–9, no. 19146, 10 Oct. 1799; XXVI, 512–14, no. 19735, 25 Jan. 1801.

6. *PSZ*, XXV, 64–8, no. 18373.

7. V. A. Zolotov, *Vneshnyaya torgovlya yuzhnoy Rossii v 1-oy ½-e XIX v.* (Rostov na Donu 1963), 137–40.

8. *PSZ*, XXIV, 614, no. 17967, 20 May 1797, § 2; XXVII, 25–7, no. 20121, 24 Jan. 1802.

9. *PSZ*, XXIV, 233–4, no. 17638, 12 Dec. 1796; Ye I. Druzhinina, *Severnoye Prichernomor'ye, 1775–1800* (Moscow 1959), 195–8.

10. *PSZ*, XXVI, 862–3, no. 20075, 12 Dec. 1801.

11. Cp. TsGIAL f. 1285, op. 1, d. 1, po pis'mu...podannomu inostrantsem Viznerom o zhelanii yego poselit'sya v Tavride (1798–9); cp. below, p. 185.

12. *PSZ*, XXV, 919, no. 19226, 21 Dec. 1799.

13. *SIRIO*, LIV, 201–8; Comte de Castres, *Relation d'un voyage sur le bord septentrional de la mer d'Azof et en Crimée dans la vue d'y établir une colonie d'émigrés* (Paris 1826), ii–iii; *Journal d'Emigration du Prince de Condé 1789–1795, publié par le Comte de Ribes* (Paris 1924), 355–9. The land involved was later re-allocated to the Nogay Tatars: A. Sergeyev, 'Nogaytsy na Molochnykh Vodakh, 1790–1832', *Izvestiya Tavricheskoy Uchonoy Arkhivnoy Kommissii* (1912), no. 48, 21.

14. de Castres, *Relation d'un voyage*, 347.

15. TsGIAL f. 383, op. 29, d. 160, ll. 2–3ob., report from Alopeus 28 Dec. 1797–8 Jan. 1798; l. 21ob., rescript to Alopeus 14 Jan. 1798.

16. Ibid., l. 21ob.

17. Ibid., l. 27, Board minutes of 10 March 1798.

18. Ibid., ll. 60–1ob, Alopeus to A. B. Kurakin, 12/23 April 1798.

19. Ibid., l. 90, same to same, 13/24 May 1798.

20. Ibid.

21. TsGIAL f. 398, op. 81, d. 95, 'po predstavleniyu Koll. Sovetnika Trappe v rassuzhdenii zhelaniya ego k vyzovu iz Shveytsarii znayushchikh razvodit' vinogradnyye sady i zemledel'tsov...' Trappe wrote from Yorkshire, England, where he was staying with friends. Scarcely had he been appointed when he had a stroke, which compelled him to retire. The Senate granted him a pension.

22. *PSZ*, XXXVI, 286–7, no. 19546, 6 Sept. 1800.

23. D. G. Rempel, 'The Mennonite Commonwealth in Russia. A Sketch of its Founding and Endurance 1789–1919', *Mennonite Quarterly Review*, XLVII (October 1973) and XLVIII (January 1974), offprint; G. G. Pisarevsky,

Pereseleniye prusskikh mennonitov v Rossiyu pri Aleksandre I (Rostov na Donu 1917), 1–40.

24. *PSZ*, xxiv, 815, no. 18263, 4 Dec. 1797.
25. TsGIAL f. 383, op. 29, d. 173, o vyshedshikh iz Shvabii v volynskuyu guberniyu dlya poseleniya v Rossii inostrantsakh...
26. K. Miller, *Frantsuzskaya emigratsiya v Rossii v tsarstvovaniye Yekateriny II* (Paris 1931), 363–6.
27. TsGIAL f. 383, op. 29, d. 160, ll. 60–10b, Alopeus to Kurakin, 12/23 April 1798.
28. Ibid., ll. 2–5, 46–58, 90, letters and enclosures from Alopeus, 28 Dec. 1797/ 8 Jan. 1798, 12/23 April, 13/24 June 1798.
29. Ibid., ll. 30–41, Alopeus' report of 18 Feb./1 March 1798; Siegfried's proposals and Board comments.
30. Ibid., ll. 40–2, 65–71, 78–89, 94–178, letters, reports, Board minutes, interdept. correspondence, March 1798–Jan. 1800.
31. In 1793, to escape from revolutionary France.
32. Theodosia.
33. de Castres, *Relation d'un voyage*, 308. Footnotes added.
34. Ibid., 309.
35. Ibid., 351–2; de Castres calls his informant Rouvier's nephew.
36. ORGPB f. 542, no. 446, ll. 9–120b., minutes of the Committee on the Establishment of the New Russian Province, 28 Dec. 1801.
37. Ibid.; cp. *PSZ*, xxvi, 102–3, no. 19347, 28 March 1800.
38. See below, p. 224.
39. A. A. Skal'kovsky, 'Tonkorunnoye ovtsevodstvo i torgovlya sherst'yu pri odesskom porte', *Trudy Odesskogo Statisticheskogo Komiteta*, no. 4, offprint (Odessa 1870), 10; further on Rouvier's sheep farming, see below, pp. 226–8.
40. *PSZ*, xxvi, 593–4, no. 19801, 22 March 1801; xxvii, 136–7, no. 20259, 9 May 1802; xxvii, 272 (actually 288)–290, no. 20449, 8 Oct. 1802.
41. ORGPB, f. 542, no. 229, l. 20b.
42. 'Mneniye Mordvinova o vyzove inostrantsev', *Arkhiv Grafov Mordvinovykh*, iii (SPb 1902), 178–82, no. 717; cp. above, p. 34.
43. Zolotov, *Vneshnyaya*, 136. For a general discussion of the background to government policy in this area, cp. N. K. Brzhevsky, *Ministerstvo Finansov 1802–1902* (SPb 1903), 126–9.
44. *PSZ*, xxvii, 143–4, no. 20270, 19 May 1802. 'Zapiski D. Mertvago', *Russkiy Arkhiv* (1867), no. 5, Appendix, 183ff.
45. ORGPB f. 542, no. 446, Dnevnyye zapiski komiteta o ustroyenii novorossiyskoy gubernii, 1801–2. The main archive of the committee is held in TsGIAL f. 1307.
46. ORGPB f. 542, no. 446, l. 670b., minutes of 11 March 1802.
47. Ibid.
48. A. A. Skal'kovsky, *Khronologicheskoye Obozreniye Istorii Novorossiyskogo Kraya*, ii (Odessa 1850), 42–4, 55 note.
49. ORGPB f. 542, no. 446, ll. 9–120b. On the Committee, and in general on the settlement and development of the S. Ukraine in the early nineteenth century, see Ye. I. Druzhinina, *Yuzhnaya Ukraina v 1800–1825 gg.* (Moscow 1970), especially 174–8.
50. A wide-ranging survey of foreign settlement in this period is given in 'Istoriya i statistika koloniy inostrannykh poselentsev v Rossii. II: Uchrezhdeniye novykh koloniy v tsarstvovaniye Imp. Aleksandra I.', *ZhMGI*, liii, ii

(October 1854), 1–34; see also the useful articles 'Fortschritte der Kolonisirung in Russland' in H. Storch, hrsg., *Russland unter Alexander I. Eine historische Zeitschrift*, 9 vols (SPb–Leipzig 1804–8), IV, 111–26, VII, 234–61.

51. See below, p. 205.
52. *PSZ*, XXVI, 805–7, no. 20035, 23 Oct. 1801.
53. They included Greeks, Bulgarians and *gagauzy*, Bulgarians who spoke a form of Turkish.
54. TsGIAL f. 383, op. 29, d. 190, l. 960b., Richelieu to Kockubey, 29 July 1803. On the Bulgarian colonies see particularly A. A. Skal'kovsky, *Bolgarskiye kolonii v Bessarabii i Novorossiyskom Kraye* (Odessa 1848) and the bibliographical introduction in I. I. Meshcheryuk, *Pereseleniye Bolgar v Yuzhnuyu Bessarabiyu 1828–1834 gg.* (Kishinyov 1965), 8–16.
55. Skal'kovsky, *Khron. Obozreniye*, II, 163–5; P. O. Morozov, 'Chernogorskiye Pereselentsy v Rossii 1803–1838', *Istoricheskiye Materialy iz Arkhiva Ministerstva Gosudarstvennykh Imushchestv*, red. V. I. Veshnyakov, vyp. I (SPb 1891), 54–107.
56. M. V. Jones, 'The Sad and Curious Story of Karass, 1802–1835', *Oxford Slavonic Papers, NS*, VIII (1975), 53–81.
57. 'Proyekt nadeleniya zemlyoy v g. Starom Kryme bratstva Les Frères de la Rédemption', *ZOO*, XXII (1900), Smes', 2–6; TsGIAL f. 383, op. 29, d. 180, Delo ob obshchestve les Frères de la Rédemption, iz'yavivshem zhelaniye chrez Grafa Lanskronskogo poselit'sya v Tavricheskoy gubernii (1802–3).
58. Skal'kovsky, *Khron. Obozreniye*, II, 75–6. The project, presented in 1804 by the Genoese brothers Lorovici (Lorovikhi), was to have been carried out in 1805. Genoese ship-owners settling in Odessa and becoming first-guild merchants or buying or building a house to the value of 300 roubles were to have a special patent and right to use the Russian flag (TsGIAL f. 383, op. 29, d. 217, l. 11 ob.–14, memo from Richelieu to Kochubey, 18 March 1804). Political developments forced the sudden departure from Genoa of the Russian College Counsellor Sankovsky, who was to have issued passports, and so stopped the project at the last moment: '1500 colonists and the vessels on which they were to reach Odessa, can no longer set out; so that they do not know what to do next' (d. 251, ll. 59 ob.–60, Richelieu to Kochubey, 13 April 1805). Sankovsky's replacement by State Counsellor Koronelli, already on his way to Italy (Ibid., note by Kochubey), failed to save the operation. See also V. F. Shishmaryov, 'Nauchnoye naslediye. Romanskiye poseleniya na yuge Rossii', *Trudy Arkhiva Akademii Nauk S.S.S.R.* vypusk 26 (1975), 161–2, 163 note 32. In 1806 the Committee of Ministers approved the recruitment of merchant seamen from Holland, Hamburg and Denmark for the Sea of Azov: *ZhKM*, I, 135, 10 April 1806.
59. Rempel, *The Mennonite Colonies*, 83–97, 101; Pisarevsky, *Pereseleniye mennonitov*, 1–59; A. Mueller, 'Die preussische Kolonisation in Nordpolen und Litauen (1795–1807) und die Mennoniten', *Zeitschrift für Ostforschung*, 22 (1973), 487–96.
60. Article by L. Weiss, in *Neue Zürcher Ztg.* (1931), no. 966, reprinted in A. Jenny und G. Jenny-Jenny, *Bilder von dem Leben u. Streben der Russland-Schweizer u. d. traurigen Ende ihrer Wirksamkeit*, NF (Glarus 1934), 84–8. The present summary draws on this and on TsGIAL f. 383, op. 29, dd. 194, 195, 243. W. Kirchner's statement, *Commercial Relations between Russia and Europe 1400–1800. Collected Essays*, Indiana Russian

and East European Series, vol. 33 (Bloomington 1966), 198–201, adds little that is new.

61. TsGIAL f. 383, op. 29, d. 190, ll. 1–3.
62. Ibid., l. 4, 30 Jan. In 1802 the Board of State Economy was subordinated to, and in 1803 it was incorporated in, the Ministry of the Interior. In the files on Ziegler the Board appears in a subordinate role, and the Minister's correspondence often did not reach it until some time after first receipt.
63. Ibid., l. 5, Vorontsov to Kochubey, 26 Feb. 1803.
64. Ibid., l. 200b., 1270b., Kochubey to Yakovlev, 1 June, Schurtter to Kochubey, 16/28 July 1803.
65. Ibid., l. 7, 14/26 May; ll. 17–18ob. 7/19 May.
66. Ibid., ll. 10–11, n.d.
67. Ibid., ll. 15–16, 92–30b. The Austrian florin, or guilder, of 60 Kreutzer (X.), was widely current in Germany. At this period, one rouble of exchange equalled nearly 3 florins.
68. Ibid., ll. 20–ob., 1 July.
69. Ibid., l. 21, Kochubey to Minister of Finance, 3 July. On 15 March 1804, one Imperial equalled 3.78 paper roubles (d. 220, l. 59).
70. Ibid., d. 190, ll. 26–ob., Kochubey to Vorontsov, 4 July.
71. Ibid., l. 32, Kochubey to Yakovlev, 4 July.
72. Ibid., ll. 27–8, Report from Kochubey, confirmed by HIH 19 July.
73. Ibid., ll. 37–40.
74. Ibid., l. 29, letter of 22 July.
75. Ibid., ll. 42–4, Kochubey to Yakovlev, 20 July.
76. Ibid., ll. 63–5.
77. Ibid., ll. 103–5, letter of 20 June/12 July.
78. Ibid., ll. 106–9, Anstedt to Vorontsov, 1/13 July.
79. Ibid., l. 112, Yakovlev to Kochubey, 12/24 Aug.; d. 205, ll. 44–5, 69–70, Richelieu and Contenius (on whom see below, p. 205) to Kochubey, 25 and 17 Oct.
80. Ibid., d. 190, ll. 82–5, Klüpfell to Anstedt, 5/17 July.
81. Ibid., ll. 80–1, Anstedt to Vorontsov, 15/27 July. Ratisbonne: French form for Regensburg.
82. Ibid., l. 127.
83. Ibid., ll. 130–1, letter 15 Aug.
84. Ibid., ll. 136–8, 175–7, Ziegler to Kochubey, 1/13 and 18/30 Aug.
85. Ibid., ll. 158–9; Prussian regulations, ll. 160–2.
86. Ibid., ll. 111–14, Yakovlev to Kochubey, 12/24 Aug.
87. Ibid., ll. 221–20b., same to same 23 Aug/3 Sept.
88. Ibid., ll. 125–ob.
89. Ibid., ll. 190–ob., Kochubey to Ziegler, Sept., n.d.
90. Ibid., ll. 193–5, Ziegler to Kochubey.
91. Ibid., ll. 221–20b., Yakovlev to Kochubey, 12/24 Aug.
92. Ibid., d. 205, ll. 118–19, Ziegler to Kochubey, 12/24 Oct.
93. Ibid., d. 190, ll. 112–226, *passim.*
94. Ibid., d. 205, ll. 118–19, Ziegler to Kochubey, 12/24 Oct.
95. Ibid., ll. 141–2.
96. Lists and figures from both Ziegler and Contenius, dd. 190, 205, *passim.* With deaths, births, flights, and new hopefuls joining on the way, numbers changed – some transports arrived more numerous than when they set out.

97. TsGIAL f. 383, op. 29, d. 190, ll. 221–20b., Yakovlev to Kochubey, 12/24 Oct.
98. Ibid., ll. 216, 229ob., Kochubey to Anstedt, 28 Sept., to Yakovlev, 23 Sept.
99. Ibid., d. 220, ll. 1–2.
100. Ibid., ll. 7–27; with slight variations, *PSZ*, xxviii, 137–40, no. 21163, 20 Feb. 1804.
101. Ibid., d. 212, ll. 14–15, Kochubey to Yakovlev, 19 April 1804.
102. Cp. *PSZ*, xxviii, 765–6, no. 21581, 31 Dec. 1804; Zh. A. Ananyan, *Armyanskaya Koloniya Grigoriopol'* (Yerevan 1969), 207–8. Purchase was the rule, even where the conditions of the original free grant were not met.
103. *PSZ*, xxviii, 154–5, no. 21177. It was drawn up in consultation with the Duc de Richelieu, who was in Petersburg during the winter. I. M. Lerner, 'Nemetskiye kolonii v Novorossiyskom Kraye', *Vedomosti Odesskogo Gradonachal'stva*, no. 236, 31 Oct. 1903, 3.
104. *PSZ*, xxviii, 177, no. 21192; cp. also above, p. 182.
105. TsGIAL f. 383, op. 29, d. 225; *PSZ*, xxviii, 260–1, no. 21254, 12 April 1804, in amplification of xxvii, 136–7, no. 20259, 9 May 1802.
106. Appendix vi.
107. TsGIAL f. 383, op. 29. d. 220, ll. 33–4, memorandum to Ziegler, 7 March.
108. Ibid., ll. 28–9, 37–43, Kochubey to Richelieu and to Contenius, 1 March, to Klüpffell, 8 March.
109. Ibid., ll. 64, 71, Kochubey to A. Czartorski (Deputy Foreign Minister), 31 March, 5 May.
110. *PSZ*, xxviii, 301–2, no. 21284, 7 April 1804.
111. TsGIAL f. 383, op. 29, d. 220, ll. 99–101, Board memorandum, confirmed by HIH, 20 March; ll. 102–6, dispatches to Lithuanian and Podolian governors, 4 June.
112. Ibid., ll. 76–7, 12/24 March 1804.
113. Ibid., ll. 80–1, letter of May, n.d.
114. Ibid., ll. 85–8, Klüpffell to Kochubey, 31 March/12 April 1804.
115. Ibid., d. 212, ll. 1–2, Otto to Kochubey, 8 Nov. 1803.
116. Ibid., ll. 4–5, 25 March, NS.
117. Ibid., ll. 12–130b., Yakovlev to Kochubey, 17/29 March; ll. 14–16, reply, 19 April.
118. Cp. C. Keller, *The German Colonies in South Russia 1804–1904*, I, trans. A. Becker (n.d. or pl. [Saskatoon, Sask., Canada, 1968]), 24–5.
119. TsGIAL f. 383, op. 29, d. 212, ll. 21–2, 37–8ob., Klüpffell to Kochubey, 28 April/10 May and 12/24 May; d. 239, l. 3, petition of 65 emigrant families (see p. 202).
120. Ibid., d. 212, ll. 26ob.–7: translated excerpt from Hamburg Gazette, no. 79, dateline Dillingen, 5 May, NS.
121. Ibid., ll. 21–2, Klüpffell to Kochubey, 28 April/10 May.
122. Ibid., ll. 37–ob., 58–ob., Klüpfell to Kochubey, 12/24 and 16/28 May.
123. Ibid., ll. 48–ob., Razumovsky to Czartoryski, 23 May/4 June.
124. Ibid., ll. 39–400b., Klüpffell to Kochubey, 12/24 May, to Czartoryski, 19/31 May.
125. Ibid., d. 239, ll. 1–140b., 20–1, 28–30, colonist petition, correspondence between Richelieu, Kochubey, Volhynian authorities.
126. Ibid., d. 212, ll. 51, 58–60, Klüpffell to Czartoryski, 19/31 May, to Kochubey, 16/28 May.
127. Ibid., ll. 51–2.

128. Ibid., ll. 510b.–53, 72–3, Klüpffell to Kochubey and Czartoryski, 19/31 May. Ulm, formerly a *Reichsstadt*, passed in 1803 to Bavaria, in 1810 (permanently) to Württemberg.

129. Ibid., ll. 61–7, 85–7, memo. from Kochubey, confirmed by HIH 11 June; Kochubey to Klüpffell, 15 June.

130. Ibid., ll. 92–8, Klüpfell to Kochubey and Czartoryski, 30 May/11 June.

131. Ibid., ll. 127–8, Kochubey to Czartoryski, 11 July.

132. Ibid., ll. 103, 129, Yakovlev to Kochubey, 30 June/12 July, 10/22 July.

133. Ibid., ll. 133–5: Note from Bavarian Amb. de Posch, 9/21 July; ll. 139–42, Kochubey to Czartoryski, 17 July; ll. 143–7, Kochubey to Klüpffell, 29 July.

134. Ibid., ll. 178–82, Klüpffell to Czartoryski, 11/23 July.

135. Ibid., l. 190, Klüpffell to Kochubey, 28 July/9 Aug.

136. Ibid., ll. 200–2, Klüpffell to Kochubey, 8/20 Sept., 223–7, same to same, 13/25 Oct.

137. Ibid., *passim*.

138. Ibid., d. 195, ll. 158–208, Ministry papers, including reports to HIH, copies of petitions from Escher.

139. Ibid., d. 212, ll. 219–20, Klüpffell to Kochubey, 10/22 Oct. 1804; d. 195, ll. 15–170b., Richelieu to Kochubey 9 May 1805, reply 22 May.

140. *PSZ*, xxiv, 641–3, nos. 18021, 18022; cp. 763, no. 18192, 8 Oct. 1797.

141. *PSZ*, xxvi, 115–28, no. 19372, 6 April 1800. The decree provides an extensive survey both of the history and of the then state of the colonies.

142. This was Contenius' own version. Public gossip ascribed to him a more romantic and elevated past. A. M. Fadeyev, *Vospominaniya 1790–1867 gg.*, 1 (Odessa 1897), 45, note.

143. Fadeyev, *Vospominaniya*, 1, 47.

144. Ibid., 1, 63–4; *SIRIO*, liv, 519.

145. Keller, *The German Colonies in South Russia*, 1, 43–4.

146. Cp. Rempel, 'The Mennonite Commonwealth', 38.

147. de Castres, *Relation d'un voyage*, 96.

148. TsGIAL f. 383, op. 29, dd. 382, 397, *passim*. An inspector's report in 1814 (d. 397, ll. 15–18) stated that in the Odessa office records were confused and some missing as far back as 1802. Whether this reflected inefficiency on the part of Contenius, whom Richelieu always portrayed as minutely scrupulous in his book- and record-keeping, or whether it was the later fault (as seems more likely) of the official subsequently in charge at Odessa, Rosenkampf, cannot be ascertained.

   Besides the usual bureaucratic vices, the Office reflected (if in somewhat grotesque form) the political trends of the time. In 1810 the Committee of Ministers received report of a conspiracy among its staff. An interpreter, Karl Oley, had planned to form a 'Corps of Knights of the Lion', which would make the Crimea over to Turkey and create him king there. He was denounced by a colonist. *Zhurnal Komiteta Ministrov 1801–1820*, ii (SPb 1891), 19.

149. *PSZ*, xxvii, 932–4, no. 20988, 17 Oct. 1803; TsGIAL f. 383, op. 29, d. 205, ll. 22–3, 27–310b., Richelieu to Kochubey, Sept. 1803, HIH rescript to Richelieu, 17 Oct. 1803.

150. In this post he succeeded General A. G. Rosenberg, who held the office briefly after the death of the former incumbent S. A. Bekleshov late in 1803.

151. I. M. Lerner, 'Nemetskiye kolonii v Novorossiyskom kraye', *Vedomosti Odesskogo Gradonachal'stva*, no. 236, 31 October 1903, 3.

152. *SIRIO*, LIV, 336.
153. TsGIAL f. 383, op. 29, d. 436, ll. 232–3, Ministry of Interior reply to Richelieu's letter of 12/24 March (?) 1818. Cp. B. Seebohm, ed., *Memoirs of the Life and Gospel Labours of Stephen Grellet*, II (London 1860), 123.
154. *SIRIO*, LIV, 336.
155. TsGIAL f. 383, op. 29, d. 436, l. 302, letter of College Counsellor Rimsky-Korsakov, i.a. praising Inzov, present head of the colonist administration: 'His predecessors, the Kherson military governors, answered every paper, but did nothing; he is inclined to act and not waste time on useless paperwork' (7 July 1818).
156. Paul's administrative reorganization of New Russia was not reversed until Oct. 1802, when this office became the Kherson Civil Governorship.
157. TsGIAL f. 383, op. 29, d. 177a, ll. 81–6, Board of State Economy summary of 2 reports, n.d.
158. Ibid., d. 178, ll. 1–15, 142–6, 172–9, Guardianship Office reports to Board, Board instructions, May 1802–April 1803.
159. Ibid., ll. 144, 189, 11 Feb., 19 May 1803.
160. Ibid., d. 269, ll. 12–22, statistical table on colonists 1801–6.
161. Rempel, 'The Mennonite Commonwealth', 38; Pisarevsky, *Pereseleniye Mennonitov*, 1–59.
162. TsGIAL f. 383, op. 29, d. 205, l. 1–ob., summarising letter from Richelieu to Guardianship Office, 22 Aug. 1803.
163. Ibid., ll. 330b., Kochubey to Richelieu 18 Oct.; ll. 62–5, Contenius to Board, 17 Oct.
164. Lerner, 'Nemetskiye kolonii'; TsGIAL f. 383, op. 29, d. 190, ll. 171–3, Vorontsov to Kochubey, 11 Sept. 1803, enclosing letter from Gervais in Iasi; d. 205, *passim*.
165. TsGIAL f. 383, op. 29, d. 190, ll. 22–5, copy of instructions, n.d. or signature.
166. *PSZ*, XXVII, 786, no. 20862, 24 July 1803; Lerner, 'Nemetskiye kolonii'.
167. Ibid.; TsGIAL f. 383, op. 29, d. 190, l. 76, Richelieu to Kochubey, 29 July; d. 205, ll. 8–11, Guardianship Office to Board, 21 Oct.
168. *PSZ*, no. 21177; cp. above, p. 198.
169. TsGIAL f. 383, op. 29, d. 269, ll. 12–22, statistical table on colonists 1801–6.
170. Ibid., d. 217, ll. 8–ob., extract from Richelieu report of 18 March 1804; d. 362, l. 490b., Ministry of Interior memorandum, April 1811.
171. Ibid., d. 212, ll. 1880b.–9, Brigonzi to Kochubey, 3 Aug.; d. 217, l. 24, Richelieu to Kochubey, 22 July.
172. Ibid., d. 212, ll. 210–11, Brigonzi to Board, 20 Sept.
173. Ibid., ll. 188, 211.
174. Ibid., d. 251, ll. 80–ob., extract from letter of 17 Oct.; cp. A. A. Klaus, *Nashi Kolonii. Opyty i materialy po istorii i statistike inostrannoy kolonizatsii v Rossii*, vypusk 1 (SPb 1869, reprinted Cambridge 1972), 21.
175. Ibid., d. 362, ll. 112–14, report by Ministry of Interior, aproached by HIH 27 Nov. 1812; ll. 151–4, Contenius to S. S. Dzhunkovsky, 5 March 1814; cp. *PSZ*, XXXII, 464–5, no. 25276, 27 Nov. 1812.
176. F. Bienemann, *Werden und Wachsen einer deutschen Kolonie in Südrussland. Geschichte der ev.-luth. Gemeinde zu Odessa* (Odessa 1893); TsGIAL f. 383, op. 29, d. 284, ...o poselenii v Taganroge nemetskoy remeslennoy kolonii, 1806–29; I. F. Pavlovsky, 'Nemetskiye kolonii v Poltavskoy gubernii v XIX v. (1808–67)', *Trudy Poltavskoy Uchonov*

Arkhivnoy Komissii, x (Poltava 1913), 97–215; H. Storch, hrsg'(*Russland unter Alexander I, Eine historische Zeitschrift* (SPb–Leipzig 1804–8), VII, 257–9.

177. TsGIAL f. 383, op. 29, d. 362, ll. 49–68, Ministry of Interior memorandum, 17 April 1811: 2,928,022 roubles *assignatsiyami*, 106,840 roubles 6 kopecks silver.

178. Ibid., dd. 159, 162, 163; *PSZ*, xxiv, 666–9, no. 18006, 20 June 1797; 815, no. 18263, 4 Dec. 1797; xxv, 5–7, no. 18305, 4 Jan. 1798; 807–9, no. 19146, 10 Oct. 1799; xxvi, 115–28, no. 19372, 6 April 1800; xxvii, 812–13, no. 20879, 1 Aug. 1803; *HBR*, 1958, 45. A useful summary of these decrees in Veshnyakov, 'Ekspeditsiya'.

179. *PSZ*, no. 18006.

180. With the exception of Riebensdorf.

181. *PSZ*, no. 19372, 118, 125.

182. Ibid., 125–6.

183. *PSZ*, xxvi, 259–60, no. 19512, 11 Aug. 1800.

184. *PSZ*, xxiv, 641–3, no. 18022, 30 June 1797, § 10; xxvi, 243–5, no. 19492, 26 July 1800, § 10.

185. TsGIAL f. 383, op. 29, d. 199, ll. 31–ob., Board (Ministry of Interior) to Guardianship Office, July 1803.

186. *PSZ*, no. 19492, § 8.

187. *PSZ*, xxv, 214, no. 18490, 21 April 1798; cp. 808, no. 19146, 10 Oct. 1799; xxvi, 121, no. 19372, 6 April 1800.

188. *PSZ*, xxvi, 299–313, no. 19562, 17 Sept. 1800 (Saratov); 635–49, no. 19873, 16 May 1801 (New Russia); xxvii, 659–70, no. 20798, 16 June 1803 (SPb); 726–31, no. 20841, 7 July 1803 (New Russia, Supplement).

189. *PSZ*, no. 19562, § 57 iv.

190. Cp. above, p. 209.

191. *PSZ*, xxiv, 525–69, no. 17906, 5 April 1797 (esp. sections VII and VIII).

192. Ibid., 672–7, no. 18082, 7 Aug. 1797.

193. *PSZ*, no. 17906, VIII, § 190.

194. See below, p. 226.

195. Pisarevsky, *Khozyaystvo i forma zemlevladeniya*, 95–9.

196. *PSZ*, xxxvii, 693–4, no. 28610, 17 April 1821.

197. A. Leopol'dov, *Statisticheskoye Opisaniye Saratovskoy Gubernii*, II (SPb 1839), 40–51.

198. S. Ya. Borovoy, *Yevreyskaya zemledel'cheskaya kolonizatsiya v staroy Rossii. Politika, ideologiya, khozyaystvo, byt* (Moscow, 1928), 194.

199. A. Florovsky, 'Neskol'ko faktov iz istorii russkoy kolonizatsii Novorossii v nachale XIX v.', *ZOO*, xxxiii (1919), 25–40.

200. *PSZ*, xl, Appendix, 41–54, no. 21779a, 3 June 1805.

201. Borovoy, *Yevreyskaya*, 41–57; Florovsky, 'Neskol'ko faktov', 28–31; N. Petrovich, 'Prinuditel'noye pereseleniye bobyletskikh krest'yan', *Trud v Rossii*, I (Petrograd 1924 = *Arkhiv Istorii Truda v Rossii*, XI), 149–63.

202. *PSZ*, xxix, 878–80, no. 22367, 23 Nov. 1806.

203. *PSZ*, xxvii, 23–5, no. 20119, 23 Jan. 1802; A. A. Kaufman, *Pereseleniye i kolonizatsiya* (SPb 1905), 12. On migration both to the Caucasus and to Siberia in the first years of the century, see N. Petrovich, 'Pereseleniye krest'yan v Sibir' v nachale XIX v.', *Trud v Rossii*, II (1924), 110–16.

204. Quoted from an official survey by Kaufman, *Pereseleniye*, 12.

205. Cp. above, p. 197.

206. For a general sketch based on the *PSZ*, see N. V. Ponomaryov, *Istoricheskiy obzor pravitel'stvennykh mer k razvitiyu sel'skogo khozyaystva v Rossii* (SPb 1880); further, Storch, *Russland unter Alexander I*, I, 229–35; V, 126–34.

207. P. Keppen (Koeppen), *O vinodelii i vinnoy torgovle v Rossii* (SPb 1832), 223, note 28.

208. Cp. above, p. 115.

209. *SIRIO*, X, 13.

210. A convenient summary is J. Eichhorn, 'Die Anfänge des Weinbaus in den Wolgakolonien', *Wolgadeutsche Monatschefte*, 1924, no. 9–10, 105–7. In 1765 Prince D. Golitsyn engaged two French wine-growers on a 3-year contract for Astrakhan: *SIRIO*, CXL, 521, 532.

211. Pisarevsky, *Khozyaystvo i forma zemlevladeniya*, 35.

212. Storch, *Russland unter Alexander I*, I, 228–9.

213. *PSZ*, XXIV, 504, no. 17847, 27 Feb. 1797; XXV, 233–6, no. 18513, 1 March 1798; Veshnyakov, 'Ekspeditsiya', 427.

214. Chernov, 'Iz istorii shelkovodstva', 96.

215. Veshnyakov, 'Ekspeditsiya', 427.

216. *PSZ*, XXIV, 793–8, no. 18240, 8 Nov. 1797.

217. *RBS*, vol. Betankur-Byakster (SPb 1908), 13–14, Bibersteyn (Baron Friedrich Marschal von Bieberstein).

218. *SA*, I, 484, 576, 708; *PSZ*, XXV, 570, no. 18865, 21 Feb. 1799; XXVII, 579–80, no. 20746, 5 May 1803; *Russkaya Starina*, C, 200; Storch, *Russland unter Alexander I*, I, 238–9, 246–7 and Table (statistics 1798–1802).

219. *SA*, I, 530. Its creation had been ordered at the time of Hablitzl's 1797 report: *PSZ*, XXIV, 793, no. 18240.

220. *PSZ*, XXVI, 45–50, no. 19290, 22 Feb. 1800, also summarised in Storch, *Russland unter Alexander I*, I, 240–6.

221. The transfer of Verdier's plantation did not have the desired result: cp. Leopol'dov, *Statisticheskoye Opisaniye*, 148–9.

222. *PSZ*, XXVI, 47, no. 19290.

223. *PSZ*, XXV, 620, no. 18935, 15 April 1799, § 13; XXVII, 579, no. 20746, 5 May 1803.

224. *PSZ*, XXVI, 48, no. 19290.

225. *PSZ*, XXVI, 48–50, no. 19290.

226. *PSZ*, XXVI, 819–21, no. 20048, 6 Nov. 1801; XXVII, 535–9, no. 20709, 14 April 1803; 577–9, no. 20746.

227. *PSZ*, XXVII, 537, no. 20709.

228. *PSZ*, XXVII, 580–4, no. 20746.

229. *PSZ*, XXVII, 727–8, no. 20841.

230. Cp. e.g. 'Kratkoye izvestiye ob uspekhakh shelkovodstva, vinodeliya i sadovodstva v poludennykh guberniyakh Rossii za 1835 god', *ZhMVD* (1836), iv, 29–31.

231. TsGIAL f. 383, op. 29, d. 390, l. 53, report of Court Counsellor Loshkarev to Ministry of Interior, 30 April 1815.

232. Skal'kovsky, *Khron. Obozreniye*, II, 129–30; cp. Chernov, 'Iz istorii shelkovodstva', 96.

233. Chernov, 'Iz istorii shelkovodstva', 97–8.

234. *PSZ*, XXV, 69, no. 18375, 13 Feb. 1798; Keppen, *O vinodelii*, 63–83.

235. *PSZ*, XXV, 72–3, no. 18375. There were well-known exceptions – for instance

the vineyards of Beketov near Astrakhan – but they merely served to prove the rule.

236. *PSZ*, xxv, 69, no. 18375; TsGIAL f. 398, op. 81, d. 1291, l. 15. In 1798 Banq was a College Assessor, and Supervisor of an Imperial vineyard at Gatchina.
237. *PSZ*, xxv, 72, no. 18375. The Board's proposals in many respects followed those of W. Friebe in his prize essay for a Free Economic Society competition of 1789 on viticulture, *Von der Kultur des Weinstocks in russichen Provinzen*. Cp. Storch, *Historisch-statistisches Gemaehlde*, ii, 426–33.
238. TsGIAL f. 398, op. 81, d. 1291, ll. 50–ob., Note approved by the Board 3 March 1798.
239. Ibid., l. 65–6, report from Seletsky, 6 May 1798.
240. Ibid., l. 67, Board minutes of 7 June 1798.
241. Ibid., ll. 73, 750b., 770b., 84–95, reports from A. D. Yeremeyev in Saratov, and from Bieberstein.
242. Ibid., ll. 103–4, Senate decree of 26 Aug. 1799 following Board report.
243. Ibid., ll. 106–20. A brief recapitulation in *PSZ*, xxvii, Appendix, 16–18, no. 20553a, Dec. 1802.
244. Ibid., l. 1370b., Board extract 'on vineyards', Jan. 1802.
245. *PSZ*, no. 20553a.
246. Cp. above, pp. 186, 188.
247. *PSZ*, no. 20533a; Storch, *Russland unter Alexander I*, v, 136–43; cp. further *PSZ*, xxviii, Appendix, 9–11, no. 21440a, 6 Sept. 1804.
248. Keppen, *O vinodelii*, 89–95; S. A. Sekirinsky, 'Nekotoryye cherty razvitiya sel'skogo khozyaystva Kryma...v kontse XVIII–1½ XIX v.', *Yezhegodnik po agrarnoy istorii Vostochnoy Yevropy za 1960 g.* (Kiev 1962), 413–14.
249. Keppen, *O vinodelii*, 89–95.
250. Sekirinsky, 'Nekotoryye', 414. Earlier evaluations were less favourable: cp. e.g. M. Ballas, *Vinodeliye v Rossii. Chast' I* (SPb 1895), 15–16.
251. *PSZ*, xxviii, Appendix, 16–19, no. 21614a, 5 Feb. 1805; Keppen, *O vinodelii*, 92–3.
252. TsGIAL f. 383, op. 29, d. 251, l. 84, extract from letter of Richelieu to Kochubey, April 1807.
253. *PSZ*, xxvii, 786, no. 20862; cp. above, p. 209.
254. Lerner, 'Nemetskiye kolonii', 3; TsGIAL f. 383, op. 29, d. 269, ll. 12–22, statistical table on colonists 1801–6.
255. Ponomaryov, *Istoricheskiy obzor pravitel'stvennykh mer*, 125; TsGIAL f. 383, op. 29, d. 229, ll. 13–240b., reports and letters from New Russian Guardianship Office, March and July 1805. Much later, in 1820, another special wine-growing colony was established in Bessarabia by Swiss viticulturists: Shabag or Shabo. See Shishmaryov, 'Nauchnoye naslediye', 136–44.
256. K. Shults, 'Neskol'ko slov o vinogradarstve v Odesskom uyezde', *Trudy Komiteta Vinogradarstva I.O.S.Kh.Yu.R.*, vypusk 1 (Odessa 1901), 172–3.
257. *PSZ*, xxiv, 670–1, no. 18009, 20 June 1797. As was the case with viticulture, the Free Economic Society had held a prize essay competition on sheep-breeding, in 1774. This produced both essays and an actual sheep-farm; it seems however to have had little effect upon official policy. Cp. *Auswahl ökon. Abhandlungen*, i, 204–22, 291–317.
258. *PSZ*, xxiv, 681–4, nos. 18092, 18093, 12–13 Aug. 1797. Except as indicated, sources for the following are K. S. Veselovsky, 'Tonkorunnoye ovtsevodstvo v Rossii', *ZhMGI* (1846), chast' 20, i, 105ff., on which is based, with addi-

tions, 'Tonkorunnoye ovtsevodstvo v Rossii, *Biblioteka dlya chteniya*, CVI (SPb 1851), iv, 1–50.
259. Veshnyakov, 'Ekspeditsiya', cxi, 168.
260. Ibid., cviii, 403–9; H. Reimers, *Sankt-Peterburg am Ende seines ersten Jahrhunderts*, ii (SPb 1805), 261–2, 391.
261. S. V. Klimova, *Istoriya proizvodstva shersti-syrtsa v Rossii v I-oy ½-e XIX v.*, kand. diss. (Moscow State University 1962), 5.
262. Müller's initial proposals: TsGIAL f. 398, op. 81, d. 555, ll. 8–9, papers found in Alexander I's cabinet, 1827.
263. The 'private speculation' mentioned above, p. 223. On this episode cp. also A. A. Skal'kovsky, 'Vzglyad na skotovodstvo Novorossiyskogo kraya. 1846–8. Stat'ya I', *ZhMVD*, xxx (1850), 375–7.
264. *PSZ*, xxviii, Appendix, 19–20, no. 21637a, 24 Feb. 1805.
265. Ibid., 11–16, 19–22, no. 21610a, 31 Jan. 1804, no. 21637a, 24 Feb. 1805. In the event the Esterhazy purchases did not take place.
266. *PSZ*, 21637a. § 6 contradicts the assertion in *Biblioteka dlya chteniya*, 18–19, that the Liechtenstein sheep were given to Sarepta and a private Volga farmer. According to Klimova, *Istoriya Proizvodstva*, 10–11, Sarepta received Liechtenstein sheep in 1807 and 1809.
267. Cp. Druzhinina, *Yuzhnaya Ukraina*, 243–4.
268. *PSZ*, xxx, 317–20, no. 23085, 12 July 1808; Skal'kovsky, *Khron. Obozreniye*, ii, 132–3.
269. TsGIAL f. 398, op. 81, d. 555, l. 14.
270. *PSZ*, xxviii, 15–17, no. 21123, 12 Jan. 1804.
271. TsGIAL f. 383, op. 29, d. 300, ll. 530b., 67, report of Kammerherr Zherebtsov on his tour of inspection, 1808. Zherebtsov gave Rouvier a bad testimonial.
272. A. A. Skal'kovsky, 'Vzglyad na skotovodstvo Novorossiyskogo kraya. 1846–48. Stat'ya I', *ZhMVD*, xxx (1850), 380–1. On Pictet see E. Pictet, *Biographie, travaux et correspondence de C. Pictet de Rochement* (Geneva–Basle–Lyons 1892), 66–75; *ZhKM*, ii, 699.
273. On Carlsthal, see E. Doering, hrsg., *Aus den Memoiren meines Vaters Friedrich Doering, eines nach Russland gesiedelten Sachsen* (Dresden und Leipzig 1903), *passim*; on Ascania, which reached its greatest heights as a sheep farm under the old colonist family of Falz-Fein: A. Druecke, *Ascania Nova. Die Geschichte einer Kolonie Anhalts in Sud-Russland*, Inaugural Dissertation, Halle 1906; L. Heiss, *Das Paradies in der Steppe. Der abenteuerliche Weg nach Askania Nova* (Stuttgart 1970 – a fictionalized recreation, also in English translation).
274. Klimova, *Istoriya proizvodstva shersti-syrtsa*, 8.
275. Ibid., 10.
276. TsGIAL f. 383, op. 29, d. 251, l. 6, note from Contenius to Ministry of Interior with financial estimates for 1805, 4 Feb. 1805; *PSZ*, xxviii, 1,241–3, no. 21909, 9 Sept. 1805.
277. Klimova, *Istoriya proizvodstva*, 10; D. G. Rempel, *The Mennonite Colonies in New Russia, A Study of their Settlement and Economic Development from 1789 to 1914*, PhD dissertation (Stanford, California 1933), 124; TsGIAL f. 383, op. 29, d. 374, ll. 1–3, report from Richelieu to Minister of Interior on use made of the 'communal fund', 6 March 1812; d. 390, ll. 122–31, 'Vedomost' o obshchestvennykh zavedeniyakh v koloniyakh vedomstva K.O.N.I.P.', May 1816.

278. TsGIAL f. 383, op. 29, d. 374, ll. 1–3.
279. Fadeyev, *Vospominaniya*, I, 98; Rempel, *The Mennonite Colonies*, 124–5, quoting i.a. Skal'kovsky, *Khron. Obozreniye*, II, 226–9.

Conclusion

1. *Zapiski F. F. Vigelya* (Moscow 1891), 21.
2. P. H. Clendenning, 'William Gomm. A Case Study of the Foreign Entrepreneur in Eighteenth Century Russia', *Journal of European Economic History*, vol. 6, no. 3 (Winter 1977), 533–48.
3. Cp. N. N. Dmitriyev, 'Pervyye russkiye sitsenabivnyye manufaktury XVIII v.', *Izvestiya Gosudarstvennoy Akademii Istorii Material'noy Kul'tury* (Moscow–Leningrad 1935), no. 116, *passim*.
4. E. P. Domar, 'The Causes of Slavery and Serfdom: A Hypothesis', *Journal of Economic History*, XXX (1970), no. 1, 18–32.
5. For a brief sketch, see my introduction to the 1972 reprint of A. A. Klaus, *Nashi Kolonii. Opyty i materialy po istorii i statistike inostrannoy kolonizatsii v Rossii*, vypusk I (SPb 1869, reprinted Cambridge 1972).

Notes to Frontispiece

The text states:
'Project for a medal marking the invitation of foreigners to Russia for settlement.

On the first side: the portrait of HER MAJESTY, with the usual subscription.

On the obverse: the Goddess of Earth or Fertility, sitting on a hillock and having on her head an urban crown, leans on a shield with the coat of arms of the Russian Empire; in her right hand she holds a key, and with her left orders Mercury, who has in his hand a palm branch, as a sign of tranquil and peaceful co-habitation, to lead the newly-arriving foreign immigrants to the places assigned to them for settlement. At the feet of the Goddess lies a cornucopia, representing outstanding wealth in all products of the earth. In the distance may be seen on one side a settler tilling the soil, on the other a new town which is being built by a river. With this the inscription: She Adds New Subjects. Beneath: *The invitation of foreigners for settlement in Russia, 1763.*'

The original is among the personal papers of the Empress: TsGADA f. 16, d. 349, l. 3. In his *Description of Russian Medals*, V. Smirnov records one struck in 1754 to commemorate the founding of New Serbia, and another of 1778 marking the migration of Greeks and Armenians from the Crimea, but nothing for the immigration of the 1760s. *Opisaniye Russkikh Medaley. Sostavil...V. P. Smirnov* (SPb 1908), 119–20 no. 237, 148 no. 283.

Bibliography

The bibliography lists all works and sources cited. A small number of other items consulted but not cited has been included.

1. MANUSCRIPT SOURCES

AN AE, Série B¹, Correspondance Consulaire: St Pétersbourg
Archives de la Bastille, Bibliothèque de l'Arsénal, Paris
Archives de la Bastille, Bibliothèque de la Ville de Paris
MAE CPR
ORGPB Bastille Archive
 fond 542: Olenin family
 fond 741: Stolpyansky papers
TsGADA, Gosarkhiv, razryad XVI: Archives of State, Internal Affairs
 fond 16: Cabinet of Her Imperial Highness
 fond 248: Governing Senate, First Department.
 fond 271: College of Mines
 fond 277: College of Manufactures
 fond 283: Chancellery of Guardianship of Foreigners
 fond 1261: Vorontsov family
TsGIAL fond 383: First Department of the Ministry of State Domains,
 op. 29, First Department of the Senate, business of the Board of State
 Economy
 fond 398: Department of Farming
 fond 1283: Department of State Economy and Public Buildings
TsGVIA fond Voyenno-Uchonyy Arkhiv (Military-Academic Archive)

2. PRINTED SOURCES
Primary Sources
a. Principal collections of documents

Arkhiv Grafov Mordvinovykh, ed. V. A. Bil'bassov, 10 vols, SPb 1901–03
Arkhiv Knyazya Vorontsova, ed. P. Bartenev, 40 vols, Moscow 1870–95
[*Buckingham Correspondence*], *Despatches and Correspondence of John, Second Earl of Buckinghamshire, Ambassador to the Court of*

Catherine II of Russia, 1762–65, ed. for the Royal Historical Society
...by Adelaide d'Arcy Collyer, 2 vols, London 1902

Chulkov, M., *Istoricheskoye Opisaniye Rossiyskoy Torgovli*, 7 vols in 21,
Moscow 1786

Polnoye Sobraniye Zakonov Rossiyskoy Imperii (Sobraniye Pervoye),
45 vols, SPb 1830

Pugachovshchina, ed. M. N. Pokrovsky, 3 vols, Moscow–Leningrad 1926–
31

[Ravaisson-Mollien, F.], *Archives de la Bastille: Documents inédits re-
cueillis et publiés par F. Ravaisson (F. et L. Ravaisson-Mollien)*, 19
vols, Paris 1866–1904

Sbornik Imperatorskogo Russkogo Istoricheskogo Obshchestva, 148 vols,
SPb 1867–1918

Senatskiy Arkhiv, 15 vols, SPb 1888–1913

Svod Zakonov Rossiyskoy Imperii, SPb 1857, XII, ii, 'Ustav o koloniyakh
inostrantsev v Imperii'

Veselago F., sost., *Materialy dlya istorii russkogo flota*, 17 vols, SPb 1865–
1904

Voltaire's Correspondence, ed. T. Bestermann, 107 vols, Geneva 1953–62

b. *Other primary sources*

*Auswahl ökonomischer Abhandlungen, welche die freye ökonomische
Gesellschaft in St. Petersburg, in teutscher Sprache erhalten hat*,
4 vols, SPb 1790–93

*Briefe über die Auswanderung der Unterthanen, besonders nach Russ-
land*, Gotha 1770

Bodemann, E., *Der Briefwechsel zwischen Kaiserin Katharina II von
Russland und J. G. Zimmermann*, Hannover–Leipzig, 1906

Bychkov, A., red., *Pis'ma i bumagi Imperatritsy Yekateriny II, khranyashchiyesya v Imp. Publichnoy Biblioteke*, SPb 1873

[de Castres], ·*Relation d'un voyage sur le bord septentrional de la mer
d'Azof et en Crimée dans la vue d'y établir une colonie d'émigrés;
par le Comte de Castres...l'un des commissaires envoyés à cet effet
par S.A.S. le Prince de Condé*, Paris 1826

[Cataneo], *Eine Reise durch Deutschland und Russland seinen Freunden
beschrieben von Johann Baptista Cataneo aus Bünden, gegenwärtigen
Pfarrer einer reformierten deutschen Colonie zu Norka in der Saratofischen Statthalterschaft an der Wolga in der russischen Tartarei in
Asien*, Chur 1787

[Catherine II], *Nakaz Imperatritsy Yekateriny II, dannyy Kommissii o
Sochinenii Novogo Ulozheniya*, ed. N. Chechulin, SPb 1907

'Pis'ma i zapiski Imp. Yekateriny Vtoroy k Grafu N. I. Paninu',
Chteniya, 1863, no. 2, 1–160

Chernov, A., 'Iz istorii shelkovodstva v Rossii', *Krasnyy Arkhiv*, CVI,
1941, 79–119

[Condé], *Journal d'Emigration du Prince de Condé 1789–1795*, ed. le Comte de Ribes, Paris 1924

[de Corberon], *Un diplomate français à la Cour de Catherine II, 1775–1780. Journal intime du Chevalier de Corberon*, ed. L. H. Labande, 2 vols, Paris 1901

Diderot, D., *Mémoires pour Cathérine II*, ed. P. Vernière, Paris 1966
Oeuvres Politiques, ed. P. Vernière, Paris 1963

Doering, E., hrsg., *Aus den Memoiren meines Vaters Friedrich Doering, eines nach Russland gesiedelten Sachsen*, Dresden und Leipzig 1903

Eisen von Schwarzenberg, J. G., autobiographical notes published in *Provinzialblatt für Kur-, Liv- und Esthland*, hrsg. G. Merkel, no. 1, 1–2, no. 2, 5, no. 3, 10–11, no. 4, 14–15, Riga 1828

'Eines Liefländischen Patrioten Beschreibung der Leibeigenschaft, wie solche in Liefland über die Bauern eingeführet ist', *Sammlung Russischer Geschichte*, hrsg. F. G. Mueller, IX, SPb 1764, 491–527

Erdmann, J. F., *Beiträge zur Kenntnis des Inneren von Russland*, 2 parts, Riga–Dorpat 1822, Leipzig 1826

Fadeyev, A. M., *Vospominaniya 1790–1867 gg.*, 2 vols, Odessa 1897 (first in *Russkiy Arkhiv*, 1891)

[Falk, J. P.], 'Zapiski Puteshestviya akad. Fal'ka', *Polnoye Sobraniye Uchonykh Puteshestviy po Rossii*, izd. Imperatorskoy Akademiey Nauk, VI, SPb 1824

[Forster, J. R.], '*A Letter from Mr. J. R. Forster, F.A.S., to M. Maty, M.D., Sec. R.S. containing some Account of a new Map of the River Volga*', *Philosophical Transactions* 58, 1768, 214–16

[Friedrich II], *Politische Korrespondenz Friedrichs des Grossen. Ergänzungsband: Die politischen Testamente Friedrichs des Grossen*, ed. G. B. Volz, Berlin 1920

The Gazeteer and London Daily Advertiser, London 31 August 1763, N.S.

Georgel, l'Abbé, *Voyage à St. Petersbourg en 1799–1800, fait avec l'Ambassade des Chevaliers de l'Ordre de Jean de Jerusalem*, Paris 1818

Gmelin, S. G., *Reise durch Russland zur Untersuchung der drey Naturreiche*, 4 vols, SPb 1770–74

Grech, N. I., *Zapiski iz moyey zhizni*, SPb 1886

[Grellet], *Memoirs of the Life and Gospel Labours of Stephen Grellet*, ed. B. Seebohm, 2 vols, London 1860

Güldenstädt, J. A., *Reisen durch Russland und im Caucasischen Gebirge*, 2 vols, SPb 1787–91

[Guthrie, M.], *A Tour, performed in the years 1795–6 through the Taurida, or Crimea...and all the...Countries on the north shore of the Euxine ceded to Russia by the Peace of Kainardji and Jassy; by Mrs. Maria Guthrie..., described in a series of letters to her husband, the editor, Matthew Guthrie, M.D.*, London 1802

Hermann, B. F. J., *Statistische Schilderung von Russland in Rücksicht auf die Bevölkerung, Landesbeschaffenheit, Naturprodukte, Landwirtschaft, Bergbau, Manufakturen und Handel*, SPb–Leipzig 1790

Indova, Ye. I., 'O rossiyskikh manufakturakh vtoroy poloviny XVIII v.', *Istoricheskaya geografiya Rossii XII – nachalo XX v. Sb. statey k 70-letiyu prof. L. G. Beskrovnogo*, ed. A. L. Narochnitsky, et al., Moscow 1975, 248–345

Ivanov, P. A., 'Delo o vykhodyashchikh iz-za granitsy v Novorossiyskuyu guberniyu zhidakh', *ZOO* xvii, 1894, 163–88

von Klingshtet, T., 'Resheniye voprosa: kotoroy iz zemnykh nashikh produktov bol'she sootvetstvuyet obshchey pol'ze i rasprostraneniyu nashey kommertsii, po chemu i razmnozheniye onogo dolzhenstvuyet byt' vsemi vozmozhnymi-sposobami pooshchrayemo', *TVEO*, chast' 1, 1765, 157–179

Lloyd's Evening Post and British Chronicle (London), xii, no. 968, 23–6 Sept. 1763, N.S.

Loit, A. and Tiberg, N., *Gammalsvenskby-Dokument*, Skrifter utgivna av kungl. Gustav Adolfs Akademien, 31, Uppsala–Copenhagen 1958

Lomonosov, M. V., *Polnoye Sobraniye Sochineniy*, ed. S. Vavilov, 10 vols, Moscow–Leningrad 1950–59

Makar'yevskiy, Fedosy, *Materialy dlya statisticheskogo opisaniya Yekaterinoslavskoy yeparkhii. Tserkvi i prikhody XVIII st.*, vypusk 2, Yekaterinoslav 1880

Merkel, G., *Darstellungen und Charakteristiken aus meinem Leben*, 2 vols, Leipzig 1839–40

[Mertvago], 'Zapiski D. Mertvago', *Russkiy Arkhiv*, 1867 no. 5, Appendix

Mirabeau, V. Riqueti, Marquis de, *L'Ami des Hommes, ou Traité de la Population*, 5 vols, 2nd ed., Avignon 1757

Müller, C., *St. Petersburg, ein Beitrag zur Geschichte unsrer Zeit in Briefen aus den Jahren 1810, 1811 und 1812*, Mainz 1813

[Ozeretskovsky], *Opisaniye Koly i Astrakhani. Iz sochineniy akad. N. Ozeretskovskogo*, SPb 1804

Pallas, P. S., *Reise durch verschiedene Provinzen des Russischen Reichs*, 3 parts, SPb 1771–6
    Travels through the Southern Provinces of the Russian Empire in the years 1793 and 1794, 2 vols, London 1802–3

Popruzhenko, M. G., 'Iz materialov po istorii slavyanskikh koloniy v Rossii', *ZOO*, xxviii, 1910, ii, materialy, 1–34

[Potemkin], 'Rasporyazheniya kn. G. A. Potemkina-Tavricheskogo kasatel'no ustroyeniya Tavricheskoy oblasti s 1781 po 1786 gg.', *ZOO*, xii, 1881, ii, 249–329

Provinzialblatt für Kur-, Liv- und Esthland, see Eisen

'Proyekt nadeleniya zemlyoy v g. Starom Kryme bratstva Les Frères de la Rédemption', *ZOO*, xxii, 1900, Smes', 2–6

The Public Advertiser, London 31 August and 23 September 1763, N.S.

[Rumyantsev], 'Arkhiv voenno-pokhodnoy kantselyarii gr. P. A. Rumyant-seva-Zadunayskogo, chast' 1 : 1767–69', *Chteniya*, 1865 no. 1, ii, 1–270

[de Saint-Pierre], *Oeuvres posthumes de J.-H.-B. de Saint-Pierre, mises en ordre et précédées de la vie de l'auteur par L. Aimé-Martin*, 2 vols, Paris 1833

Sbornik voyenno-istoricheskikh materialov, vypusk 6: Bumagi Potemkina, ed. N. Dubrovin, SPb 1893

Shcherbatov, M. M., *Neizdannyye Sochineniya*, Moscow 1935

Schlözer, A. L., *Von der Unschädlichkeit der Pocken in Russland und von Russlands Bevölkerung überhaupt*, Göttingen–Gotha 1768

A. L. Schlözers öffentliches und Privatleben, von ihm selbst beschreiben. Erstes Fragment, Göttingen 1802

Schmidt, S. O., 'Proyekt P. I. Shuvalova 1754, "O raznykh gosudarst-vennoy pol'zy sposobakh" ', *Istoricheskiy Arkhiv*, 1962, no. 6, 100–18

von Sonnenfels, J., *Grundsätze der Polizey, Handlung und Finanzwissen-schaft. Erster Theil*, 3rd ed., Wien 1770

Storch, H., 'Ueber die Bevölkerung. Ein staatswirtschaftlicher Versuch', *Journal von Russland*, hrsg. J. H. Busse, 2ter Jg., 2ter Bd., 12tes St., Junius 1795, 337–71

[de Tott], *Memoirs of the Baron de Tott. Containing the state of the Turkish Empire and the Crimea, during the late war with Russia... The second edition. To which are subjoined, the strictures of M. de Peysonnel*, 2 vols, London 1786

Trudy Vol'nogo Ekonomicheskogo Obshchestva, see Klingshtet

'Vedomost' o chisle sposobnykh i nesposobnykh k khlebopashestvu kolo-nistov, 1769', *Trudy Saratovskoy Uchonoy Arkhivnoy Komissii*, 1887, II, Saratov 1889, vypusk 1

Veynberg, L. B., ed., *Materialy dlya istorii Voronezhskoy i sosednikh guberniy*, t. XVI, Voronezh 1890

[Vigel'], *Zapiski F. F. Vigelya*, Moscow 1891

Vinsky, G., *Moyo Vremya*, SPb 1914

[Vorontsov], 'Iz pisem gr. S. R. Vorontsova k gr. A. A. Bezborodko', *Russkiy Arkhiv*, 1879 no. 1, 83–111

Waltner, E. J., *Banished for Faith*, Freeman 1968

[Züge], *Der russische Colonist oder Christian Gottlob Züges Leben in Russland. Nebst einer Schilderung der Sitten und Gebräuche der Russen, vornehmlich in den asiatischen Provinzen*, 2 vols, Zeitz-Naumburg, 1802–3

Zhurnal Komiteta Ministrov, 1801–1820, 2 vols, SPb 1891 (no more published)

Secondary Sources

a. Reference works, catalogues, and specialized bibliographies

Dashkevich, Ya. R., *Armyanskiye kolonii na Ukraine v istochnikakh i literature XV–XIX vv.*, Yerevan 1962

Entsiklopedicheskiy Slovar' Brokgauz-Efron, 186 vols, SPb 1890–1907

Funck-Brentano, F., *Catalogue des Manuscrits de la Bibliothèque de l'Arsénal*, t.9 *Archives de la Bastille*, Paris 1892

Long, J., The German-Russians. A Bibliography of Russian Materials. . . . Santa Barbara–Oxford 1978

Lyublinskaya, A., sost., *Otdel Rukopisey Gosudarstvennoy Publichnoy Biblioteki. Dokumenty iz Bastil'skogo Arkhiva, Annotirovannyy Katalog*, Leningrad 1960, typescript

Russkiy Biograficheskiy Slovar', 25 vols, 1895–1919

Schiller, F. P., *Literatur zur Geschichte und Volkskunde der deutschen Kolonien in der Sowjetunion für die Jahre 1764–1926*, Pokrowsk an der Wolga 1927

Stumpp, K., *Das Schrifttum über das Deutschtum in Russland. Eine Bibliographie*. 3rd ed., Stuttgart 1971

Svodnyy katalog russkoy knigi grazhdanskoy pechati 1725–1800, 5 vols and suppl., Moscow 1962–75

b. Other secondary sources

Adamczyk, T., *Furst G. A. Potemkin. Untersuchungen zu seiner Lebensgeschichte*, Emsdetten 1936

Alefirenko, P. A., *Krest'yanskoye dvizheniye i krest'yanskiy vopros v Rossii v 30–50 gg. XVIII v.*, Moscow 1958

Aleksandrenko, V. N., *Russkiye diplomaticheskiye agenty v Londone v XVIII v.*, 2 vols, Warsaw 1897

Amburger, E., 'Der fremde Unternehmer in Russland bis zur Oktoberrevolution im J. 1917', *Tradition: Zeitschrift für Firmengeschichte und Unternehmerbiographie*, 4, 1957, 337–56

Die Anwerbung ausländischer Fachkräfte für die Wirtschaft Russlands vom 15. bis ins 19. Jahrhundert (Osteuropastudien der Hochschulen des Landes Hessen, Reihe I, Bd. 42), Wiesbaden 1968

'Hugenottenfamilien in Russland', *Herold*, vol. 5, 1963–5, 125–35

Russland und Schweden 1762–72. Katherina II, die schwedische Verfassung und die Ruhe des Nordens (Historische Studien, hrsg. E. Ebering, Heft 251), Berlin 1934

Ananyan, Zh. A., *Armyanskaya koloniya Grigoriopol'*, Yerevan 1969

'K voprosu o zaselenii yuga Rossii armyanami vo 2-oy ½-e XVIII v.', *Izvestiya A.N. Armyanskoy S.S.R. (obshchestvennyye nauki)*, 1963, no. 5, 45–54

Arbat, Yu., *Farforovyy gorodok*, Moscow 1957

Arsh, G., *Eteristskoye dvizheniye v Rossii*, Moscow 1970

Auerbach, H., *Die Besiedelung der Südukraine in den Jahren 1774–78* (Veröffentlichungen des Osteuropa-Instituts, München, Bd. 25), Wiesbaden 1965

Babintsev, M., 'Uchastiye nemtsev Povolzh'ya v vosstanii Pugachova', *Za kommunisticheskoye prosveshcheniye*, Engels, 1941, no. 1 (20), 60–7

Baburin, D., *Ocherki po istorii Manufaktur-Kollegii*, Moscow 1939

Bagaley, D., 'Kolonizatsiya Novorossiyskogo Kraya i pervyye shagi yego po puti kul'tury', *Kievskaya Starina* xxv–xxvi, April 1889, 27–55; May–June 1889, 438–85; July 1889, 110–48

Balagurov, Ya., *Olonetskiye gornyye zavody v doreformennyy period*, Petrozavodsk 1958

Ballas, M., *Vinodeliye v Rossii*, chast' 1, SPb 1895

Barkhudaryan, V. B., *Istoriya Novo-Nakhichevanskoy Armyanskoy Kolonii (1779–1861 gg.)*, Yerevan 1967 (in Armenian, Russian summary and documents 455–77)

Bartlett, R. P., 'Culture and Enlightenment: Julius von Canitz and the Kazan' *gimnazii* in the Eighteenth Century', *Canadian–American Slavic Studies* (1980)

'Foreign Settlement in Russia under Catherine II', *New Zealand Slavonic Journal*, NS, 1974, no. 1, 1–22

'J. R. Forster's Stay in Russia 1765–6: Diplomatic and Official Accounts', *JbfGO*, NF, 23, 1975, Heft 4, 489–95

'Scottish Cannon-Founders and the Russian Navy 1767–1785', *Oxford Slavonic Papers*, NS, x, 1977, 51–72

Bauer, G., bearb., *Geschichte der deutschen Ansiedler an der Wolga seit ihrer Einwanderung nach Russland bis zur Einführung der allgemeinen Wehrpflicht (1766–1874), nach geschichtlichen Quellen und mündlichen Ueberlieferungen*, Saratow 1908

Bayburtyan, V. A., *Armyanskaya koloniya Novoy Dzhulfy v XVII veke*, Yerevan 1969 (English summary, 151–66)

Bazhova, A. P., 'Iz yugoslavyanskikh zemel' – v Rossiyu', *Voprosy Istorii*, 1977, no. 2, 124–37

Beheim-Schwarzbach, M., *Hohenzollernsche Colonisationen*, Leipzig 1874

Belikov, T. I., *Uchastiye kalmykov v krest'yanskoy voyne pod rukovodstvom Ye. I. Pugachova*, Elista 1971

'Belovezhskaya nemetskaya koloniya', *Pamyatnaya knizhka Chernigovskoy gubernii* (Chernigov 1862), 129–62

Belyavsky, M. T., *Krest'yanskiy vopros v Rossii nakanune vosstaniya Pugachova*, Moscow 1965

Bennigsen, A., 'Un mouvement populaire au Caucase au XVIII siècle. La "Guerre Sainte" du *sheikh* Mansur (1785–91), page mal connue et controversée des relations russo-turques', *Cahiers du Monde Russe et Soviétique*, v, 1964, no. 2, 159–205

Beratz, G., *Die deutschen Kolonien an der unteren Wolga in ihrer Entstehung und ersten Entwicklung. Gedenkblätter zur 150. Jahreswende der Ankunft der ersten deutschen Ansiedler*, ed. J. Schönberger, A. Bier, G. S. Löbsack, 2nd ed., Berlin 1923

Beyträge zur Kunde Preussens, see Hagen

Bienemann, F., *Werden und Wachsen einer deutschen Kolonie in Südrussland. Geschichte der evangelisch-lutherischen Gemeinde zu Odessa*, Odessa 1893

von Bilbassoff, B., *Geschichte Katharina II*, 2 vols in 3, Berlin 1893

Bibliography 331

[Bogdanov–Ruban], *Istoricheskoye, geograficheskoye i topograficheskoye opisaniye Sanktpeterburga...sochinyonnoye g. Bogdanovym...a nyne dopolnennoye i izdannoye...Vasil'yem Rubanom, Izdaniye pervoye*, SPb 1779

Bonwetsch, G., *Geschichte der deutschen Kolonien an der Wolga* (Schriften des Deutschen Auslandisinstituts, Stuttgart, no. 2), Stuttgart 1919

Borovoy, S. Ya., *Yevreyskaya zemledel'cheskaya kolonizatsiya v staroy Rossii. Politika, ideologiya, khozyaystvo, byt*, Moscow 1928

Buchholtz, A., *Geschichte der Juden in Riga*, Riga 1899

Bylov, M., 'Nemtsy v Voronezhskom kraye (istoriko–statisticheskiy ocherk)', *Pamyatnaya knizhka Voronezhskoy gubernii na 1894 god*, Voronezh 1894, 111–26

Chenakal, V. L., *Watchmakers and Clockmakers in Russia, 1400–1850*, trans. W. F. Ryan, Antiquarian Horological Society Monograph no. 6, n.p., 1972

Christie, I. R., 'Samuel Bentham and the Western Colony at Krichev, 1784–87', *SEER*, XLVIII, no. 111, 1970, 232–47

Clendenning, P. H., 'William Gomm. A Case Study of the Foreign Entrepreneur in Eighteenth Century Russia', *Journal of European Economic History*, vol. 6, no. 3, Winter 1977, 533–48

Conze, W., *Hirschenhof, die Geschichte einer deutschen Sprachinsel in Livland* (Neue Deutsche Forschungen, Bd. 3), Berlin 1934

Defourneau, M., *Pablo de Olavide ou l'Afrancesado (1725–1803)*, Paris 1959

Dmitriyev, N. N., 'Pervyye russkiye sitsenabivnyye manufaktury XVIII v.', *Izvestiya Gosudarstvennoy Akademii Istorii Material'noy Kul'tury*, no. 116, Moscow–Leningrad 1935

Domar, E. P., 'The Causes of Slavery and Serfdom: A Hypothesis', *Journal of Economic History*, XXX, 1970, no. 1, 18–32

Donnelly, A. S., *The Russian Conquest of Bashkiria, 1552–1740*, New Haven–London 1968

Donnert, E., *Johann Georg Eisen (1717–1779). Ein Vorkämpfer der Bauernbefreiung in Russland*, Leipzig 1978

Druecke, A., *Ascania Nova. Die Geschichte einer Kolonie Anhalts in Süd-Russland*, Inaug. Diss., Halle 1906

Druzhinina, Ye. I., 'Klassovaya bor'ba krest'yan Yuzhnoy Ukrainy v pervoy polovine XIX v.', *Yezhegodnik po agrarnoy istorii vostochnoy Yevropy za 1964 g.*, Kishinyov 1966, 572–83

Kyuchuk-Kaynardjiyskiy Mir 1774 g., Moscow 1955

Severnoye Prichernomor'ye, 1775–1800, Moscow 1959

'Volneniya kolonistov Novorossii i Yuzhnoy Bessarabii', *Problemy istorii obshchestvennogo dvizheniya i istoriografii. K 70-letiyu M. V. Nechkinoy*, Moscow 1971, 102–09

Yuzhnaya Ukraina v 1800–1825 gg., Moscow 1970

Dubrovin, N., 'Brat'ya Potemkiny na Kavkaze', *Russkiy Vestnik*,

332   Bibliography

CXXXVIII: Nov. 1878, 1–55; Dec. 1878, 483–561; CXXXIX: Jan. 1879,
    65–102; April 1879, 825–83
Dukes, P., 'Catherine II's Enlightened Absolutism and the Problem of
    Serfdom', W. E. Butler, ed., *Russian Law: Historical and Political
    Perspectives*, Leyden 1977, 93–115
*The Emergence of the Superpowers. A Short Comparative History of
    the U.S.A. and the U.S.S.R.*, London 1970
Eckhardt, J., *Livland im 18ten Jahrhundert*, 2 vols, Leipzig 1876
'Economie et Population. Les doctrines avant 1800', *Institut d'Etudes
    Démographiques, Travaux et Documents*, Cahiers 21, 28, Paris 1954
Eichhorn, J., 'Die Anfänge des Weinbaus in den Wolgakolonien', *Wolga-
    deutsche Monatshefte*, 1924, no. 9–10, 105–7
Elias, O.-H., 'Zur Lage der undeutschen Bevölkerung im Riga des 18ten
    Jahrhunderts', *JbfGO*, NF, 14, 1966, Heft 4, 481–4
Esper, T., 'The Odnodvortsy and the Russian Nobility', *SEER*, XLV, no.
    104, Jan. 1967, 124–34
d'Estrée, P., 'Une Colonie franco-russe au XVIII s.', *Revue des Revues*,
    1896, no. 19, 1–16
'Fermiers généraux et femmes galantes: un policier homme de lettres,
    l'inspecteur Meusnier (1748–57)', *Revue Retrospective*, N.S., XVII,
    July–Dec. 1892, Paris 1893, 217–76
Etterlin-Adliswil, J., *Die ehemaligen Schmeizerkolonien in Russland, die
    Ukraine, die Krim, das Donezgebiet, der Kaukasus, die Wolga und
    ihr Gebiet*, Zürich–Bern, 1945 (typescript)
*Die evangelisch–lutherischen Gemeinden in Russland. Eine historisch–
    statistische Darstellung*, hrsg. vom Zentral-Komite der Unterstützungs-
    Kasse für evangelisch–lutherischen Gemeinden in Russland, 2 vols,
    SPb 1909–11
Fadeyev, A. V., *Ocherki ekonomicheskogo razvitiya stepnogo Predkav-
    kaz'ya v doreformennyy period*, Moscow 1957
Rossia i Kavkaz pervoy treti XIX v., Moscow 1960
Ferguson, A. D., 'Russian Landmilitia and Austrian Militärgrenze (A
    Comparative Study)', *Südostdeutsche Forschungen* 13 (1954), 137–58
Fieldhouse, D. K., *The Colonial Empires*, London–New York 1966
Fisher, A., *The Russian Annexation of the Crimea, 1772–1783*, Cambridge
    1970
Florovsky, A. V., 'Neskol'ko faktov iz istorii russkoy kolonizatsii Novorossii
    v nachale XIX v.', *ZOO*, XXXIII, 1919, 24–40
von Frantzius, G., *Die Okkupation Ostpreussens durch die Russen im
    7-Jährigen Kriege, mit besonderer Berücksichtigung der russischen
    Quellen*, Berlin 1916
Gaysinovich, A. I., 'Tsekhi v Rossii v XVIII v.', *Izvestiya A.N. S.S.S.R.,
    otdeleniye obshchestvennykh nauk*, 1931, no. 5, 523–68
Georgi, J. G., *Geographisch-physikalische und naturhistorische Beschreib-
    ung des russischen Reichs zur Uebersicht bisheriger Kenntnisse von
    demselben*, Königsberg 1797

Versuch einer Beschreibung der russisch-kayserlichen Residenzstadt Sanktpeterburg und der Merkwürdigkeiten der Gegend, SPb 1790, Riga 1793

Geraklitov, A. A., *Istoriya Saratovskogo Kraya v XVI–XVIII vv.,* Saratov–Moscow 1923

Gessen, Yu., *Istoriya yevreyskogo naroda v Rossii,* 2 vols, Leningrad 1925

Giesinger, A., *From Catherine to Khrushchev. The Story of Russia's Germans,* Battleford, Sask., 1974

Got'ye, Yu., 'Iz istorii peredvizheniy naseleniya v XVIII v.', *Chteniya,* 1908, no. 1, Smes', 1–26

Griffiths, D. M., *Russian Court Politics and the Question of an Expansionist Foreign Policy under Catherine II, 1762–1783,* PhD dissertation, Cornell U. 1967

Häberle, D., *Auswanderungen und Koloniegründungen der Pfälzer im 18ten Jahrhundert. Zur 200-jährigen Erinnerung an die Massenauswanderung der Pfälzer und an den pfälzischen Bauerngeneral N. Herchheimer...,* Kaiserlautern 1909

Hafa, H., *Die Brudergemeinde Sarepta, ein Beitrag zur Geschichte des Wolgadeutschtums* (Schriften des Osteuropa-Instituts in Breslau, Neue Reihe, Heft 7), Breslau 1936

[Hagen], 'Preussens Schicksale wahrend der drey schlesischen Kriege. Von dem Regierungsrath Hagen', *Beyträge zur Kunde Preussens,* hrsg. C. G. und C. H. Hagen I, Königsberg 1817, 525–67

Hans, N., 'François Pierre Pictet, Secretary to Catherine II', *SEER,* XXXVI, 1957–8, 481–91

Hauben, P. J., 'The First Decade of An Agrarian Experiment in Bourbon Spain: the "New Towns" of the Sierra Morena and Andalusia, 1766–75', *Agricultural History,* 39, no. 1, Jan. 1965, 34–40

Haumant, E., *La Culture Française en Russie, 1700–1900,* Paris 1910

Hayes, R., 'The German Colony in County Limerick', *North Munster Antiquarian Journal,* vol. 1, no. 2, Oct. 1937, 45–53

HBR, see *Heimatbuch* and Sch.

Heimatbuch der Ostumsiedler, later *der Deutschen aus Russland,* Stuttgart 1954–

Heiss, L., *Das Paradies in der Steppe. Der abenteurliche Weg nach Ascania Nova,* Stuttgart 1970

Hoare, M. E., *The Tactless Philosopher: Johann Reinhold Forster 1729–1798,* Melbourne 1976

Hösch, E., 'Das sog. "griechische Projekt" Katharinas II', *JbfGO,* N.F. 12, 1964, Heft 2, 168–206

Ioannisyan, A. R., 'Armyanskoye natsional'no-osvoboditel'noye dvizheniye v 60-kh gg. XVIII v.', *Izvestiya A.N. S.S.S.R. (istoriya i filosofia),* III, 1946, no. 2, 135–44

Rossia i armyanskoye osvoboditel'noye dvizheniye v 80-kh gg. XVIII st., Yerevan 1947

Ischchanian, B., *Die ausländischen Elemente in der russischen Volkswirt-*

schaft. Geschichte, Ausbreitung, Berufsgruppierung, Interessen und ökonomisch-kulturelle Bedeutung der Ausländer in Russland, Berlin 1913

Istoricheskiy ocherk Odessy k stoletnemu yubileyu so dnya zavoyevaniya, Odessa 1889

Istoricheskiye svyazi i druzhba ukrainskogo i armyanskogo narodov, Sbornik materialov nauchnoy sessii, I, Yerevan 1961; II, Kiev 1965; III, Yerevan 1970

'Istoricheskoye obozreniye vodvoreniya inostrannykh poselentsev v Rossii', *ZhMGI,* LII, Sept. 1854, 35–78

'Istoriya i statistika kolonii inostrannykh poselentsev v Rossii, ii', *ZhMGI,* LIII, ii, Oct. 1854, 1–34

Jenny, A. und Jenny-Jenny, G., *Bilder von dem Leben und Streben der Russland-Schweizer und dem traurigen Ende ihrer Wirksamkeit,* Neue Folge, Glarus 1934

Jones, M. V., 'The Sad and Curious Story of Karass, 1802–35', *Oxford Slavonic Papers,* NS, VIII, 1975, 53–81

Jones, R. E., *The Emancipation of the Russian Nobility, 1762–1785,* Princeton 1973

Kabuzan, V. M., 'Krest'yanskaya kolonizatsiya Severnogo Prichernomor'-ya (Novorossii) v XVIII-1-oy ½-e XIX vv. (1719–1857)', *Yezhegodnik po agrarnoy istorii vostochnoy Yevropy za 1964 g.,* Kishinyov 1966, 313–24

Zaseleniye Novorossii (Yekaterinoslavskoy i Khersonskoy Guberniy) v XVIII–1-oy ½-e XIX vv., Moscow 1976

Karidis, B. A., *The Greek Communities in South Russia: Aspects of their Formation and Commercial Enterprise 1774–1829,* M.A. thesis, University of Birmingham 1976

Katayev, I. M., *Na beregakh Volgi. Istoriya Usol'skoy votchiny grafov Orlovykh,* Chelyabinsk 1948

Kaufmann, A. A., *Pereseleniye i kolonizatsiya,* SPb 1905

Keller, C., *The German Colonies in South Russia, 1804–1904,* I, trans. from German by A. Becker, n.d. or pl., [Saskatoon, Sask., Canada 1968: the original, Odessa 1905]

Keppen (Koeppen), P., 'Ob inorodcheskom, preimushchestvenno nemetskom naselenii Peterburgskoy gubernii', *ZhMVD,* 1850, no. 11, 181–209

O vinodelii i vinnoy torgovle v Rossii, SPb 1832

Khachaturyan, V. A., 'Administrativno-pravovoye polozheniye astrakhanskikh armyan vo 2-oy ½-e XVIII v.', *Izvestiya A.N. Armyanskoy S.S.R. (obshchestvennyye nauki),* 1963, no. 12, 57–68

'Naseleniye armyanskoy kolonii v Astrakhani vo 2-oy ½-e XVIII v.', *Izvestiya A.N. Armyanskoy S.S.R. (obshchestvennyye nauki),* 1965, no. 7, 77–87

'Poseleniye v Astrakhani', *Literaturnaya Armeniya,* 1972, no. 4, 92–7

Kirchner, W., *Commercial Relations Between Russia and Europe 1400–*

1800. Collected Essays, Indiana Russian and East European Series, vol. 33, Bloomington 1966

Kizewetter, A. A., 'Otzyv o sochinenii G. G. Pisarevskogo "Iz istorii inostrannoy kolonizatsii v Rossii v XVIII v." ', *Otchot o 52-om prisuzhdenii nagrad gr. Uvarova*, SPb 1912, off-print

Klaus, A. A., *Nashi Kolonii. Opyty i materialy po istorii i statistike inostrannoy kolonizatsii v Rossii*, vypusk 1 (no more published), SPb 1869, reprinted Cambridge 1972

Unsere Kolonien. Studien zur Geschichte und Statistik der ausländischen Kolonien in Russland, trans. H. Toews, Odessa 1887

Klimova, S. V., *Istoriya proisvodstva shersti-syrtsa v Rossii v 1-oy $\frac{1}{2}$-e XIX v.*, kandidatskaya dissertatsiya, Moscow State University, 1962

Klyuchevsky, V. O., *Sochineniya*, 8 vols, Moscow 1956

Koch, E., *Die deutschen Kolonien Nordrusslands. Eine siedlungswirtschaftsgeographische und kulturhistorische Untersuchung*, Inaugural dissertation, Würzburg 1931, Gera 1931

Koch, F. C., *The Volga Germans in Russia and the Americas from 1763 to the Present*, Pennsylvania U.P., University Park and London 1977

Koeppen, P., *Ueber die Deutschen im St. Peterburgischen Gouvernement*, SPb 1850

Kohls, W. A., 'German Settlement on the Lower Volga; A Case Study: The Moravian Community at Sarepta, 1763–1892', *Trans. Moravian Historical Society*, XXII, ii, Nazareth 1971, 47–99

Korobkov, N., *Semiletnyaya Voyna*, Moscow 1940

Korshunova, T. T., comp. and intro., *Russkiye Shpalery. Peterburgskaya Shpalernaya Manufaktura*, Leningrad 1975

'Kratkoye izvestiye ob uspekhakh shelkovodstva, vinodeliya i sadovodstva v poludennykh guberniyakh Rossii za 1835 god', *ZhMVD*, 1836, iv, 27–64

Kuhn, W., *Die jungen deutschen Sprachinseln in Galizien. Ein Beitrag zur Methode der Sprachinselforschung* (Deutschtum und Ausland, Studien zum Auslanddeutschtum und zur Auslandkultur, hrsg. G. Schreiber, Heft 26–7), Munster 1930

Kusheva, E., 'Saratov v tretey chetverti XVIII v.', *Trudy Nizhne-Volzhskogo Oblastnogo Nauchnogo Obshchestva Krayevedeniya*, vypusk 35, chast' 2, Saratov 1928, 1–58

Lang, D. M., 'Count Todtleben's expedition to Georgia 1769–71, according to a French eye-witness', *Bulletin SOAS*, 13, London 1949–50, 878–907

Langhans-Ratzeburg, M., *Die Wolgadeutschen. Ihr Staats- und Verwaltungsrecht in Vergangenheit und Gegenwart*, Berlin 1929

Leonhard, R., *Agrarpolitik und Agrarreform in Spanien unter Carl III*, München u. Berlin 1909

Leopol'dov, A., *Statisticheskoye Opisaniye Saratovskoy Gubernii*, 2 parts, SPb 1839

Lerner, I. M., 'Nemetskiye kolonii v Novorossiyskom kraye', *Vedomosti Odesskogo Gradonachal'stva*, Odessa: no. 231, 25 October 1903, 2–3; no. 236, 31 October 1903, 3

Letiche, J., ed., *A History of Russian Economic Thought, Ninth through Eighteenth Centuries*, Berkeley and Los Angeles 1964

Lewin, E., *The German Road to the East: an account of the 'Drang nach Osten' and of Teutonic aims in the Near and Middle East*, London 1916

Lodyzhensky, K., *Istoriya russkogo tamozhennogo tarifa*, SPb 1886

Lyublinskaya, A. D., 'Bastiliya i yeyo arkhiv', *Frantsuzskiy Yezhegodnik za 1958 g.*, Moscow 1959, 104–26

Lyubomirov (Lyubomirow), P. G., *Ocherki po istorii russkoy promyshlennosti*, Moscow–Leningrad 1947

'Zaseleniye Astrakhanskogo kraya v XVIII veke', *Nash Kray*, no. 4, Astrakhan 1926, 54–77

Die wirtschaftliche Lage der deutschen Kolonien des Saratower und Wolsker Bezirks im Jahre 1791, Pokrowsk an der Wolga 1926

McGrew, R. E., 'Dilemmas of Development: Baron H. F. Storch (1766–1835) on the Growth of Imperial Russia', *JbfGO*, NF, 24, 1976, Heft 1, 31–71

Macler, F., 'Rapport sur une mission scientifique en Galicie et en Bukovine (juillet–août 1925)', *Revue d'Etudes Arméniennes*, VII, i, 1927, 11–175

Madariaga, I. de, 'Catherine II and the Serfs: A Reconsideration of some Problems', *SEER*, LII, no. 126, January 1974, 34–62

Maksimov, S., 'Ocherk russikh pereseleniy v posledniye poltora veka', *Morskoy Sbornik*, LIV, no. 8, Aug. 1861, 189–234

Markova, O., 'O proiskhozdenii tak nazyvayemogo Grecheskogo Proyekta (80-yye gg. XVIII v.)', *Istoriya S.S.S.R.*, 1958, no. 4, 52–78

Matthäi, F., *Die deutschen Ansiedlungen in Russland. Ihre Geschichte und ihre volkswirtschaftliche Bedeutung für die Vergangenheit und Zukunft*, Leipzig 1866

Matviyevsky, P. E., 'O roli Orenburga v russko-indiyskoy torgovle v XVIII v.', *Istoriya S.S.S.R.*, 1969, no. 3, 98–111.

Mavrodin, V. V., 'Die Teilnahme deutscher Ansiedler des Wolgagebiets am Pugačevaufstand', *Jahrbuch für die Geschichte der UdSSR*, 7, 1963, 189–99

'Ob uchastii kolonistov Povolzh'ya v vosstanii Pugachova', *Krest'yanstvo i klassovaya bor'ba v feodal'noy Rossii. Sbornik statey pamyati I I. Smirnova=Trudy Inst-a Istorii A.N. S.S.S.R.*, Leningradskoye Otdeleniye, vypusk 9, Leningrad 1967, 400–14

Maykov, P. M., *Ivan Ivanovich Betskoy. Opyt yego biografii*, SPb 1904

Meshcheryuk, I. I., *Pereseleniye Bolgar v yuzhnuyu Bessarabiyu, 1828–34 gg.*, Kishinyov 1965

'Pervoye massovoye pereseleniye Bolgar v nachale XIX v.', *Izv. A.N. S.S.S.R., moldavskogo filiala*, 1953, no. 3–4 (11–12), 65–97

Miller, K., *Frantsuzskaya emigratsiya v Rossii v tsarstvovaniye Yekateriny II*, Paris 1931

Morozov, P. O., 'Chernogorskiye pereselentsy v Rossii 1803–1838', *Istoricheskiye materialy iz Arkhiva Ministerstva Gosudarstvennykh Imushchestv*, V. I. Veshnyakov, ed., vypusk 1, SPb 1891, 54–107

Mueller, A., 'Die preussische Kolonisation in Nordpolen und Litauen (1795–1807) und die Mennoniten', *Ztschft für Ostforschung*, 22, 1973, 487–96

Nedosekin, V., 'O diskussii po krest'yanskomu voprosu v Rossii nakanune vosstaniya Pugachova', *Izvestiya Voronezhskogo Gos. Pedagogicheskogo Instituta*, 63, 1967, 326–46

Nersisyan, M., *Iz istorii russko-armyanskikh otnosheniy*, 1, Yerevan 1956

Neuschäffer, H., 'Der livländische Pastor und Kameralist Johann Georg Eisen von Schwarzenberg. Ein deutscher Vertreter der Aufklärung in Russland zu Beginn der zweiten Hälfte des 18. Jahrhunderts', *Russland und Deutschland=Kieler Historische Studien*, 22, hrsg. U. Liszkowski, Stuttgart 1974, 120–43

Katharina II und die baltischen Provinzen, Hannover–Döhren 1975

Nolde, B., *La Formation de l'Empire Russe. Etudes, Notes, Documents*, 2 vols, Paris 1952–3

Orlov-Davydov, V. P., 'Biograficheskiy ocherk gr. V. G. Orlova. Sostavlen vnukom yego gr. V. P. Orlovym-Davydovym', *Russkiy Arkhiv*, 1908, no. 7, 301–96; no. 8, 429–507; no. 9, 67–86; no. 10, 145–214; no. 11, 297–303; no. 12, 465–507

Osterloh, K. H., *Joseph von Sonnenfels und die österreichische Reformbewegung im Zeitalter des aufgeklärten Absolutismus. Eine Studie zum Zusammenhang von Kameralwissenschaft und Verwaltungspraxis*, Lübeck–Hamburg 1970

Paustovsky, K., 'Sud'ba Shar'lza Longsevilya', *Sobraniye Sochineniy*, VI, Moscow 1969, 7–52

Pavlenko, N. I., *Istoriya metallurgii v Rossii XVIII v. Zavody i zavodovladel'tsy*, Moscow 1962

Pavlovsky, I. F., 'Nemetskiye kolonii v Poltavskoy gubernii v XIX v. (1808–67). Po arkhivnym dannym', *Trudy Poltavskoy Uchonoy Arkhivnoy Komissii*, x, Poltava 1913, 97–215

Pazhitnov, K., *Problema remeslennykh tsekhov v zakonodatel'stve russkogo absolyutizma*, Moscow 1952

Peterson III, C. B., *Geographical Aspects of Foreign Colonization in Pre-Revolutionary New Russia*, PhD dissertation, Washington 1969

Petrovich, N., 'Pereseleniye gosudarstvennykh krest'yan v Sibir' v nachale 19 v.', *Arkhiv Istorii Truda v Rossii*, XII=*Trud v Rossii*, II, 1924, 110–16

'Prinuditel'noe pereseleniye bobyletskikh krest'yan', *Arkhiv Istorii Truda v Rossii*, xi = *Trud v Rossii*, i, 1924, 149–63

Pictet, E., *Biographie, travaux et correspondence de C. Pictet de Roche-mont*, Geneva–Basle–Lyons 1892

Pisarevsky, G. G., *Iz istorii inostrannoy kolonizatsii v Rossii v XVIII v.*, Moscow 1909

Khozyaystvo i forma zemlevladeniya v koloniyakh Povolzh'ya v XVIII i 1-oy ½-e XIX v., Rostov na Donu 1916

'Nizhneye Povolzh'ye v tretey chetverti XVIII v.', *Izvestiya Pedagogi-cheskogo Fakul'teta Azerbaydzhanskogo Gos. Univ., obshchest-vennyye nauki*, xiv, Baku 1929, 221–9

Pereseleniye prusskikh mennonitov v Rossiyu pri Aleksandre I, Rostov na Donu 1917

Vnutrenniy rasporyadok v koloniyakh Povolzh'ya pri Yekaterine II, Warsaw 1914

Polons'ka-Vasylenko, N. D., 'The Settlement of the Southern Ukraine 1750–75', *Annals of the Ukrainian Academy of Arts and Sciences in the U.S.A.*, Summer–Fall 1955, New York 1955

Polunin, F., *Novyy i Polnyy Geograficheskiy Slovar' Rossiyskogo Gosudar-stva*, 6 parts, Moscow 1788–9

Polyansky, F., *Gorodskoye remeslo i manufaktura v Rossii v XVIII v.*, Moscow 1960

Ponomaryov, N. V., *Istoricheskiy obzor pravitel'stvennykh mer k razvitiyu sel'skogo khozyaystva v Rossii*, SPb 1880

Popov, N., *V. N. Tatishchev i yego vremya*, Moscow 1861

Pushkaryov, I., *Opisaniye Sanktpeterburga i uyezdnykh gorodov sankt-peterburgskoy gubernii*, 4 parts, SPb 1839–41

Pylayev, G. I., *Ocherki po istorii yuzhnoslavyanskoy i moldavano-volosh-skoy kolonizatsii v Rossii v 50–60kh gg. XVIII v.*, kandidatskaya dissertatsiya, Moskovskiy Gos. Pedagogicheskiy Inst. im Lenina, Moscow 1950

Raeff, M., 'Der Stil der russischen Reichspolitik und Fürst G. A. Potem-kin', *JbfGO*, NF, 16, 1968, Heft 2, 161–93

Red'ko, F. A., *Kolonizatsionnaya politika russkogo tsarizma i nemetskiye kolonisty na Ukraine (s kontsa XVIII do nachala XX st.)*, avtoreferat kandidatskoy dissertatsii, Kievskiy Gos. Univ., Kiev 1952

Reimers, H., *Sankt-Petersburg am Ende seines ersten Jahrhunderts*, 2 vols, SPb 1805

Rempel, D. G., *The Mennonite Colonies in New Russia, A Study of their Settlement and Economic Development from 1789 to 1914*, PhD dissertation, Stanford, California 1933

'The Mennonite Commonwealth in Russia. A Sketch of its Founding and Endurance 1789–1919', *Mennonite Quarterly Review*, xlvii, October 1973, and xlviii, January 1974, and off-print

'From Danzig to Russia: The First Mennonite Migration', *Mennonite Life*, 24, 1969, no. 1, 8–28

Robinson, E., 'The Transference of British Technology to Russia, 1760–1820: A Preliminary Enquiry', B. Ratcliffe, ed., *Great Britain and her World 1750–1914. Essays in honour of W. O. Henderson*, Manchester 1975, 1–26

Ruban, V., *Lyubopytnyy mesyatseslov na 1775 g.*, SPb 1775

[Rychkov], *Topografiya Orenburgskaya, to yest' obstoyatel'noye opisaniye Orenburgskoy Gubernii, sochinyonnoye...Petrom Rychkovym*, 2 vols, SPb 1762

Safonov, S., 'Ostatki grecheskikh legionov v Rossii, ili nyneshneye naseleniye Balaklavy', *ZOO*, i, 1844, 205–38

Sch., 'Geschichte der einsamen deutschen Bauernkolonie Riebensdorf in Zentralrussland', *Deutsche Post aus dem Osten*, 1939, no. 4–5, 8–13, reprinted with additions in *HBR*, 1958, 35–45

Schmidt, D., *Studien über die Geschichte der Wolgadeutschen, Theil I* (no more published), Pokrowsk–Moscow–Kharkov 1930

Schmoller, G., 'Die preussischen Kolonisationen des 17ten und 18ten Jahrhunderts', 'Zur inneren Kolonisation in Deutschland', *Schriften des Vereins für Sozialpolitik*, XXXII, 1866

Schünemann, K., *Die Bevölkerungspolitik Oesterreichs unter Maria Theresa*. Bd. 1 (Veröffentlichungen des Inst. zur Erforschung des deutschen Volkstums im Süden und Südosten in München und des Inst. für ostbayrischen Heimatforschung in Passau, Bd. 6), Berlin 1936, no more published

Sekirinsky, S. A., 'Nekotoryye cherty razvitiya sel'skogo khozyaystva Kryma i prilegayushchikh k nemu zemel' Yuzhnoy Ukrainy v kontse XVIII – 1-oy ½-e XIX vv.', *Yezhegodnik po agarnoy istorii vostochnoy Yevropy za 1960 g.*, Kiev 1962, 403–18

Selifontov, N. N., 'I. K. Boshnyak, kommendant gor. Saratova, 1774', *Russkaya Starina*, XXVI, 1879, 199–216

Semevsky, V. I., *Krest'yane v tsarstvovaniye Imp. Yekateriny II*, 2 vols, SPb 1901–3

Krest'yanskiy vopros v Rossii v XVIII i 1-oy ½-e XIX v., 2 vols, SPb 1888

Semyonov-Tyan-Shansky, V. P., red., *Rossia, Polnoye Opisaniye Nashego Otechestva*, 11 vols, SPb 1899–1913

Sergeyev, A., 'Nogaytsy na Molochnykh Vodakh, 1790–1832', *Izvestiya Tavricheskoy Uchonoy Arkhivnoy Kommissii*, 1912, no. 48, 1–144

Shafranov, P. A., 'Otzyv o knige G. G. Pisarevskogo "Iz istorii inostrannoy kolonizatsii v Rossii v XVIII v." ', *Chteniya*, 1909, no. 4, Smes', 28–46

Shafonsky, A., *Chernigovskogo Namestnichestva Topograficheskoye Opisaniye, s kratkim geograficheskim i istoricheskim opisaniyem Maliya Rossii...1786, Izdal M. Sudiyenko*, Kiev 1851

Shcherbatov, M. M., 'Statistika v rassuzhdenii Rossii', *Chteniya*, 1859, iii, 1–96

Shishmaryov, V. F., 'Nauchnoye naslediye. Romanskiye poseleniya na

yuge Rossii', *Trudy Arkhiva Akademii Nauk S.S.S.R.*, vypusk 26, 1975
Shpilevsky, M. M., 'Politika narodonaseleniya v tsarstvovaniye Yekateriny II', *Zapiski Imp. Novorossiyskogo Univ.*, vi, Odessa 1871, 1–178
Shul'ts, K., 'Neskol'ko slov o vinogradarstve v Odesskom uyezde', *Trudy Komiteta Vinogradarstva I.O.S.Kh.Yu.R.*, vypusk 1, Odessa 1901, 172–6
Sinner, P., 'Kurzgefasste Geschichte der deutschen Wolgakolonien', *Beiträge zur Heimatkunde des deutschen Wolgagebiets*, Pokrowsk (Kosakenstadt) 1923, 5–28
Skal'kovsky, A. A., *Bolgarskiye kolonii v Bessarabii i v Novorossiyskom kraye*, Odessa 1848
Khronologicheskoye Obozreniye Istorii Novorossiyskogo Kraya, 2 vols, Odessa 1850
Pervoye tridtsatiletiye Odessy 1793–1823, Odessa 1837
'Sravnitel'nyy vzglyad na Ochakovskuyu oblast' v 1790 i 1840 gg.', *ZOO*, i, 1844, iv, 262–3
'Tonkorunnoye ovtsevodstvo i torgovlya sherst'yu pri Odesskom porte', *Trudy Odesskogo Statisticheskogo Komiteta*, no. 4, off-print, Odessa 1870
'Vzglyad na skotovodstvo Novorossiyskogo kraya. 1846–1848. Stat'ya I', *ZhMVD*, xxx, 1850, 356–401
Smith, A. E., *Colonists in Bondage. White Servitude and Convict Labour in America, 1607–1776*, Chapel Hill 1947
Sokolov, N. S., *Raskol v Saratovskom Kraye. Opyt issledovaniya po neizdannym istochnikam.* T. 1: *Popovshchina do pyatidesyatykh godov nastoyashchego stoletiya*, Saratov 1888
Solov'yov, S. M., *Istoriya Rossii s drevnyeyshikh vremyon*, ed. L. Cherepnin, 29 vols in xv, Moscow 1959–66
Spitzer, F. *Joseph von Sonnenfels als Nationalökonom*, Inaugural Dissertation, Bern 1906
Stählin, K. von, *Aus den Papieren Jacob v. Stählins. Ein biographischer Beitrag zur deutsch–russischen Kulturgeschichte des 18ten Jahrhunderts*, Königsberg–Berlin 1926
Steiner, G., 'J. R. Forsters und Georg Forsters Beziehungen zu Russland', *Studien zur Geschichte der russischen Literatur des 18ten Jahrhunderts*, hrsg. H. Grasshof und U. Lehmann, ii, Berlin 1968, 245–311
Stepermanis, M., 'Aizkraukles K. F. Šulcs un viņa sabiedriskā darbība (C. F. Schoultz of Aizkraukle and his public work)', *Latvijas Ūniversitātes Raksti, filologijas un filosofijas fak.*, serija iii. 5, 1935, 105–68
'J. G. Eisen et ses luttes pour l'abolition du servage en Livonie et en Courlande', *Pirmā Baltijas vēsturnieku konference Riga 1937*, Riga 1938, 501–7
'Pirmās ciņas par dzimtbušanas atcelšanu Vizdemē 1750–1764 (The first struggles to abolish serfdom in Latvia 1750–1764)', *Izglītibas Ministrijas Menešrakts*, 1931, no. 10, 275–93; no. 11, 438–53

Stolpyansky, P., *Peterburg, kak voznik, osnovalsya i ros Sankt-Piterburkh*, Petrograd 1918

Storch, H., *Historisch-statistisches Gemaehlde des russischen Reichs*, 6 parts, Riga–Leipzig 1797–1802

hrsg., *Russland unter Alexander I. Eine historische Zeitschrift*, 9 vols, SPb–Leipzig 1804–8

Strod, Kh. P., 'Vliyaniye torgovoy politiki rossiyskoy imperii na razvitiye sel'skogo khozyaystva Latvii v XVIII v.', A. K. Biron, red., *Ekonomicheskiye svyazi Pribaltiki s Rossiyey. Sb. statey*, Riga 1968, 146–72

Strumilin, S., *Ocherki ekonomicheskoy istorii Rossii*, Moscow 1960

Stumpp, K., *Die Russlanddeutschen. Zweihundert Jahre unterwegs*, Freilassing 1966; English translation by J. S. Height, *The German Russians. Two Centuries of Pioneering*, Bonn–NY 1967

The Emigration from Germany to Russia in the years 1763–1862, Tübingen n.d. [1972]

Tastevin, F., 'Les calvinistes français en Russie', *Feuilles d'Histoire du XVII au XX s.*, 4, 1910, 197–206

Tatarincev, A. G., 'Zum Widerhall des Pugačev-Aufstandes im Saratower Gebiet. Aus der Geschichte der deutschen Kolonisation in der zweiten Hälfte des 18. Jhdts', *Zeitschrift für Slawistik*, XIII, 1968, 196–206

'Tonkorunnoye ovtsevodstvo v Rossii', *Biblioteka dlya chteniya*, CVI, iv, 1851, 1–50

Tooke, W., *The Picture of St. Petersburg. From the German of Henry Storch*, London 1801

View of the Russian Empire during the Reign of Catherine the Second, and to the Close of the Present Century, 3 vols, London 1799

Tower, T., *Memoir of the late Charles Baird, Esq., and of his son Francis Baird of St. Petersburg and 4, Queen's Gate, London*, London 1867 (private printing)

Troitsky, S. M., 'Novyy istochnik po istorii ekonomicheskoy mysli v Rossii v seredine XVIII v. ("Rassuzhdeniye o rossiyskoy kommertsii" sekretarya senata F. I. Sukina)', *Arkheograficheskiy Yezhegodnik za 1966 g.*, Moscow 1968

Urry, J., *The Closed and the Open: Social and Religious Change Amongst the Mennonites in Russia (1789–1889)*, unpublished D.Phil. dissertation, Oxford 1978

Utas, J., *Svenskyborna. Historia och öde fran trettonhundra till nu*, Stockholm 1959

Vas'kin, N. M., 'Pomeshchich'e zemlevladeniye v Astrakhanskom kraye vo vtoroy polovine XVIII v.', *Problemy Istorii SSSR*, v, 1976, 181–93

Velitsyn, A. A. (pseudonym of Paltov), 'Inostrannaya kolonizatsiya v Rossii', *Russkiy Vestnik*, CC–CCI, 1889, no. 1, 155–77; no. 2, 3–32; no. 3, 98–130; no. 6, 187–222

Veselovsky, K. S., 'Tonkorunnoye ovtsevodstvo v Rossii', *ZhMGI*, 1846, chast' 20, i, 105ff

Veshnyakov, V. I., 'Ekspeditsiya Gosudarstvennogo Khozyaystva 1797–1803', *Russkaya Starina*, CVIII, 1901, 195–205, 403–22; CXI, 1902, 151–70, 427–38

Veuclin, V. E., *L'Amitié franco-russe, Ses origines. Le Génie Français et la Russie sous Catherine II. Documents inédits recuillis par V. E. Veuclin*, Lisieux 1896

Les Lyonnais et la Russie au siècle dernier. Mémoire présenté au Congrès des Sociétés savantes à la Sorbonne en 1896, Lyon 1896

Vitevsky, V. N., *I. I. Nepluyev i Orenburgskiy Kray v prezhnem yego sostave do 1758 g.*, 5 parts, Kazan 1889–97

Wieczynski, J. L., *The Russian Frontier. The Impact of Borderlands upon the Course of Early Russian History*, Charlottesville 1976

Wiegand, G., 'Russland im Urteil des Aufklärers Christoph Schmidt genannt Phiseldek', hrsg. E. Lesky, u.a., *Die Aufklärung in Ost- und Südosteuropa*, Köln–Wien 1972, 50–86

Woltner, M., *Das wolgadeutsche Bildungswesen und die russische Schulpolitik* (Veröffentlichungen des Slavischen Inst. a.d. Friedrich-Wilhelms–Univ., Berlin, no. 17), Leipzig 1937

Yakushkin, V., *Ocherki po istorii russkoy pozemel'noy politiki v XVIII i XIX vv. Vypusk I: XVIII v.*, Moscow 1890

Yastrebov, V., 'Greki v Yelizavetgrade', *Kievskaya Starina*, VII, April 1884, 673–84

Yatsunsky, V. K., 'Rol' migratsiy i vysokogo yestestvennogo prirosta naseleniy v zaselenii kolonizovavshikhsya rayonov Rossii', *Voprosy Geografii*, Sb 83, 1970, 34–44

'Rol' Peterburga v promyshlennom razvitii dorevolyutsionnoy Rossii', *Voprosy Istorii*, 1954, no. 9, 95–103

Yukht, A., 'Armyanskiye remeslenniki v Astrakhani v 1-oy ½-e XVIII v.', *Izvestiya A. N. Armyanskoy S.S.R. (obshchestvennyye nauki)*, 1958, no. 1, 37–54

'Indiyskaya koloniya Astrakhani', *Vosprosy Istorii*, 1957, no. 3, 135–43

'Pravovoye polozheniye astrakhanskikh armyan v 1-oy ½-e XVIII v.', *Izvestiya A. N. Armyanskoy S.S.R. (obshchestvennyye nauki)*, 1960, no. 12, 47–60

Yurovsky, L. N., *Saratovskiye Votchiny. Statistiko-ekonomicheskiye ocherki i materialy iz istorii krupnogo zemlevladeniya i krepostnogo khozyaystva v kontse XVIII i v nachale XIX stoletiya*, Saratov 1923

Zagorovsky, V. P., *Istoricheskaya Toponimika Voronezhskogo Kraya*, Voronezh 1973

Zagorovsky, Ye. A., 'Inostrannaya kolonizatsiya Novorossiyskogo kraya v XVII v. (po povodu issledovaniya prof. G. G. Pisarevskogo, "Iz istorii inostrannoy kolonizatsii v Rossii v XVIII v.")', *Izvestiya Odesskogo Bibliograficheskogo Obshchestva pri Imp. Novorossiyskom Univ.*, II, vypusk 8, March 1913, 103–18

Voyennaya kolonizatsiya Novorossii pri Potemkine, Odessa 1913

Zagoruyko, V., *Po stranitsam istorii Odessy i Odesschiny*, vypusk 1, Odessa 1957

Zherbin, A. S., *Pereseleniye Karel v Rossiyu v XVII v.*, Petrozavodsk 1956

Zlatkin, I. Ya., *Istoriya Dzhungarskogo khanstva (1635–1758)*, Moscow 1964

Zolotov, V. A., *Vneshnyaya torgovlya yuzhnoy Rossii v 1-oy ½-e XIX v.*, Rostov na Donu 1963

Zutis, Ya., *Ostzeyskiy vopros v XVIII v.*, Riga 1946

Index

Bruce, Countess 33
Brunswick 252
Budapest 196, 202
Budzhak Tatar Horde 139
Bug, river 117, 124, 134, 138
Bukhara 7, 150, 158
Bulgarians 111, 124, 127
  colonists 62, 80, 84, 137–9, 141,
    188–9, 204, 207–8, 211, 212, 220
Bury, British weaver 146
Buturlin, Count, Senator 43–4

Cadiz 158
Cambrai 252
cameralism 2, 24, 54
Canel, river 242
Canitz, civil servant, projector 61
Carcassonne 175
Carlsthal, sheep colony 228
Carolina 60
Carpathians 196
Caspian Sea 17, 25, 117–18, 153–4
Castella, entrepreneur 221
Castres, Comte de, émigré 185–6,
  206
Catherine II, Empress 1–4, 25–6, 31–
  43, 46–7, 50–1, 55–6, 61, 77, 100–
  1, 106, 128, 131, 157–8, 171, 174,
  177, 180–1, 209, 237, and *passim*
  accession 17, 30
  and Livonia 77, 85–94, 174
  Instruction 31, 115
  policies, political–economic theory
    25–6, 31–2, 85–8, 91–2, 106–8,
    141–3, 145–6, 176, 197, 217,
    230–2
  voyage down the Volga 94–5, 101
Catholics 131
Caucasus 3, 37, 49, 104, 117–24, 139–
  40, 152, 189, 216
Caucasus Line 118–20, 218, 221–3
Cayenne 57
Chamberlain, entrepreneur 233
Chancellery
  for Imperial Estates 55, 82
  'for migration' 10
  of Guardianship for Foreigners 43,
    47–9, 52–6, 61–3, 66–76, 81–9,
    91–7, 99–103, 107–8, 119, 143–4,
    147, 152–6, 160–6, 168–71, 177,
    217, 230–3 and *passim*
  Petersburg Police Chancellery 162
  Provincial Chancelleries
    Astrakhan 36, 69–70, 75, 81, 105
    Moscow 12
    Orenburg 48
    Petersburg 42

Saratov Voyevoda's Chancellery 70–
  1, 96, 99, 154, 156–7
Chanony, entrepreneur 171–3,
  250–1
Charter and Statute to Towns of the
  Empire 121, 178
Charter to Mennonites 184, 197, 204
Chechuliy, recruiting agent 62
Cherkassk, town 120
Chernigov, province 84
Chernyshev 34, 94
  Count I. 33
  Count Z. 33, 83, 90, 93
Chevalier, colonist 251
Chief Judge
  New Russia 205
  Saratov 75, 98, 222
China 25, 158
Chorny Yar 49
Colbert 25
collective responsibility 102
Colleges 47
  Little Russian 63, 79, 109, 217
  Livonian, of Justice 61
  Medical 31, 163
  Military 42, 117, 119
  of Foreign Affairs 17, 21–2, 35–7,
    39–42, 55, 61, 66, 152–3
  of Manufactures 16, 36, 143–4, 217,
    231
    Office 143–4, 164–9, 311 n.180
  of Mines 143, 166, 171, 178
  Treasury 75
    Office 90
colonies
  artisan 163, 212
  in Astrakhan 149–54
  in Ukraine 77–80, 129–31, 163,
    188–212
  Kalmyk 10
  Livonian, *see* Hirschenhof
  military 130, 136, 214–15
  of other European powers 2, 29–30,
    57–8
  private 33–4, *see poselitel'* settle-
    ment
  Serbian, *see* New Serbia
  Volga 69–75, 80–1, 94–108
  vyzyvatelskiye 63–4, 97
commerce
  Baltic 85–90
  Buturlin on 43–4
  Eastern 7–8, 17–18, 25, 81, 151–2,
    153–4
  French 172
  in 1763 Manifesto 49
  in tobacco 78, 104, 107, 169–70